ELECTRONIC PHOTOGRAPHY

Computer Graphics Technology and Management Series

Series Consulting Editor: Carl Machover

AutoCAD: Methods and Macros (No. 2989)
Jeff Guenther, Ed Ocoboc and Anne Wayman

VersaCAD Tutorial: A Practical Approach to Computer-Aided Design (No. 3003)
Carol Buerhens, CADD Specialist,
CR/CADD a division of Consolidated Reprographics

DataCAD for the Architect (No. 3075)
Carol Buerhens

AutoCAD Programming (No. 3093)
Dennis N. Jump

The C-4 Handbook: CAD, CAM, CAE, CIM (No. 3098)
Carl Machover

ELECTRONIC PHOTOGRAPHY

John J. Larish

COMPUTER
GRAPHICS
TECHNOLOGY
AND
MANAGEMENT
SERIES

TAB Professional and Reference Books

Division of TAB BOOKS
Blue Ridge Summit, PA

TPR books are published by TAB Professional and Reference Books, a division of TAB BOOKS. The TRP logo, consisting of the letters "TPR" within a large "T," is a registered trademark of TAB BOOKS.

Published by **TAB BOOKS**
FIRST EDITION/FIRST PRINTING

Library of Congress Cataloging-in-Publication Data

Larish, John J.
Understanding electronic photography / by John J. Larish.
p. cm.
ISBN 0-8306-8315-1 ISBN 0-8306-3315-4 (pbk.)
1. Electronography. I. Title.
TK415.L37 1990
621.36'7—dc20 89-48414
CIP

Questions regarding the content of this book should be addressed to:

Reader Inquiry Branch
TAB BOOKS
Blue Ridge Summit, PA 17294-0850

Acquisitions Editor: Larry Hager
Technical Editor: Steven L. Burwen
Produciton: Katherine Brown
Book Design: Jaclyn J. Boone

Cover photograph by Amy S. Friend

Trademarks

Mavica, ProMavica, and **Trinitron**	Sony Corp.
Maxxum	Minolta
Xapshot	Canon U.S.A., Inc.
USA TODAY	Gannett Publishing Co.
Kodak, Megapixel, Eikonix, Video Visualizer, Megaplus, ColorEdge, Ektachrome, Kodachrome, T-Max, Ektapress, Ektar, Create-a-Print and **Ektatherm**	Eastman Kodak Co.
Fujix, Pictography 1000, and **Jetgraphy 3000**	Fuji Photofilm Company
Scanmaster II and **Pixelmaster**	Howtek, Inc.
Imapro and **Photographics 3000**	Imapro Corp.
Barneyscan	Barneyscan Corp.
Appletalk and **QuickDraw**	Apple Computer Inc.
Macintosh	license, Apple Computer Inc.
Array	Array Technologies Inc.
Visual Presenter	Elmo Mfg. Corp.
Polaroid	Polaroid Corp.
MicroVAX	Digital Equipment Corp.
Targa, Vista, TrueVista, NuVista, and **Vidi/o Box**	TrueVision, Inc.
QuickCapture and **ColorCapture**	Data Translations, Inc.
Digital Darkroom	Silicon Beach, Inc.
Image Studio and **Color Studio**	Letraset, Inc.
GraphisPaint	Aba, Inc.
IBM, PS/2, AT, and **MCA**	International Business Machines Corp.
PC Vision Plus	Image Technology, Inc.
T9506	Toshiba America, Inc.
Pixel-Planes	University of North Carolina
Pixar	Pixar Corporation
Pixel Machine	AT&T
Alice	Telephoto Communications, Inc.
PicturePower®	PictureWare, Inc.
DVI	Intel Corporation
Leafax	Leaf Technology, Inc.
Fotovix	Tamron Industries, Inc.
Calibrator	Barco Industries, Inc.
Beam Matrix	Matsushita Electric Corp.
ColorQuick	Tektronics, Inc.
Cycolor	Mead Corporation
PhotoMac	Avalon Development Group

Trademarks (*cont.*)

PostScript, Pagemaker, Adobe Illustrator and **Photo Shop**	Adobe Systems, Inc.
Image-Pro Color	Media Cybernetics, Inc.
The Darkroom	Picsus, Inc.
ImagePaint	Imageware Research and Development, Inc.
Pantone	Pantone, Inc.
Laserpaint Color II	Laserware, Inc.
Photo Management Workstation	National Digital Corporation
SPARC	Sun Microsystems, Inc.
4cast	DuPont, Inc.
PhotoStream	Associated Press International, Inc.
Newsline and **PhotoTouch II**	Crosfield
Picture Desk	Reuters.

Contents

Foreword

The present and future of electronic imaging are as exciting as anything we will find in space and, in immediacy, far more useful to mankind. However, perhaps no modern communication technology is so little understood or its future so greatly ignored by the general public.

The average consumer can master the directions for connecting his VCR to his television or learn how to run his camcorder, but how the opaque, blank-appearing tape can hold an image and how it plays back is a complete mystery. Even the knowledgeable computer operator tends to see imaging only in terms of his immediate needs and use.

Yet the present and future possibilities of video imaging, both still and moving, computer databanks, telephonics, laser disc, chip, and optical-disk data recording and storage, plus the instant transmission of information and reproduction of image information anywhere in the world represents very real teachnology within our grasp today—or just around the corner. Also, many technologies are interrelated and can or will communicate with each other.

Surprisingly, there have been few if any comprehensive books to guide the interested and knowledgeable, no less the novice. True, individual scientific papers have been available at conventions as well as popular newspaper and magazine articles covering individual elements of electronic imaging.

However, no one has attempted to fit all the present electronic jigsaw pieces of the puzzle together and to relate them to real, economically practical applications. No one has compiled a comprehensive glossary of terms with understandable definitions so it all makes sense. No one has dared to predict the incredible future as it will be or could be—until now.

Foreword

Is there anyone in a better position to author an easy-to-read yet complete book on electronic imaging, past, present and future than John Larish? He is president of Jonrel Imaging Consultants, a company specializing in new concepts and technology in imaging and electronics. Larish was also the developer of the AutoStudio, a complete hybrid electronic and silver halide portrait photography studio, a product for which he holds patents. He has studied at the Electronic Engineering Department at the University of Dayton. He is also thoroughly familiar with silver sensitive emulsion technology, having been a manager for a photofinishing plant. He is a much sought after speaker in the U.S. and overseas. He has authored many articles for popular and technical journals, and has been published by the Society of Motion Picture and Television Engineers and the Biological Photographers Association. He is a charter member of the Computer Press Association and is currently co-Editorial Director and Publisher of *Electronic Photography News*.

At any electronic or photographic convention, a puzzled member of the press knows he can usually find the up-to-date answers on who is or will be doing what, why, and how by "asking John." And it's not his considerable physical height that helps him see over the heads of other members of the press and pick up things they miss.

Larish's enthusiasm for electronic imaging and its future is well-balanced by his equally solid grounding in business administration and marketing. He holds a BS in business administration from Empire State College, spent 15 years working for the Eastman Kodak Company in such diverse areas as international marketing for Africa, the Middle East, and Japan, supervised a customer service group, and served as a senior market intelligence analyst with special emphasis on electronics, new products, and markets.

Describing this book as "An amalgamation of principles, how things work, equipment, and applications," Larish adds, "It really represents a challenge for me—to put my arms around this thing called electronic photography—what it is, what it can and will be."

Whether electronic photography itself is now and will remain in good arms or hands remains to be seen, but the explanation of it certainly is.

Herbert Keppler
Publishing Director
Popular Photography

Introduction

The electronic still camera has been the dream of many inventors over the years. You've seen it in science fiction movies and stories as well as in the comic pages. Articles on the "someday it will come world" talked about the uses of electronic still photography; these came soon after the first television images appeared, but neither the equipment nor the desires of the consumer of photography were ready for electronics.

Then came Sony's 1981 announcement of their "revolutionary still camera." To some, it was an answer to a dream. It didn't take some gurus long to say that conventional photography was dead. This was the filmless camera that had the ability to view images on the same display medium that people had in their homes—their home color-television set. No developing, no dependence on limited natural resources such as silver, no waste—it was an entirely clean product. Although the concept was in place in the early 1980s, only now are actual, purchasable electronic-photography systems coming into reality.

You might wonder why all the false starts, the high expectations, the dreams, but when you think about it, isn't that the evolution of technology? Even the invention of roll photographic film for amateur cameras by Hannibal Goodwin, and the creation of instant photography by Edwin Land were evolutionary; each was a further advancement of technologies that grew over a period of years. The only difference now is that the rate of technological change is much faster. Where once it took two or more generations for a change, now it almost seems to happen overnight.

In their original August 24, 1981, press release, Sony public-relations people were quick to point out that there had not been a major change in photographic processes since Daguerre had invented the original product.

That might have been PR hype, but there really was some degree of truth in it if you forget about the evolution of photography. Today, some 43 companies have signed a pact that has set a standard for the first electronic-video photo still system, mostly based on the work of Sony. Now they've developed the most recent (July, 1988) Hi-band still video standard, which is designed to match the efforts of video tape makers with Super VHS, ED Beta, and high-band 8-mm video.

Although none of these standards reach the quality levels of HDTV (high-definition TV) or 35-mm silver-halide film, still video is one of the most exciting and revolutionary new tools to appear in the market, now that it has become a real product for the professional and also for the amateur.

Although the first development efforts were from Sony, the greatest development and marketing efforts most recently, both for a product and for application of the medium, have been from Canon, those people from Japan who gave us the famous Canon AE-1 single-lens reflex camera used by so many as their start on the road to 35-mm photography. It has not been an easy introduction for Canon, especially with the continuing evolution of silver-halide films. Often, when some new development occurred in electronic photography, there was at the same time a new conventional film announcement. Too often there has been a direct comparison of silver halide to electronics, and the result has never been very flattering. However, when has new technology ever had an easy time? There were those who laughed at Jobs and Wozniak and their garage-developed computer, but there were those, who became a majority, who saw the real revolution we had at hand with the Apple computer.

Computer graphics and computer art have been primarily the province of original image creation. With the advent of new capture devices like electronic still cameras combined with computer capture boards that allow us to digitize these images easily, we are seeing more and more use of the electronic photographic image.

Although we are only at the start of real electronic photography, we will see more and more combining of images. Considering this graphic application along with the need and capability for desktop publishing of graphics and images, electronic photography will be an important new tool for the further communication of ideas, much like early graphic images opened people's minds to the capabilities of presenting information more quickly and clearly. The words of the old sage were never more true, "A picture is worth a thousand words," especially if it is an electronic photo image available immediately for our use.

This book would not have been possible without the dedicated assistance of several people. Rose Ellen Larish spent many hours laboring over this manuscript. Jim and Sue Larish's proofreading suggestions were very appreciated and useful, as were those of valued friends Keith and Phyllis Hackleman.

Bert Keppler's foreword sets a dramatic stage for the start of this book. My *Electronic Photography News* Copublisher Don Franz encouraged me in learning more about this growing field and he shared some of his EPN articles for this book. Elliott Novak, a recognized expert in electronic photography, was a great help.

In addition, there were the numerous members of companies marketing products, such as Sony Corporation, who readily answered questions and provided press photos. Finally, there were the numerous people who attended programs and classes that I led in the field of imaging because each person added to my knowledge, just as I hope I contributed in a small way to increasing their knowledge.

Cardinal John Henry Newman, said in 1864, "Growth is the only sign of life" and electronic photography offers us the opportunity of growing—professionally, aesthetically, and technically.

1

Electronic Still Photography

If products are known by the company they keep, certainly electronic photography has become a significant factor in the world of imaging. With companies such as Sony, Canon, Nikon, and Eastman Kodak Company entering the field of electronic photography, there is the promise for real growth and significant product development.

Although Eastman Kodak Company and other manufacturers have continued the development of silver halide image photography, Polaroid, Kodak, and other companies such as Fuji and Konica are working on a variety of technologies, including the development of new camera sensors, printing technology, and digital storage systems.

Silver halide has been the principal means of image capture for more than 100 years and will continue to be a major imaging system for many years to come. Electronic imaging, on the other hand, using still image capture, display, and reproduction, promises to be one of the great growth areas of the next several years.

There is no question that we are becoming an electronically oriented society. Whether it is the home consumer, news media, medical profession, or industry in general, we are becoming highly computer-oriented—highly image-dependent—and this reinforces the positioning of electronic photography today. There is a revolution taking place in the ways of capturing images, storing images, and using these in a variety of applications, both commercially and for general usage.

THE FIRST ELECTRONIC STILL VIDEO CAMERA

Electronic photography began with the introduction of the Sony video still camera called MAVICA, an acronym for *ma*gnetic *vi*deo *ca*mera.

Announced on August 24, 1981, it was to be several years before Sony delivered a professional camera called the "ProMavica."

The initially proposed MAVICA embodied the most advanced electronic technology that was available at the time in magnetic recording, CCD's, and IC semiconductors. The new MAVICA system used no photographic film and thereby eliminated the need for developing and printing processes. Sony's announcement said that their new still camera was "an epoch-making innovation in the history of still photography." The Sony release went on to add that "the conventional camera has seen some improvements over the years such as the change from dry plate to film, use of electronics in certain parts, and the reduction of size and weight. However, for more than 140 years, since the invention of Daguerre of France, there has been no fundamental change in the concept and technology of photography, in which materials are recorded on film through chemical reactions of photosensitive materials."

Sony's original announcement indicated a revolution was about to take place in still photography (Fig. 1–1). Akio Morito, president of Sony, was quoted as saying that Sony would become "the Kodak of electronic photography."

While Sony continued the development of their MAVICA system (Fig. 1–2), Canon introduced their still video system. By the time a new Hi-band standard was introduced in July 1988, 43 equipment manufacturers (Table 1–1) of both photographic and electronic equipment had joined in the approval of the latest Hi-band standard. The standard established in 1984 for still video photography closely matched the performance of the VHS video tape system of that time. The resolution of the still video system was slightly better than VHS, but not significantly.

What has happened from Sony's original announcement to today's electronic photography is the evolution of an analog system that closely parallels the existing television systems of today and the beginnings of the digital photography systems of the future (Fig. 1–3).

Before I talk about products available for electronic photography today and how you might use them, first I want to define electronic photography. In this book, *electronic photography* is used to refer to a unique medium in which the image is captured electronically, either through a camera or by some other means, to create an analog or digital electronic record of the image. The image can be a black-and-white or color image, but it must be a photorealistic representation as opposed to an artist's rendition.

To most people, electronic photography is still video photography. The still video system (SVS) uses a 2-inch magnetic floppy disk to record 50 analog fields or 25 analog frames consisting of two interlaced fields (Fig. 1–4). The images often are thought to be digital because of the disk, but they are not.

Announcement

SONY CORPORATION

7-35 KITASHINAGAWA 6-CHOME, SHINAGAWA-KU, TOKYO, 141 JAPAN

August 24, 1981

Revolutionary Video Still Camera Called "MAVICA" Disclosed by Sony
— Newly Developed Magnetic Disk Called "MAVIPAK" Used —

Sony Corporation today announced that it has developed a revolutionary video still camera, embodying fully the advantages of advanced electronic technology in magnetic recording, CCD and IC semiconductors.

Called the MAVICA system, the new magnetic video still camera uses no photographic film and therefore does not require developing and printing processes which are indispensable to conventional chemical photography. This new video still camera represents an epoch-making innovation in the history of still photography.

The conventional camera has seen some improvements over the years, such as the change from dry plate to film, the use of electronics in certain parts, and the reduction of size and weight. However, for more than 140 years since the invention by Daguerre of France, there has been no fundamental change in the concept and technology of photography, in which images are recorded on film through chemical reactions of photo-sensitive materials.

Sony's MAVICA system replaces each chemical processes with an electromagnetic system. The MAVICA is no larger than a conventional 35mm single-lens reflex camera. An image that comes through the lens is converted into electronic signals by a solid-state imager called CCD (Charge Coupled Device), previously developed by Sony. The signals are recorded on a very small magnetic disk called MAVIPAK that Sony has developed for the new camera system.

The newly developed memory medium called MAVIPAK can record 50 still color pictures. The recorded pictures can be viewed immediately on the home TV set through a specially designed playback unit called the MAVIPAK Viewer. MAVIPAK pictures require no developing or printing processes such as required in chemical photography. It is expected that hard copies of color pictures can be produced from the MAVIPAK by means of a new color printer now under development by Sony.

Fig. 1-1. The original Sony press release announcing Mavica.

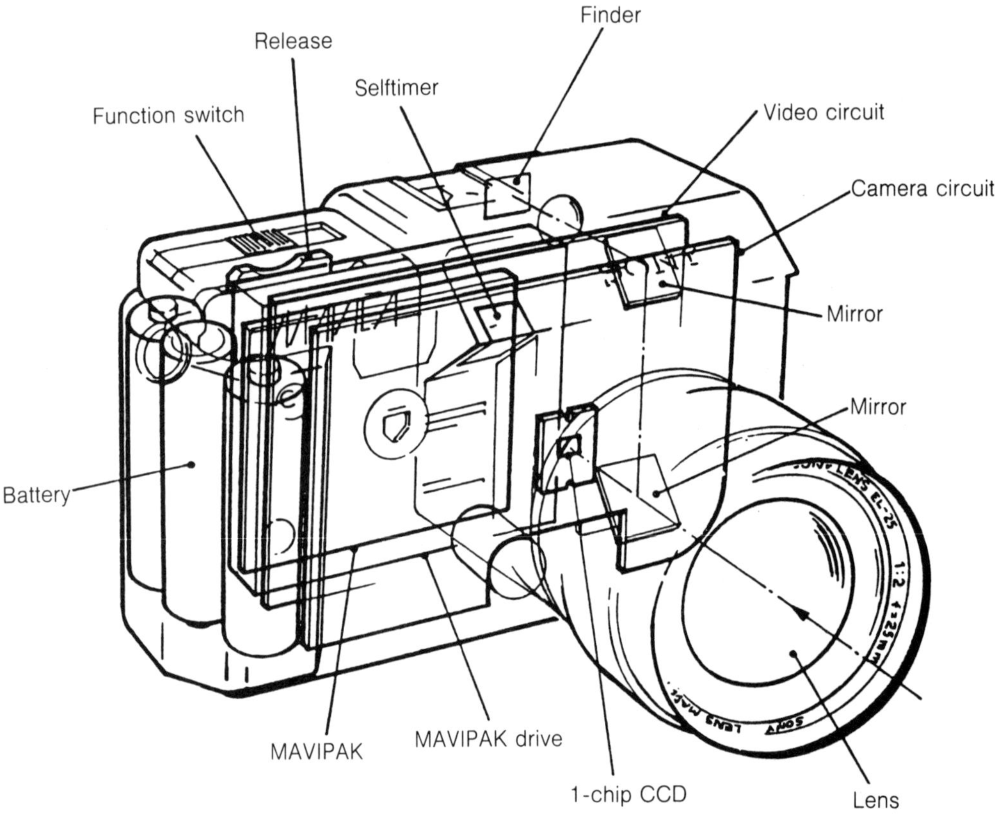

Fig. 1-2. The original perspective view of the Mavica.

Two different standards are used for electronic still cameras that are commercially available. There is the original standard that was approved in 1982 (Table 1–2). Sony, the originator of the first still video system, learned the lessons of video-tape-recording standards. When home video recording appeared as the Beta system from Sony, they made no effort to create a single standard. As a result, along came VHS and the battle lasted for more than a dozen years before the market finally declared its preference for VHS.

A Hi-band standard announced in July, 1988 kept the same media and tracks but changed the recording specifications (Table 1–3). The resolution of the new Hi-band standard is over 400 horizontal lines and provides an image quality much like the new Super VHS and ED-Beta video-tape standards.

Table 1-1. Electronic Still Standardization Committee Members (as of July, 1989).

Ashai Optical Co., Ltd.	Mitsubishi Electric Corporation
BASF Aktiegesellschaft	NEC Corporation
Canon, Inc.	NEC Home Electronics, Ltd.
Casio Computer Co., Ltd.	Nihon Polaroid Corporation
Chinon Industrial, Inc.	Nikon Corporation
Citizen Watch Co., Ltd.	Olympus Optical Co., Ltd.
Copal Co., Ltd.	Philips International B.V.
Columbia Magnetic Products Co., Ltd.	Ricoh Company, Ltd.
Dai Nippon Printing Co., Ltd.	Samsung Japan Electronics Co., Ltd.
Eastman Kodak Company	Sankyo Seiki Manufacturing Co., Ltd.
Elmo Co., Ltd.	Sanyo Electric Co., Ltd.
Fuji Photo Film Co., Ltd.	Seiko Co.
Hitachi, Ltd.	Seiko Epson Co.
Hitachi Maxell, Ltd.	Sharp Corporation
Kasei Verbatim Corporation	Sony Corporation
Keystone Camera of Japan, Ltd.	Space-Wide Enterprises Co.
Konica Corporation	TDK Corporation
Kyocera Corporation	Thompson-Japan K K Co.
Mamiya Camera Co., Ltd.	3M Company/Sumitomo 3M Ltd.
Matsushita Electric Industrial Co., Ltd.	Toshiba Corporation
Minolta Camera Co., Ltd.	Victor Company of Japan, Ltd. (JVC)

In addition to the still video camera, there are many other ways of creating an electronic photograph—from capturing images with conventional video cameras to specialized scanners (chapter 2), and then processing them using a variety of tools available for personal computers (chapter 3).

Although the Sony announcement shook many areas of the world, by the time of the 1982 Photokina in Cologne, West Germany—one of the world's largest photo shows—the camera was an exhibitcase item with private demonstrations at the Sony headquarters for Sony GmbH in West Germany.

The first major commercial introduction of a still video system with a product available for sale was from Canon. Their mid-year 1986 press announcement caught many people by surprise because Sony was considered the originator and had been expected to be the first to reach the market.

Today's still video photography products include cameras for both the professional and the general photographer. Among the professional cameras available, Canon offers several models; Nikon has a unique black-and-white camera designed for the press market; Minolta has a back for their Maxxum camera; Fuji is still feeling out the market in locations outside of Japan; and new products are available or promised from several other

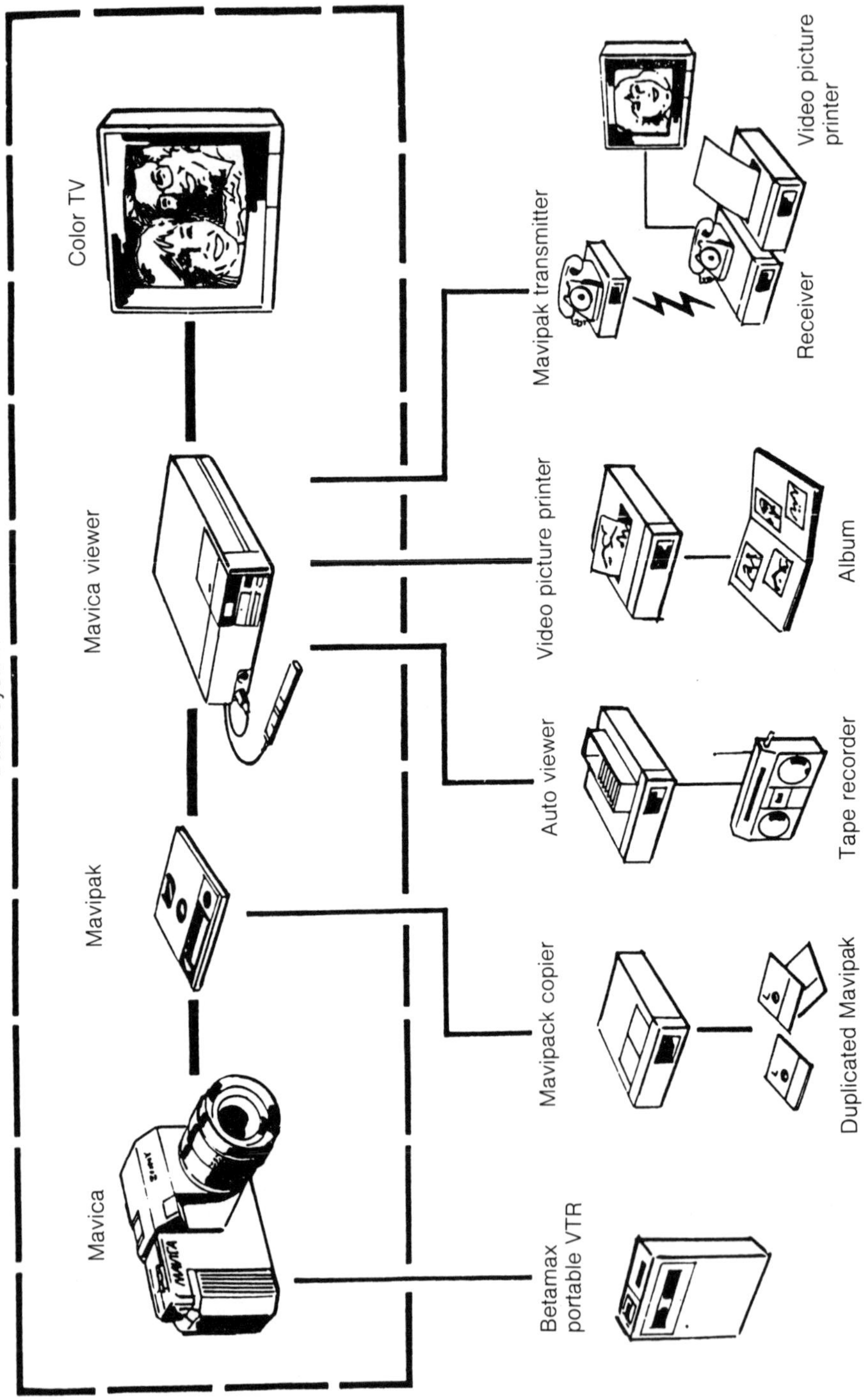

Fig. 1-3. The originally envisioned Mavica system.

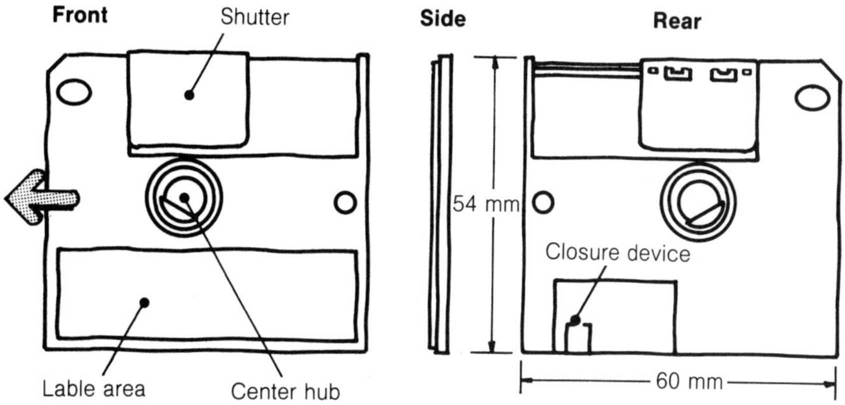

Fig. 1-4. The 2-inch still video floppy disk.

manufacturers. For the general photographer, there is the Canon Xapshot and Sony MVC-1 Camera, which followed by a year the Casio camera that ultimately was withdrawn from the market because of its increased price. Other cameras are now available from Fuji, Panasonic, Sanyo, Konica, and others.

Table 1-2. Original Still Video Photography Standard.

1. Recording system	
Luminance	FM modulated reording system (NTSC/PAL System)
White peak	6.0 MHz
Synch. peak	1.5 MHZ
Frequency deviation	1.5 MHz
White clipping	None
Recording current (Optimum)	7 MHz
Color Signal	R-Y, B-Y differential color lines. Subsequent FM-Modulated recording in accordance with Still Video Floppy System.
2. Disk Sheet	In accordance with Still Video Floppy System
Thickness	40 μm
Magnetic sheet	Metal sheet or equivalent
3. Disk Pack	In accordance with Still Video Floppy System
Dimensions	60 × 54 × 3.6 mm (W × H × D)
4. Track	In accordance with Still Video Floppy System
For picture/sound	From track 1 to 50 digital data
Cue track	Track 52
Track pitch	100 micron

Table 1-3. Hi-Band Still Video Photography Standard.

	Original	Hi-Band
Luminance	FM modulated recording system (NTSC/PAL System)	Same
White peak	6.0 MHz	9.7 MHz
Synch. peak	1.5 MHZ	7.7 Mhz
Frequency deviation	1.5 MHz	2.0 MHz
White clipping	None	Less than 250%
Recording current (optimum) color signal	7 MHz R-Y, B-Y, differential color lines. Subsequent FM-modulated recording in accordance with Still Video Floppy System.	9 MHz Same

What does all of this activity mean? Many manufacturers are seriously developing new equipment for electronic imaging and trying to find markets. Throughout this book will be short feature stories about market applications that will provide some new ideas and ways others have found to use electronic photography.

Electronic photography is here today. Understanding how it works and becoming familiar with its principles and components will help you better understand the product and how it can be used.

ELECTRONIC ANALOG PHOTOGRAPHY—THE BASICS

Nature is basically analog (Fig. 1–5, color section). The brightness of an object can have any value, and many gradations are possible on the object, both in color and density. Everything from the division of time into small units on the face of a clock or the shadings of the petals of a rose are all analog. When television was originally developed, it was too expensive to try to create a true digital system. Even today, with the lowered costs of components, digital is only now becoming cost-competitive to analog systems.

The still video camera serves as a means to convert an image in front of the camera into an electrical signal. It is a one-dimensional signal with only one value in any moment of time. If you look across an image, however, there are many values at different positions of the image. The image is actually two-dimensional, and the trick is to make it into a one-dimensional electrical signal.

By scanning the image one line at a time, in what is called *raster*, you can establish a pattern that is reproducible. The sensing of the image is done by rapidly moving a point across the image one line at a time and sensing at each point the electrical difference of color brightness of the image under the sensing point. This series of values spread over time is called the *video signal*. Scanning proceeds horizontally from the upper left corner across the image, with each line being called a *scanning line*. One complete scan of the image is called a *field*; a second interlaced scan of the same image is placed together with the first scan, forming a *frame*.

For standard television images, the ratio between the vertical and the horizontal lines is 3:4. In the new High-Definition Television (HDTV) systems planned (discussed in chapter 7), the ratio reaches 1.95:1.

Resolution is determined by the number of horizontal lines that can be viewed separately. In the 1950s, the National Television Systems Committee (NTSC) set up the original U.S. television color standard with a maximum line capability of 525 lines resolution. (European systems reach 625 lines resolution.) The bandwidth of the signal information requires 1 MHz for each 80 lines of horizontal resolution. This makes meaningful the change in bandwidth of the Hi-band recording format for still video as compared to the originally developed format.

Basically this discussion was about a monochrome system. Where does the color come from? The color is another part of the analog signal. The NTSC color system carries the monochrome image as a luminance signal, called the *Y signal*. The color is carried in two different parts called *I* and *Q*, which stand for *Inphase* and *Quadraturel*, because the two signals are carried on a single color subcarrier signal, one at 0 degrees and the other at 90 degrees or quadrature. The Hi-band width is 1.5 MHz, and the Q signal is selected so that it is only 0.5 MHz. The amplitude of the color signal represents the saturation values of the image, while the phase of the color subcarrier represents the hue of the image. Hue on a television set is referred to as tint, while the saturation control is called color. In the most recent changes of specification to Hi-band for recording, the color signal has remained at 1.5 MHz, while the luminance signal has been expanded greatly to increase the line resolution.

There are many tools and standards for measuring the quality of the color signal—test patterns, gray-scale response—that all provide information on the resolution performance of the video system. For color, test bars can show the system color performance as well.

Artifacts are a great concern with video images, not unlike dirt on a photographic negative or transparency. *Signal-to-noise ratio* (S/N) is a measurement of the amount of noise between the system and the actual image recorded. Signal-to-noise ratios of 40 or below are very apparent as snow, or white spots, in a picture. Most still video systems handle noise very well, with the exception of low light levels that generally will begin to show the inherent noise of the camera-sensing device.

Very few noise problems exist with single-chip still video cameras. With the addition of multichip cameras, with one chip providing the luminance information and one chip providing the chroma information, the potential exists for increased noise by off-registration or other mechanical failures. The advantage of the dual-chip camera is that no longer is the camera signal divided into three equal parts for red, green, and blue, but the full value of the CCD electrical recording capabilities are available from the single chip, resulting in improved speed and resolution in the still camera.

ANALOG STILL VIDEO PHOTOGRAPHY

With analog still video photography, the electronic signal that is recorded on the 2-inch magnetic floppy disk is similar to the signal recorded on conventional video tape (Fig. 1–6). Because of the use of the floppy disk, many people think that the system is a digital system; it is not! The 2-inch floppy disk is one of the limitations still to be overcome for higher resolution electronic still systems. If the still video floppy disk were a computer disk similar to that being used in laptop computers, the disk capacity would be between 740 kilobyte (Kb or K) and 1 megabyte (Mb), depending on the manufacturer. Another limitation is the capability of the CCD sensors, which are currently at a high point of 600,000 pixels in the Canon Model 760 camera. New sensor technology will be available, and I discuss this in chapter 2. Digital systems are beginning to appear, but it might be some time before we see an actual digital system available for sale. I will have more to say on this later.

The main components of the analog video system are discussed in this section. The first component is an optical system, which is the same as the optical system of a conventional silver halide still camera. The difference usually is that the sensors used to capture the electronic image are much smaller than the conventional 35-mm film so that a lens used on an interchangeable-lens still video camera actually has four times the magnification of a lens used with 35-mm film. For example, a 50-mm lens used with an electronic sensor would be the equivalent of a 200-mm lens used with a 35-mm camera. This means that the development of wide-angle lenses is a greater challenge for the still video camera designer. Long focal lenses for sports use or law enforcement surveillance are already available at lower prices than equal focal length lenses for 35-mm cameras. It becomes a much easier task at the long-focal-length end of the spectrum because a 1000-mm lens is equal to a 4000-mm lens in 35-mm photography. Also, the center portion of the lens is used, which gives the greatest area of flat imaging and sharpness.

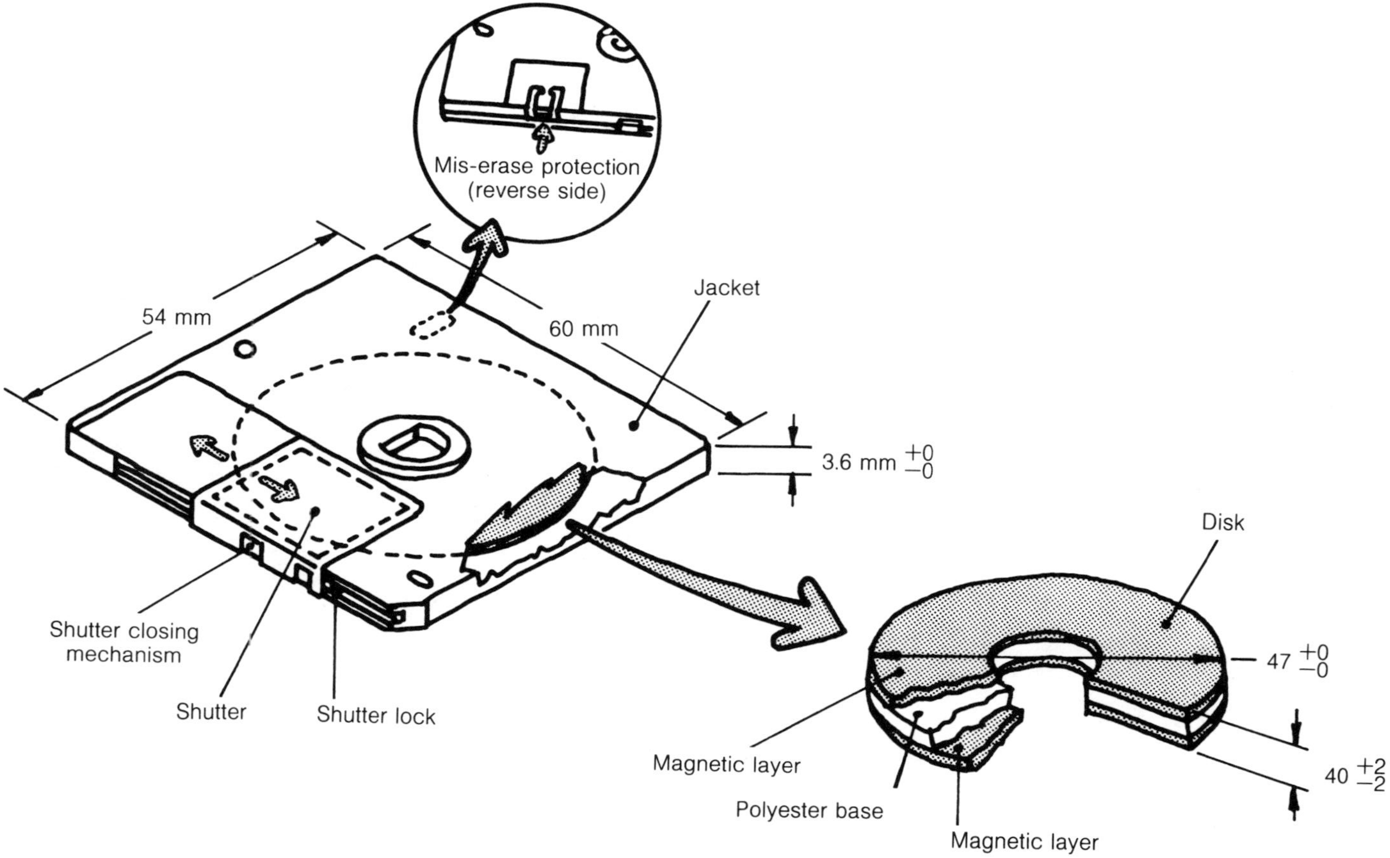

Fig. 1-6. A cut-away diagram of the 2-inch video floppy disk.

All of the cameras produced have optical viewfinders. Either single-lens reflex or viewfinders have proved to be the easiest approach to electronic photography. To date no company has used an electronic image viewfinder. With the advent of the new, small, liquid-crystal screens (LCDs), direct electronic viewing of the image being recorded might be possible in a future generation of camera.

The second major element of the still video camera is the solid-state sensor, which captures the image that comes through the lens electronically. Sensors are either charge-coupled devices (CCDs) or metal-oxide-semiconductors (MOSs).

Sensors are available in either monochrome or color to allow full color image rendition. The sensors available today, even for the Hi-band cameras, exceed the current NTSC format for U.S. video. With the advent of HDTV systems with higher resolution, the sensor could be one of the limiting factors because the cost of higher resolution sensors makes up an important part of the product cost of the camera. For example, the change from the 350,000-pixel sensor of the Canon RC-701 to the new 600,000-pixel sensor contained in their RC-760 camera caused the price of the basic camera to almost double. Much of this cost was attributed to the new sensor.

Working with the sensor is an entire system of electronics that converts the sensor output into a conventional color video signal. Although this is not new technology, the application of very large scale integrated circuits (VLSI) has been a major factor in the ability to reduce the size of the cameras to that of a conventional film camera.

Storage of today's still video images is on a video floppy disk. Conveniently called a 2-inch floppy disk, the circular magnetic disk is actually 47-mm in diameter, or slightly under 2 inches. The outer dimension is 60-mm wide by 54-mm high and is contained in a plastic jacket that has a shutter that moves aside by a camera or player mechanism to protect the disk surface. The lock on the shutter releases automatically when the disk is inserted into the drive. When the disk is removed, the mechanism relocks itself.

An erase protection device is included on the reverse side of the disk. If this tab is removed, no further recordings can be made on the magnetic material, much like conventional computer disks.

The recording surface has a total of 52 tracks (Fig. 1–7). Video, audio, and ID signals can be recorded from track 1, which is at the outermost point on the disk, to track 50 near the center. Signals cannot be recorded on track 51; track 52 is used for a cue signal recording that controls playback. Each track, from 1 to 50, actually records one field of video information. For frame recording, which includes two fields, a second field signal is placed on the track adjacent to the first. The disk revolves in a counterclockwise

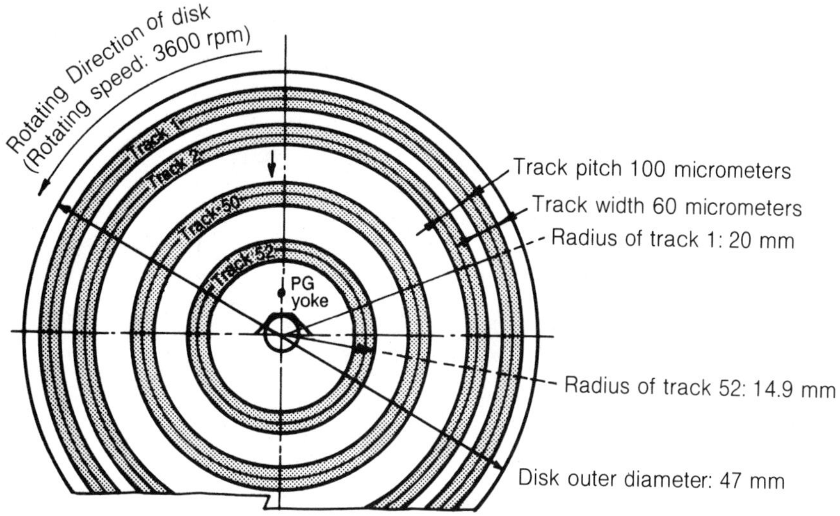

Track pattern (recording side)

Fig. 1-7. The still video floppy disk track pattern.

direction at 3600 revolutions per minute for NTSC and 3000 for PAL recording.

One important function contained within the magnetic disk is the hub, the center of the magnetic disk. When the floppy disk is placed in the drive, it is important that it be centered precisely for positioning both the track and the head. Several design features have been incorporated to ensure accuracy and interchangeability of the disks. The rotating spindle and magnetic sheet rotate as one piece. A magnet contained in the rotating spindle and a magnetic plate in the hub assure stable head-to-disk contact without any slippage (Fig. 1–8).

The playback of a field picture or one track of information is a fairly easy task. The playback of a frame picture, or two side-by-side tracks, presents an interesting challenge. The head that is doing the reading must have two gaps and coils that are 0.1 mm apart. Sony's solution to this problem was the development of a thin-film double-gap head that was used in the original MVR-5500 ProMavica.

Data recording on the disk presents another challenge. Although some areas are well defined, such as field or frame and track number, other data elements are options of the individual camera manufacturer, and there is always the possibility of some incompatibility of the data presentation. The standard bit allocation for data appears in Fig. 1–9.

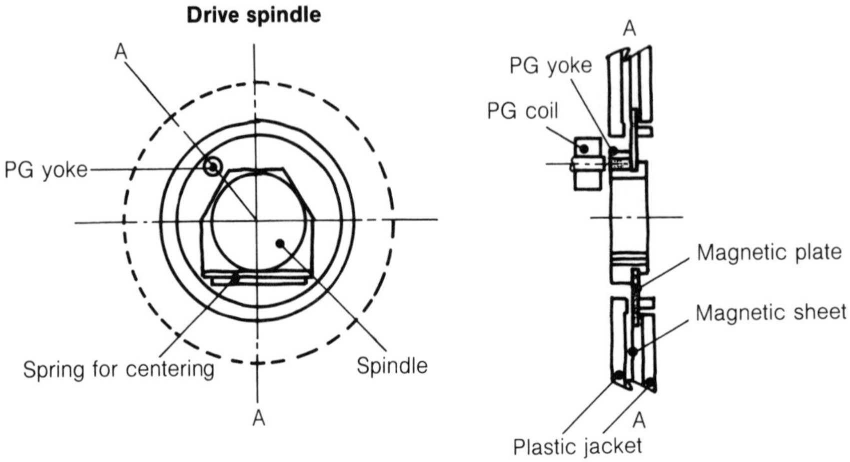

Fig. 1-8. Diagram of the hub assembly of the 2-inch video floppy disk.

The magnetic floppy disk also allows for the recording of either 5, 10, or 20 seconds of audio per track using digital signals that are memorized in a semiconductor memory device (RAM) and then read out to the disk. The actual recording takes place in analog form and requires the addition of a 6-MHz center frequency that is recorded on the main track. The time-compression speed is fixed by the readout speed from the memory against the sound length (period), which can be recorded on one track. Available time-compression ratios include 1:320, 1:640, 1:1280 for NTSC. For PAL/SECAM systems, available ratios include 1:272, 1:544, and 1:1088. At the 1:1280 compression ratio, 20 seconds of audio are available per track.

The sound quality closest to the original sound can be obtained if a low-compression ratio is used. Because of the relationship of modulation ranges, video images and sound cannot be recorded on the same track. It requires two tracks combined properly at recording. If a longer time is needed, requiring the use of more than two tracks, control codes and other key codes are recorded in order to provide continuity of sound. The tracks related to video image and sound, or sound and sound, can be reproduced easily while at the same time the tracks need not be adjacent to be related continuously to each other.

ADVANTAGES OF ELECTRONIC STILL PHOTOGRAPHY

The still video camera requires no chemical processing during developing and printing. The images can be viewed at once on an office or home TV screen or printed using a video-printer. Disks are erasable and are easily

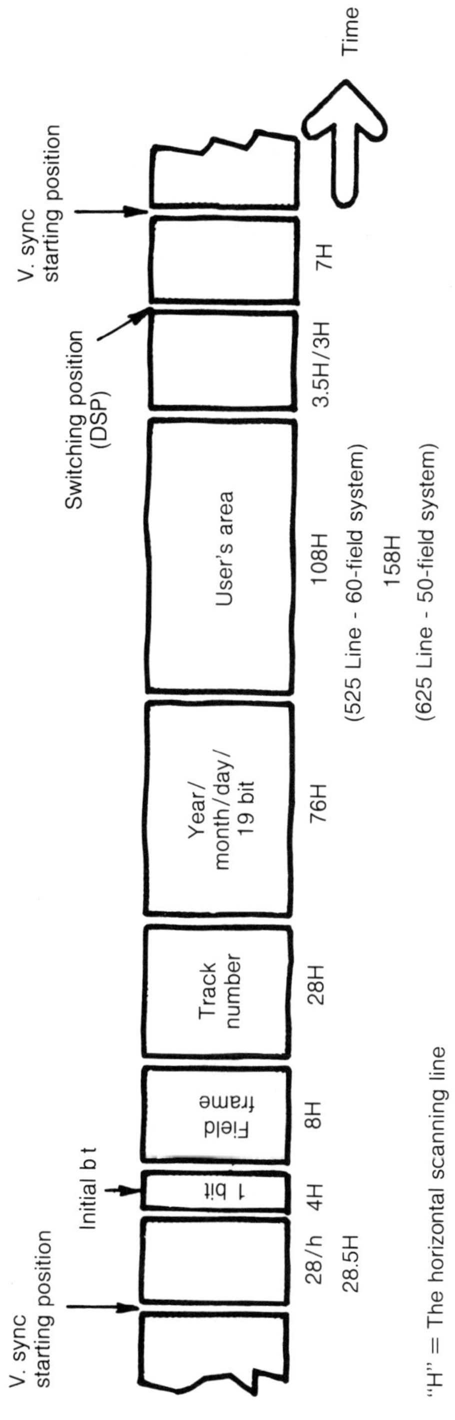

Fig. 1-9. The bit allocation for the ID code on the still video camera disk.

inserted in the camera. The 2-inch floppy disk holds 50 field images or 25 frame images in a very small amount of storage space. Still cameras can be connected by way of conversion devices to conventional computer systems and linked to printers in homes and offices (Fig. 1–10, color section).

Despite all of these advantages, it will still be a problem to change the viewing habits of the user from hardcopy prints to a combination of soft images on a screen or viewing device with the alternative of hardcopies. The solution partly depends on the changing display technology as well as the speed and quality of the printing capabilities. Although sales are estimated at 4,000,000 units/year in three to four years, much will depend on the changing tastes of the viewing public. Some of the features of the video media include:

- Video imaging can be prepared easily by anyone.
- Minimum amount of time is spent in preparing.
- Low cost of available software.
- Ease of adaptation to existing personal computers.
- Images can be transmitted rapidly.
- Random access viewing is possible through multidisk players or DAT conversion devices.

FEATURES OF ELECTRONIC STILL VIDEO CAMERAS

What are some of the major features of electronic still video cameras? First, they offer the opportunity of recording up to fifty images on a 2-inch floppy disk housed in a hard plastic shell. The images are viewable immediately on an ordinary TV screen and can be printed on a wide variety of printers designed for color still image printing (these are covered in chapter 5).

Both color and black-and-white cameras are available (Fig. 1–11, color section). These analog electronic images can be converted into digital images that can be processed using a variety of image-processing devices available for computers (see chapters 3 and 5). Processing can include modifying images, combining or improving them, or even creating new art forms from original electronic still video images.

Another key feature of electronic still video cameras is compatibility. Disks from one camera or system can be played in another system of the same type (standard or Hi-band). With the wide range of players available from various manufacturers, it is possible to integrate still video photography into existing systems, production systems, security systems, and a wide range of other potential applications. Available cameras range from simple point-and-shoot cameras to cameras with the optical sophistication of the best 35-mm single-lens reflex cameras.

SYSTEM CHARACTERISTICS

Today two different formats are available for still video recording. The normal band spectrum, which was approved as a standard in the early 1980s, includes a signal that closely resembles the signal and performance of standard VHS tape (Fig. 1–12, color section). A frequency spectrum of the normal band signal carries the same color signal information as the new Hi-band contains. The major difference between the original and the improved Hi-band system is the width of the luminance portion of the signal, which was extended from about 10 MHz to better than 15 MHz. In addition, the white peak frequency was moved to 9.7 MHz from 7.5 MHz, providing better sharpness and definition. From 360 lines, the new Hi-band still video format provides approximately 500 lines of resolution (Fig. 1–13).

The challenge was, and will continue to be, the need for greater sharpness with still pictures when compared to motion video images. The eye forgives many of the artifacts and the loss of sharpness with motion video images, but still video images are frozen on the screen and the eye becomes more critical and more demanding of image quality.

The resolution of today's still video systems remains the limiting factor in still video photography. There are other ways to create electronic photographic images, particularly from existing photographs (prints, negatives, or transparencies) or by directly scanning images of products or other items. The limits of resolution can be overcome with available equipment, but the current NTSC system offers a particularly low resolution that directly affects the quality potential of the still video image.

The best comparison might be to show the pixel count of the images and compare these to what the eye actually can see (Table 1–4). These numbers are only an approximation because it is difficult to develop exact comparisons in each medium. The bottom line is that the current NTSC and potentially HDTV will not resolve at the power of the eye. On the other hand, neither do normal newspaper images, but laser printers and 35-mm negatives certainly go beyond the resolving capability of the eye.

AVAILABLE STILL VIDEO CAMERAS

Since the first 1981 press announcement of the Sony MAVICA, at least a dozen manufacturers have demonstrated prototype video cameras. Currently half of these have brought products to the U.S. market; others have released their cameras only in Japan. The overall impact has been dramatic. Although most of the early cameras were normal band cameras, most of the cameras introduced in 1989 have been Hi-band, which take advantage of the improved definition capabilities of the new still video standard (Table 1–5).

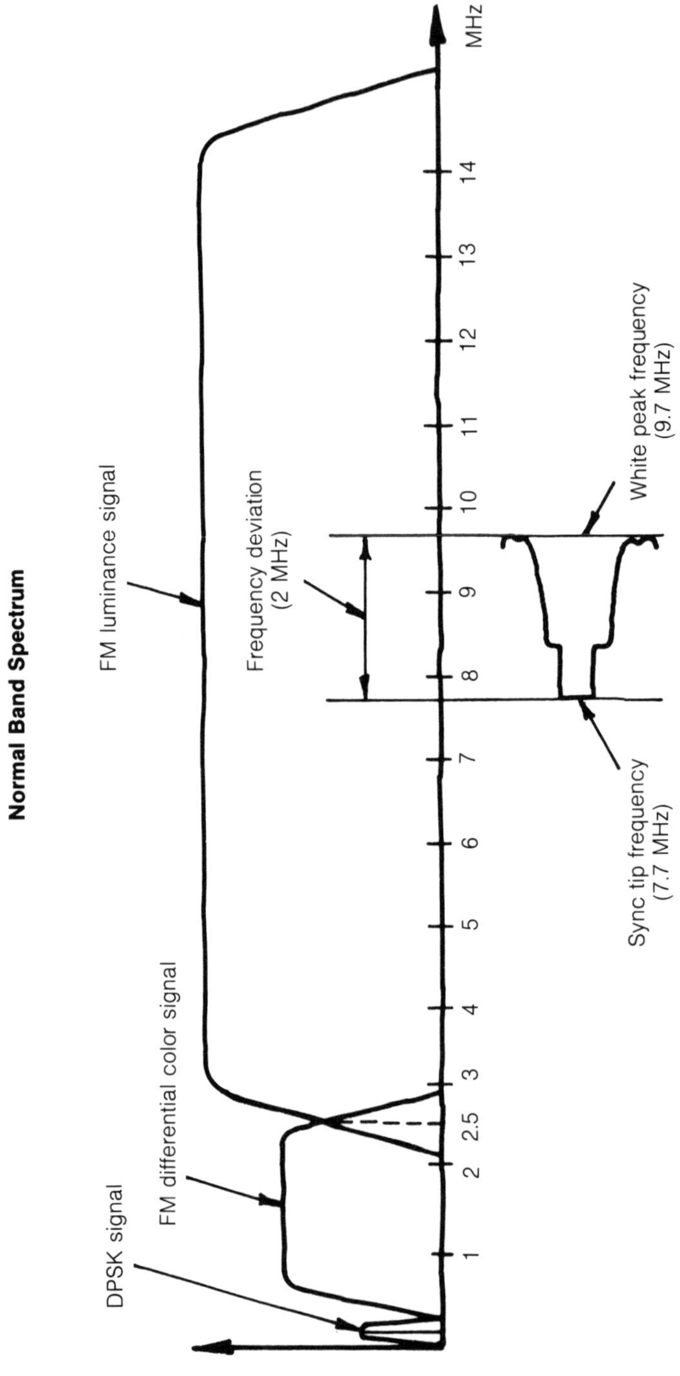

Fig. 1-13. The frequency spectrum of recording signals for Hi-band still video cameras.

Table 1-4. Imaging-System Comparisons.

Imaging System	Number of Pixels
Eye, 8 × 10 image	1,893,376
NTSC, full screen	262,144
HDTV, full screen	1,048,576
Laser printer (300 dpi), 8 × 10 image	7,200,000
Offset printed magazine, 133 line screen, 8 × 10 image	1,415,120
Newspaper, 65–85 line screen, 8 × 10 image	338,000
35 mm black-and-white Negative, full frame	8,640,000

Cameras are beginning to fall into two major categories. Professional cameras are designed with interchangeable lenses or other features that make them flexible for industrial, commercial, or government work. General-use cameras, usually priced below $1000, are aimed at the nonprofessional consumer of photography. The cameras are generally "point and shoot" types designed with the simplest of controls and, in some cases, with the built-in capability to allow direct playback of recorded still video images.

The following sections discuss most of the still video camera manufacturers, the products that they offer, and what their designs mean.

Sony

Sony's marketing efforts for still video photography began with the introduction of the MVC-A7AF still video camera recorder. Featuring a single-lens reflex with a 6× zoom lens, the 12-mm to 72-mm (f1.4–f1.7) lens was the equivalent of a 35-mm 48-mm to 288-mm lens. Audio capability includes up to 9.6 seconds of audio converted from analog into digital signals and compressed onto one track of the floppy disk.

In addition to the camera, the ProMavica includes the initial product line, two still video recorders, the MVR-A770, the MPR-5500, and a still video player, the MVP-2500.

Additional equipment available from Sony includes program-editing controllers, program controllers, and dye sublimation printers designed to meet the needs of these systems.

Sony has considered not only the professional but the general photographer with the announcement of the MVC-C1 Mavica Hi-band still camera. The camera is easy to use and offers simple point-and-shoot operation. Weighing just over one pound and measuring 5 3/4 × 2 1/4 × 4 inches (w × h × d), the Mavica MVC-C1 unit is designed to fit in the palm of a hand.

Table 1-5. A Summary of Available or Announced Analog Still Video Cameras.

Canon
RC-760—Still video camera with 600,000-pixel CCD, field and frame modes
RC-701—Color still video camera with 380,000-pixel CCD
RC-701 BW—Monochrome still video camera with 380,000-pixel CCD
RC-470—Hi-band format, compact dual-lens, autofocus camera
*RC-250/Xapshot—Hi-band still video camera with playback, CCD

Casio
*VS-101—280,000-pixel MOS sensor

Chinon
*Zoom lens still video camera, multi-beam auto focus
Still video camera back for CP-9AF camera

Copal
Prototype still video camera

Fuji
*Fujix EX-20—400,000-pixel CCD, ISO 160
*Fuji ES-30TW—Hi-band, 400,000-pixel CCD, tele/wide lens

Konica
*KC-300—300,000-pixel CCD

Minolta
SB 70S/90S—Still video backs for the Maxxum 7000 and 900 cameras

Nikon
QV-1000C—Monochrome camera with 380,000-CCD, lenses

Olympus
VCC-102—Hi-band, still video camera, zoom lens, 360,000-pixel CCD

Panasonic
AG-ES10—Hi-band, still video camera, 360,000-pixel CCD

Pentax
*EI-C70—Hi-band, auto-focus zoom lens, 360,000-pixel CCD

Sanyo
SVC-05—Compact electronic still video camera, 380,000 CCD

Sony
*MVC-C1—Hi-band, "personal" Mavica, 280,000 MOS
*MCV-A10—Hi-band, Audio Mavica (9.6 sec., audio), 280,000-pixel MOS
MVC-2000—ProMAVICA, Hi-band format, single 380,000-pixel CCD
MVC-5000—ProMavica, Hi-band, 2-chip each 380,000-pixel CCD

Vivitar
V-2000—Still video camera, 360,000-pixel CCD

Yashica
*Samurai V-70—Hi-band, 3X zoom lens, auto focus, 390,000-pixel CCD

*Cameras intended for general photography

Designed for the Hi-band video standard, the Mavica camera system provides quality still images with up to 300 lines of resolution. The camera features a lightweight disk drive mechanism and high-density integrated-circuit technology developed by Sony.

There are two components in the new Sony Mavica system, the MVC-C1 camera and the MAP-T1 player/adapter. A fixed-focus f/2.8 15-mm lens is used that provides focusing as close as 1.5 meters, or 4.5 feet (Fig. 1–14). Shutter speed is 1/60 to 1/500 second, with a built-in electronic flash. In the automatic mode it can take nine shots/sec. (field mode) or four shots/sec. (frame mode). Automatic exposure coupling range is EV 9 to 17, with the flash automatically activated in all but the EV 9 setting (Table 1–6).

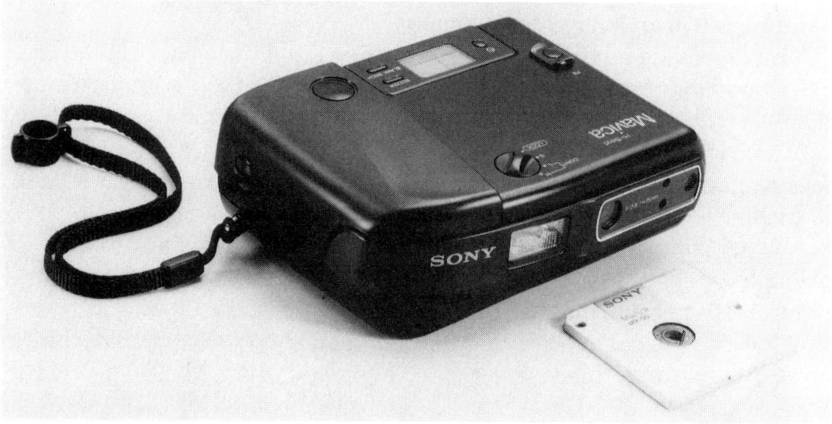

Fig. 1-14. The Sony Mavica Still Video Camera and Mavipak Disk.

Table 1-6. Specifications for the Sony Mavica MVC-C1.

Frames per disk:	50 frames (in field recording)
Lens:	15-mm f2.8 fixed focus from 1.5 m
Imaging pixels:	2/3-inch MOS-image sensor
Shutter:	1/60 - 1/500 sec
Flash:	Automatic
Photometer system:	Direct photometer with central-focus for image sensor
Strobe:	Parallel automatic flash strobe
Resolution:	Record/playback: 300 lines of horizontal resolution
	Playback: 400 lines of horizontal resolution
Shooting mode:	S: 1-shot advance
	CONT L: 4 shots/second continuous
	CONT R: 90 shots/second continuous

In addition to single-picture shooting, the camera offers continuous high-speed still-image recording at four or nine pictures per second. This allows intricate high-speed shooting of sports subjects or industrial images.

Some camera functions include a self-timer (10 second delay), "blank-search" for forward or reverse seeking of unused fields/frames on the disk, a pre-stand-by mode that determines exposure, and a shut-off system that automatically turns off power after five minutes of no usage. The video data is recorded in the Hi-band format, with 300 horizontal lines and 400 vertical lines for playback.

A 6-volt rechargeable nickel cadmium battery powers the camera. If unused for five minutes, a power-off feature automatically turns off the camera to conserve the battery. The BP-C1 battery pack plugs into the back of the camera or the player. It uses a 6-volt nickel cadmium system that can be recharged in an hour with an adapter.

An output signal that goes into the video input terminals of television sets is available from the MAP-T1 player/adapter. For TVs without a video input, an F-adapter can be used. This unit is only 131 mm (w) × 94 mm (d) × 30 mm (h), and weighs 250 grams without battery pack. In addition to operating with the common battery pack, the unit will also work with a 9V ac adapter.

Either automatic (5-second intervals) or manual playback modes are available for sequential showing of the recorded images. A remote control unit RM-C1K permits the user to select specific images.

The two pieces offer a simple point-and-shoot system that can be coupled to any home television system. Equipped with a 280,000-pixel MOS image sensor, the MVC-C1 camera has a sensitivity equivalent of ISO-80 film.

The introduction of the general Mavica fulfilled a promise made several years ago by Sony Chairman Akio Morita at the announcement of the original Mavica that they would have a camera in the $600 to $700 range in the near future. Although it was not an overnight achievement, the camera is now a reality.

Where does Sony see a market for this general-purpose Mavica camera? For families, it could be instant viewing of vacation pictures or making visual memos while shopping for anything from coats to homes. Athletes can analyze individual performances.

Fashion design and real estate are three areas in which the system can be used when visual impressions are important. Department stores could use it to merchandise their offerings electronically to customers; businesses can enhance presentations; and the MAVICA products can be linked to other electronic equipment such as computers or telecommunications equipment.

Sony, the oldest announced manufacturer of electronic still video cameras, recently has announced a new ProMavica two-chip camera. With two separate chips, one for chroma (color) and one for luminance—both chips containing 360,000 pixels—the improved sharpness is dramatic because the full 360,000 pixels are available for the luminance signal. This dual-chip design means that the images are much sharper than can be obtained with a single-chip camera containing alternating stripes or dots of color.

The Sony two-chip camera, the MVC-5000, already has seen service with *USA Today* with direct separations for color printing being made through a computer (Fig. 1–15). This final set of separation films gave *USA Today* quality capabilities from original images. The camera's two chips pick up luminance and chroma separately. As a result, the camera produces more than 500 lines of horizontal resolution. (See Table 1–7.)

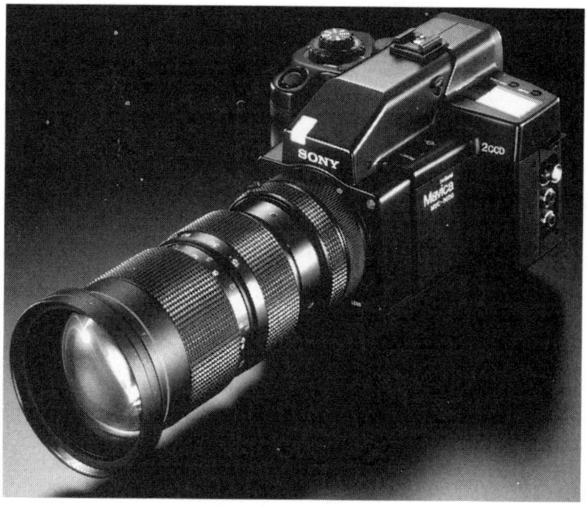

Fig. 1-15. The Sony MVC-5000 Hi-band ProMavica Electronic Still Video Camera.

There is a built-in narration microphone on the rear of the camera with the ability to record 9.6 seconds of audio on a single track. The camera comes with a bayonet mount, and an MCL-200N lens adapter allows a variety of Nikon lenses to be used on the camera.

Sony also has created a new ProMavica MVP-660 Hi-band ProMavica player with a rotation jogger to help move faster across a disk (Fig. 1–16).

Canon

Canon was the first company to actually introduce a still video camera system into the marketplace, in mid-1986. Fujio Mitarai, president of Canon

Table 1-7. Specifications for the Sony MVC-5000 Still Video Camera Recorder.

Recording format:	Still video floppy
Video:	Chrominance: -Y, B-Y differential color-line sequential FM recording
Audio:	Time-compressed FM recording 9.6 sec/track)
Recording mode:	Hi-band/normal band selectable
Recording mode:	EIA monochrome, NTSC color
Imager:	Two 2/3" interline transfer CCD image sensors
Picture elements:	380,000 pixels each (768H × 493 V)
Viewfinder:	TTL optical viewfinder, viewing area 90%
Photometer:	TTL center-weighted
Shutter:	Focal-plane, 1/15-1/2000 sec
Flash synch:	1/180 sec
White balance:	Self-adjusting automatic white balance/3200k/ 5800k/memory
Shutter mode:	Single, 3 images/sec continuous/self timer/interval
ID recording:	Year, month, day, hour, minute, second, aperture value, shutter speed
Video-recording mode:	Frame/field selectable
Exposure-control system:	Programmed AE, shutter priority AE, aperture priority AE, manual
Horizontal resolution:	500 TV lines (recorder, Hi-band)
	360 TV lines (recorder, normal band)
Recording capacity:	Frame recording: 25 pictures
	Field recording: 50 pictures
	Frame picture with audio recording: 16 pictures
	Field picture with audio recording: 25 pictures
	(audio only: 480 sec.)
Input:	External microphone input Remote control (for RM-S7) Hot shoe

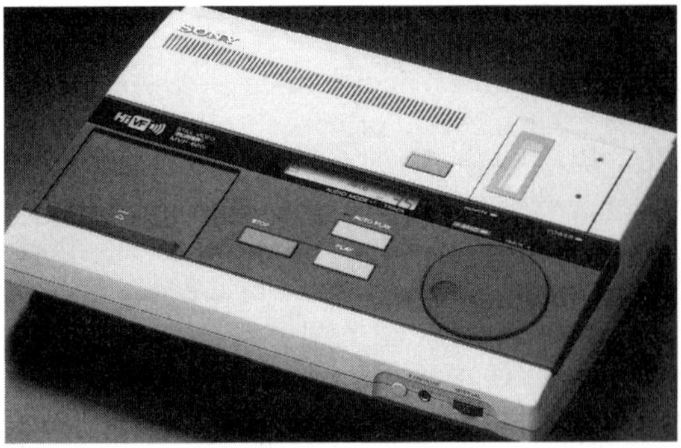

Fig. 1-16. The Sony MVP-660 Hi-band ProMavica Player.

U.S.A., was quick to point out at the product introduction that, "The system was designed and is being built exclusively by Canon. The design team drew on the company's expertise in cameras, optics, video, and office machines, including copiers."

The first camera announced by Canon was the RC-701, which uses 380,000-pixel sensor to produce 50 images on a standard 2-inch video floppy disk. The initial product line included an RT-971 transceiver for transmitting color or black-and-white images over ordinary phone lines in three minutes, the RP-601 printer, an ink-jet printer for making hardcopies up to 3 5/8 × 4 13/16 inches, and the RR-551 recorder for instant picture playback on conventional TV sets. In addition, a Video Visualizer (chapter 2) was introduced as a replacement for an overhead projector, along with a laminator for creating a gloss surface on the ink-jet-produced prints.

Initial testing of the Canon system was done at the 1984 Summer Olympics by the Japanese newspaper, Yomiuri Shimbun. Pictures were transmitted from Los Angeles and ran in the evening edition in color the same day.

It wasn't long before the Canon RC-760 still video camera appeared at the end of 1987 (Table 1–8). Using a new 600,000-pixel sensor that delivers 480 lines of horizontal resolution, the new CCD delivers 1212 pixels horizontal and 500 vertical. A vertical pixel design has produced a significant sharpness increase and is certainly a welcome development. The new CCD uses a line-transfer technique and on-tip RGB stripe filter. The camera operates in the normal band but provides a much sharper image than previous Canon electronic still video cameras.

In addition to resolution, the camera's color quality was dramatically improved as well. The RC-760 has fully automatic white-light balance and

Table 1-8. Specifications for the Canon Still Video Camera RC-760.

Pickup element:	Color 600,000-pixel CCD image sensor
Light-metering system:	TTL full aperture, using an SPC; center-weighted average metering
Exposure-control system:	Shutter-priority AE, 3-mode program AE
Shutter:	Rotary sllt shutter
Shutter speed:	1/8 - 1/2000 sec
Flash X- synch speed:	1/80 sec
White balance:	Auto tracking/manual
Shooting speed:	Single, 2, 5, and 10 images/sec in field mode; single, 2, 4, or 6 images/sec in frame mode
ID data	Month, day, year, hour, minute, second, Av, Tv, and 4-digit number

also a nine-position manual control to allow accurate color reproduction in a variety of typical conditions. This, coupled with the ability to record either frames or fields, produces the maximum possible sharpness. Both the RC-701 and RC-760 cameras were designed for the professional with interchangeable lenses and other functions.

Some of the other features in the new camera include frame or field selection, a brighter laser-matte split-prism viewfinder and a new standard lens, a Canon 13–52-mm f1.8. The RC-760 has built-in encoding and records the year/month/day and hour/minute/second; shutter speed and aperture; and a four-digit identification code. This information can be superimposed on the video and print image (Fig. 1–17 and 1–18, color section).

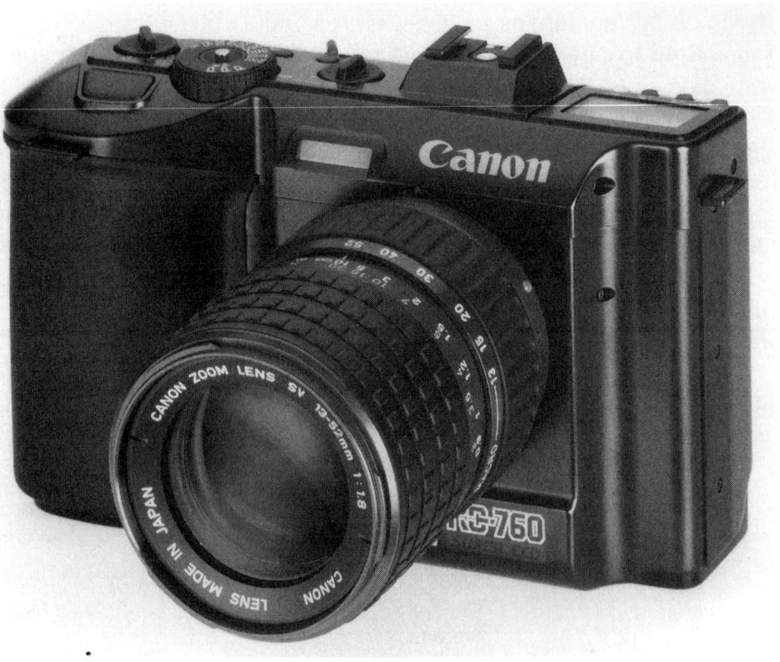

Fig. 1-17. The Canon Still Video Camera RC-760.

The RC-760 camera attracted much attention from areas such as law enforcement because the camera uses normal 35-mm camera lenses. Because of the size of the sensor, a gain factor of four occurs in the focal length of the lens so that a 500-mm lens becomes a 2000-mm lens. The

500-mm 35-mm camera lenses are available at a much lower cost than 2000-mm lenses.

The need for surveillance photography in the marketplace also brought another version of the RC-701—a black-and-white-only imaging camera that removed the color stripes from the sensor, thus substantially increasing the speed. Speeds in six-digit ISO numbers have been reported for images captured using the black-and-white RC-701 camera. Especially interesting to law-enforcement agencies is the lens capability of the RC-701 black-and-white camera. The gain of 4:1 on lenses allows the use of existing 35-mm photography lenses of 1000 mm to serve the same purpose as expensive 4000-mm lenses. In addition, the surveillance photography disks can be reused so that a more economical method of surveillance photography is possible along with a greater variety of optics.

The Xapshot RC-250 camera was introduced by Canon with the general photography market in mind. There was a small amount of uncertainty about the name of the camera because it appeared initially as the RC-250, then as the Zapshot, and most recently as the Xapshot (Fig. 1–19). On this Hi-band still video camera, everything is automatic, including the flash (Table 1–9). Canon's compact RC-250 (which resembles a pair of binoculars) has a 1/2-inch CCD imager, measures 142 mm (w) × 107 mm (d) × 33 mm (h), and weighs 500 grams without battery pack. It has a fixed-focus 11-mm f/2.8 lens, with a focal distance of from 1 meter to infinity. The automatic exposure coupling range is EV 8 to 18, with an AE exposure control system and a 1.5 EV backlight compensation. The built-in flash

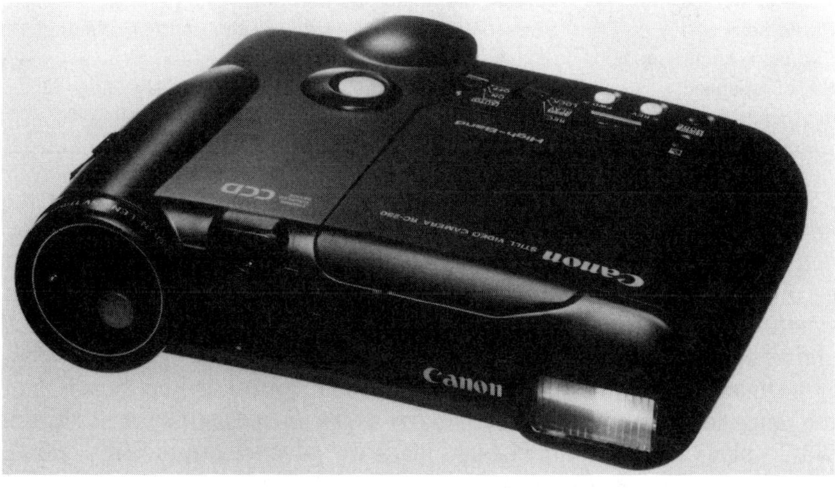

Fig. 1-19. The Canon Xapshot RC-250 Still Video Camera.

Table 1-9. Specifications for the Canon Xapshot (RC-250) Still Video Camera.

Image pickup element:	CCD image sensor
Transfer method:	Full-frame transfer
Construction:	Single virtual phase drive
Screen size:	6.4 mm (H) × 4.8 mm (V) (Equivalent to 1/2-inch size)
Number of picture elements:	786 horizontally
Coloring method:	RGB pure color stripe filter (on-chip)
Output method:	R-G-B separate outputs
Anti-blooming method:	Recoupling of charges by anti-blooming gates
Recording method:	Field recording (complies with Hi-band standard of the Association of Electronic Still Camera Makers)
Luminance signal:	FM recorded
Color signal:	Sequential FM recording of color differential lines
Coloring method:	NTSC format
Lens:	Fixed focus
Focal length/aperture:	11 mm
Effective range:	1.0 to Infinity
Macro mechanism:	Activates when the macro switch is in the on position; focusing point in macrophotography: 30 cm from the CCD image pickup surface
Viewfinder:	Real image secondary imaging finder
Shutter:	Two-blade programmed lens shutter
Shutter speed:	1/500 to 1/30 sec
Electronic flash synchronizing speed:	1/125 sec
Release method:	Electronic release
Photometry:	External Photometric sensor (SPC) and CCD signal
Exposure-control method:	Programmed AE (f2.8 to f22)
Shooting-speed:	Single-frame shooting and continuous shooting - 3 frames per sec

automatically fires at EV 8 or lower and can be turned on manually for fill-in or off. Shutter speeds are 1/30 to 1/500 second, with 1/125-second flash synch. Accessories include a BP-4C battery pack, pin cable, battery charger, and ac coupler (Fig. 1–20).

Operating the camera is extremely simple. Push the eject button and the hinge cover on top pops open. Insert a disk and press the cover closed. With a blank disk, the camera automatically advances to the first frame. Slide the main switch to Record, look through the viewfinder, compose the picture, and press the shutter release button.

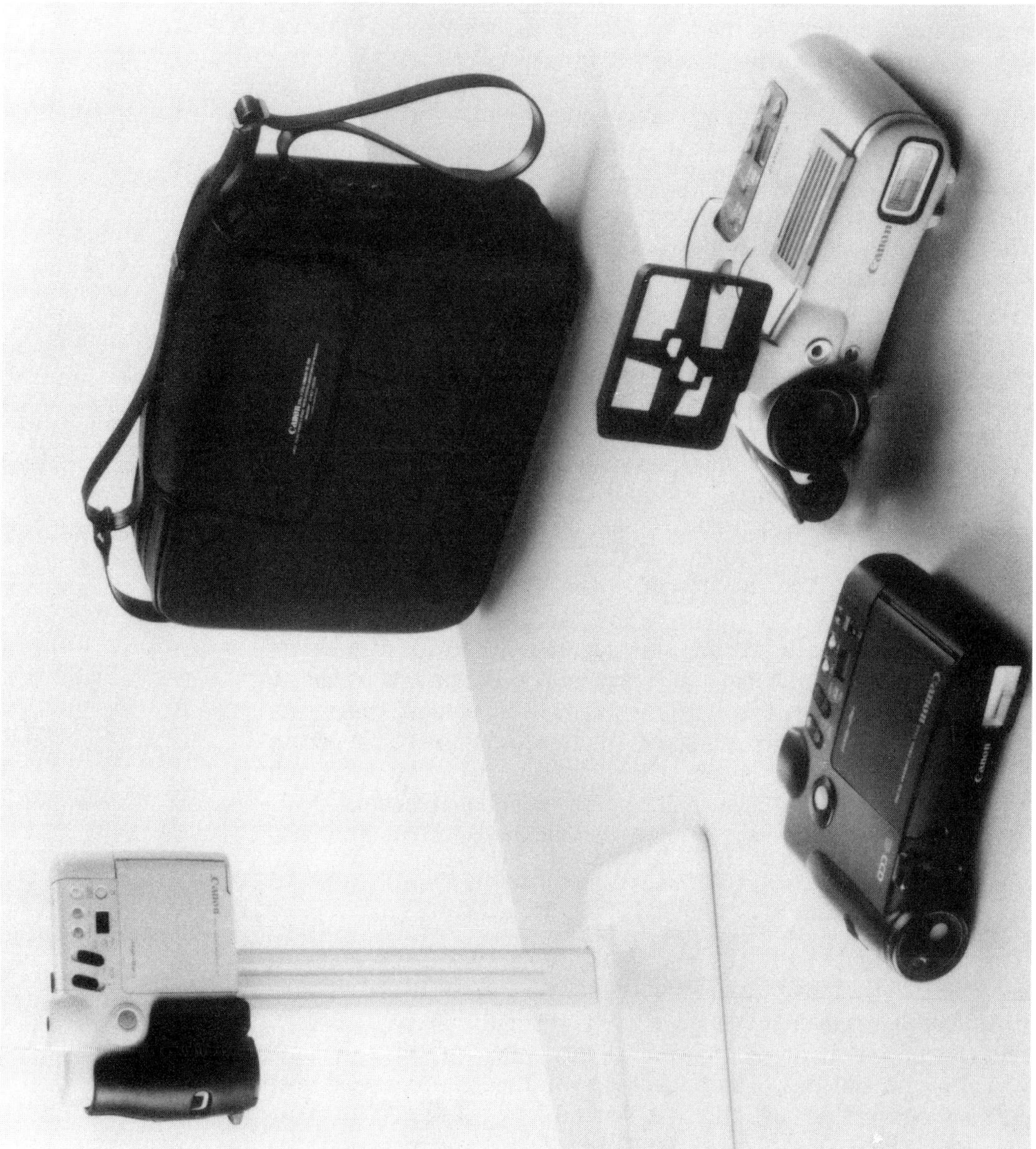

Fig. 1-20. Accessories for the Canon RC-250 Xapshot.

Playback is just as easy. One end of a cable plugs into the camera, the other connects to a TV set the same way as a cassette recorder. Select Play and the first frame appears on the television. Press the camera's Forward button to advance through the frames. Press reverse to review earlier frames.

To erase an image, slide the main switch to Erase, press the Forward or Reverse button to locate the desired image, then press the Erase Mode button and the shutter release. This three-step procedure is a safety precaution to prevent accidental erasures.

With the addition of the Xapshot, Canon was now ready to face a broader market with still video products for both the professional and general photographer.

Canon provided a point-and-shoot for the professional with the introduction of the RC-470 camera. This camera looks a great deal like the simple point-and-shoot 35-mm cameras that had become so popular. It is designed in the more conventional camera shape, with a right-hand extended body/hand-grip, autofocus and built-in automatic flash. Dimensions are 148 mm (w) × 71 mm (d) × 87 mm (h), and weight is 600 grams without battery pack. Using the new Hi-band circuitry along with a 360,000-pixel 1/2-inch sensor, high resolution of more than 400 TV lines, both horizontal and vertical, are achieved. The RC-470 offers the option of frame or field recording.

A bifocal lens on the RC-470 has been adopted with a wide-angle 9 mm (equivalent to 48 mm for 35-mm cameras) and tele-16 mm (equivalent to 86-mm lenses for 35-mm cameras). The lens is made up of moving elements in the front and rear that permit better resolution and more stable performance. Lenses move on the optical axis for greater accuracy with a full aperture of f2.0 at the wide angle and f2.5 in the telephoto position.

The camera rangefinder works in the dark and will even find subjects without contrast. No moving parts are involved so that reliability is very high for the rangefinder.

Shutter speed also covers a wider range, from 1/30 to 1/1000 second, with flash sync speed of 1/150 second. The automatic exposure coupling range is EV 6.7 to EV 18 in the field mode and EV 7.7 to EV 18 in the frame mode, with an AE exposure-control system.

Shooting speeds are single, five and 20 exposures/second in the field mode, and single and five exposures/second in the frame mode. Other camera functions include a self-timer (10-second delay), flash control (auto, on, off), disk initial setting (Normal, Skip/Insert; in which Normal and Skip set the head to the next-to-last track recorded and Insert sets the track to the first recordable track), and auto code setting (on/off, with choice of year/month/day or hour/minute/second). Battery pack BP-4P is an option, with CR-2032 lithium battery back-up. A battery charger (BC-24P) and car battery cord (CB-12) also are offered as options (Fig. 1–21).

The Canon RV-301 Still Video Player offers a choice of Hi-band (500 horizontal lines) or normal (350 horizontal lines) resolutions. An optional remote-control unit allows direct random access of any selected image, and the player can erase either a single image or an entire floppy disk. If chosen, the track number can be displayed in the upper-right corner of the TV screen, and the year/ month/ day or hour/ minute/ second and code number can be displayed in the lower right corner.

The RV-301 also offers "interval play" for continuous display, with auto advance selected from 1 to 99 second intervals. A scan mode allows 10 images/second to be displayed. Other selectable speeds are 2.5 or 10 images/second (in the field mode) and 2 images/second (in the frame mode). The RV-301 also has an auto-disengage function for removing the head from the disk when the display of a single image exceeds 30 minutes, or when power is off. Power is ac. This is one of several still video player/recorders that are marketed by Canon.

Kinji Kikuchi, Canon's vice president, announced to the press in November of 1988 that he looked forward to combined total sales of still video cameras reaching the 10 million level within four to five years. This is significantly higher than other industry estimates of 4 to 5 million units during that period.

Eastman Kodak

Kodak was not about to let their competitors steal all of the electronic still video glory. In mid-1987, Kodak introduced a line of products for still video use, with the exception of a still video camera. At their initial press conference introducing electronic photography products, Kodak showed a hand-built model of a camera, but it still has not appeared on the market (Fig. 1–22).

The initial line of products announced by Kodak included a multidisk recorder/player that could play up to 1500 images from a cartridge. The SV7500 still video multidisk recorder handles field or frame images with a tray capacity of 30 still video floppy disks. The individual trays have an erasable nonvolatile memory that allows each image to be categorized into 1 of 20 categories using a hand-held remote control. In addition, a serial port permits computer-controlled operation and two-way communications.

Kodak has continued to add components in addition to their widely accepted video printer and transceiver equipment. A recent copy-stand type camera is another element that I discuss later in chapter 2.

Kodak has primarily played a wait-and-see game with still video products, not unlike the marketing strategy of Japanese manufacturers who for so many years allowed U.S. companies to do the basic research and product development, and then begin their marketing efforts when the product became accepted.

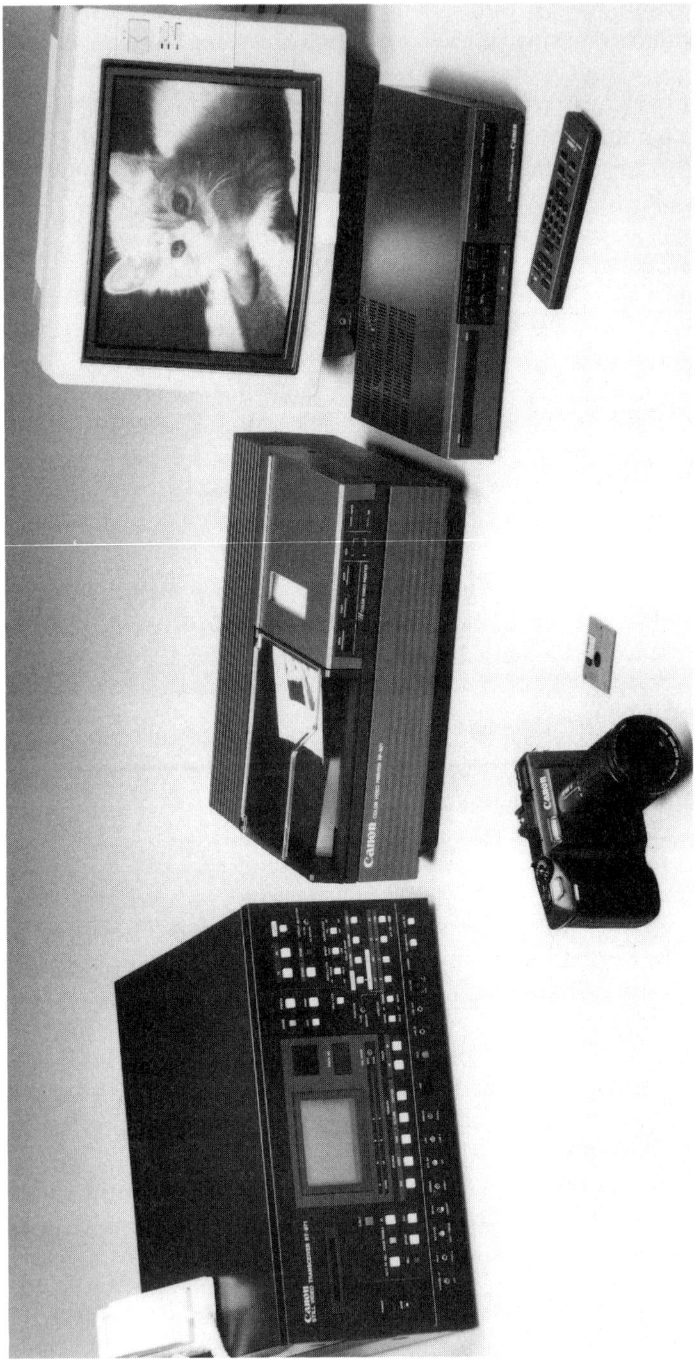

Fig. 1-21. A complete Canon Still Video System.

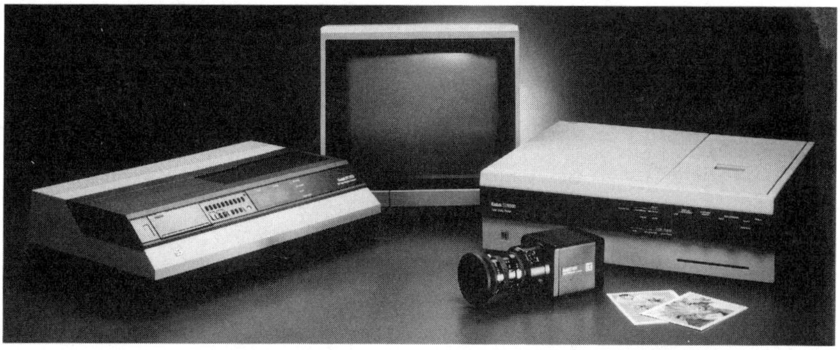

Fig. 1-22. Some of the Kodak Still Video System. On the left, the SV7550 Multidisk Recorder; on the right, the Kodak SV6550 Color Video Printer; and in the foreground, one of their CCD cameras.

Casio

Casio was one of the first electronic still video cameras designed for the general market and offered for sale in the United States. At the time of the original announcement, in June 1987, at the Consumer Electronic Show in Chicago, Casio showed a simple camera which was intended originally to sell well below $1000, but that ultimately was priced much higher. The Casio camera is able to play back its images directly into a television set. The camera uses a 280,000-pixel MOS sensor and a F2.8 fixed-focus lens that provides coverage from 1.0 meters to infinity. When coupled with the automatic exposure control, shutter speeds vary from 1/8 second to 1/1000 second.

Chinon

Chinon created a prototype electronic still back for its CP-9AF single-lens reflex camera. Using a 380,000-pixel sensor, the record-only back easily replaces the conventional film back on the camera.

Chinon earlier had shown a dedicated electronic still video camera but was now showing the prototype version for their top-of-the-line 35-mm camera.

Copal

At the 1984 Photokina in Cologne, West Germany, Copal exhibited a prototype still video camera. At the 1986 Photokina, the company announced the availability of various video components, including shutters, lenses, and video floppy drive units. In 1988, the still video component line was expanded still more.

Their products include a VFS-2 compact focal-plane shutter assembly for a 2/3-inch color imager. A single motor sequentially controls shutter cocking, and five frames/second are possible. The maximum shutter speed is 1/1000 second, and the fastest synchronizing speed for electronic flash operation is 1/125 second. The dual-focal-length VFL-2 lens permits a changeover from wide angle (10 mm) to telephoto (20 mm) by sliding the lens along a guide pole. The lens has diaphragm openings at f2.8, f5.6, and f11.

Fully compatible with all 1-inch video floppy disks, the VFD-2 video floppy drive is a compact dc brushless drive only 58 mm (w) × 65 mm (d) × 20 mm (h) and weighing only 100 grams.

Copal acknowledges that it supplies many of the components for the Casio still video system, but insists that it recommended to Casio that the system be improved further before going into production.

Fuji

Fuji did not begin its entry into still video imaging with cameras. The Fujix TV photography system was designed to take film images and transfer them to video floppy disks. This service, available in Japan beginning in 1984 for photofinishers, was an experiment to permit the conversion of conventional color negative photographic images to still video images.

The first Fuji still video camera appeared in 1985. It was the result of combining technology from media-manufacturing techniques for high-performance magnetic materials, camera medical systems, and a variety of optical instruments. The Fujix ES-1 camera, designed with a 2/3-inch, 380,000-pixel CCD, continues to be marketed actively in Japan. Fuji's latest still video cameras are the Fujix ES-20 (Fig. 1–23) and the Fujix ES-30TW.

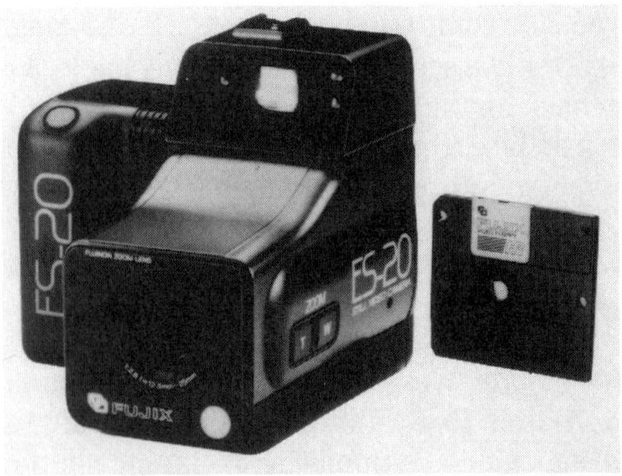

Fig. 1-23. The Fujix ES-20 Still Video Camera.

The Fuji Fujix ES-20 Still Video Camera has a 2/3-inch 400,000-pixel CCD imager, a 2× zoom lens, auto-focus, and programmed exposure. This field/frame camera permits 50/25 images to be made at the touch of a button. Built-in auto-white balance automatically adjusts for natural color. Automatic color control of the subject takes into account illumination or weather conditions, even outdoor or indoor lighting (Table 1–10).

Table 1-10. Specifications for the Fujix ES-20 Still Video Camera.

Recording system:	Frame recording/field recording (conforms to industry standard)
Image sensor:	2/3-inch 400,000-pixel CCD imager
ISO frame recording:	Equivalent to ISO 80 (can be upgraded to ISO 160)
ISO field recording:	Equivalent to ISO 160 (can be upgraded to ISO 320)
Lens:	TV-FUJINON f2.8, f12.5–25.0 mm
Viewfinder:	Abada-type bright frame finder
Focusing:	Infrared-ray active auto-focusing (with focus memory provided)
Photometry method:	TTL through-aperture metering (center-weighed light reading)
Shutter:	Electronic control method vertical run metal focal plane
Shutter speed:	1/2–1/1000 sec
Picture-taking speed:	Continuous picture taking—5 picture/sec
Auto flash function:	Exclusive electronic flash works automatically, even for daytime synch

It also features TTL center-weighted metering system, an electronic shutter with speeds from 1/2 to 1/1,000 sec., continuous shooting at five frames/sec., and a track-skip mode that permits post-exposure recording of audio in conjunction with the Fujix P7A Player. With the player, 9.6 seconds of audio can be added to each image in the field mode (recorded under the track-skip mode). The narrative or sound effect is compressed 640:1 and recorded onto an adjacent track. The P7A also features NTSC format, playback only with field/frame and color/black-and-white selection, frame-by-frame advance, random access, and automatic repeating.

Fuji provides an entire series of recorders and players, including recorders with audio capability (Fig. 1–24).

Konica

With the introduction of the Konica KC-300, another general-market product has appeared. Konica first showed electronic still video equipment in 1985 in a series of designs that looked very similar to earlier Super-8

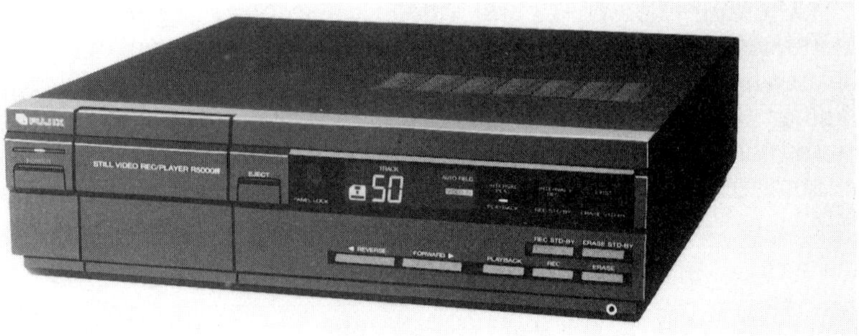

Fig. 1-24. The Fujix R5000H Hi-band-compatible Still Video Recorder Player.

general motion-picture cameras. The Konica SVC-40 still video camera used an autofocus, CCD image sensor-based camera for imaging on video floppy disks. The autofocus system featured a 12- to 36-mm f1.4 zoom lens and a switchable manual focus override. The SVC-40 replaced the original SVC-20, first available in 1985. The image sensor was a 2/3-inch CCD with 300,000 pixels. An LCD display showed frame number, recording mode, exposure, single or continuous shooting, date, and time (Fig. 1–25, color section).

Next came the Konica KC-400 with a 380,000-pixel, 1/2-inch sensor. The latest KC-300, with reduced price and improved features, has a 300,000-pixel sensor and offers the option of field and frame recording. An f2.8 12-mm fixed-focus lens is combined with a programmed AE exposure control system 7 EV (1/15 second f2.8) to 18 EV (1/2000 second, f11).

The camera has an AE program that incorporates a fixed iris and CCD electronic shutter as well as automatic strobe flash for low brightness and close-up conditions. The CCD is made up of a vertical-transfer CCD that transmits the electric charge of the photodiode and horizontal transfer CCD that read the electric charge for each pixel and a sweeping drain that removes unnecessary electric charges.

At the photosensitive part, unnecessary electric charges such as heat and noise are swept out the sweeping drain through the vertical CCD, emptying the photodiode. This process opens the shutter and becomes the starting point of exposure. Light passing through the lens focuses on the CCD. Conforming to the brightness level, electric charges of different potential are generated and stored, and when the shutter signal is input, the electric charge of the signal is transferred to the vertical transfer CCD (the time up to this point is the shutter time) and then stored by high-speed transfer.

The shutter speed can be controlled by shutter pulse, permitting a highly precise exposure control compared with a mechanical shutter. Other manufacturers have many patents on the technologies employing CCDs, but the Konica camera is one of the first to utilize these coupling techniques to advantage in the camera.

The KC-400 offered three continuous shooting speeds:

- High speed at 20 exposures/second
- Medium speed at 6 exposures/second
- Low speed at 2 exposures/second.

Recording is on a 2-inch video floppy disk, in NTSC compatible format. Autodating can be added by superimposing the data on the video signal. A playback unit, the KP-300, also is available to complete the package for TV viewing.

Minolta

When Minolta designers were creating their Maxxum family of cameras, they happily designed a still video back that can be used with their 7000 and 9000 35-mm single reflex cameras (Fig. 1–26). Incorporating the disk drive and a 2/3-inch CCD image sensor, it allows these cameras to convert quickly from conventional film to electronic still photography. The challenge still remains that the lenses are multiplied by a factor of four, meaning that the normal 50-mm lens immediately becomes a 200-mm lens. With Minolta lenses, a supplementary diopter lens reduces this to a factor of two but with a loss of lens speed. With surveillance photography, this is an advantage; for regular photography, this still makes a normal lens a telephoto lens. Date and exposure number capability are available, as well as field- and frame-selectable recording.

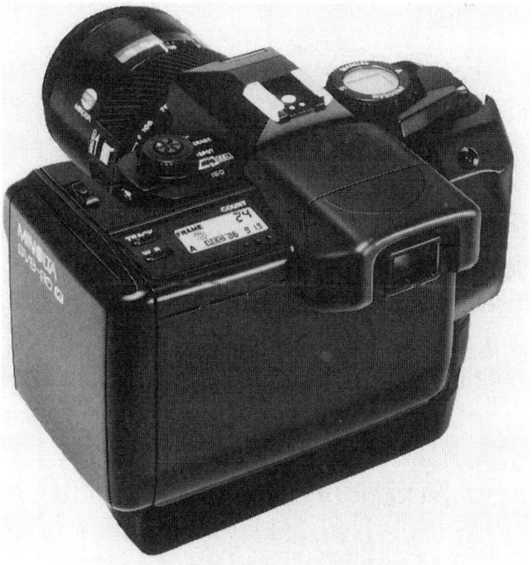

Fig. 1-26. The Minolta Still Video Back for their 7000 and 9000 35mm single-lens reflex cameras.

Nikon

Nikon is another of the companies that has shown prototype equipment at major world trade shows and only recently has brought to market a black-and-white still video camera called the QV-1000C. The camera has created a great deal of attention in the newspaper area because it is the still video camera with the highest sensitivity that has appeared to date, with a rating of 1600. The camera has a variable shutter with speeds of from 1 to 1/2000 second. Using a center-weighted TTL metering system, a choice of aperture priority, shutter priority, program or manual exposure controls are available.

Single frames can be exposed or a continuous sequence of 4 or 20 frames per second. The user can select three film-speed equivalents: ISO 400, 800, or 1600, which doubles when the camera is set for continuous high-speed operation. The QV-1000C camera has two Nikkor interchangeable zoom lenses: the f1.4 10–40mm and the f2.0 11–120mm. A lens adapter also allows photographers to use standard Nikkor lenses with the video camera. A special reset recording method reduces the time between shutter release and recording on the 2-inch video floppy disk and permits 20 images/second to be shot with the CCD sensor function (shutter speed 1/1000 second, mirror locked up, only for field picture).

With a 380,000-pixel sensor, the QV-1000C provides images in most light conditions needed for press photography and has the ability to provide images at the last minute for press deadlines. Even with the 380,000 pixel sensor, with no color filters, it still does not meet the minimum requirements that have been set by many photojournalists of 1 Mbyte or more pixels for ultimate sharpness in their images.

Olympus

Olympus Optical Co., Ltd.'s first still video system was a unique modular system with advancements both in design and capability. The Olympus V-100 still video camera had a different shape, compact design and a great deal of modular functionality when used with the V-200 playback processor. Actually, the V-100 and V-200 were the same shape and could be plugged together for a very compact package. However, the V-200 requires ac power, while the V-100 used batteries, so it was necessary to be near a power outlet for reviewing images.

The Hi-band V-100 Camera used a 1/2-inch 360,000-pixel CCD imager with a 9–27-mm f2.8 zoom lens that focused as close as 0.85 meter. For right-handed people, the unit fit neatly into the palm, with a strap that went around the back of the hand to keep the unit from being dropped. The zoom and exposure buttons lay conveniently under the fingers, making this unit very comfortable to use (Fig. 1–27).

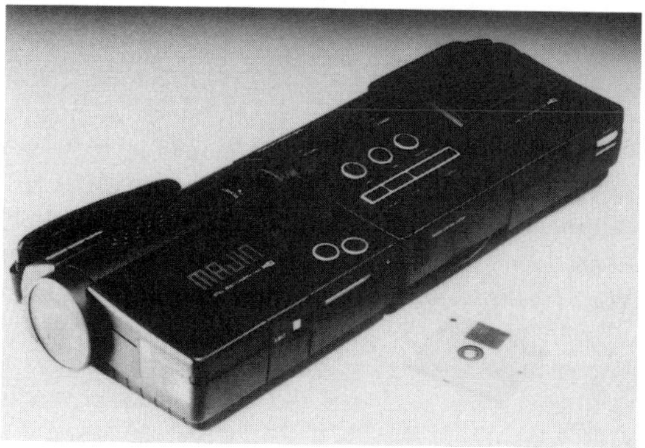

Fig. 1-27. The Olympus V100 Still Video Camera modularly attached to the V200 Playback Processor.

The camera used programmed AE with automatic backlight compensation to control the exposure, with an electronic shutter speed of from 1/8 to 1/2000 second. The built-in flash was synchronized at 1/30 second and was activated automatically in low light or backlight conditions. The camera could shoot at a frame rate of 15 frames per second. Designed for Hi-band recording, automatic exposure compensation and assistance was provided in other difficult lighting conditions. A patterned light measurement was utilized via the CCD of the camera. Data recording capability was included for year/month/day and track numbers.

Continuous shooting mode was selectable from 5, 10, or 15 pictures/second. The camera is 137 mm (w) × 165 mm (d) × 59 mm (h) and weighs 840 grams without batteries. A nickel cadmium battery pack was provided.

When used with the V-200 playback processor, the two units formed a single unit with a variety of playback functions, including the ability to provide multiscreen playback 4, 9, 16, or 25 pictures at one time. Digital effects such as solarization and negative-reverse imaging could be accomplished at the touch of a button on the playback unit. Adjustable intervals for individual pictures are selectable from 1 to 99 seconds with high-speed continuous playback of up to 15 pictures/second being possible without gaps between pictures. A picture being played back could be recorded on the disk. All of these functions could be handled with an optional remote control. The unit is 205 mm (w) × 137 mm (d) × 62 mm (h) and weighs 1100 grams.

Hi-band output is available with the V-300 Recorder/Player. This unit is significantly larger than the V-200 and also offers high-speed playback at 2, 5, or 10 pictures/second. It records at the same 2, 5, or 10 pictures/second rate (in field mode only). The unit is capable of more than 500 lines of horizontal resolution.

The VC-102 is Olympus's latest still video camera (Table 1–11). It represents the lessons learned from the V-100.

Table 1-11. Specifications for the Olympus V-102 Still Video Camera.

Recording system:	Hi-band still video system
Recording capacity:	50 field images per disk
Imaging device:	1/2-inch CCD with 360,000 pixels
Sensitivity:	Corresponding to ISO 100
Lens:	10-27 mm f2.8 power zoom lens
Working distance:	46 cm—infinity
Viewfinder:	Optical TTL viewfinder
Focusing:	Passive autofocus system with AF illuminator
Shutter:	CCD electronic shutter; shutter speed 1/30-1/2000 sec
Exposure control:	Programmed AE with automatic flash activation in low light and backlight
White balance control:	Automatic
Flash:	Built in
Continuous shooting modes:	5 or 15 pictures/sec
Data recording:	Year/month/day

Panasonic

Panasonic Industrial Division of the Matsushita Electric Industrial Co. has introduced the AG-ES10 Hi-band still video camera for business applications. The optical components are being supplied by Canon, Inc. The camera has a 1/2-inch 360,000 pixel CCD imager, auto-focusing, white balancing and exposure; tele/wide convertible lens; four continuous shooting modes with 15, 10, 5, and 1 frame/sec.; and a five-digit data imprinting unit.

The unit is targeted for producing picture catalogs for used-car dealers, real estate agents and others, and will be marketed by year end. With vertical and horizontal resolution of more than 400 lines, it allows frame or field recording. Weighing only 1 1/2 pounds, including battery, the camera has a simple design yet includes many functions. You can select a wide angle (9 mm f2.0) or telephoto (16 mm f2.5) lens with both the image and viewfinder, and the illumination angle of the strobe flash changes automatically as the focal points change. Infrared autofocus provides clear images even in dim lighting.

With the AG-ES10, 16 shots per second can be recorded in continuous mode. Like so many of the other still video cameras, easy-to-read liquid crystal multidisplays provide information on date, time, and track number.

There is even a six-digit user-selectable ID number. For locations where potential hazards exist or if you want to make unobserved recordings such as outdoor nature scenes or scientific observations, a wireless remote-control option is available.

Numeric keys on the camera let you program a 6-digit ID number. Designed as a point-and-shoot camera, this camera could find many applications in schools, hospitals, and other similar locations. In addition to the new Panasonic camera, the AG-ES100 portable floppy player is available with a horizontal resolution of more than 500 lines and features an advance/reverse search and automatic time setting for playback. It uses a professionally popular jog dial much like the jogging dials available on professional video-tape recorders.

On-screen displays are possible for information such as date, time, track number, and camera 6-digit ID numbers. The AG-ES100, like many of the other new Hi-band products, has a separate Y/C S-video output terminal that allows the maximum quality to be obtained by completely separating the chroma and luminance information of the video recording. The same wireless control unit designed for the camera also is usable with the video floppy player.

Pentax

Pentax has shown a prototype still video system with an integrated recorder playback designed for Hi-band electronic still video recording.

The Pentax camera has a 3× zoom and features a built-in erase head. The date and time of the image are also clearly identifiable by a recording that is built into the camera. Using a 360k half-inch sensor, field recordings are made that also allow an adjunct audio adapter to place 10 to 20 seconds of audio per frame. The zoom lens is an 8 to 24 mm f2.8 to f5.6 and focuses from 0.6 meters to infinity.

Sanyo

The Sanyo SVC-05 compact electronic still video camera is aimed at the general photographer. Featuring a 390,000-pixel CCD sensor, the camera is designed for field recording only and includes autofocusing, autostrobe flash, and auto-white-light balance. Continuous recording of either 7 or 15 fields per second is possible.

In addition to the SVC-05 camera, Sanyo is also marketing a still video recorder with the capability of both field and frame recording. Operable by remote control, the unit will display recorded information. An audio-recording capability is available with an audio adapter with ten seconds of audio per image.

Vivitar

The Vivitar still video camera offers a choice of unusual focal-length lenses with either a 9-mm f2.0 or 16-mm f2.5 lens. This is the equivalent of a 35-mm lens on a 35-mm camera, or a 60-mm lens. Using a 360,000-pixel CCD sensor, both field and frame modes have a horizontal resolution of 400 lines.

A sensor within the camera measures the color temperature of the scene being recorded for totally automatic white-light balance adjustment. The incorporated electronic flash has a 1.5-second recycling time with a choice of manual or automatic operation. An LCD panel in the camera informs the photographer of the date, time, and track number, and also has provision for a user-selectable number. All of this information is recorded on the disk during the recording.

Capable of field- or frame-mode recording, the desired mode is selected with a switch that can be changed at any time on the disk.

What has made all of these new cameras possible is primarily the standardization to one of two formats for still video recording. The advent of the Hi-band recording has opened many new possibilities for still-video camera usage.

Color CCD imagers, with greatly increased use in camcorders, have made a whole new range of cameras possible, meeting the greater demands of Hi-band recording. When you combine these new cameras with the use of transceivers for industry and commercial applications as well as with the variety of high-speed color output printers, all of the chemistry is right for the greatly expanded use of electronic photography.

Although the variety of cameras that are available continues to grow (Table 1–5), the key is the application of the cameras to actual professional needs and for the serious general photographer who would like another tool such as a camera that could be used within the environment of the home entertainment center, and possibly even with a computer to create totally new art forms as the future of electronic photography evolves.

SOME BASICS OF THE DIGITAL WORLD

Earlier I discussed analog signals and the fact that the world is made up of images that are analog in nature. Everything—from the watch we look at to the various shades and hues of nature that surround us—is analog. Conventional video recording is analog—continuous both in value and in time. A digital signal contains both value and time as noncontinuous values. The value or amplitude must be a digital value with a certain number of bits, and the time also must be a value in equal steps of time. The process for converting time into values is called *sampling*, and the process for converting the value or amplitude into discrete values is called *quantizing*.

Before discussing digital still photography, it might be good to first discuss something of digital imaging technology. Today we commonly relate digital imaging to the screen of a computer. This is not necessarily a true digital image, but it gives us a place to start talking about digital imaging. Whether it is a personal computer or a system connected to a mainframe, the information that appears is in digital form.

Whether we see a picture or simply text, what always appears is a digital image displayed in a converted video form on a raster-scanned CRT. It is easiest to represent numerical values in digital form through the use of integers in which a certain number of bits are represented as powers of two. The problem with integer numbers is that they go in steps of 1 with no fractional values. Floating-point numeric representations that do not have the limitations of integers are being used more and more in computers.

An analog waveform has a continuously varying value and time. To convert this to a digital signal, both the value and the time must be changed to noncontinuous values. The amplitude is represented by a digital integer with a certain number of bits. Time is represented as a series of those values taken at equal steps in time. The process of time determination is called sampling, and the conversion of the amplitude is quantizing. Together these are called analog-to-digital (A/D) conversion or digitizing. This conversion process is an approximation but has become much more refined with the improvement of A/D conversion devices and the use of higher sampling rates. If the sampling rate is low, the result is a very inaccurate representation of the signal. If the sampling rate is high, an almost exact copy of the original, both for color and density, can be achieved.

In the case of color, the red, green, and blue information is handled as three complete, separate sets of data, producing three complete sets of digital information. Three A/D circuits are used, and the encoding is done simultaneously.

In digitizing an image, you create a series of adjacent points in the image in the same pattern that the camera tube or solid-state imaging device originally scanned the image. These individual points are picture elements, or pixels. When reconstructing the image for display, each pixel is shown either as a small rectangle or square filled with a color calculated from the number of color bits representing that pixel or as a shade of gray if a black-and-white image is being recorded. If the resolution of a system is low, it is possible to see the individual pixels, resulting in a fuzzy picture with the individual pixels showing; this is called *pixellation.* The degree of pixellation depends on how far you are away from the image and the corner-to-corner diagonal of the screen. A large viewing screen can appear sharp with a fewer number of pixels, whereas a small viewing screen requires a large number of pixels to appear sharp.

Two things are discarded from the normal analog video signal. The *blanking interval*, or the time when the screen is blank between individual screen fields, and synchronizing signals that ensure the synchronization of the video system, are not needed in digital storage. The computer remembers where a picture begins and ends, and these individual signals can be eliminated. The arrangement of adjacent pixels and lines into a continuous memory without the video components is called a *bitmap*.

Another important consideration in digital storage is the number of bits per pixel, which determines how many colors can be displayed simultaneously. Values ranging from 1 to 32 bits/pixel are used in various systems. The difference is that the amount of storage required increases greatly as the number of bits per pixel increases. A 1-bit/pixel system displays two colors. These can be black and white, yellow and green, or whatever two colors are chosen. There is no gray scale with 1-bit/color. On the other hand, most commercial scanners and other devices use 8 bits to 12 bits/color, resulting in color capabilities of over 1 million colors at the 12-bit/color level.

Contouring, or distinct steps of shading in an electronic digitized image, occurs when too few bits/pixel are used. The color of the image appears in steps. Although the effect on the image is almost artistic in the form of a posterization, the contouring disappears at the 8 bit/pixel level.

One other artifact that occurs in digital images is *aliasing*, or stair-steps. In aliasing, diagonal lines appear to step, or have a jagged effect. This is especially true with alphabetical characters such as an upper case A. In gray-scale systems, anti-aliasing generally is provided, which averages the difference between the steps and reduces the effect of stair-stepping.

DIGITAL STILL VIDEO PHOTOGRAPHY

The fall of 1988 saw the release of the first Fuji digital still camera. Using an SRAM card with a built-in battery for maintaining the memory, each card stores 9 or 18 megabits of information. The memory card was developed jointly with Toshiba. The 8-bit/color signal receives pictures from a 400,000-pixel CCD sensor, with pictures being recorded entirely in the field mode or using half of each sensor. Although the first camera records ten images on its recording medium, it is expected that this will be increased to around 40 images per card at a later date by using image compression.

The camera is a fixed-focus 16-mm lens with a 1/60 to 1/2000 electronic shutter. The camera operates at a fixed f5.6 and at f4 with a flash. The camera weighs only 400 grams, which is slightly less than one pound.

Compact in size and simple because of the slide-in card, the recording capability eliminates all mechanics, motors, and drives, and should increase substantially the life expectancy of batteries and power-supply components.

With the digital image, there is no deterioration in resolution, and copies can be made at fast transfer rates rather than at the slower transfer rates of analog systems. Recorded images also can be transferred to optical disks and digital audio tapes (DATs), and sound can be added during the transfer process. The Fujix DS-1P is compatible with personal computers, word processors, communication equipment, and other office automation devices.

The Fujix DS-1P digital still camera uses a 400,000-pixel CCD imager and has a fixed-focus f5.6 16-mm lens (Fig. 1–28). The automatic flash is built-in, and the camera itself weighs approximately 14 ounces. In addition to the camera, a digital card player is provided for reproducing images from the memory card (Fig. 1–29).

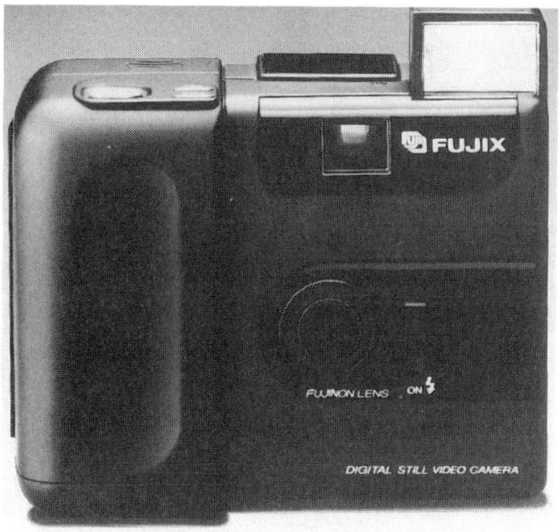

Fig. 1-28. The Fujix DS-1P Digital Still Camera.

A dramatic example of the ruggedness of an all-digital camera came at a major photographic trade show. I saw one of the digital Fuji cameras dropped by a demonstrator. The camera case cracked, but the lenses remained intact. The camera continued to function perfectly, producing the same quality images as before the camera was dropped. With the lack of moving parts, the camera is certainly much simpler and more rugged.

Fuji has recently announced the DS-X digital still camera (Table 1–12). It offers a flatter camera design.

Since the time of the original announcement of the Fujix digital still camera, Toshiba Corporation and Fuji Photo Film Company now have joined together in developing a digital still camera system. The industrial system has been introduced and a commercial version is due in 1991.

Table 1-12. Specifications for the Fujix DS-X Digital Still Camera.

Recording method:	Digital recording on SRAM
Image sensor:	2/3-inch 400,000-pixel FIT-CCD imager
Lens:	F3.5 f 15 mm (fixed focal point) in macro—30 cm from lens
Shutter:	Electronic shutter 1/30–1/500
Exposure control:	Programmed AE F3.5 1/30 sec.—F16 1/500 sec.
Images stored:	IM-18X card, up to 12 images or 6 with higher resolution
	IM-9X card, half above amount
Data compression system:	Sub sample/ADPCM
Flash:	Built-in auto flash

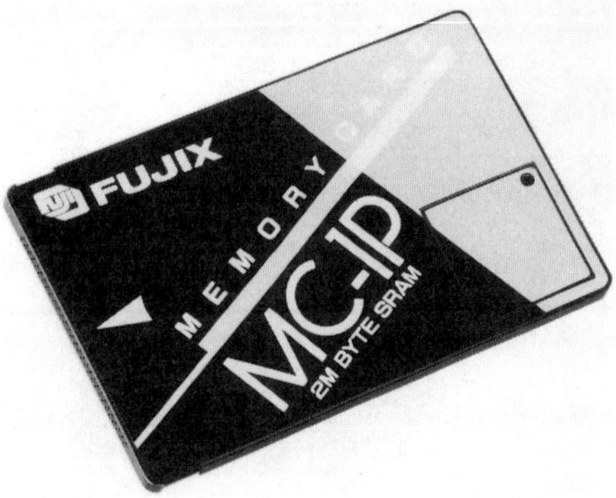

Fig. 1-29. The Fujix Digital Memory Card.

Current designs have 400 horizontal pixel resolution, with a goal of 430 for production models.

The advanced version of the IC card will incorporate the 4 Mb NAND-type EEPROMs (electrically erasable programmable read-only memory) that Toshiba recently discussed at a recent Solid-State Circuits conference. Further development is aimed at a 200 Mb IC card, which, in conjunction with a 16:1 image-compression system, would enable the card to store 50 images (like the 50-field analog video floppy systems presently available). Both companies also are working on an image-storage subsystem based on digital-audio-tape (DAT) technology. This "electronic photo album" would be able to record up to 1000 images on a single 120-minute DAT cassette.

The IC card camera will be the first application of Toshiba's new technology. The NAND-structured memory has eight memory cells connected to a single switching transistor, reducing the cell size to one-sixteenth that of a conventional EEPROM and permitting a 4-Mb device to be manufactured using a 1-micron CMOS process. In addition to reducing the number of chips used in the camera's IC card from 20 to 5, the nonvolatile EEPROM eliminates the need for back-up power required with SRAM cards (Fig. 1–30).

"The memory portion of the semiconductor-based system is too expensive, considering the current cost of microchips," said Shozo Iijima, Toshiba's chief engineer. "So our main objective is to lower memory cost without affecting the picture quality."

The Toshiba data-compression technique uses the discrete-cosine-transform method. This method divides the image into blocks, removes the high-frequency elements of the image signal, and transforms the signal into code. The system design being developed by Fuji and Toshiba is expected to be complete by the early part of 1990. They will then ask other camera and electronic manufacturers to standardize the digital-card camera format, much as was done with the 2-inch floppy video format in 1982. This will be the initial application of Toshiba's EEPROM.

Additional peripheral equipment has been developed by Toshiba for use with the IC card camera. An electronic album, based on a digital audio tape (DAT) recorder, can record up to 1000 pictures on a single 120-minute DAT cartridge. Users also can add audio messages that play concurrently

Table 1-13. Specifications for the Toshiba Digital Still Camera System.

Memory Card Camera IMC-100	
Pickup element:	2/3-inch 400,000 pixel FIT-CCD
Flash:	Built in, 4 shots/sec.
Lens:	Build in macro
White balance:	Auto
Continuous shooting:	5 frames/sec.
Power source:	Ni-Cd battery pack
Memory Card	
Capacity:	IC-18S- 18 Mb 12 images in normal mode, 6 images in high quality mode
	IC-9S- 9Mb, 1/2 capacity of IC-18S
Memory Card Player IP-100	
Resolution:	Horizontal more than 400 TV lines
	Vertical more than 400 TV lines
Digital Picture File	
Capacity:	1,000 photos (120 min. DAT Tape)

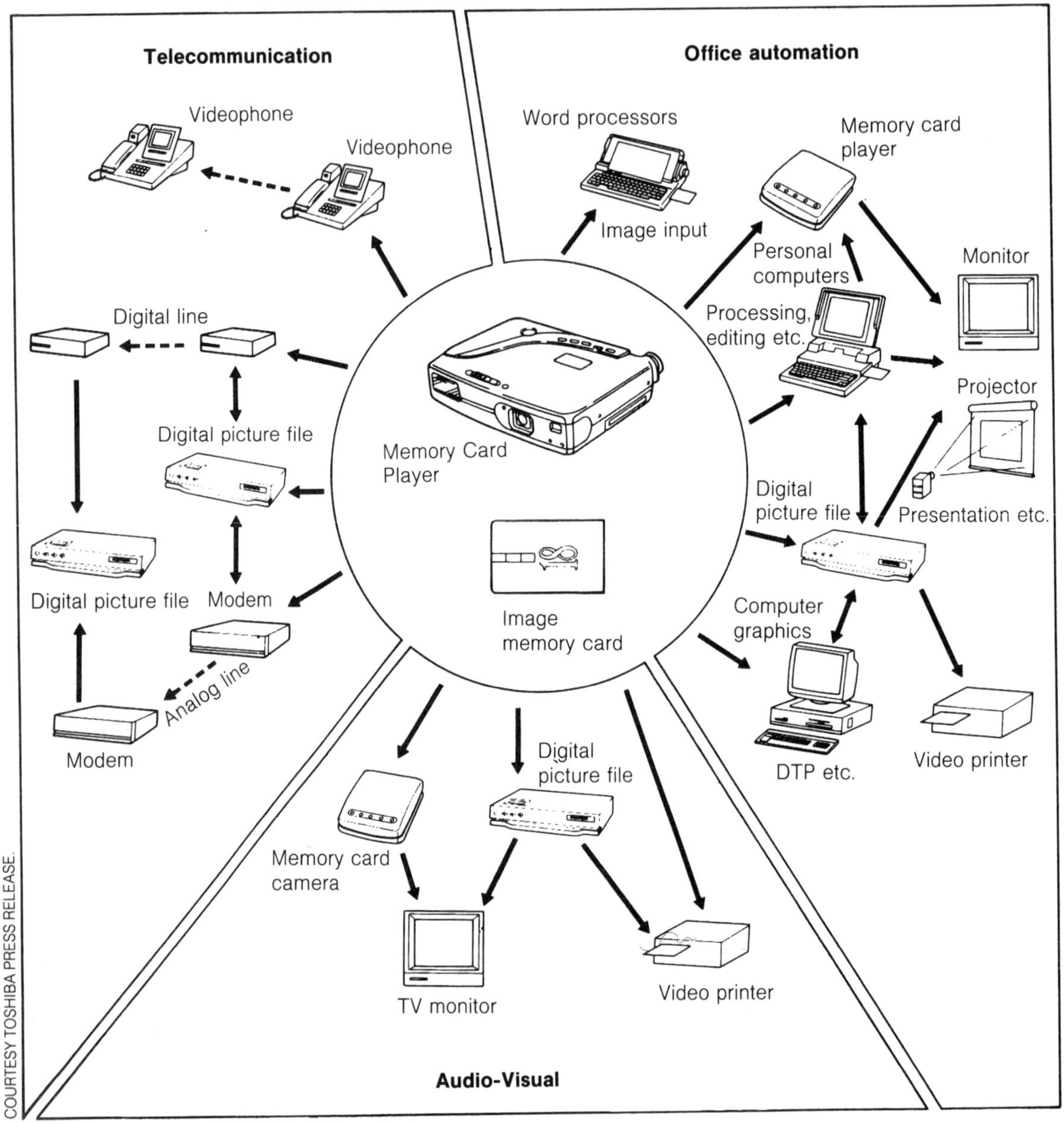

COURTESY TOSHIBA PRESS RELEASE.

Fig. 1-30. The applications of the Toshiba Digital Card Camera System.

with the photo images. The DAT player is equipped with a random-access function so that any image can be retrieved by keying its number (Table 1–13).

The potential uses for the digital camera are exciting and have been recognized by even Eastman Kodak Company. "The image quality achievable through digital technology is much higher than what is possible with the analog still floppy video," noted K. Bradley Paxton (vice president and general manager for Kodak's Electronic Photography Division). "A digital electronic still camera can be rugged and compact."

So the future certainly could lie with digital photography, but for today the evolution of still video systems allows an excellent working tool for both the professional and the serious general photographer.

APPLICATION STORIES

Electronic Photography in the Beauty Shop

The Salon System from New Image Industries could be revolutionary for beauty shops. Customers, both male and female, are photographed electronically, and this image appears on a monitor screen. Using a pull-out control drawer, the operator can show over 100 hair styles substituted for be shown, simulating color mixing. For that special hair style, cutting and trimming can be done on the individual's electronic photograph.

Cosmetic makeovers can be simulated using different lipsticks, eye liners, and mascara, etc. Clothing and jewelry changes also can be part of the makeover. A hardcopy print can be produced for the customer to see the finished changeover.

USA Today *and Electronic Photography*

USA Today is using an all-Sony still video system, from camera to prepress image processing. Currently they have a prototype of the new Sony Hi-band 2-CCD chip camera; a portable Hi-band still video player for field use; two image transceivers, one to send and the other to receive; a color video printer that creates near-photo quality for hard copy prints for proofing and archiving; and a prototype of the Sony electronic publishing system (SEPS) based on a Sony NEWS workstation that corrects and enhances the electronic image and converts it from digital format to YMCK separations for SCITEX image processor.

Frank Folwell, associate photography editor of *USA TODAY*, says, "Sony's digital-image transceiver—which is really the key to getting images back to the newsroom fast—is very quick and easy to use. When our photojournalists are on assignment, they need to send their shots via standard telephone lines. A still video image sent by the Sony transceiver takes about 3 1/2 minutes, and the newest model of the transceiver is even faster. In contrast, a comparable film-based transmission system can take as long as 30 minutes just for transmission."

Speed is important in deadlines (Fig. 1–31, color section). *USA TODAY* saves minutes in the transfer of images to their Scitex processor because they never have to convert the electronic image to film or scan. The SEPS system takes the digital color image directly from the Sony transceiver, and using Sony-developed software, filters out the video noise that interferes with image quality and converts the digital photo signal to YMCK electronic color separations. *USA TODAY* sees the ability to go from a still video directly to prepress processing completely electronically as a tremendous advantage. More importantly, the SEPS system is able to take any video signal—camcorders, video-tape recorders, computers equipped with video boards, video copy stands—all can generate images for transmission and translation to the prepress processor.

With the SEPS, correction, enhancement, storage and, transfer of images can be accomplished, everything that the electronic darkroom should do.

An example of the use of the electronic system was a recent NBA playoff game photographed with the new ProMavica camera, MVC-5000. They received the images at 9:30 p.m., 14 minutes after tip-off, and they felt that these were the best still images that they had ever seen. They could not see the difference between still video images and conventional photographs. Although *USA TODAY* does not say that still video is a replacement for film (nor should it be), it will play an important role in the emerging electronic newsroom of tomorrow.

J. C. Penney Communicates with Electronic Photography

With ProMavica systems, J. C. Penney dramatically lowers the cost and increases the speed with which buyers overseas communicate with the company's Dallas headquarters. Systems installed in Penney offices in Hong Kong, Singapore, Seoul, Taipei, and Osaka enable buyers to transmit full-color still images of merchandise over phone lines via Sony's SFU-1000 Still Image Transceiver to buyers in Dallas. "The ProMavica system is a major tool assisting us in merchandise procurement," says Bill Johnson, J. C. Penney Vice President and Director of Public Affairs and Company Communications. "It enables our people to greatly reduce time in getting new items sourced and delivered. We also save time and money by avoiding express shipment of multiple samples to the U.S."

Sony systems in each location include a ProMavica MVC-A7AF camera, player/recorder, and SFU-1000 Still Image Transceiver. Images captured on a reusable Mavipak diskette with the camera are transferred to a recorder/

player, then viewed and edited. Selected items are then transmitted to buyers in Dallas (in about two minutes) for display on a TV monitor or for printing out on the Sony UP-5000 color video printer.

An important transceiver feature is auto reception. "The ability to send and receive images automatically without an operator being present is absolutely critical to our system operations and success," says Ed Sample, J. C. Penney Special Projects Manager. "Depending on the country, we have a 14- or 15-hour time difference with the Far East. With Sony transceivers, images are waiting for our Dallas buyers when they get to the office. This reduces the impact of the time difference and shortens action time."

Other advantages of the ProMavica system are flexibility and the ability to use any video source as input. "The ability to use various video sources, from 8-mm video to broadcast quality cameras, gives us a great deal of flexibility with regard to picture resolution and color clarification," explains Johnson.

Sample adds, "Quality can be achieved based on specific need. If body style and silhouette is needed, a field transmission suffices. For thread count and fabric detail, we may use a broadcast quality camera. Flexibility is the key. Output is also flexible. The Sony printer offers hard copy, or transparency options for use in presentations. Images can also be displayed on any standard RGB or NTSC video monitor."

ProMavica performance meets J. C. Penney's expectations. "System reliability has been exceptional," says Sample. "Downtime has been less than 1/50th of one percent during our first four months of operation."

Industrial Recording with Electronic Photography

General Public Utilities Nuclear Corporation in Reading, Pennsylvania, a holding company known as GPU Nuclear, owns and operates nuclear power plants and utilities in the Northeast—including the Oyster Creek and Three-Mile Island nuclear facilities, Jersey Central Power and Light, Metropolitan Edison, and Pennsylvania Electric.

For reasons of safety, efficiency, and government regulation, the welds in the thousands of feet of steel-alloy piping must be inspected regularly. "In some plants there are pipes running from the thirteenth floor to the basement," says Bill Jeitner, Supervisor of Material/Deposits for GPU Nuclear. In order to analyze conditions, Jeitner's group of six laboratory technicians periodically visits GPU facilities. "There may be eight-hundred areas we have to document in the field at each site," Jeitner says. "In the past we viewed each individually through a microscope and reproduced them on instant film. The problems were the cost of film was becoming increasingly prohibitive, and the required engineering report was a massive document." Although instant prints provided a means of hard-copy documentation, they could not be duplicated quickly and offered only a small-scale view of trouble spots.

In order to make field documentation easier and reporting less bulky and expensive, GPU Nuclear purchased two Kodak SV7400 Still Video Recorders, a Kodak SV1300 Color Monitor, and a Kodak SV6500 Color Video Printer.

"Now we can take our video camera and a Kodak recorder and monitor on-site and shoot all the replicas directly to disk," Jeitner says. He overlays the weld location data with a video typewriter. "We can code in the pipe name, indicate the lead of the pipe, enter a location identification . . . then have it reproduced with each image," notes Jeitner. Instead of returning from the site with a large bundle of instant pictures, Jeitner and crew now capture all images on a handful of Kodak SV50 Still Video Floppy Disks.

Once recording is complete, using still video equipment offers additional advantages to GPU Nuclear. "When one of our facilities is shut down for a scheduled outage, it's a very expensive proposition," Jeitner says. "We have to have all the contractors in to review the damage, see where scaffolding will be erected and discuss each repair."

Jeitner displays the images to contractors on the Kodak SV1300 Color Monitor. "In this way, the service contractors and our coordinators can examine exactly what needs to be done and get a much clearer picture of the work to be scheduled," he says. His coded-in data also becomes much more relevant and useful with this system. "For instance, they can now see each problem area in color and enlarged detail, and the coding information gives them a precise location."

Jeitner's group is still required to file an engineering report and uses their Kodak SV6500 Color Video Printer to produce thermal prints of selected replicas. The printer also provides selected reference images to engineers in charge of particular aspects of a project and helps document conditions of various components sent from the field to the lab for analysis.

TV-Photo System Finds a Commercial Market

One still video system already has chalked up quite a success. The Fujix TV-System, which was introduced to the Japanese domestic market in April, 1985, already has become established in many commercial applications. Reports from Japan indicate Fuji Photo has sold several thousand systems to date.

The TV-Photo System was the first practical application for the 2-inch video floppy disk, which served as an alternative to videocassettes for viewing either prints or color negative frames on home television. Customers would take their photographs or negatives to a Fujicolor photofinishing lab, which would record up to 48 images on the 2-inch floppy disk. The initial price was ¥1400 from color prints and ¥2100 from color negatives (about $5.80 and $8.75 at that time). These video floppy disks then could be played back through the Fujix TV-Photo Player.

A survey of early TV-Photo customers indicated that they bought the disks for group viewing (46%), system flexibility (44%), and prints arrangement (39%). In response to the question about how they use the system, they indicated family album (61%), record of sports, hobby, etc. (26%), and business presentation (24%).

In 1986, Fuji had added some additional elements to the system. A Multivision System permitted 16 players to be controlled by a personal computer, with random-access to any of the 768 images (16 × 48), for a business presentation on 16 TV monitors. The Video Print System for hardcopy prints on color photographic paper of the images stored on the video floppy disk offered customers the ability to send disks and have prints made of selected images.

The system has been expanded to include a Still Video Camera and a Recorder/Player that records signals from a video camera, VCR, TV, video disk, or personal computer onto the 2-inch floppy and plays back any 2-inch video floppy onto the TV screen (which can be any size, including projection units). The Recorder/Player also can be used for editing and duplicating, and a Synchronizer allows narration or music to be added.

Although consumer acceptance has been good, the commercial applications have further fueled the growth of the system. The ability to rerecord the floppy disks encourages users to "take more pictures."

Still video offers some advantages over "movie video," including ease of editing and updating; quick turnaround in software production; lower cost of program creation and maintenance; and random-access capability.

Note that within Japan, the Fujicolor Service group is the largest photofinisher, permitting the installation of early Fujix floppy-disk production equipment. The ready availability of facilities elsewhere for creating video floppy disks from a variety of "hard-copy" images is lacking.

With the exception of Eastman Kodak subsidiaries in Australia, France, Norway, the U.S.A., and the United Kingdom, there are no dominant ties between equipment developers and retail imaging facilities that present the same opportunities for making the programs so readily available. Consequently, the success enjoyed by the Fujix TV–Photo system might not be duplicated outside of Japan for a while.

2

Capturing Images

The still video camera depends on either a CCD or MOS device as the initial image-capturing device. The CCD or MOS sensor is the equivalent of a piece of film with the ability to record electronically what the lens of the camera sees. It is only in the last few years that cost-effective imaging devices have appeared. Patent literature is filled with new variations and modifications of basic sensors, using them for camera focusing, for white-light balancing, for all of the various functions needed by the complete electronic still video camera.

In addition to the still video camera, it is possible to capture images in a variety of other ways. Image scanning can be accomplished with a scanner that looks much like the top of a copy machine. Other scanners look like a rotating drum, and some scanners even look like conventional video cameras.

Then there is the actual use of video cameras for image pickup. With the advent of HDTV cameras, higher resolution is possible than ever before. Finally, there is the linear CCD and the implications of this device for the future of electronic photography.

Added together, each of the different forms of image capture gives us a unique opportunity to increase the use of electronic photography. Whether we talk in terms of a complete still video camera, a scanner, a motion video camera adapted to still work, or unique uses of the linear CCD pickup, all these open new horizons for the use of electronic photography and the capture of images electronically and in full color (Table 2–1).

My aim here is to create the broadest possible understanding of the technologies involved and the opportunities for utilizing these new tools and to make the knowledge of them available to you so that electronic photography will become as familiar as conventional film photography.

Table 2-1. Comparison of Image-Capture System.

	Minimum Detectable Signal* (lux sec)	Exposure Range
Solid-State Array		
Theoretical	1×10^{-5}	
Prototype	3.5×10^{-5}	50,000:1
Commercial Still Video Camera	10^{-2} to 10^{-3}	4,000:1
Vidicon (Avg)	3×10^{-4}	200:1
Silver halide film		
Ektachrome 400	2×10^{-3}	100:1
Kodacolor Gold	4×10^{-4}	1,000:1

*at wavelength = .555 microns

NTSC CAMERA SIGNAL PROCESSING

Camera signal processing generally includes color matrixing, gamma correction, aperture correction, and NTSC encoding. The sensor and color filter array (CFA) being used will influence the matrix. One of the reasons for altering the camera signals is to produce the signals necessary to create the desired image on the TV monitor.

A linear matrix is used to obtain the negative lobes. Without going into detail, I'll just say that the signal-to-noise ratios of the RGB signals are decreased and noise increases as a result.

Applying aperture correction increases the amplitude of the horizontal and vertical high-frequency information, compensating for modulation transfer function (MTF) falloff due to the camera lens and photosite aperture.

The three output RGB signals are combined into a single composite video signal via the NTSC encoder. It is the sum of the 4.2-MHz bandwidth luminance signals and two lower bandwidth color-difference signals. The luminance signal, weighted relative to the brightness sensitivity of the eye, is composed of 59% green, 30% red, and 11% blue.

Because the sensitivity of the eye to color is much lower than to brightness, much lower bandwidths are used for the color information. The cyan-orange chrominance axis for the I (in-phase) component is low-pass filtered to 1.5 MHz. The orthogonal Q component, falling along the magenta-green axis, is low-pass filtered to 0.5 MHz.

Interestingly enough, despite the limitations of the NTSC standards, many television sets have filters that pass only about 3 MHz of the 4.2-MHz luminance bandwidth. Comb filters introduced in 1978–79 sets allow the full 4.2 MHz to pass but utilize only 0.5 MHz of the chrominance bandwidth.

In 1984, RCA introduced TV receivers that processed the full 1.5-MHz chrominance bandwidth. Still, the NTSC image suffers from two flaws: 1) The appearance of horizontal lines across the entire picture (resulting from the interlaced scanning technique), and 2) dots crawling uphill on the edges of colored objects (a result of simultaneous transmission of chrominance and luminance information). Both can be reduced by digital processing. Full-frame storage also helps.

New techniques are being developed to improve the image quality within the NTSC format. Despite the limitations of the format, its full potential has yet to be realized.

THE BASICS OF CCDs

Charge-coupled devices (CCDs) have been developed only in the last few years to the state of excellence and resolution capabilities we see today. CCDs have improved substantially because of the ability to produce large-scale integrated circuits and the continued development of memory chips. The defense industry certainly has made a great contribution to the development of CCDs. Images that have come back from distant planets are primarily examples of either area or linear CCDs, and the development of the technology in the 1970s has led to the exciting products that we have today—electronic still video cameras and the great variety of camcorders that are common household items today.

The solid-state sensor operates on a principle similar to the scanning of a TV signal in a tube camera, except that the scanning is performed in a different way. A discrete array of elements (each called a pixel, or picture element) has the light from the object imaged onto it (Fig. 2–1).

A photoconductive material similar to that used in the vidicon provides the light sensitivity. However, whereas the photoconductor in the vidicon is a smooth undifferentiated layer on which the scanning beam defines the picture element, the solid-state sensor requires that each individual picture element be delineated by an appropriate electrode accessed by means of a metallic lead. As a result, this makes the solid-state sensor more expensive to manufacture. In beam-addressed devices such as the vidicon, changes in scan velocity, beam landing error, point spreading (blooming), and peripheral nonorthogonal landing contribute to spatial anomalies. This gives the solid-state sensor a much better positional accuracy.

Other comparisons between the two basic types of sensors show that with a solid-state sensor, the input capacitance of the first stage of the preamplifier can be as much as a hundred times smaller than that of the

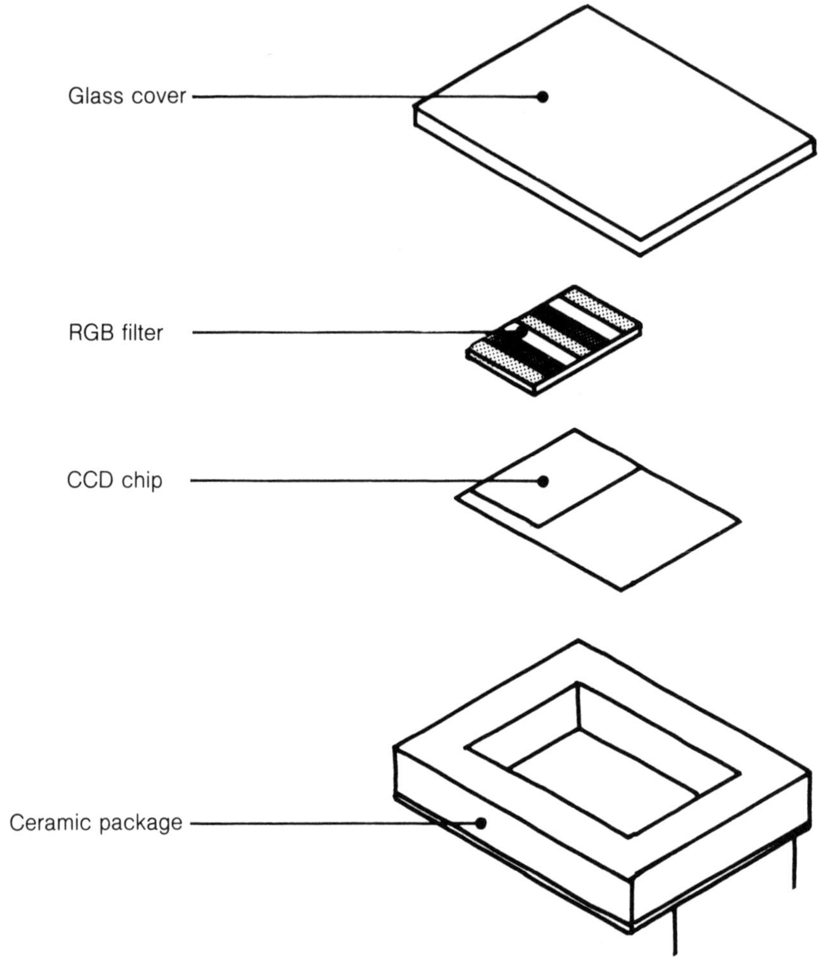

Fig. 2-1. Components of a typical charge-coupled device (CCD).

vidicon. This, in turn, enables the amplifier noise to be about ten times smaller, requiring less electronic signal processing.

A major disadvantage of the vidicon, obviously, is its physical size. Although this might not be a problem for traditional TV-type cameras, which are designed to be held on the shoulder, it makes it impossible to use in compact hand-held still video cameras.

These solid-state sensors that are suitable for electronic photography cameras can be grouped into three categories: frame-transfer charge-coupled device (CCD) arrays; interline transfer CCD readout arrays; and matrix (x-y)-addressed arrays such as the charge injection device (CID) and metal-oxide semiconductor (MOS) photodiodes.

In the frame-transfer CCD, there are two distinct sections with similar structures—an imaging area and a storage area. The brightness information recorded on the imaging (pixel, or picture element) section must be transferred to the storage section before the new brightness information can be sensed (the so-called sample-and-hold).

Interline transfer devices interleave the storage and transfer sections with the photodetector sections. Thus, the effective photosensitive aperture is about one-third of the total pixel area. This provides less sensitivity than the full-frame transfer design, but gives better resolution and is considered to give better color picture quality with mosaic color filters. With the matrix-addressed approach, all the pixels can be read sequentially, which facilitates high-speed signal processing.

Most of us are aware that three sensor systems split the incoming light into three distinct color components through the use of a beam splitter. The red light is then picked up by the red sensor, the green light by the green sensor, and the blue light by the blue sensor. Today's compact CCD sensor cameras use only a single sensor. In that case, how is the color created with a single sensor camera?

The color is created through the use of a repetitive pattern of color filters, called a *color filter array* (CFA). Although I won't go into too much detail, I'll review two separate approaches to single-chip color camera designs, recognizing that the choice of CFA has a significant effect on the system image quality.

The feasibility of a single-sensor solid-state color video camera was reported first in 1978 by the Kodak Research Laboratories team of P. Dillon, D. Lewis, and F. Kasper in their article "Color Imaging System Using a Single CCD Array," (IEEE Transactions on Electron Devices, Vol. ED-25, Feb. 1978, pp 102–107). A 100 × 100 pixel CCD imager was covered by the checkerboard primary color pattern. The NTSC video signal has three components: a luminance signal Y and the two color difference signals, I and Q.

Each pixel is covered with a color filter that allows only that color to pass. Half the pixels are covered with the green selective filter alternating across the checkerboard, while the remaining half are divided equally between red- and blue-sensitive filters. Although this pattern reduces the red and blue resolution compared to the green, the dominant component of the luminance signal comes from the green sensor—and high-frequency luminance information has a much greater effect on image quality than high-frequency color information.

A separate approach uses complementary filters. This was employed by Hitachi Corp. on its VK-C2000 MOS camera, the first single-chip camera available in the U.S. The CFA consists of an equal number of cyan (CY), yellow (YE), white (W), and green (G) filters.

Two vertically adjacent rows are scanned simultaneously and the information separated to produce independent yellow, white, green, and cyan signals. After these signals are amplified, they are combined to form the luminance signal Y and red and blue information according to the following equations:

$$Y = W + CY + YE + G$$
$$R = (W+YE) - (G+CY)$$
$$B = (W+CY) - (YE+G)$$

These signals are processed further to reduce fixed-pattern noise spikes that result from mismatches in the characteristics of the sensor's MOS switches and fed into low-pass filters. A special *G matrix* circuit is used to form the high-resolution green signal from the weighted differences of the wideband luminance and low resolution R and B signals. The RGB signals are gamma corrected (to compensate for nonlinear voltage vs. light output curves) and recombined to form the Y, R–Y and B–Y signals. The Y luminance signal is further enhanced to sharpen horizontal image edges.

Regardless of whether primary or complementary filters are used or not, various configurations have been employed. With frame-transfer CCD sensors, vertical stripe filters provide satisfactory quality color. Checkerboard patterns can be varied, or the patterns can be shifted, as shown in Fig. 2–5. This shift produces a greatly improved horizontal sharpness but with the loss of some diagonal sharpness compared to the regular checkerboard designs.

Area imaging CCDs, which started out at a level of 200,000 pixels, are now able to record up to four million pixels on specialized sensors. Although the four-million pixel sensor is not an everyday item, it certainly does show that the technology has a lot a growing room, just as we have seen silver halide products improve tremendously over the years.

The basic operating principle of the CCD is called *charge-coupling* (Fig. 2–2). Extremely small amounts of electrical charge called *packets* are created in specific locations in the silicon semiconductor material. These *storage elements* are created by the field of a pair of what are called *gate electrodes*, which are very close to the surface of the silicone. By placing the storage elements adjacent to each other, the voltages on adjacent gate electrodes can be alternately raised and lowered, causing individual charge packets beneath them to be passed from one storage element to the next. Because each of these packets can be a different size, the line of elements becomes a very simple analog shift register.

All CCDs are basically shift registers because they transfer their charge

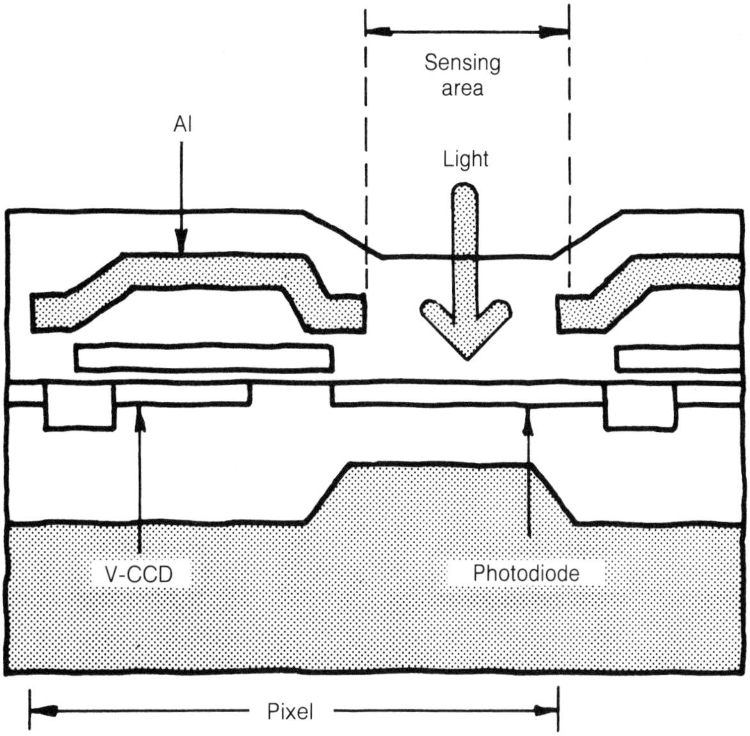

Fig. 2-2. A cross-section of a conventional CCD image sensor showing the light path along with the light sensitive photodiode which acts as a gate electrode.

to the next adjacent element very efficiently while the amount of charge in each packet stays the same, even after it has been passed from one element to another. The individual points can be compared to small batteries that hold their charge until they are passed over to one end, at which they become an analog signal. A key point to remember is that the CCDs are basically analog devices with the information coming to a register. In the case of a color CCD, alternating stripes of red, green, and blue are placed over the face of the CCD, and the signal then becomes individual records of red, green, and blue voltages.

The image-sensing function utilizes another of the characteristics of silicon semiconductor devices. This is the *photoelectric effect*, by which free electrons are created in the region of silicon illuminated by photons from the ultraviolet to the near infrared range. When the silicon absorbs light striking its surface, a proportional number of free electrons are generated. With the normal sensor consisting of 300,000 to 600,000 individual points, the number of free electrons generated at each point is proportional to the incident light striking that surface. If a lens is used to create this light image on the surface, it will be a photo-like reproduction of the scene. Based on the exposure time, the light generates a time and intensity-proportional electrical-charge packet. These charge packets then are transferred by charge-coupling and the signals finally transferred, with the value of each charge packet corresponding to a picture element, or pixel, when transferred.

The camera sensors used are composed of a series of horizontal and vertical rows, or an xy array of elements. You will note that some CCDs are listed as horizontal transfer and some as vertical transfer. This is one of the characteristics of individually designed CCDs.

CCD CHARACTERISTICS

CCDs work best at low temperatures, but modern designs allow them to work in temperatures up to 150° if the memory registers have had special cells designed in to assure the quality of the produced signal.

Speed is one of the limiting factors of current CCDs. Most still video cameras are in color, ranging from EI 100 to EI 160. Monochrome still video cameras have considerably higher speeds because it is not necessary to have the three alternating stripes of red, green, and blue, so all of the pixels are available for the collection of photons of energy.

A new, more efficient generation of sensors is under development that transfer energy directly to the underside of the sensors so that more surface energy can be collected. This means a higher-speed sensor is possible in the future. These new sensors, designed primarily for new high-definition television systems (HDTV), should be available in the coming year.

One advantage of CCDs is greater reliability. Compared to previous vacuum picture tubes, CCDs offer a very reliable low-power device that has the capability to accept large amounts of light without causing any damage to photosensitive surfaces. The manufacturing technology for CCDs parallels the manufacturing technology for other solid-state devices, which generally has very high reliability with proven dependability. Although initial losses might occur because of production artifacts, once the units have been successfully produced, their dependability is extremely high.

All CCDs have a certain amount of noise. Recent CCDs have noticeably improved signal-to-noise ratios (S/N) compared to their predecessors. This results in better low-light-level performance with less noise in the image. Noise in an image appears as granular spots. The actual CCD registers, the heart of the CCD devices, are practically noiseless because they lack the junctions and other design points of most chips. When you see noise in a video system, it is probably coming from adjacent circuits in the system rather than the CCD itself.

Earlier I mentioned that CCDs of up to four million pixels have been produced (Table 2–2). These specialized application sensors are not yet economical enough for use in ordinary electronic photography. Part of the limitation is the packing density possible with the normal CCD technology. Although many more elements can be put onto the surface of a CCD because it requires no electrical contacts, CCDs still require physical gate elements. The new designs planned for the high-definition television sensors move the need for these elements to a different surface so that the entire surface can be used for creating higher-resolution sensors.

Table 2-2. Selection of Available Area Scan CCD Sensors.

Vendor	Model	Number Pixel	Speed (Mil. Pix./Sec)	Dynamic Range (dB)	Minimum Signal (Electron)
Fairchild	CCD222	488 × 380			
Kodak		570 × 484	10		20
Kodak		192 × 240	Up to 46		2000
Kodak	Megapixel	1035 × 1320	14	63	35
Kodak	KAF-4200	2048 × 2048		65	
Photometrics	512 × 512		90	6	
Sony	XC-117	510 × 492	15		
Tektronix	TK2048M	2048 × 2048			10
Thompson	TH7866	488 × 550	70		
Westinghouse	ETV-2000		10	56	
VSP Labs	SC505	604 × 485	11		

CCDs have come a long way since they were introduced in the mid-1970s. The first CCDs had less than 200,000 pixels. Today commercial color sensors are available with 600,000 to 800,000 pixels, with specialized sensors reaching four million pixels. However, the basic principles of the CCD—the ability to convert photons to electrons, transport these electrons, store them, and provide an analog output—remains the same. Continuing development has resulted in their becoming more cost effective than ever before.

The choice today is between silicon CCD or MOS metal-oxide sensors. Silicon provides a uniquely photosensitive surface with a wide latitude. The spectral sensitivity of the silicon sensor is very wide, ranging from ultraviolet to near infrared. In addition, manufacturing facilities are well developed for working with silicon in the fabrication of arrays.

The image from CCDs can be transferred in several different ways. A mechanical shutter can be used to expose the array and keep it in the dark while the image is being read. A frame-and-transfer device can be used in which a complete field is transferred as a field of charge. Finally with interline transfer CCDs, the devices are organized with columns of pixels interlaced with nonsensitive columns of charge transfer registers.

Another type of device is the charged injection device (CID) pioneered by General Electric in the late 1970s. A group of people purchased the Electronic Camera Operation Division of General Electric Co. in 1987 and called the new company CIDTEC.

In a CID, a charge is placed on each of the elements. When light strikes the element, the amount of charge required to bring the element back to a reference level is a measure of light that has reached a pixel. The major advantages of the CID over the CCD are its resistance to blooming an image and its resistance to defects in the array. With healing algorithms developed for conventional CCDs and other new algorithms, both blooming and pixel healing have been effected within the conventional CCD.

Here's how CIDs developed. Scientists at GE used the photosensitive characteristics of silicon to produce a simple x,y addressable array of photosensitive capacitor elements that evolved into the first CID camera in 1972. Like a CCD array, each pixel can be uniquely addressed.

However, unlike a CCD imager, which transfers collected charge out of the pixel collectors during readout (and hence erases the image stored on the sensor), the CID array does not transfer charge from site to site. Instead, the displacement current is read when collected charge packets are shifted between capacitors within individually selected pixels. This displacement current is proportional to the stored signal charge, which is proportional to the amount of light that falls on the pixel site.

The displacement current is amplified, converted to a voltage, and combined into a composite video signal that accurately quantifies the photon energy collected at each pixel site. Readout is nondestructive because the charge remains intact in the pixel collectors after the signal level has been determined. To clear the array for new frame integration, the row and column electrodes in each pixel are switched momentarily to ground (grounded), releasing, or injecting, the charge packets into the substrate.

This principle of operation makes CID technology fundamentally different from other imaging techniques, giving rise to a number of technical advantages that can be used to solve imaging problems. For instance, the nondestructive readout capability of CID cameras makes it possible to introduce a high degree of exposure control to low-light viewing of static scenes. By eliminating the charge-injection step of "zeroing" each pixel site, multiple-frame integration is achieved. This step can be viewed on a video monitor without affecting the imaging process, permitting the optimum exposure to be determined for recording. This integration could proceed for a period of milliseconds to several hours. However, for long integration periods, the sensor must be cooled to reduce the buildup of thermally-generated dark current in the semiconductor. This controlled-illumination integration process is especially useful in astronomy.

CCD imagers exhibit blooming or smearing under high intensity nonuniform light. This is because of charges spilling from oversaturated elements to adjoining pixels or the shift registers (charge-transfer mechanisms) during readout. Thus, adjacent pixel areas are affected and become saturated also. Optical overloads are confined to the illuminated pixels in CID imagers, because the charge does not transfer from the pixel collectors. This inherent antiblooming performance provides accurate image detail, even under extreme lighting conditions. That makes the CID particularly suited for missile tracking, semiconductor pattern recognition, and factory inspection in which reflections and the appearance of bright objects create brilliant highlights within a properly exposed image.

The contiguous pixel structure of CID arrays further contributes to accurate imaging because there are virtually no opaque areas between pixels (needed with CCD imagers for the transfer of the coupled charge) where image detail is not recorded. This is important in applications in which precise dimensional data is critical, such as determining object edges for inspection, measurement, positioning, and tracking. CID cameras are being used in precision gauging equipment to make measurements accurately to half a micron.

Because each pixel in the CID array can be addressed individually, different readout and processing options can be employed. A *progressive-scan* readout allows an image processor to analyze one row of information while readout continues to the next line. CID cameras from CIDTEC offer high-speed readout of 60 frames/second. If the full-frame information is not needed, the readout can be confined to a limited number of lines, with a resulting increase in readout speed.

A rapid-scan feature of these cameras allows the user to define multiple areas of interest, or *windows*, for readout at normal rates while scanning at a very high rate between windows. The selective data extraction increases readout speed and reduces data volume, facilitating high-speed processing. This capability is especially valuable for target acquisition, in which several objects must be tracked simultaneously individually at rates of up to several hundred images per second as they move through the field of view. Windowing also is used for high-speed inspection in which specific sections of a pharmaceutical bottle, for example, are read out for processing to check cap placement or verify expiration dates and lot codes.

Random-access CID arrays (RACIDs) allow specific pixels to be addressed in any sequence for selective readout at maximum scanning rates. Readout sequence is software controlled. RACIDs are being used in star tracking and celestial navigation, in which only designated stars are followed.

Freeze-frame applications of CID cameras permit them to capture and read asynchronous high-speed events. An example of this is the recording of the image of a fast-moving bottle. The camera is triggered by the appearance of the bottle, rather than being a slave to the *vertical blanking interval*, the period between frames, when scanning returns to the top of the array in preparation for new frame readout. Asynchronous image capture is achieved by utilizing the inject inhibit function to hold the image momentarily until scanning of the next full frame begins, permitting readout of the complete image. A CID camera's 60 frame/second capability can capture asynchronously and read out well over 1800 images/minute, even higher if windowing or less-than-full-frame scanning is used.

Why aren't more CIDs being used in imaging? At present, they are being made only in monochrome versions, but that doesn't preclude the addition of color filters. There is also a 25% to 100% price premium, mainly because of the lower numbers of CID arrays being manufactured. However, the primary reason is that the development of CIDs has lagged far behind that of CCDs. Now that the manufacturing process has been perfected, we should see many more CID arrays finding their way into CCD strongholds—maybe even into specialized still video systems (Fig. 2-3).

Photodiode arrays might best be described as a mass of individual photoelectric cells in miniature, picking up images and generating direct photo current. Although the concept would suggest greater sensitivity and faster operation, the complexity of the structure makes fabrication difficult and leads to many problems in uniformity of response.

When it comes to color, silicon's panchromatic characteristics are another reason why CCDs are based on silicone technology. For broadcast applications and when highest quality is desired, three dichroic beam splitters are used to separate the image into red, green, and blue single-sensor components. This yields the highest quality and certainly is evidenced in the quality of the images seen on today's television. This is also a very expensive solution because it does require three complete systems for handling the three different signals. On the other hand, where high resolution is desired above the current standard NTSC values, the three-chip solution is necessary. The three separate signals are also attractive for use in printing because the three separate signals already are prepared for electronic handling.

As I mentioned in chapter 1, a two-chip solution is being used already in the latest Sony ProMavica. A dichroic beam splitter delivers the image to two arrays, with one array receiving a green signal and providing complete luminance information, and the other sensor receiving a pattern of alternat-

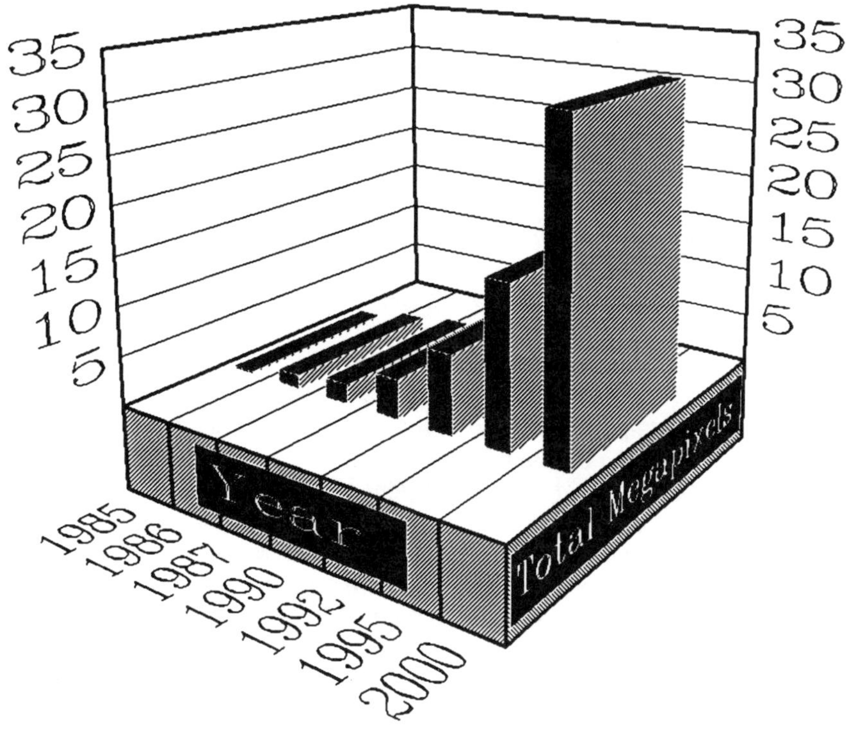

Available solid-state camera sensor resolution

Fig. 2-3. The possible development curve for future CCDs using the doubling rule, which indicates that with electronic solid state devices, new versions are double the value of the old versions. This chart was prepared originally in 1985, and the 1990 objective was reached in 1989 with a 4-million-pixel sensor.

SOURCE: JONREL IMAGING CONSULTANTS

ing red and blue filters to produce the chrominance signal. This is a lower-cost solution that produces a high-quality result, although not up to the level of the true three-chip image.

The most common use of the CCD chip is in a single-chip format for camcorders and for electronic still video cameras. A color-filter pattern is placed on the face of the array, either on alternating pixels or in columns of pixels. Most of the time the colors are not equal, with green occupying half of the pixels and red and blue occupying 25% each.

The high cost of CCD chip manufacture, particularly the higher-resolution chips, is a direct result of the limits of production yield with today's technology. Although this is not a totally significant consideration on the small sensors used for camcorders and electronic still video cameras, even these require healing algorithms that allow averaging two different pixel densities in the event of the loss of a single pixel. This technology has been well developed and is commonly used. In the case of high-resolution sensors—sensors that might be used for scientific measurements, astronomy studies, etc.—quality becomes of the utmost importance because a single lost pixel could be mistakenly interpreted as, in the case of astronomy, an object in the heavens. The higher-resolution sensors quite often are offered in prices dependent on the number of defects allowed. This allows the sale of sensors that are not totally perfect for some applications, while those applications requiring absolute perfection will justify a higher price.

Noise is a matter of great concern in any imaging device. Generally, signal-to-noise (S/N) ratios involve problems generated by the initial stages of detection and amplification that follow the initial signal information from the sensor. The greater the signal-to-noise ratio, the less the low light level of the signal will be affected by noise. A general rule of thumb is that as the resolution of a sensor increases, the noise increases because of the smaller light-collecting area of a sensor. In addition, if the readout rate increases, the noise increases as well. It should be noted that on sensors, such as the four megapixel sensor, the maximum readout is ten frames per second.

One of the real surprises is the dynamic range potential of the silicon sensor. This often can be seen in moving a CCD camera through a variety of light conditions and watching the effect. The dynamic range that can be handled is even greater than the range of highlights and shadows that most conventional silver halide systems can handle. This will change, however, with the advent of higher resolution sensors with smaller cell sizes. As the individual elements of sensors are reduced to gain higher resolution, the dynamic range will also be reduced. This matter of resolution is one that requires continuing study. Some of the new sensors that have been made available offer much higher resolution but at considerable cost. However, with the advent of new 4- and 16-megabit DRAMs, some of the technology being developed for the manufacture of these new devices could have a significant impact on the cost-effective production of higher-resolution sensors with improved characteristics as well.

NEW SENSORS

Two Japanese manufacturers have announced two-million pixel CCDs. A 16.5 × 10.0 mm chip with 1920 × 1035 pixels has been developed by NEC for high-definition TV cameras, office automation equipment, and medical and image processing. The company claims that a separate structure for receptors and picture elements (pixels) permits this high-density circuit integration. It uses 1.4 micron lines. To eliminate blooming under intense lighting conditions, the company has developed a vertical overflow drain design. The readout speed is 74.25 MHz (Fig. 2–4).

Toshiba claims to be already test manufacturing its 1920 × 1036 16.2 × 10.5-mm CCD chip with a 210 mA/lux sensitivity and a dynamic range of 72 dB. It employs a highly photoconductive, amorphous silicon first layer, with storage diodes being located in the second layer. Through the use of the two-layer approach, smearing is reduced because the amorphous silicon layer prevents light from reaching the transfer channel directly. The readout speed of the Toshiba CCD is 74.25 MHz. The double-channel horizontal read registers are driven at 37.125 MHz.

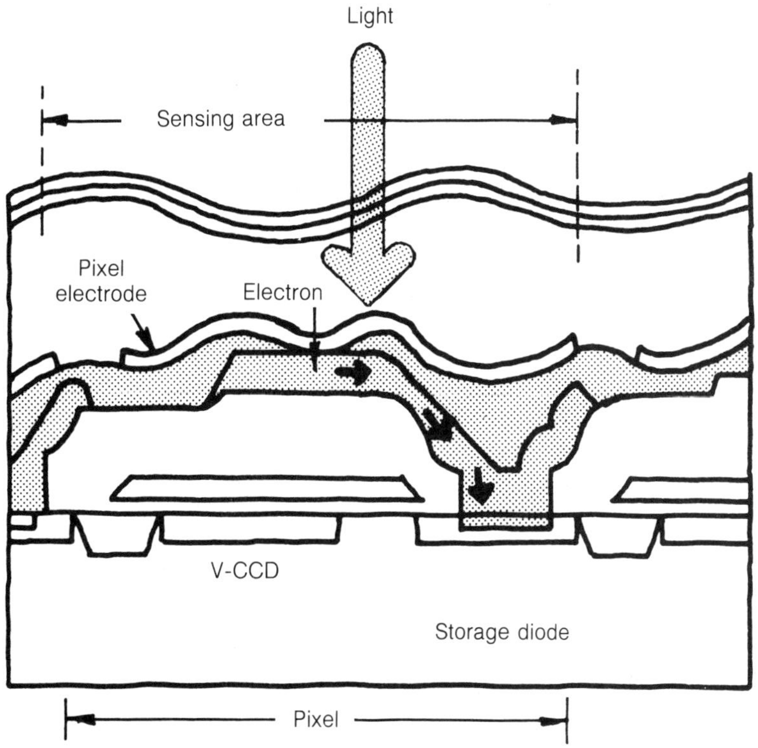

Fig. 2-4. A cross-section of the design of the NEC 2-megapixel CCD image sensor showing the overflow design that provides more surface for image capture.

Fuji has introduced a 2/3-inch, 800,000-pixel CCD camera developed by their semiconductor technology engineers. Part of their Fujix FV-X high-resolution CCD camera, the unit will produce 500 horizontal lines and is designed for high-band still video image recording. The camera uses a standard C-mount 2.32× zoom lens. Output is RGB, NTSC, or S-Jack signal, which provides more flexibility for this camera than most. The sensor is an interline-transfer-type CCD imager.

Kodak's four Megapixel KAF-4200 sensor was the first public announcement of a sensor of this size. Earlier CCD sensors from Ford Aerospace, TI, Thompson CFI, Tektronix, and others have been aimed at the military and intelligence markets and have had high costs and limited availability.

As you look at this new four-megapixel sensor, you see the strong family resemblance to the earlier 1.4-megapixel sensor that was introduced a couple of years ago. Each pixel is a 9-×-9-micron square arranged in 2048 vertical columns and horizontal rows, a close resemblance to four of the original chips joined together. As a matter of fact, they are produced with four to a wafer instead of nine per wafer. The actual imager size is 18.4 × 18.4 mm.

The new sensor can capture 10 frames per second, a speed similar to the original, but each pixel has twice the light-capturing ability of the original sensor. For color applications, the sensor can be used with a filter wheel to obtain RGB color information.

PHOTOSENSITIVE ELEMENTS

There are three basic groups of photosensitive elements: the photodiode, the photocapacitor, and the photoconductor. The photodiode has an implanted element at the top that is designed to collect a high electric field with a well for charge collection. The photocapacitor has a thin polysilicone gate above an oxide. Finally, the photocapacitor consists of a photoconductive film such as hydrogenated amorphous silicon that is located on top of an interline CCD of an addressable diode ray. This approach yields high energy, provides a large area of sensitivity, and resists blooming by providing internal antiblooming.

The most often used sensors are frame-transfer sensor CCDs, interline transfer CCDs, and MOS photodiode arrays. The interline transfer CCD is by far the most popular.

TUBE-BASED CAMERAS

Although we no longer hear about them as often nor see them in products available for the general market, imaging tubes are still a source of high-resolution imaging.

The original Vidicon tubes from RCA were a product of the 1960s. Today high-resolution Vidicon tubes are available in resolutions of up to 1600 TV lines.

Modern video tubes are of the photoconductive type. The first vidicon tube was developed by RCA in 1949 and consists of a photoconductive target that is scanned directly by a low-velocity beam. The photoconductive material used varies the different type tubes. They have such names as Plumbicon, Saticon, and Newvicon; however, all of these tubes operate on the same principles.

Basically, a vidicon consists of a layer of photoconductive material that changes its resistance in inverse proportion to the intensity of light falling on it. The light emitted from the object is focused onto the faceplate, and creates resistance variations across the photoconductive layer that represents the object.

A beam is swept continually across this layer at rates and patterns determined by various formats. A bright spot on the layer has a low resistance and consequently produces a high voltage, while less light results in a lower voltage. The voltage pattern generated during the sweep eventually determines the intensity of light that you see as the phosphor on your video monitor is swept by a corresponding beam.

Tube design has not changed since its inception. In the Vidicon tube, an electron beam scans a photosensitive conducting surface. This beam then produces the analog signal with the front side functioning as a positive voltage with respect to the back side, which has a near-zero voltage.

When a light pattern is focused on the face of the tube, conductivity increases in the illuminated areas and the back side charges to a more positive value. The electron beam then reads the signal by depositing electrons on the positively charged area to provide a signal at the signal electrode. The image surface of the tubes can be made of silicon, lead oxide, zinc telluride, or antimony trisulfide.

Vidicon tubes are still found commonly in television broadcast cameras, but they also appear in some of the high-resolution electronic-imaging systems. The Vidicon tube has certain inherent limitations compared to CCDs. These include such problems as image burning, in which the same image is kept on the tube for a length of time and results in a remembered image on the surface; sensitivity to extremes of illumination, resulting in loss of surface in the tube; and dirt deposits, which can be caused by mishandling of the tube or by particles remaining within the tube causing permanent loss of surface points. This dirt could have been left in the tube at the time of manufacture and can fall on the photosensitive surface when the tube is upended, causing a permanent loss of information at that particular point.

Tubes have served the needs of the image capture field for more than 30 years. Some of the highest resolution devices have been produced for the military surveillance market. Tubes using electrostatic deflection have reached resolutions of up to 6000 lines, a figure well beyond current CCDs.

CCDs, however, appear to be the choice in a multitude of commercial applications, including electronic photography, high-definition television cameras, and other electronic still image capturing areas. The electronic tube will still find a place for high-resolution, low-light-level applications, particularly those in the military surveillance market. The tube market will continue to be affected by future developments, where most of the effort will be concentrated in the area of the CCD.

SCANNING TECHNOLOGY

The CCD array scanners currently are limited in scan resolution. Although some of the new CCD array sensors offer 2000 × 2000 pixel image-capturing capability, linear-array sensors are available in arrays of up to 5000 to 6000 pixels wide. *Linear arrays*, or *linear-imaging devices*, are a single line of sensor elements on a long, narrow chip. The most common use of linear arrays is in digital copiers and facsimile machines in which the subject is generally a line pattern. When the information being scanned is moved or the sensor is moved relative to the material being captured, a high-resolution TV-type picture is produced. Linear arrays are basically monochrome devices, but development is underway for tricolor sensors offering simultaneous red, green, and blue scanning of images.

In some cases, in capturing images of reflected or transmitted light material or even three-dimensional still objects, the sensor is moved mechanically, electronically, or by means of a scanning mirror.

Most desktop scanners that have been available to date have had a maximum resolution of 300 dots per inch. Based on an 11-inch wide scan, these devices generally use a sensor such as the 3456-element line sensor made by Fairchild Weston Systems, the CCD-151. If used across an 8 1/2-×-11-inch page, a 400-dot-per-inch resolution is achieved. A number of desktop scanner manufacturers are now advertising 600 and 800 dot-per-inch levels. These are achieved primarily by averaging adjacent picture elements to form the in-between element. This is a very effective way of creating what appears visually to be a more detailed image.

To date, color desktop scanners have been 300 dots per inch, with a selection at lower resolutions. Higher-resolution capabilities are possible with 35-mm film scanners because of the use of the complete linear array over a smaller surface. This technique is used in the camera-type linear-array scanners such as those available earlier from Eikonix and currently available from AT&T and Chinon in monochrome and Array Technology in full color.

Market prediction companies indicate a continuing development of desktop scanners with a continuing price decline, as well as increased demand for both monochrome and color scanners (Fig. 2–5).

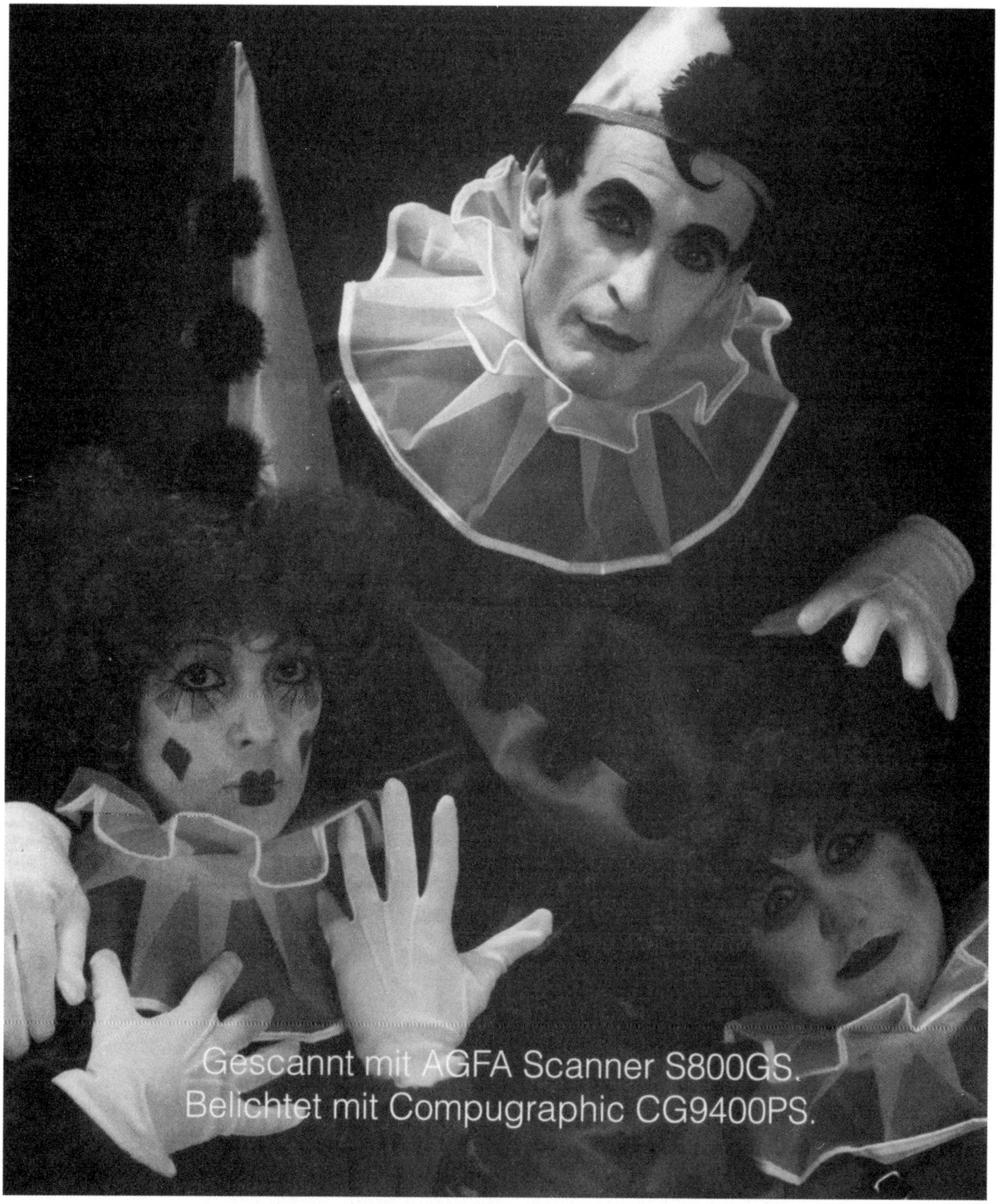

Fig. 2-5. A sample scanned image from a monochrome 800 dpi Agfa S800GS Scanner.

A wide range of monochrome and color scanners are available in both desktop and camera format. The desktop scanners look like, and are closely related to, the top of a typical copy machine with the ability to scan a flat piece of material or, in some cases, transmitted light material. The image is scanned once for monochrome and three separate times for color. The camera-type scanners usually look like a conventional silver-halide copy camera. They offer the ability to move the scanner in and out to maximize the resolution by filling the image frame with the scanned image. A carrier is provided in 35-mm film scanners that place the slide in a light path and are totally self-contained with no external movement, all movement of the sensor is internalized.

Here are some observations on scanners from an interview in *Electronic Photography News* with Clifford L. Hersh. Hersh is Vice President of Engineering for a new company, Array Technologies, Inc., of Oakland California.

"Resolution has a lot of meanings in the industry. It is often equated with the number of dots that a scanner can record in a file. We generally call that the addressability, or addressable resolution of the scanner. There is another kind of resolution, which is how much image data can be captured, and that depends on something else called the spot size of the scanner, which is how big is the smallest piece of information that the scanner can capture.

"The term used to describe, in general at least, the true resolution or the spot size of the scanner is the number of line pairs that the scanner can capture, which is if there is alternating black and white lines, how many lines can there be—how close can the lines get together—before the black lines are at 25% level and the white lines are at 75% level, so that the difference between them is half a full scale. There is a very objective function in the sense that it is easy to measure and there are many charts around to measure it with.

"The number of pixels that the scanner has is its addressability—its addressable resolution, and that has to do with how big a file it can produce. In both scanners and film recorders you see some very large numbers, but these numbers are many, many times the number of line pairs that either the scanner or film recorder can resolve.

"Generally, scanners use some sort of filter which approximates the response of the human eye. One of the great difficulties is that the way that the human eye actually computes color is not particularly well understood and the optical filters we use, at best, are a crude approximation. An example of that crudeness is if you take those color filters and use them to scan the light out of a prism or a diffraction grating. The appearance of that in the scan will be a nice, smooth transformation from red through yellow and orange to green, yet if you look at a rainbow—which is the same effect—you see clearly defined bands of color with very little variation of color inside the band. Because of this substantial difference in the way that your eye actually perceives color and the results that you gain from the color model, any scanning process is going to produce color errors which go by the name of metamorism, which technically just means substituting one color for another.

"Eight bits per color gives a dynamic range generally of 256:1, and 12 bits per color gives a dynamic range of 4000:1. Generally a piece of film has a dynamic range of approximately 5000:1. To really capture the information on a piece of film requires a dynamic range of 16,000:1, which is currently beyond the ability of even the best scanners. Dynamic range is one of those things that the more you have [of it], the more you want because it determines how fine the details [are that] you can get and how subtle the details you can get out of the film are.

"Generally there are two basic methods of scanning currently. One uses a solid-state sensing device, which is usually some sort of photodiode and some method of connecting them. The other more traditional scanner uses a photomultiplier tube. The advantage of a photomultiplier tube is that it has very high speed and a very high dynamic range. The disadvantage of a photomultiplier tube is that it is very unstable and usually uses not more than one color per channel in a scanner. The photodiodes are generally either connected with transistor switches or charge-coupled devices. The advantage of the charge-transfer devices is that they make the connection process easier at the expense of smearing the pixels together somewhat and making it rather questionable whether you can recharge them correctly.

"There are more ways of sensing light, but those are the only two which are currently used in commercially available scanners, partly because those two methods work very well and are relatively established technology and have yielded good results.

"With the photomultiplier tubes you digitize the data as quickly as you can and that has to be very, very fast because you have one sensor getting all of the data for the entire scan. With the photodiodes basically you let light accumulate on the photo diode which essentially knocks [out] electrons. The photodiode is reverse-biased, making a capacitor out of it, and then the light actually knocks electrons out of the capacitor and thus reduces the charge on it. The process of reducing the charge measures the light. The way that the charge which remains is measured is that you recharge the photodiode and see how much current was required. The difficulties are that if you don't recharge the photodiode completely, the next time you expose it you will get some of the last images pixels in the next one. Also if you don't recharge it completely, you can't measure how much charge it took to recharge it correctly. It becomes very important to have some system where the photodiode can be exactly recharged.

"There are two important kinds of processing. One is sharpness correction which basically accommodates effects of the lens and dynamic problems of the integrated circuit. Every lens creates essentially a bump where you would prefer to have a very sharp spot. Fortunately the shape of that bump is well known and it is caused by the diffraction of the iris. In theory, if you know the f-stop, you can compensate for it exactly. In practice, because the spot that the f-stop produces is a circle in the center of the array and somewhat elliptical at the edges of the array, the problem becomes slightly more difficult.

"The other difficulty is that every electronic method of scanning has certain patterns that it imposes on the image which create artifacts which look much like a piece of cloth. They tend to have lines in them and those lines are caused by one line of the sensor being slightly more sensitive than another, or the light being slightly brighter when one line is scanned, or the time applied to one line [being] slightly more or slightly less than the next, or the dark current of one line being slightly more than the next. In general, they create a linen-like look and they make pictures unusable. One level of processing which is necessary for most any scanner is to compensate for these differences and [to] remove the linen effect.

"The other important piece of processing is color correction. No matter what you do, you have a problem scanning color because you don't necessarily know the distribution of light and you don't have good control over the exact nature of the medium that the light was allowed to go through before it got scanned; you don't know the temperature of the light and many other aspects of it.

"Your filters aren't perfect. If you had narrow enough filters, sharp and pure enough filters, the red filter would only let red light through, [and] it would take a huge amount of light to scan. So what happens basically is that even though the red filter lets mostly red light through, it lets a little green light through and a little blue light through. The green filter, being in the middle, is the worst of all. When you are trying to make something which only looks at green, you have a problem. Yellow is half green . . . and a worse situation is if you only looked at green light with the green filter and only looked at red light with the red filter and . . . scan something that is yellow, it would look black.

"It becomes a very complicated process to get the colors right, partly because unlike the human eye which essentially becomes the definition of color—everybody sees the color they expect to see—the problem with the scanner is that when people see a photograph they want to see in this photograph the colors they expect to see. Unlike the sensing mechanism, which is self-reference, you actually have to have a very good model.

"Color correction becomes very important. In general, it is done two different ways. One is that the scanner itself does some color correction and the other is that a post-processing workstation does some color correction. How much is done in the scanner and how much is done in a post-processing environment depends on the application more than the technology.

"There are basically two things that affect the speed of a scanner. One, if you scan 512 × 512 you scan 256,000 dots more or less. If you scan 4k × 4k you scan 16 million dots. Now assuming that both scanners are the same speed in terms of how many dots they scan, 16 million dots is obviously going to take 64 times as long as 256,000 dots because there are 64 times as many dots. If you go to 8k × 8k it becomes 256 times as many dots, and that's a lot of dots. The other problem is that when you scan 4k × 4k you have to be much more careful about what a dot is, namely the quality associated with each dot goes up because you will want to do some post-processing which is going to introduce a level of noise.

"Video scanners generally can get away with a low dynamic range and they are usually what people mean by 'fast' because the picture is always moving and you don't really see noise in a moving picture. On the other hand in a still picture, like print or photography, the slightest amount of noise looks terrible and part of it is. Unlike your TV, people take a picture and get right up to it. They want it to look good even when they're close even though you can't see what's in the picture from there. You have a lot of differences between still photography and motion photography and just like a professional still photograph is vastly higher resolution than a single frame of a movie, in the same way a high-resolution scanner needs much more resolution and much more color quality than a television camera.

"Unfortunately all of these things require an increase in the amount of information, and the raw information that you get in scanning is photons. In film scanning you have some control over how many photons you get. In every other kind of scanning you are stuck with what the world offers and so you are basically up against a bad choice. The more light you have, the more information you get. The more unusual you have made the scene, if it is a real one, and the less versatile your system is, the more light it requires to scan. Generally, for instance in television cameras, they take what they can get and they have noisier scans in lower light.

"Scanners are pretty much the same—the more light you have, the more information you can get and the faster you can finish the scan. The information requirement is so much higher in a high resolution scanner than it is in a television camera. The voltage, the time, and the light level are usually much higher.

"The other difficulty is that high resolution scanners are generally used in applications where the exactness of color and dynamic response are critical, such as photography, printing and publishing where artifacts (because the image isn't moving), especially correlated artifacts like lines across the image, can't be allowed to exist at all because they become very visible. The human eye can perceive correlated information even when it is less than one least significant bit of the data field. It is very important to have data whose background noise level is higher than the artifacts because the background noise level is all that conceals them. Since you need a background noise level that is higher than the artifacts and you need to have a very high dynamic range, you need a lot of bits.

"The trick basically is that if you want at least 4000:1 dynamic range, which is 12 bits of data, and you have to have the artifacts down below 14 bits or 1 part in 16,000 and 2 bits of fairly good noise. That makes for an excellent 12 bit scan but requires more than 12 bits to represent it.

"Scanning will benefit more from digital signal processing, and the advances there, and large scale chip integration, namely bigger chips. Since scanning is information related, the more dots you get at one time, the more information you gather at one time, the less time it takes to finish the scan. Scanning a million pixels is ten times as efficient as scanning 100,000 so the advances in VLSI will help.

"The biggest single help for scanning in the future will be storage space. Bigger disks and more memory are really what will help scanning most. When people talk about 4k × 4k and 8k × 8k, they are talking about absolutely massive data files. Even the temporary buffering in memory, since the scanning process requires that this data you're taking be put somewhere between the time you scan it and the time you get it on a disk and the signal processing, requires that some amount of it be buffered. Both large disks and larger memories will make a huge difference. The other obvious difference is that DSP chips are becoming cost effective ways of drastically improving scanning."

Desktop Scanners

Most of the desktop scanners available today are monochrome scanners. These scanners started as line scanners, the kind you might find in a copy machine, but they have become highly developed gray-scale scanners. They have progressed from the days of the copy machine version of scanners, that is, units that used as their basic technology the input side of several manufacturers' copy machines, to equipment that produces an entire series of halftones, some 64 scales of gray, some 256 scales of gray, depending on the design of the software. Color was the next step and in many cases, equipment was available for color before black and white from manufacturers such as Mitsubishi. Although the Mitsubishi scanner was not common under that name, it appears in the trade dress of a number of other manufacturers with significant changes to accommodate each manufacturer's perceptions of the need of the marketplace.

Desktop-scanning equipment operates much like the familiar personal copy machine. A color scanner usually has a resolution selection of 50, 150, or 300, or variations of these. The material to be scanned is placed on a flat glass surface and covered with a lid much like a copy machine. In the case of a transmitted-light adaption such as that done by Imapro, a moving light source is used that provides a transmission light source for scanning transparencies up to 11 inches wide (Fig. 2–6). The image is scanned to create three independent image files, one each for red, green, and blue. A problem you discover early on is the variation in file format. File formats allow the scanner and computer to format information consistently, and there is a great variety of formats, including TIFF (Tagged Image File Format) that is very commonly used. Other formats include EPS, IMG, GEM, PX, PCX, and MSP.

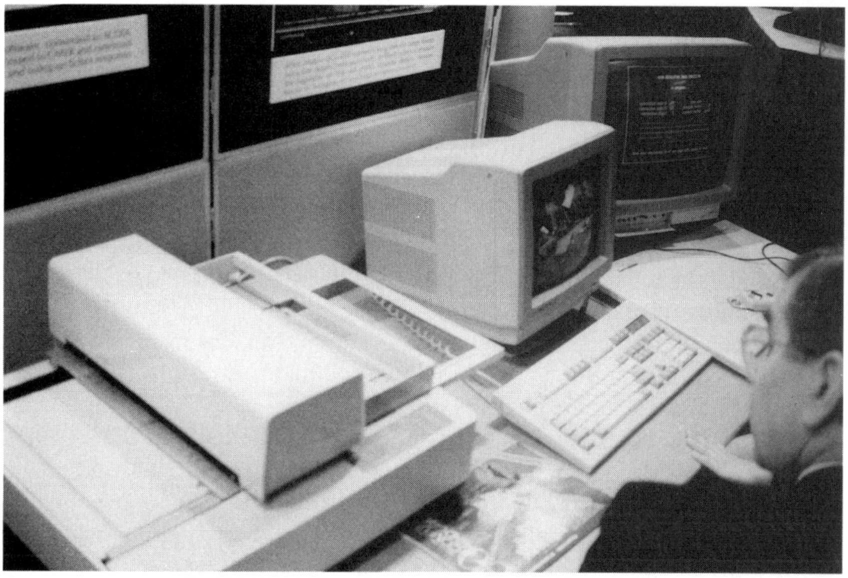

Fig. 2-6. The Imapro Color Scanner includes both a reflective and transmissive light source.

Resolution is determined by two factors. One is the scanner resolution. Because most color scanners to date have been 300 dots per inch, this is a basic limitation in output capability. In addition, the number of bits per color creates another limitation because anything less than six bits per color results in *contouring*, or a series of sharp differences between different colors, such as in a face.

Another problem with color-image scanning is the file size. Although a color page with a 300-dot-per-inch scanner can require 1 megabyte of memory, higher-resolution systems can result in image files of 60 to 100 megabytes for a single image. There are solutions to this information storage problem, and I discuss them in chapter 3.

It might help to review the different desktop scanners currently available. The Howtek Scanmaster II employs a single CCD and an all-electronic RGB color-separation method. A combination of rapidly strobing fluorescent lamps, custom dichroic filters, and phosphors are combined to create the illumination system that moves across the face of the platen and precisely reads the data. The Scanmaster II offers user-selectable fixed scan rates of 75, 100, 150, 200, and 300 DPI, or adjustable rates from 30 to 300 DPI using an asynchronous line-oriented interface. A line of high-resolution red, green, and blue information is buffered and sent at the host's request. The scanner waits until this task is complete rather than disrupt the entire I/O system.

Under command from the host computer, the Scanmaster II can modify the color balance of an image. Correction tables are calculated by a program in the host computer, which in turn generates new look-up tables for downloading to the Scanmaster II.

A windowing function allows the Scanmaster to scan a specified area of a document from 1/2 inch to a full 8 1/2- × 11-inch size. In addition, a zoom function allows the user to specify the number of pixels in each direction of the window. The scanner scans the document and transmit the exact number of pixels specified.

The maximum scanning speed of the Scanmaster II is 45 ms per line. At 300 DPI, it can scan an 8 1/2- × 11-inch document in approximately 2.5 minutes (assuming no host overhead).

Using Scan-it, scanned images can be saved in a variety of file formats, including TARGA, VISTA, TIFF, and Howtek SIM in the IBM PC environment and PICT 2 and RIFF in the Mac II environment.

The Imapro color scanner goes one step beyond the Howtek Scanmaster II with a transmitted light source added to the scan capability. In addition, a series of modifications to the Imapro scanner gives greater image integrity and quality. With the addition of the transmitted-light capability, a single scanner can be used for either reflected color materials, such as color photographs, color advertisements, original color artwork, or color transparencies up to 11- × 14-inch size.

35-Millimeter Transparency Scanners

Transparency scanners for 35-mm film produced a great deal of interest because so much of today's photography is done in the 35-mm original format. This provides a standard size for conversion to electronic images for electronically created presentations, image enhancement, and particularly image transmission. The Barneyscan was one of the earliest available dedicated scanners for 35-mm transparencies. The Barneyscan, as well as most other 35-mm film scanners, comes with its own software package that provides for scanner calibration, color correction, resizing, cropping, and also unsharp masking for edge enhancement.

The Barneyscan scanner has a resolution of 1024 × 1520 with each pixel sampled at 8 bits per color. The total of 24 bits of color produce 16.8 million hues. Each of the 1024 sensor elements is calibrated individually. This data then is stored and used to correct each pixel. This assures quality and uniformity. The scanner output formats include TIFF, TARGA, TARGA BIGPIC, Lumena 16 and 32, RIFF, PICT, PICT 2, Sunraster, and Artisan.

The unit offers a proprietary NetScan option to allow local-area network operations on TOPS, Ethernet, and Appletalk for easy interface to other major workstations from Digital Equipment Corporation, Silicon Graphics, Apollo, and others.

The Barneyscan light source is a commercially available quartz halogen lamp with an average life of 3000 hours. The light is guided by fiberoptics through the slide without any heat to the slide. This prevents the transparency from buckling during the required three scans.

For PC/AT and compatibles, the Barneyscan requires a minimum of 1.5 megabytes of RAM. Its interface card takes an empty PC/AT slot. It is also necessary to have a VISTA, TARGA 16, 24, or 32 frame buffer or a work-alike to display the scanned image on a color monitor. For Macintosh II, the interface card takes an empty NUBUS slot. The scanner also needs a display card and 2 megabytes of memory.

The scan time is about three minutes depending on slide density, with monochrome slides being scanned in 30 seconds. Exposure is set with an internal auto-white exposure control.

The Howtek Scanmaster 35 is a specially adapted version of the Leaf scanner. With a resolution of 1333 × 2000 DPI, the image is scanned by a CCD array using an RGB filter wheel and fluorescent lamp. Data is transferred at a 100 kbytes per second sustained rate with the output selectable as either 8 bit or 12 bits per color.

The Nikon 35-mm LS-3500 scanner scans images at 4096 × 6144 pixels. Red, green, and blue are read in 8-bits per color, offering a palette of 16.7 million colors (Fig. 2–7).

The image is scanned by a 4096-element linear CCD using a mechanical scanning mechanism involving a moving stage screw-driven by a stepping motor. The scanning time is approximately 15 seconds for each color. The software for the Nikon film scanner provides a series of functions. These include negative/positive or reversal selection, shading correction, density

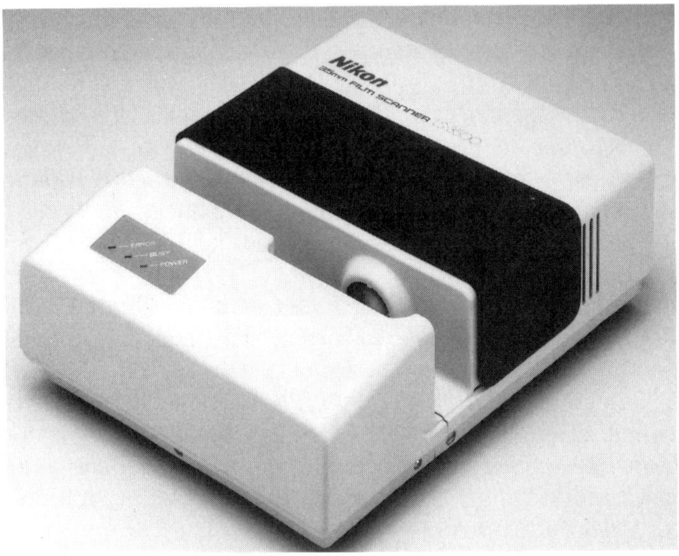

Fig. 2-7. The Nikon 35mm LS-3500 Film Scanner.

conversion (culling), binary processing (slice level selectable), dither matrix (seven types, from 3 × 3 to 6 × 6), and trimming (by specifying address area). Image correction includes exposure, tone-wedge gamma, and color-balance correction in both manual and automatic modes. Images are transferred as sequential red, green, and blue screens.

Drum Scanners

If you have ever visited a magazine publisher or other location that specialized in color reproduction, you have probably seen the large drum scanners used for high-resolution scanning of reflective or transmitted-light original photographs. These machines, which look like giant lathes, produce extremely high-resolution output, digital images, or direct screen separations for reproduction purposes.

Priced in a six-figure range, these scanners represent a high state of the art in graphic reproduction and often are used in enhancement systems for initial digitalization of imaging.

Although not your everyday electronic still camera or desktop scanner, these drum scanners represent a unique state of the art in digital reproduction.

An image can be scanned at a sampling pitch ranging from 25 to 1000 microns, depending on the machine. For some machines, the potential exists for up to 24 bits per color, which assures an almost absolute digital reproduction of the image.

Linear-Array Camera Scanners

Linear-array camera scanners often look like video cameras, but they are designed in many cases for higher-resolution output. Used for copying color prints, art work, or color transparencies, linear-array scanners also can be used for nonmoving still objects to obtain high-resolution images.

There are four versions of the linear-array camera scanner. In one version, the scanner is moved incrementally by a stepping motor to form a complete scan of the image. If it is a color system, three individual scans, one each for red, green, and blue, are made. These separate records are maintained in separate files and are available for processing and other uses such as halftone output or direct color imaging.

The second method is to move the head electronically as the Array scanner. The Array scanner generates color files that can then be handled in a variety of software programs. The third method is the use of a mirror that allows a linear array to look across a piece of copy and create an image line-by-line.

Finally, the last type moves the information in front of the camera. This is referred to as a digital line scan camera.

One of the pioneers in this field was the Eikonix scanner, which was purchased by Eastman Kodak Company and is no longer available today. The Eikonix 1412 imaging camera system provided a 4096 × 4096-pixel image with a dynamic range of up to 12 bits per pixel per color (Fig. 2–8). This camera could scan a minimum width of 16 mm with no maximum restrictions. Transmission, reflection, or 3D objects were limited only by the design of the camera station, which looked like an enlarger/copy stand. Using a 55-mm MicroNikor for most cases, this digital scan camera met very high quality standards for scanning.

To capture an image, an Eikonix digital camera scanned the photo original art or object using a light-sensitive linear array in the camera. This linear array recorded the amount of light coming from the subject as a series of precise digital values with three separate scans, one each for red, green, and blue. The linear array, with its 4096 individual elements, provided information for the camera to transfer to the computer by stepping the array across the image field of view up to 5200 times. This method produced over 20 million pixels of image definition. Each pixel represented as many as 1024 gray-scale levels or up to 16 million different color hues.

The Array Scanner-One (AS-1) is a high-resolution digital color camera. The camera scans color and graphic gray-scale images at resolutions of up to 4096 × 4096 pixels. Other user-selectable resolutions include 512 × 512,

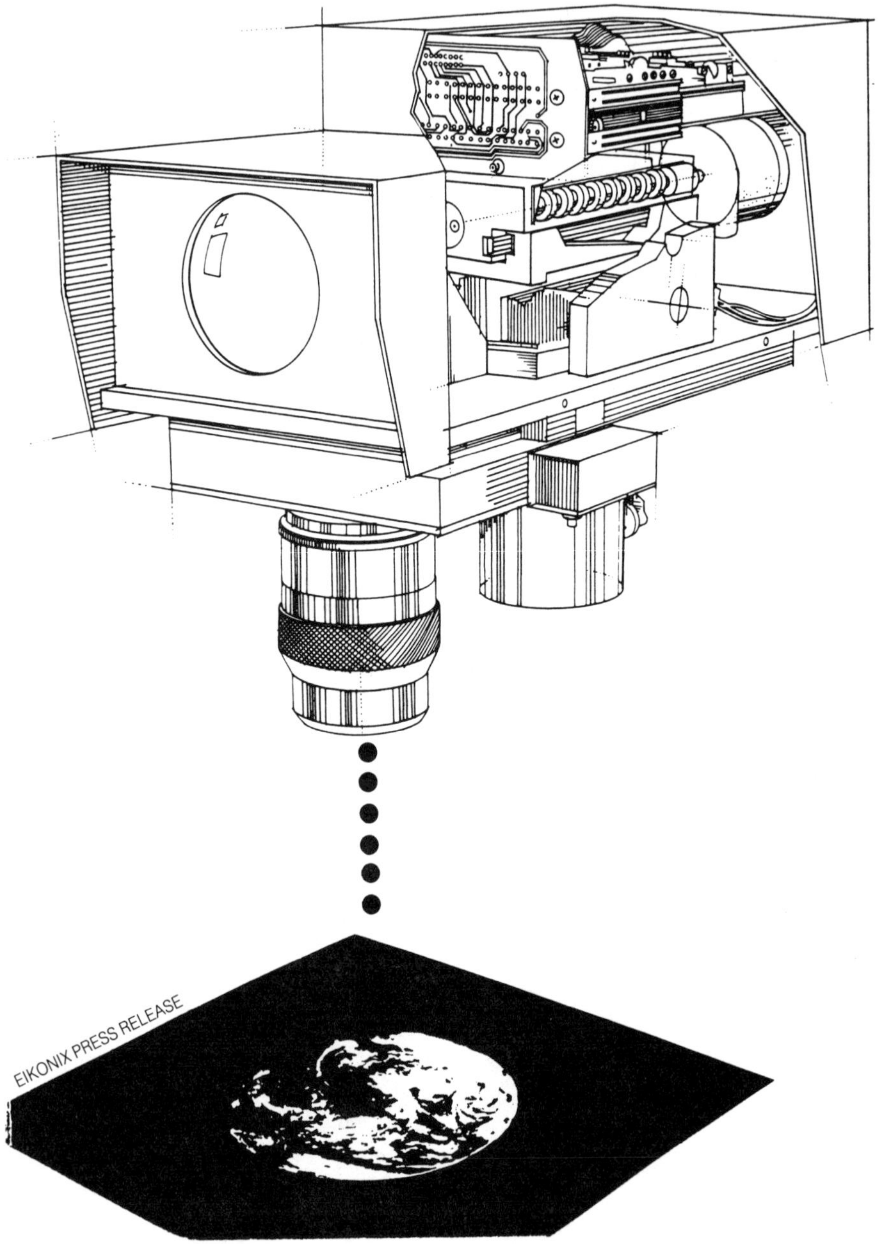

Fig. 2-8. A cross section of the Eikonix Digital Imaging Camera.

1024 × 1024, and 2048 × 2048. The optical resolution of the system has a maximum of 1700 line pairs. The system uses a proprietary motion control and square-image-assembly technology. A square color-image sensor with a transverse sense-line array of photodiodes with 3310 active elements takes rapid snapshots of the target image. One-pass color and high-speed image acquisition gives the operator rapid control over imaging parameters such as focus and luminance.

Ultraprecise motion control and high-speed image assembly are used to create a raster file in a frame buffer or on a hard disk. A pop-up menu interface gives the operator control over a variety of tools by using a mouse, bitpad, or computer keyboard. Image resolution, dynamic range, aspect ratio, and color values are specified by the operator. Automatic installation, start-up calibration, and input and output gamma correction minimize the operator learning curve.

The dedicated digital signal processing hardware is contained on a board that is placed on the AT bus and SCSI interfaces to connect with workstations and PCs. Standard file formats are supported, such as TIFF 24/48 and encapsulated Postscript.

An example of a mirror technique is the Chinon Image Scanner N-205 (Fig. 2–9). Using a linear CCD, monochrome scanning resolutions of 100, 120, 150, and 200 DPI are achieved. A single scan of a conventional typewriter-size-page document at 200 DPI requires a minimum of 12.8 seconds. Designed primarily for documents rather than photographs, the technology does provide a good example of a scanner providing a direct digital interface, with two-way parallel interface board connecting directly to an IBM PC/AT at either 9600 or 19,200 baud.

The Fairchild model CAM-1600R is an industrial-grade line-scan camera with a monochrome resolution of 3456 elements. The CAM-1600R is designed for high-resolution document scanning, but it does offer an example of a line scanner. The camera includes a timing signal generator for control of the camera, an analog module for processing the camera video output, a pixel locator module for interfacing the camera and the digital processing equipment, and a power-supply module.

The primary output of the CAM-1600R line-scan camera is an analog waveform showing the spatial distribution of incident illumination intensity along a scanned monochrome line. Conversion of the optical input into an analog signal is accomplished by a monolithic CCD image sensor containing 3456 detecting elements aligned in a single row. If an object is transported past the field of view of the camera, a complete two-dimensional image of the object can be constructed from the series of line-scanned data.

I should point out that the Chinon image scanner and the Fairchild line-scan camera are designed for industrial applications such as document scanning or, in the case of the Fairchild unit, industrial production lines for

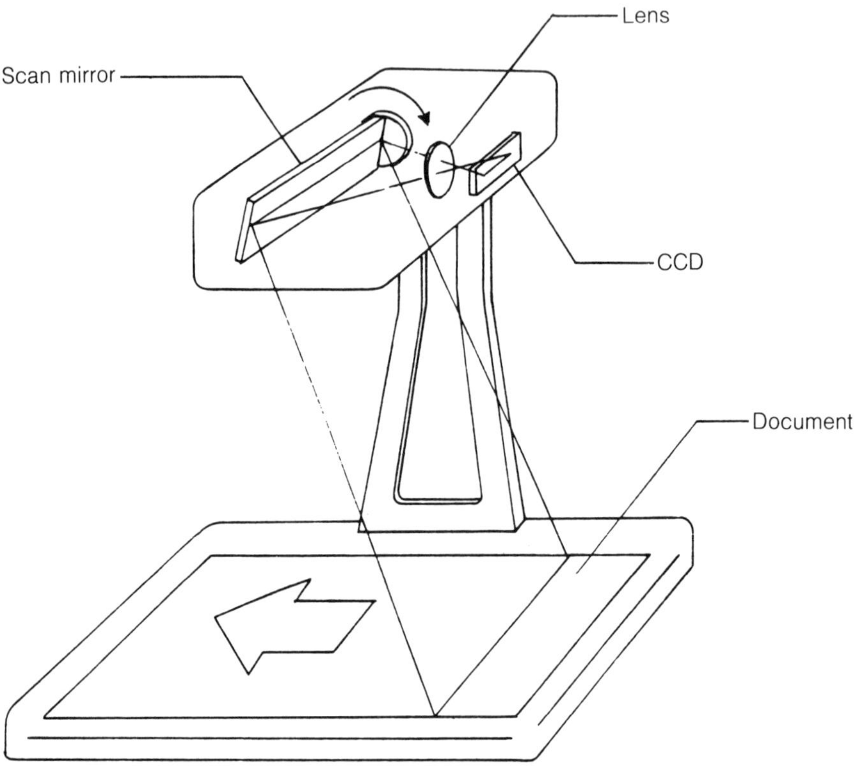

Fig. 2-9. A sketch showing the scanning mirror of the Chinon Image Scanner N205.

actually creating images of moving objects. Both represent another way of using scanning technology that has potential color applications and for capturing complete electronic photographs.

Although these are only four examples of the use of linear-array technology, more applications can be expected since the advent of 8000-pixel linear arrays. New tricolor linear arrays have rows of red, green, and blue sensitive elements all included in a single sensor array.

An example of more recent linear arrays is the MN3666 CCD linear image sensor from Matsushita Electronics. It scans A3 documents with a 24 lines/mm resolution, equivalent to 7500 pixels. It has a dynamic range of 73 dB (at 25 degrees C) and an after image of 8% at 100V. The chip size is 70.8 × 1.38 mm, and the present scanning data transfer rate is 10 MHz, which will be increased as the capacity of the driving circuits improves.

VIDEO CAMERAS

Even with the limitations of the NTSC system and the only slightly higher resolution of the current PAL and SECAM systems, video cameras are finding extensive use as electronic photography tools. When used with available image-capture boards, NTSC video cameras as well as the visual-presentation devices with copy stands, make excellent electronic photography tools. In addition to these systems, several cameras are available that produce resolutions higher than NTCS cameras, sometimes exceeding 1000 horizontal lines of resolution.

A variety of video-camera stands have appeared from manufacturers such as Elmo, Kodak, and Fuji. Most of these are simple combinations of available CCD cameras and convenient controls for camera operation.

The Elmo Visual Presenter EV-308 takes any visual source—notes, charts, color pictures, slides, photographs, diagrams, and three-dimensional or moving objects—and transfers these into dynamic images either on a recording medium or to the frame grabber of a computer system for digital storage (Fig. 2–10). The EV-308 uses a motor-driven zoom lens to provide close-up viewing of tiny objects and small text. A built-in transmission light source is available for slide reproduction. Equipped with a 300,000-pixel color CCD camera, the Visual Presenter uses a 1/2-inch interline-transfer CCD.

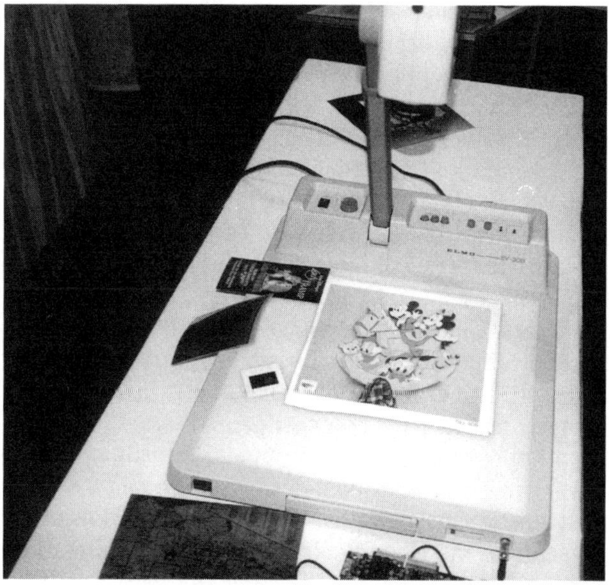

Fig. 2-10. The Elmo Visual Presenter EV305.

The Kodak SV-5000 Video Transfer Stand was part of Kodak's original announcement of electronic photography products, and converts slides and prints into video signals. Using a daylight balance system for both slide illumination and a ring light for print illumination, the NTSC video output of the transfer stand can be sent to a color monitor, still video recorder, or a transceiver for direct transmission or to a frame-grabbing board in a computer. Inputs include 35-mm 2 × 2-inch slides or color prints from 3 1/2 × 5 to 9 × 12 inches. The originally supplied camera used a Newvicon tube.

The latest version of the Kodak video transfer stand, the SV-5010, now has a CCD camera with an RGB output that allows transfer to computer image boards. It is completely compatible with the Kodak SV-6500 series color video printers (Fig. 2–11).

The Canon RE-550 Video Visualizer has been a popular input device for many companies marketing photo-imaging systems (Fig. 2–12). The CCD video camera module on this unit provides 380,000 pixels (780 horizontally and 490 vertically) to provide a highly detailed picture. The camera unit itself has an RGB pure color stripe filter and an RGB output. Equipped with an f1.2 zoom lens, output is possible either directly to a monitor, to a video printer, to a still video transceiver, or a still video recorder (Table 2–3).

The Fujix video camera/processor FV-5000 is another of the complete image capture stations (Fig. 2–13). With a 2/3-inch 400,000-pixel CCD imager, it provided the highest resolution available until the announcement of the Fujix FV-X high-resolution CCD camera with the first 2/3-inch 800,000-pixel interline transfer CCD imager. The FV-X camera provides a horizontal resolution of a full 500 TV lines. The Fujix FV-X has both RGB and NTSC video output with S-jack capabilities for use with systems with separate luminance and chroma.

The variety of cameras available for image capture in color is wide. Canon provides a mixture of half-inch and 2/3-inch cameras with 2/3-inch CCDs with 380,000 pixels. The CI-10 MK2 is an NTSC camera with a CI-10 MD2 RGB camera available as well. One of the significant changes that begins to appear with these cameras is the improved signal-to-noise ratio. The S/N ratio for the original CI-10 camera was 43 dB for chrominance and 46 dB for luminance. Currently the signal-to-noise ratio is 46 dB or better, which means a better color image is possible.

The Canon CI-20 CCD family of cameras uses a half-inch pickup still with 380,000 pixels and an RGB color stripe.

In addition to providing a transfer stand, Elmo also provides a means for capturing original images from slides or 16-mm and 8-mm movies. The Elmo film-to-video transfer units use a half-inch color 300,000-pixel CCD. The original design of the Elmo equipment employed a less than 300,000-pixel sensor with the result that the images lacked sharpness. Now, with the

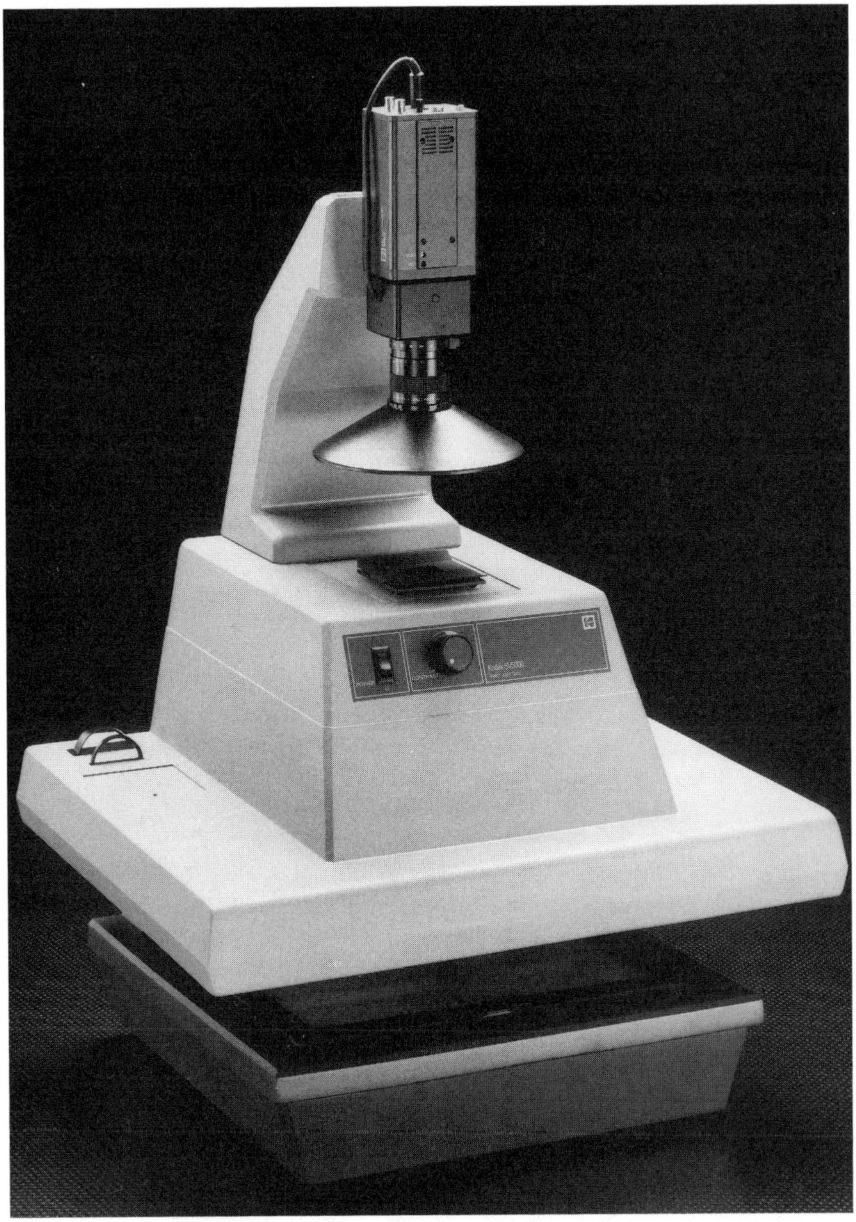

Fig. 2-11. The Kodak CCD 1000RGB camera is now a standard component on the improved SV5010 Video Transfer Stand. The system can be used to capture images of prints or slides. It has a built-in slide and print illuminator.

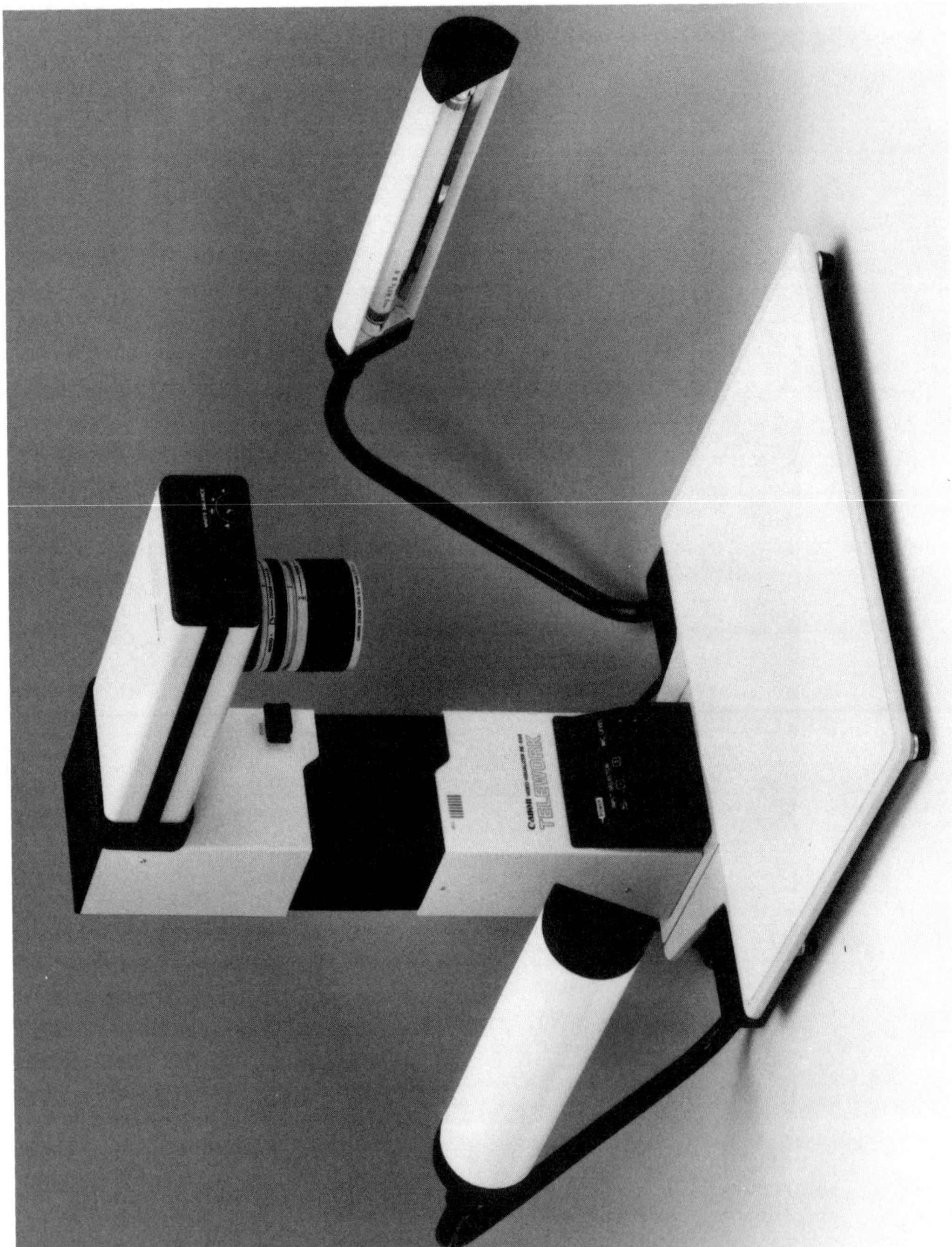

Fig. 2-12. The Canon Video Visualizer RE550.

Table 2-3. Specifications for the Canon Video Visualizer RE-550.

Type:	Compact color video camera built-in image input unit
Video output signal:	Video 2 channels
Lens:	8.3-16 mm f1.7-2.2 zoom lens with macro
Display document range:	8 1/4" × 11 11/16" (max.) 2 15/16" × 4 1/8" (min.)
External input:	Selecting one of 2 video channels and 2 audio channels
Microphone:	Built-in: input terminal for external microphones (0.35 mm mini-jack) with mixing volume
Lighting:	6W fluorescent lamp × 2

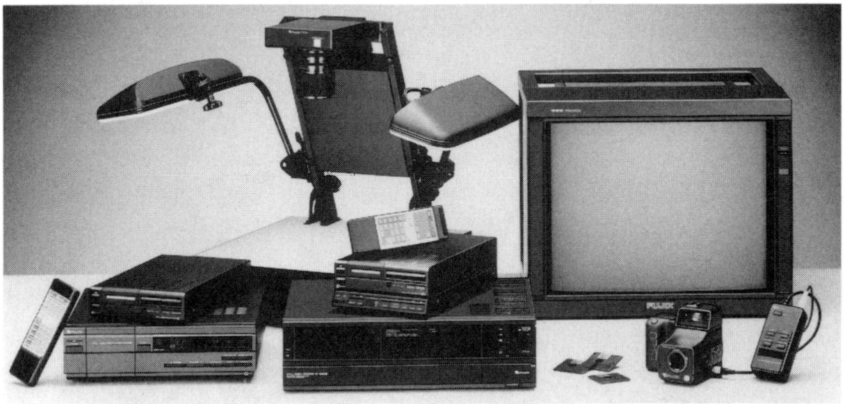

Fig. 2-13. The Fujix Video Camera/Processor FV5000.

change to the 300,000-pixel sensor, a resolution of 370 horizontal TV lines is possible.

In addition to the conventional NTSC cameras, higher resolution cameras are available such as the Megaplus camera from Kodak's Videk operation (Fig. 2–14). The Megaplus camera was one of the first available CCD cameras with a 1-megapixel monochrome sensor. Developed for scientific applications, JVC, Sony, and Nikon have all marketed this type of camera. These cameras have resolutions ranging from 700 to 1100 horizontal lines and are normally not compatible with conventional NTSC television systems. However, they can be used with frame grabbers that allow the analog-to-digital conversion of images of greater resolution.

A super-high-resolution (SHS) system is available now from Sony. The 1050-line vertical SHS output of 31.5 kHz can be digitized or converted to NTSC.

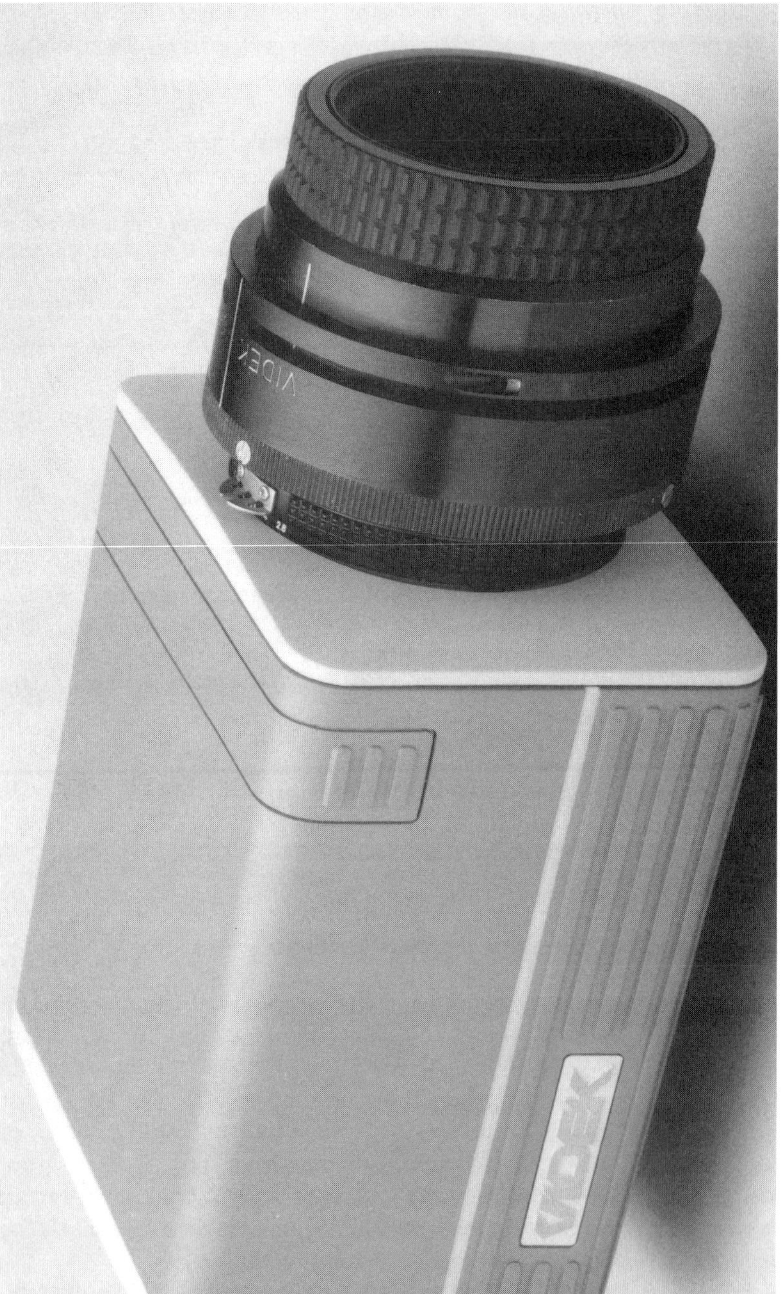

Fig. 2-14. The Videk Megaplus Camera, from one of Kodak's companies, is a monochrome solid-state camera capable of imaging 1.4 million picture elements.

The SHR-10P camera head, camera-control unit SHR-10, and a Super-Fine-Pitch Trinitron monitor GDM-1920 produce 1000 lines horizontal and either 1025 lines interlaced or 525 lines in noninterlaced mode. A built-in shutter protects the 2/3-inch MF Saticon picture tube. The 3:4 aspect ratio screen scan is at 60 frames/second and delivers 950 lines of resolution.

Nikon has produced an HDTV still video camera and an HDTV frame store memory. Using a 1-inch Saticon image pickup tube, images are 1920 × 1035 pixels with 8 bits/color. The system uses the HD1125/60 (BTA S-001) standard. The unit has high sensitivity and a high-speed input of 0.3 seconds/frame.

Another approach to image capture of negative and transparency film images is the TRV-30SF unit from Elmo Co. The design of the system permits it to scan the films through mylar/plastic pages/holders. This eliminates the need to take the films, particularly the slides, out of their filing sheets, view them on the TV monitor, and then return them to the holder. The converter features a 300k pixel CCD imager, 2.5× zoom lens, a VTR for recording the video image, and a low-wattage 12W lamp.

A final video system that shows a new direction is the Polaroid 8801 CCD still video system. This black-and-white system includes a CCD camera with a 600,000-pixel sensor developed by Polaroid, a control unit, and a Polaroid printer for creating black-and-white prints. The resolution is 378 × 486 pixels in standard mode. In the high-resolution mode, the camera produces a Polaroid-designed high-resolution signal with a resolution of 1134 × 486 pixels for storage on Super-VHS recorders. With 256 levels of gray, images appear photolike in final form. This is the first publicly shown product that indicates the most probable direction Polaroid will take in electronic still imaging. The High-Resolution CCD Still/Video System is now officially called the Polaroid 8801 CCD Still/Video System.

The key element that makes the system work is digital enhancement. The potential areas of application cited by Polaroid include investigation, surveillance, quality assurance, and photojournalism. In addition to the three basic components (the video camera, control unit, and video printer), the still/video system has a video monitor and a large format, high-resolution black-and-white analog monitor for soft viewing of the enhanced image to be printed.

A Super-VHS VCR is an available option for recording the enhanced image. Other options include a digital interface for use with personal computers and a modem for image transfer by telephone.

The system specifications and performance characteristics of the three Polaroid basic components are:

1. A video camera with still-frame capability that uses a single CCD imager with frame transfer to record either standard (378 × 486 or 183,708 pixels) or high-resolution (850 × 486 or 413,100 pixels).

2. A control unit that does analog-to-digital conversion, digital processing/enhancement, and digital-to-analog conversion.
3. A high-resolution video printer.

The other components listed above such as the monitors, Super-VHS VCR, digital interface, and modem are added cost items. The present system is black and white only. Polaroid has displayed color prints, but these were made from color separations imaged onto Polaroid color print film. A true color system is under development but is some time away.

Polaroid's 8801 Still/Video System is only capable of black and white output. This factor, together with the system's cost, could limit newspaper interest until the color version is available. Polaroid specifically has avoided using the Still Video Floppy Standard, with its inherent limitations on resolution. Although the newly established Hi-band still-video floppy standard has raised this resolution level, hard-copy output using this resolution level is still limited.

The approach of upgrading a video or analog signal that Polaroid has taken provides an interesting means of resolution improvement. It will be interesting to follow its degree of success and the markets served by this new electronic still photographic system.

With all of the options available in addition to still video cameras, electronic photography is real option with great potential for future growth (Table 2–4). This growth will depend on some of the products mentioned in chapter 3 in the processing and transmission of images, along with the electronic darkroom, which is a significant innovation and will be available soon. These are discussed in chapter 6.

Table 2-4. Comparison of Electronic and Silver Halide Systems.

Product	Pixel Resolution (000's Omitted)
Canon RC-760 (CCD imager)	600
Sony ProMavica MVC-5000 (2 CCD Imagers)	760
Kodak Videk Megaplus (CCD Imager—Digital)	1,400
110 film negative (VR 100)	4,000
35mm film negative (Kodacolor Gold 100)	20,000

APPLICATION STORIES

Medical Analysis

At the Veterans Administration Medical Center in San Diego, Dr. Robert Myers is using a Data Translation high-resolution frame grabber in a MicroVAX system for the analysis of nerve biopsies. Electronic images are captured in the electronic microscope, false coloring added, and calculations performed on each sample.

TIME Magazine Covers the Olympics Electronically

Time Magazine used the ProMavica system as an "editing and viewing" system to enhance photo coverage of the Summer and Winter Olympics in Seoul and Calgary, according to *Time* picture editor Michele Stephenson.

Photographers at both events used film cameras to take photographs. Slides were then scanned with a Tamron 35-mm capture unit, stored on the ProMavica recorder, and transmitted using a pair of Sony transceivers. The received images were reviewed by Stephenson and other *Time* editors to make decisions on photo selection. ProMavica images also were used for positioning pictures on page layouts. Once photos were selected, Stephenson instructed picture editors in the field to send the final images.

"We use a Crosfield System to transmit, via satellite, camera-ready high-resolution color photographs," Stephenson explains. "However, transmission can take 20 to 60 minutes per picture. With the ProMavica system we transmitted a color image from Calgary or Seoul to New York City in 3 minutes. It allowed us to view and select photos under consideration rather than just have editors attempt to describe them over the telephone. By the time the picture was scanned and transmitted via the Crosfield system, we had already completed the layout using the ProMavica image for positioning."

"The ProMavica system allowed us to get late-breaking news pictures from long distances into the magazine right up until deadline," says Stephenson. "The system was a great help in covering the Olympics because it saved a lot of time and gave us the advantage of seeing the images we were talking about, which helps us make better editorial judgments. I also like the fact that our pictures could be transmitted overnight and (be) ready for editing when we came in the morning."

Electronic Photographs and the Titanic

The Toko DR72 Microfreezer helped make history by capturing the first images seen in 73 years of the *Titanic*. The ultracompact size and state-of-the-art performance of the DR72 digital-video-image storage system made it the ideal choice of the Woods Hole Oceanographic Institute for its search for the HMS *Titanic*. The DR72 was used to record video images in a deep diving submersible sled called the *Argo*.

The *Argo* contained a camera, the DR72 and other equipment. The sled was tethered to the USS *K. Knorr* by approximately three miles of I/O control and video cable. Using a powerful strobe light for illumination, the *Argo* utilized the DR72 to record high-resolution images from an intensified camera during each brief flash of the strobe. In turn, the DR72 transmitted the images repeatedly to an image processor with recursive filtering capability on board the search ship, thus canceling out interference and noise that would otherwise have masked the *Titanic's* detection.

From a systems designer's point of view, the ultracompact DR72 is a functional block that can replace larger and more costly external frame storage devices. It is switchable to 525 or 625 scan standards, with either single- or dual-frame capability, field or frame selectable. Both last image hold and one-shot modes of operation can be selected via a TTL level input control connector. A TTL-level record output signal is available for control of external systems, such as an X-ray machine. Standard connector types are used throughout.

Performance characteristics match or exceed those of rack-mounted systems. Frame composition is 512 pixels × 480 lines, with 7-bit (128) gray-level resolution for NTSC video. The digital sampling rate is approximately 10 MHz. Memory storage capability is 256,000 words by 7 bits.

In addition to undersea research, applications for the DR72 include integration into imaging systems for medical, military, ultrasound, robotics, security, and computer graphics.

Surgery and Electronic Photography

Today surgeons are looking into the smallest cavities of the human body with a clarity not possible a few years ago. This is due in part of the efforts of researchers at the Laser Research Center of Cedars-Sinai Medical Center in Los Angeles, California.

"The Laser Research Center is a collaborative effort built upon investigations into the use of lasers in surgical procedures," says Dr. Warren Grundfast, Assistant Director of Surgery at Cedars-Sinai and Director of the Laser Research Center. "In looking for ways to transmit the laser's energy, we turned to fiberoptics and discovered a variety of new uses for these tiny glass fibers that provide a unique view inside the body."

In addition to the laser, Grundfest and his colleagues developed very thin, flexible endoscopes that use optical fibers to transmit light to small body cavities such as blood vessels and ducts. They can work with a laser and simultaneously examine the affected tissues and structures.

The endoscopes require a video camera and monitor for image display. The endoscopic examination or surgical procedure is displayed on the monitor and recorded on video tape.

Because endoscopic procedures can take a long time, they produce a tremendous amount of data and use a great deal of video tape. Although video tape provides complete documentation of the procedure, it is time consuming to review and does not offer a hard copy of the information.

"From the start of our research, getting hard copy documentation was a problem," Grundfest says. "Transferring video images to print form required converting the video tape to film, reviewing the film to select the scenes or images we needed and then making prints. It could take weeks to get the prints and was expensive. We needed a better way."

"With a Kodak SV6500 Color Video Printer we now produce still images from video tape simply by pressing a button to capture the scene displayed on the monitor and pressing another button to print it," says Dr. Jacob Segalowitz, clinical research fellow at the Center. "Within 90 seconds, we have a high-quality color print that provides the color and detail of the image on the monitor."

The ability to produce prints immediately on site has enabled researchers at the Center to do many things not previously possible.

"In the laboratory, still video prints allow us to compare in an easy and timely fashion different scenes or sequences using the endoscope or the laser," Grundfest explains. "We can also capture images in a way that allows us to quantify the results of our research. For example, by examining a series of prints from a procedure, we can see how much more of a vessel we might need to open. This is important in an experimental setting because it helps guide our research."

The clinical area, too, has benefited from the arrival of the SV6500, as surgeons use the Kodak Printer to capture and print images right in the operating room.

"The SV6500 lets us evaluate what we're doing during surgery as well as after," Grundfest says.

"For example, in bypass surgery small irregularities often develop when veins are sewn together in the legs. These irregularities are revealed through a tiny endoscope called an angioscope. The only way to document the repairs to the veins is to capture the images during the procedure. We then file the prints in the patient's record."

Researchers at the Laser Research Center also are using still video prints for publication. "It's essential in a research setting to be able to provide quality prints for publication, but this has always been a problem with endoscopic research," Segalowitz says. "Now with the SV6500 we can quickly and easily produce color images that illustrate the results of our research and are suitable for reproduction."

Cancer Cell Studies

Researchers at the Exploratory Sciences Division of Eastman Kodak Company in Rochester, New York are using video microscopy and digital-imaging technologies to study the reactions of cancer antigens (substances that stimulate the production of antibodies) in live tumor cells. Their goal is to develop new tools for diagnosing and combating various forms of cancer.

"The experiments we conduct generate a lot of information, and that produces two problems," says Kodak's Dr.Robert Belly, research associate in the Exploratory Sciences Division. "The first is how to distill data into a meaningful form. The second is how to best convey our results to our colleagues and others in the field."

Data can be presented in two ways, Belly says. One is by providing quantitative summaries, i.e., by using numbers to show relationships and differences. The other is by using pictures.

"The images from our cell research can be black and white or color," he says. "Black-and-white pictures usually contain raw or unprocessed images and may yield very little information. By adding color to these images in proportion to the gray-scale intensity, we can see much more detail."

Many images can be required to interpret data from a single cell. Generally people want to see the untouched black-and-white image plus subsequent enhanced versions, Belly says.

The traditional method for producing pictures is to use black-and-white or color film. By attaching a camera to the microscope, researchers can take photographs as they examine a specimen. A camera also can be used to capture images displayed on a video monitor. The prints are then processed and distributed or filed.

Although film offers the highest-resolution hard copy, classical photography has some disadvantages in applications related to microscopy, Belly says.

"By the time we've taken a roll of film and waited for processing, we may forget what's on the roll. Also, when the camera is attached to the microscope, we have no control over exposure and don't always know whether the image will be a good one," he explains.

Today, Belly and his colleagues are supplementing conventional photographs from their research with high-quality, continuous-tone thermal prints, in color and black and white, produced with the Kodak SV6510 Color Video Printer.

A recent addition to the family of Kodak Still Video Products, the SV6510 Printer is integrated into the laboratory's imaging workstation, which includes a Zeiss Axiovert microscope, charge-coupled device (CCD) and silicon intensifier target (SIT) cameras, and a MicroVAX II computer. Image-processing software created especially for biological research provides a wide range of image enhancement and quantitative-analysis capabilities.

"Light passes through a sample on the microscope, and the image is captured by the CCD or video camera," Belly says. "From the camera, the image is passed to the image processor and then to the computer for storage on a hard disk. Once captured and stored, the image can be retrieved, displayed, enhanced, analyzed and now printed thermally."

The printer is connected to the workstation through its RGB analog input. A switch on the printer's rear panel is used to select black-and-white or color printing. Front-panel controls allow adjustments to color, contrast, and black level.

"The SV6510 Printer is a powerful tool," Belly says. "Within a minute and a half, we can produce a print that faithfully represents the cell structure displayed on the computer screen."

Still Video Photography at the Political Convention

One of the first significant trials of the Polaroid 8801 Still/Video System was at the Democratic Party's National Convention held during July 1988 in Atlanta, GA. Two components of the system were used in a joint effort with the Associated Press. The images were recorded using the camera, and the image signal was upgraded with the controller. The resulting high-resolution, analog signal then was transmitted directly into the special AP "electronic darkroom" installed at the convention site. The AP, in turn, transmitted these images promptly to the large electronic darkroom in their New York City headquarters and to member newspapers and news magazines.

Although capabilities, not economics, were the main considerations in testing the new Still/Video System in a major news event, such usage addressed a key concern in the photojournalism field. By electronically capturing and transmitting high-resolution images, the normal silver-halide photographic steps of photographing, developing, and then scanning were bypassed. Immediate all-electronic handling of photographic-quality images was possible with the first hard copy or print appearing only at the receiving newspaper's Wirephoto machine.

3

Processing and Transmitting the Electronic Photograph

One of the most important benefits that electronic photography brings to us is the ability to process the image either to create additional effects, correct artifacts in the image, or improve on the original as only the photographer would by retouching or print control.

At the same time, we have the ability to send images from point-to-point using new transmission tools. Never before have there been such powerful tools to expand the creative dimensions of the photographer and to serve the many needs of the researcher and photo practitioner.

What has made all of this possible is the development of new solid-state chips that contain affordable highly integrated digital-signal-processing capability, analog-to-digital conversion for inputting images, and digital-to-analog conversion for outputting images (Fig. 3–1). Today new digital-signal-processing chips are reaching submicron dimensions, continually gaining in speed, and in general doing things that no one ever dreamed of before.

Digital-signal processing (DSP) is not just the province of the electronic photograph. There are numerous other applications for digital processing and analog-to-digital conversion for such things as digital audio, modems, and even the instrument panels and systems in automobiles. Some might say that these new developments are not related to the needs of electronic photography, particularly the higher state of integration of circuits and the development of application-specific ICs (ASIC).

These new developments have allowed the cost-effective development of the new world of electronic photography products. Without this new technology, we would not have the image processing and transmission systems we have today nor would we have the many electronic still video

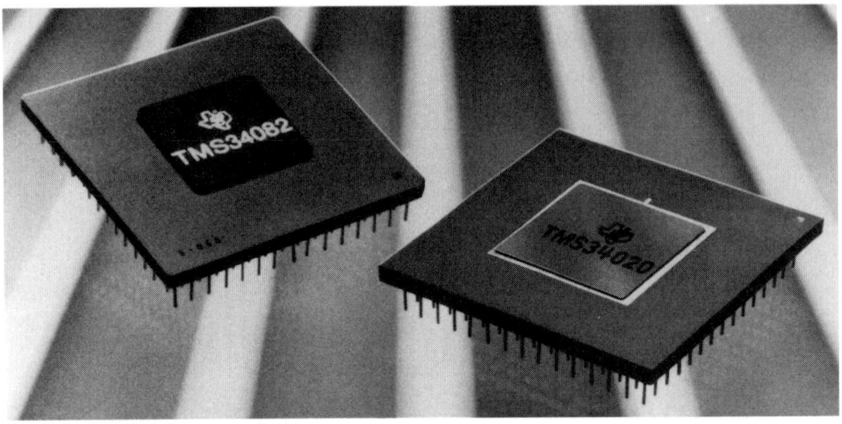

Fig. 3-1. From Texas Instruments, the second-generation high-performance TMS34020 Graphics System Processor (right) and the high speed Floating-Point Processor (left) for use in high-speed graphics systems. These are 100 times faster than current systems.

cameras that have already reached the marketplace. With the advent of computer-assisted design tools, the day is very close when an application-specific integrated circuit (ASIC) can be ordered using components out of a vendor's library of cells. This development will produce more powerful and lower-cost electronic chips for processing electronic photographs.

We can clearly identify three major areas of development in new chip technology. First, there are A-to-D converter chips that allow the conversion of, for example, a signal from an electronic still video floppy disk to a true digital signal in full color. These digital signals can be processed with a minimum of 6 or 8 bits of color information for each red, green, and blue channel. Then there is the actual DSP function, which provides the ability to process the signal. This can employ a technology called *floating-point arithmetic*, which involves an additional coprocessor chip to provide high performance and number-crunching capability in the microcomputer (Fig. 3–2).

To understand the importance of arithmetical capabilities, you have to remember that digital signals are composed entirely of numeric values. Any change you make in a value, for example, if you want to enlarge or reduce an image, is done by recalculating the numerical values for each point in the image. With a pencil and paper, this would be next to impossible. With the computer, especially as our computers operate at faster and faster speeds, these number-crunching jobs are easy. In digital-signal processing, all values are expressed numerically. Numbers are expressed in floating-point format. This is more accurate than fixed-point numerical representation in

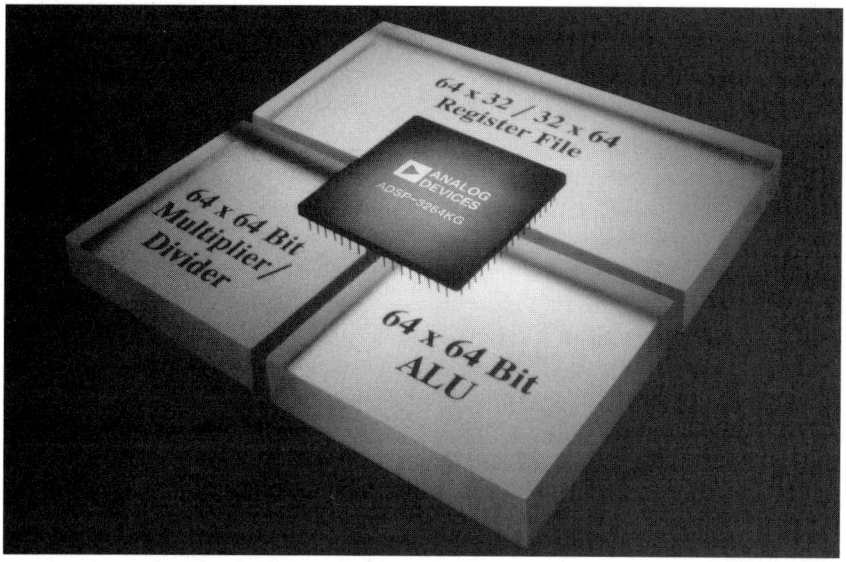

Fig. 3-2. Analog devices ADSP-3264 single-chip Floating-Point Arithmetic Unit sustains 31 MFLOPS throughout for single- and double-precision operations.

which the decimal point or the binary point is assigned to a specific location in a string of bits allotted for numerical data. With floating-point processing, larger dynamic ranges of values are handled within the same word width.

A 32-bit processor doing integer arithmetic uses all 32 bits to represent each whole number. A 32-bit floating point processor splits each word into a 24-bit field for the mantissa and an 8-bit field for the exponent. Floating point numbers frequently require *normalization*, in which the most significant digit of the mantissa contains a nonzero number. This means the mantissa has no leading zeros.

To ensure that various manufacturers of floating-point processors conform to the same criteria in representing and using floating-point numbers, the IEEE has established the 754–1985 standard. This standard specifies rules for representing, rounding, truncating, and defining the accuracy of floating-point numbers.

The IEEE defines three formats for floating-point numbers. Single-length, or single-precision, format, uses 32 bits comprising a 24-bit mantissa and an 8-bit exponent. Double-precision uses 64 bits, permitting a 53-bit mantissa with an 11-bit component. Extended-precision format uses 80 bits, 64 for the mantissa, and 16 for the exponent.

A "building block" floating-point chip can be used in a variety of applications, including as a coprocessor or complex-instruction-set-computer

(CISC), or as an element of a custom host processor. Reduced-instruction-set-computer (RISC) designs in particular require floating-point units as one element of the processor.

Performance for floating-point processors is measured in millions of floating-point operations per second, or MFLOPS. Floating-point performance for supercomputers is generally between 100 and 1000 MFLOPS. Until recently, floating-point processors for microcomputers provided speeds in the fraction of MFLOPS realm. However, new technologies are beginning to push microcomputers to a level where they are approaching the lower levels of supercomputers.

The final element of the new chip technology is the digital-to-analog converter (DAC) (Fig. 3–3). The DAC makes it possible to use a standard CRT to view a computer-generated image. Although the computer operates in the digital world, the monitor operates in the analog mode. The DAC changes the digital signal into an analog signal. To meet the photorealistic standards expected of processing workstations, images of 2048 × 2048

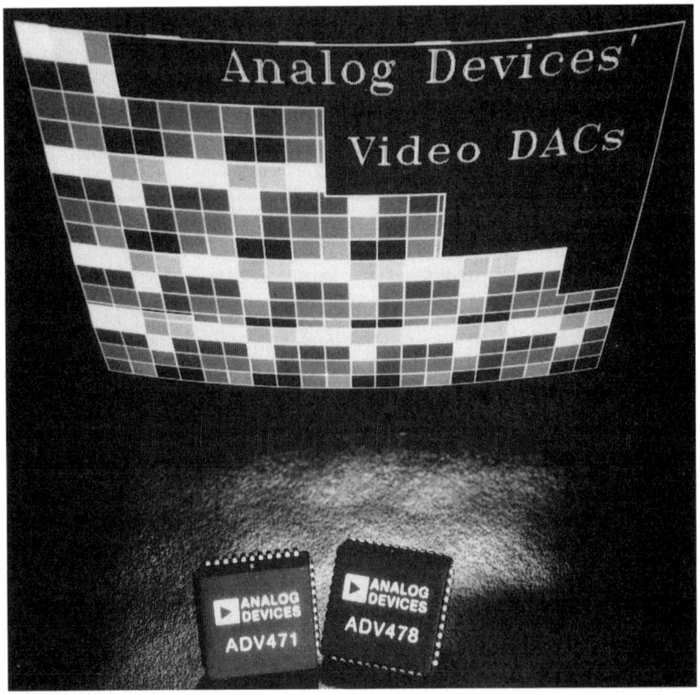

Fig. 3-3. The 6-bit ADV471 and 8-bit ADV478 compatible RGB DACs from Analog Devices feature internal RAM for 256-color palette resolution and separate RAM for 15-color overlay.

pixels are required. With operating speeds of anywhere from 200 to 500 MHz, today's monitors must be improved well beyond their current maximum operating speeds of 100 MHz if we want to obtain all of the information from a high-resolution image. For color, timing accuracy becomes very critical because of the complexity of the signal being processed and stored. Any errors in the signal appear as color or image artifacts. ICs meeting these needs are being produced and monitor screens and printing devices will soon follow, but it will take time to meet these demanding requirements.

One practical application for digital-signal processing will be high-definition television technology. One of the HDTV proposals includes a partially analog, partially digital signal that could be transmitted over current broadcast facilities. Receivers with digital-processing capabilities would be needed to see the entire HDTV image, but present receivers would have the same level of picture that they have today. This, combined with potential of electronic still photography, can be the driving force behind the development of digital-signal processing designed strictly for color-image processing.

Today chips for DSP processing are being produced by Texas Instruments (TI), Motorola, National Semiconductor, Fujitsu, and a host of other firms. Given both the competition and the need, there is a need for continued research and development in this field.

IMAGING BOARDS

In the early 1980s, we were only beginning to see computers leave the area of purely textual displays and switch to a combination of text and low-resolution graphics. Even at this early stage in the evolution of microcomputer, boards for imaging were being developed. The few imaging boards that were available at that time were differentiated from a graphics board by the fact that they had an A/D converter chip on the board. All of the processing of the A/D converter was done by the host computer. Today, both the imaging boards and graphics boards have become very sophisticated and promise to offer even more capabilities in the future. Many of these boards have their own CPU, along with coprocessors and very large areas of memory for image storage during processing. Before taking a look at some of these imaging boards, you should understand that there are several different architectures, each of which requires a different board that might operate differently.

Right now the great debate is between the NuBus developed at the Massachusetts Institute of Technology in the late 1970s and the several other bus architectures already extant from others such as IBM. The NuBus (see Fig. 3–4) was a relatively obscure development until Apple incorporated it into the Macintosh II. For the Macintosh user, it is an accepted

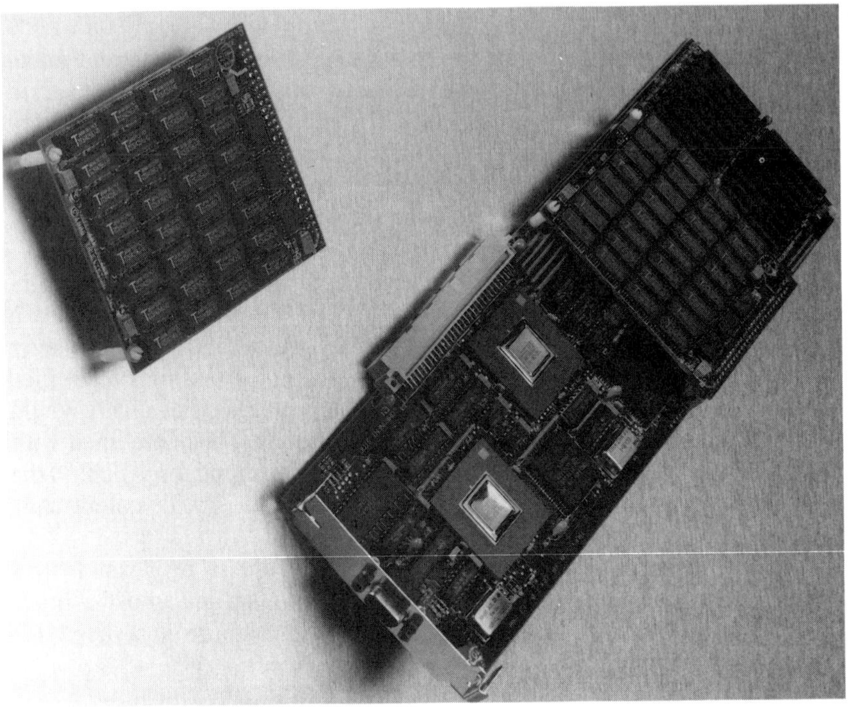

Fig. 3-4. The NuVMX (foreground product) provides users of a NuVista Video Graphics Card with additional memory for image processing, program code storage, and other needs. The daughter-board snaps onto a NuVista card (see background card) and provides 2, 4, or 8 Mb of DRAM for use in sophisticated applications.

standard, even with its limitations of transfer rates. Now the proposed extended-industry standard architecture (EISA) is challenging this bus as is the Microchannel Architecture (MCA) developed as part of the IBM PS/2 line of personal computers.

Part of the reason for the great interest in the bus structure is that the bus can be compared to the pipeline through which all processing flows in a computer platform. Electronic photographs present a great challenge because the higher resolution of the electronic photograph requires that very large amounts of data have to be moved through the bus. Original buses available would allow movement of possibly 500 kb/sec through the bus. This does not present a problem with the simple video image. However, if the resolution increases to, for example, 4096 × 4096 pixels with 12-bits per color depth this requires over 50 Mb of data to be moved. Also, the transmission interval would be 100 seconds—an eternity for a computer.

The EISA and MCA buses propose to move data at a speed of 5 Mb/sec or higher. Part of this problem has been overcome by performing some, if not all of the operations, on the imaging board and by not using the bus or the CPU. However, it would be far more desirable if the full capacity of the computer could be used.

In addition to the three new buses, the VME bus and the Intel Multibus 2 also are commonly used where higher throughput capacities are needed. An advantage of the VME bus is its widespread use in industrial applications and the speed of the bus, which can exceed 100 Kb/sec with some device outputs. This factor increases the technical expertise available on the bus and more importantly decreases the cost associated with its production.

High-resolution color imaging on personal computers was pioneered by an AT&T "intrapreneurial" venture, the Electronic and Photographic Imaging Center (EPICenter) founded in mid-1984. This later became TrueVision, Inc., when the employees purchased the company in the last quarter of 1987. TrueVision, Inc., produces the Targa imaging board, one of the most widely recognized of the high-end imaging boards for the IBM PC/XT, AT, and compatibles. Several hundred third-party companies offer imaging software that utilizes the Targa boards.

The Targa (TrueVision advanced-raster-graphics adapter) occupies the middle range of the TrueVision product family, providing spatial resolutions of up to 512 × 482 pixels. Although each Targa model has fixed pixel depth (8, 16, 24, or 32 bits/pixel), they all provide real-time image capture, genlock, zoom, independent horizontal and vertical panning, and many other features (Table 3–1).

The original product of TrueVision is the image-capture board (ICB). This is the original frame-capture card for the IBM PC, XT, AT, or compatible. With this board, you can capture full color images from any conventional video source in real time and display them on analog, RGB, or composite video monitors at resolutions of up to 256 × 240 pixels. Its 16 bits per pixel enables the ICB to produce continuous tone images with good quality and realism particularly when combined with the moderate spatial resolution (Table 3–2).

The TrueVista video graphic adapter represents the newest and most powerful of TrueVision's products. Each capture-and-display model offers high spatial resolution, a 32-bit graphic processor, NTSC or PAL compatibility, true color and color-mapped modes, programmable resolution of 8, 16, or 32 bits per pixel, and up to 4 Mb of high-speed video memory, all on a single slot board. AT Vista models are available for AT bus machines, and NuVista products are available for Macintosh II computers.

With the TrueVista family, it is possible to establish images of 1024 × 1024 × 132 bits, 2048 × 1024 × 16 bits, or 2048 × 2048 × 8 bits. All of these are user selectable. All of the TrueVista products use the Texas Instrument

Table 3-1. Comparisons of TrueVision Targa Boards.

	TARGA 8	TARGA M8	TARGA 16	TARGA 24	TARGA 2
Color Resolution	256 levels of grey	256 grey levels; or 256 colors from a palette of 16,777,216	32,768 colors	16,777,216 colors	16,777,216 colors
Input Signals	RS 170 compatible (black and white) video	4 RS-170 compatible (black & white) video channels, or analog RGB (for sequential color capture); Digital RGBI input (for pass-through of of CGA output)	RS 170A compatible (color) video Analog RGB	Analog RGB	Analog RGB
Output Signals	RS 170 compatible (black and white) video	Analog RGB Monochrome, RS-170 composite video	RS 170A compatible (color) video Analog RGB	Analog RGB	Analog RGB
Overlay Capability		Overlay live input with memory (one entry in color lookup table	Overlay live input with memory (1 bit)		Overlay live input with memory (1 bit) and 128 levels of mix for blending live input with memory (7 bits)
Memory	8 bits/pixel 256K bytes	8 bits/pixel 256K bytes	16 bits/pixel 512K bytes	24 bits/pixel 768K bytes	32 bits/pixel 1,024K bytes
Overscan	Optional	Optional	Included	Optional	Optional

340101 graphics processor to perform graphic manipulations at high speeds. The display from the TrueVision is noninterlaced, flicker free, and has square pixels. It has the ability to pan across the entire video memory, along with QuickDraw compatibility (Table 3–3).

To gain the full capability of the Targa and TrueVista series of graphic adapters, TrueVision also has created a product to convert NTSC video signals between RGB and composite or S–video. The Vidi/O Box, a stand-alone unit, provides a link between composite video-based cameras, monitors, and VCRs and RGB-based devices, such as the Targa and TrueVista boards (see Fig. 3–5). The product also will handle conversion between RGB and the emerging S-video standard, which supports Super VHS and ED Beta VCRs and other devices. This really takes some of the mystique out of bringing different signals together into common input and output channels.

Table 3-2. TrueVision ICB Specifications.

Resolution mode:
  256 pixels by 240 pixels by 32,768 colors (15 bit/pixel)
Input signal:
  NTSC composite video (for image capture)
Output signals:
  NTSC composite video
  Analog RGB and sync
Bit-mapped display:
  128k bytes
Connectors:
  1 RGB (out)
  2 Composite (in, out)
Programmable options:
  Location of active area on screen
  Application process interrupt on vertical blanking interval or specified pixel
  Odd or even field capture
  Interlaced or noninterlaced video output
Display memory contention:
  less than 1 percent
Border color:
  black
Power:
  0.5 amps at 5 volts
  0.25 amps at 12 volts
  0.25 amps at -12 volts
ICB Settings and Adjustments:
  Interlaced or noninterlaced capture and display
  Image centering in screen
  Color adjustment (monitor)
  Hue, saturation, and contrast adjustment (input signal)
  Genlock adjustment (i.e., video camera or VCR/video disc player)

Another source for color-image processing is a series of boards created by Data Translation. The QuickCapture is a real-time frame grabber for the Macintosh II (see Fig. 3–6). This frame-grabber board and software offers 640 × 480 square pixel resolution, 64 gray levels, cable, and several advanced-image-processing functions, including editing, enhancing, and analyzing images. The QuickCapture also is supported directly by several software packages, including Silicon Beach's Digital Darkroom, Letraset's Image Studio, and Aba's GraphistPaint II Photoretouching Package. Other models of the QuickCapture can handle 24-bit color information as well as the 256 gray levels.

The ColorCapture from Data Translation is a color frame-grabber board and software for capturing, processing, and displaying color video

Table 3-3. TrueVision TrueVista Specifications.

Feature	ATVista 1M	ATVista 2M	ATVista 4M	NuVista™ 2M	NuVista 4M
PC Host	IBM PC AT	IBM PC AT	IBM PC AT	Macintosh II	Macintosh II
Data Bus Width	8 or 16	8 or 16	8 or 16	8, 16, 32	8, 16, 32
Video Memory	1 Mbyte	2 Mbyte	4 Mbyte	2 Mbyte	4 Mbyte
Maximum Addressable Resolutions					
32 bit	512 × 512	1024 × 512	1024 × 1024	1024 × 512	1024 × 1024
16 bit	1024 × 512	1024 × 1024	2048 × 1024	1024 × 1024	2048 × 1024
8 bit	1024 × 1024	2048 × 1024	2048 × 2048	2048 × 1024	2048 × 2048
Look-up Tables	3 × 2 kbytes	4 × 2 kbytes	4 × 2 kbytes	4 × 2 kbytes	
Alpha Channel	no	yes	yes	yes	yes
On board TI34010	yes	yes	yes	yes	yes
Row Table	yes	yes	yes	yes	yes
NTSC Compatible	yes	yes	yes	yes	yes
PAL Compatible	yes	yes	yes	yes	yes
Genlock	yes	yes	yes	yes	yes
Zoom (programmable)	yes	yes	yes	yes	yes
Pan	yes	yes	yes	yes	yes
VMX Expansion	2–10 mbytes	2–10 mbytes	2–10 mbytes	2–8 mbytes	2–8 mbytes
Video Memory Upgrade	no	2 mbyte	no	2 mbytes	no

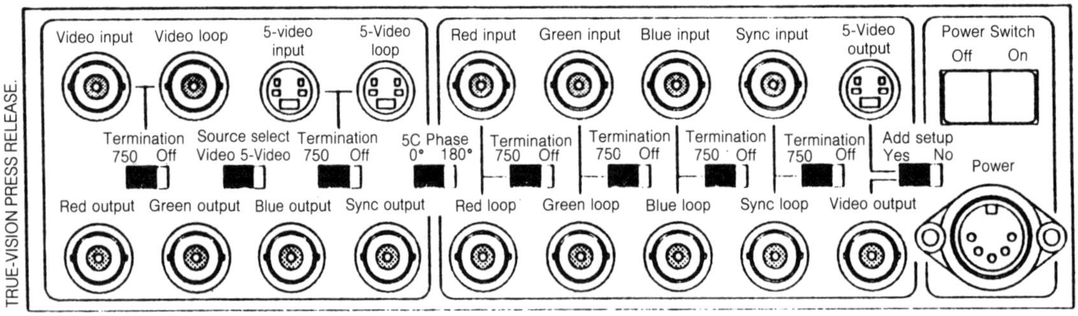

Fig. 3-5. The rear panel of the VidiIO box shows the variety of connection capabilities for both input and output information.

images on the IBM PS/2 MCA computer or compatible. The board plugs into any one of the available expansion slots in the IBM PS/2.

ColorCapture acquires images from an RGB color video source in real time (1/30th sec) and displays them on an RGB video monitor with 640 × 480 square pixel resolution, and up to 32,768 colors. Standard NTSC or PAL

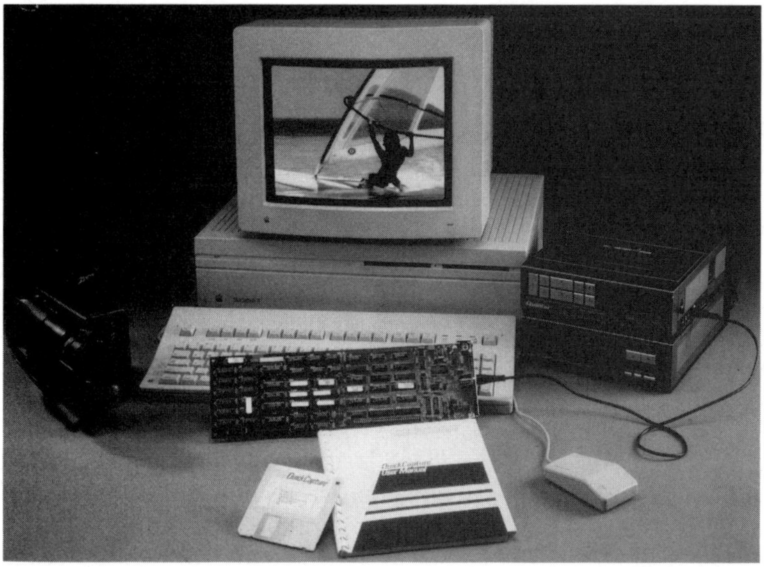

Fig. 3-6. Data Translations DT2253 QuickCapture is a frame-grabber board and software for capturing, processing, and displaying images on Macintosh II computers.

composite color devices also can be used if connected to a video-conversion device.

Images also can be displayed on a PS/2 VGA system monitor. Sophisticated color-mapping routines are used to optimize color mapping and resolution for the best possible display on a VGA color monitor. ColorCapture also includes a programmable overlay feature that allows a full color overlay of text or graphics on top of a live video image.

Another approach comes from Rapid Technology Corporation, which utilizes an array process coupled with application-specific software packages for IBM or compatible personal computers. The ASAP-32 (Pacific Array Processor) is well suited for image processing. It consists of a 32-bit floating-point processor that operates at 13.5 MFLOPS. The board includes a 2k × 32-bit ROM that has the basic mathematical, vector, matrix, and I/O functions permanently programmed into it. It also has two fast program RAMs that can be downloaded with application-specific software, higher-level algorithms, and functions from the host PC.

The board also has a double data buffer RAM with 4k × 32 bits each, for transferring data between the PC and floating-point processor. Both data buffers are dual ported, which allows pipeline processing and permits a continuous stream of successive operations much like a physical pipeline. While the floating-point processor is operating on one set of data, the PC can load simultaneously the next set. This unique design concept circumvents the need for a large data buffer usually associated with array processors.

The Variable-scan 100-AT frame grabber is useful in processing images from nonstandard cameras. The VS-100-AT from Imaging Technology, Inc. supports high-resolution image acquisition of up to 1024 × 1024 pixels and interfaces with virtually all of the video sensors commonly used for such things as microscopy.

Although most image processors are limited to acquiring images from more commonly supported RS-170 and CCIR cameras, the VS-100-AT also interfaces with newly available CCD sensors such as line-scan cameras, X-ray scanners, and high-resolution video cameras. A new 768 × 512 image-capture mode provides square pixel acquisition and display when working with CCIR cameras.

There are a number of boards that will capture color images from video sources. These boards digitize video images from standard VCR or video cameras for storage and manipulation by PS/2 or compatible personal computers. The new RAMCorder boards from Sigma Designs replace the dedicated graphics adapters, scanners, and monitors usually required. Ramcorder boards interface with any home video camera or VGA-equipped PC. Resolutions range from 640 × 480 pixels with 16 shades of gray to 320 × 200 pixels with 256 shades of gray. A color monitor can be connected to the boards to display the imported signal.

If there is the need to interface a high-definition TV (HDTV-MUSE) system to NTSC, Matsushita Electric Industrial Co. and Mitsubishi Electric Co. have developed jointly new LSI converters that convert HDTV-MUSE signals into NTSC-compatible signals. Mitsubishi provided the image-signal-processing ICs while Matsushita supplied the audio ICs for the converters. With this system, any future HDTV video camera or VCR can still be used with current imaging boards.

Macintosh II computers are being given more attention as image-processing platforms. The Mercury MC-3200NU adds to the Macintosh a 20-MFLOP, 10-MIP engine with up to 8 Mb of memory that provides near-supercomputer floating-point-processing power (Fig. 3–7). This addition to the Macintosh 68020 microprocessor allows the Macintosh to handle multitasking operating system (OS) calls, the user interface, or the display while the MC-3200NU simultaneously performs number crunching. This greatly enhances the Mac's ability to display and process complex digital images at high speeds.

The Mac DSP24MC is a 24-MFLOP floating-point accelerator card for the Macintosh II from Spectral Innovations. The DSP card is based on the AT&T DSP-32C digital-signal-processing chip. The NuBus interface supports 16-bit transfers at 5 MB/sec.

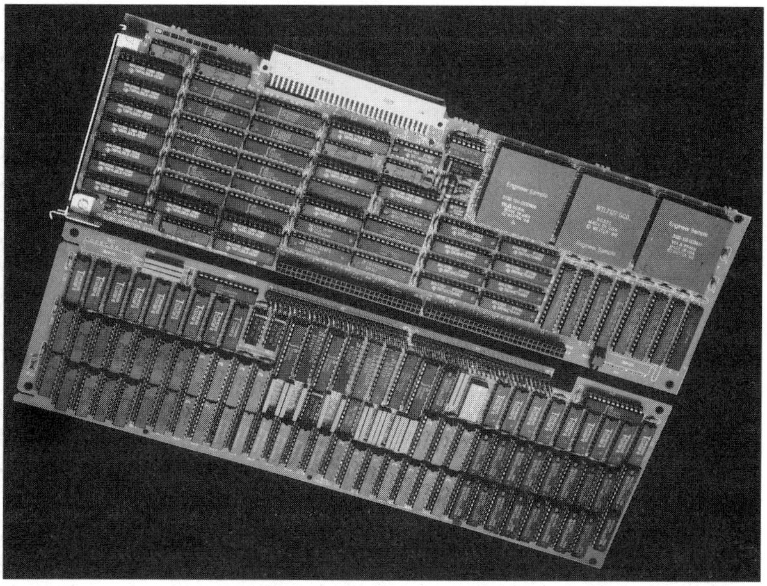

Fig. 3-7. Mercury Computer Systems MC3200NU board operates at 10 MIPs and 20 MFLOPS as a coprocessor for the Macintosh II.

A straightforward frame-grab device is the PCVISION Plus Frame Grabber, Image Technology's most basic processor. This single-slot board is installed in a PC and permits the acquisition, storage, and display of video images at 30 frames/sec. Specially designed frame-memory-access modes overcome some limitations of the personal computer's architecture, accelerating the transfer of pixels between the host and the PCVISION Plus frame grabber. A broad spectrum of software allows the immediate processing of images at a 512 or 640 pixels horizontal resolution.

Toshiba has employed their own digital-signal-processing chip, the T9506, in creating the IP-9506 PC/AT image processor, a high-performance board designed for integration into a variety of PC XT and AT-based systems (Fig. 3–8). The processor can access memory at a maximum speed of 60 Mb/sec. In a three-channel configuration, it can access all channels in parallel at 5 Mwords/sec (32-bit word length). With the use of multiple image processors in the same PC, you can achieve even greater speeds through parallel processing.

Another approach to image processing is the Graphex Parallel Image Processor (GPIP), which provides an ultra-high-resolution display of over 2 million pixels in a 1668 × 1280 × 24-bit display.

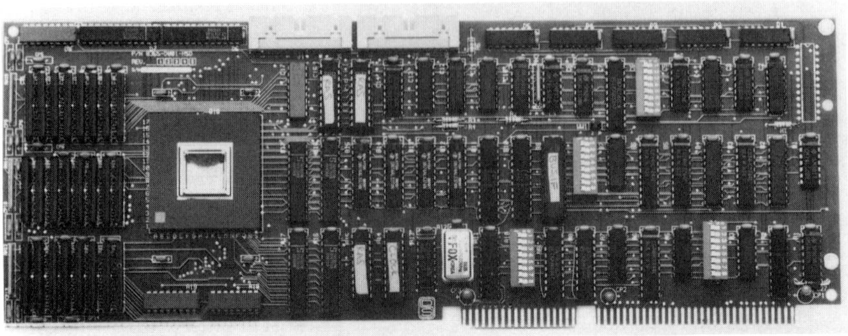

Fig. 3-8. Toshiba's 9506 IBM PC/AT Image Processor Board brings advanced image processing to PC-based computer systems. Based on Toshiba's 32-bit T9506 Digital Signal Processor, this unit has access to third-party boards through the DT-connect fast I/O bus.

The advanced process architecture of the GPIP incorporated an array of 32-bit RISC microprocessors working in parallel to control the manipulation of 384 to 864 Mb of random-access memory. Together, this array of microprocessors, memory, custom designed ICs, high-speed image multiplexing, and I/O interface circuitry constitutes the GPIP.

Essentially, all of the data of the high-resolution image is stored in the GPIP, eliminating the common input and output bottlenecks. An internal data flow in excess of 450 Mb/sec is maintained by using direct-access memory and extremely high computational power created by using parallel processors with throughput up to 180 MIPS.

Proprietary high-speed image compression and multiplexing circuitry allow a full 8000 × 8000 pixels to be read during first image capture with display updates every 1/60th sec. The GPIP can be connected to a multitude of host systems (VAX, SUN, IBM PC/AT, and compatibles).

TOTAL SYSTEMS AND IMAGING ENGINES

Image processing requires a unique combination of speed, large amounts of memory and, for color, the ability to handle three completely separate pieces of information in total synchronization. Although this has been solved by many of the previously discussed imaging boards, there are processing platforms, or engines, being developed dedicated to the handling of images that rival supercomputers in their processing power.

One example was a unique device shown a few years ago created by the University of North Carolina at Chapel Hill. The Pixel-Planes is a raster graphics system that provides a chip for every pixel of a 512 × 512 display × 72-bit deep image. Using 2048 custom 3-micron nMOS chips (63,000 transistors in each operating at 10 million microinstructions/sec), it allows total instant parallel processing of images. Although this is a very unique experiment intended to broaden thinking, several dedicated engines and systems provide a good off-the-shelf solution to handling image processing.

Stellar Departmental supercomputers use custom-design, parallel, multiprocessor architecture and very high-bandwidth technology to execute a sustained 20 to 25 million instructions and up to 80 MFLOPS. With an additional scaler accelerator option, the performance can be boosted to a sustained 35 MIPS and a peak of 100 MFLOPs (Fig. 3–9). This system provides tremendous powers for image processing in a variety of machines.

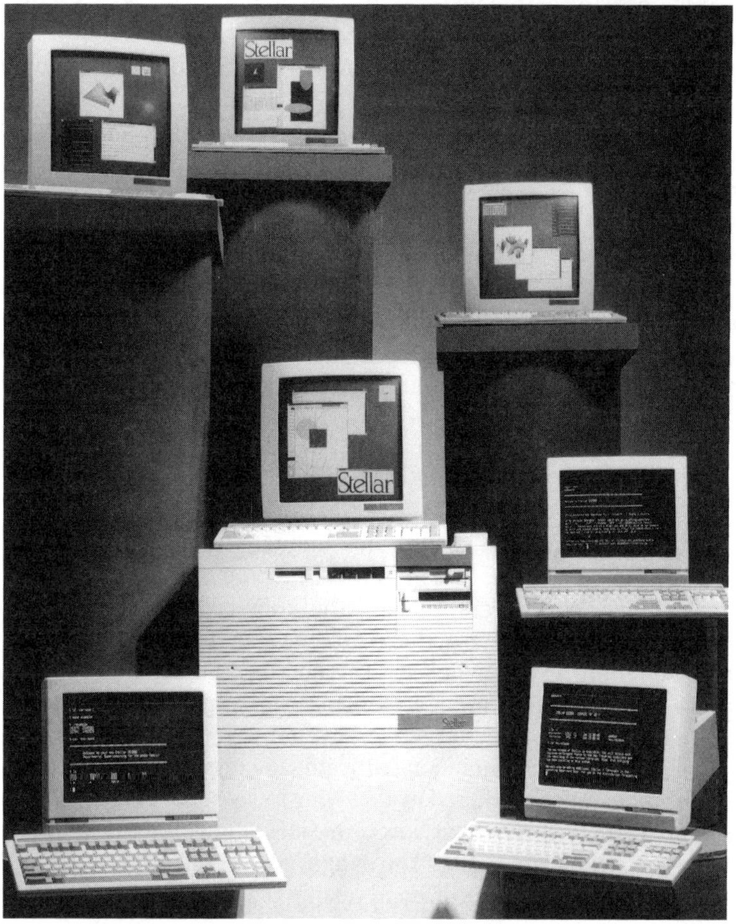

Fig. 3-9. The Stellar DS1000 Departmental Supercomputer supports a broad range of DEC VAX/VMS-compatible and coexistent features.

Pixar computers have been dedicated for image-processing applications. The Pixar image computer is capable of maximum general-purpose pixel-processing power when compared to a nonimage dedicated computer, with up to 192 Mb of image memory. Its video display resolution is 1024 × 768. The Pixar II can accommodate up to 108 Mb of image memory and has a display resolution programmable up to 1280 × 1024. Pixar image computers are based on a pixel-based architecture.

The AT&T Pixel Machine is a family of image and graphics processors based on parallel architecture with ratings of 410 MIPS and 820 MFLOPS. The PXM-900 series encompassed five modular processors, all upgradable. With highly parallel architecture and large, tightly coupled image memories, configurations can contain up to 82 floating-point processors with over 800 MFLOPS of peak processing power. Each PXM-900 consists of four functional units, a high-speed parallel interface, a transformation pipeline, a parallel array of pixel nodes, and a video controller.

Each processor is a fully programmable AT&T DSP 32-point processor and can be tailored for individual needs. The Pixel Machine can have up to 48 Mb of image memory, 32 bits per pixel (RGBA), and 32-bit floating-point depth buffer.

Other complete system manufacturers sometimes use VME-based platforms, IBM PC or compatible platforms, or specially designed systems for image and graphics processing. Graphics processing is very closely akin to the processing of real photographic images with the real photographic image requiring a greater depth of pixels for color realism as well a higher resolution to achieve photorealistic imaging.

IMAGE COMPRESSION

A digital photographic image is a redundant image in which the same information can appear more than once. One type of redundancy is where the same color is at different pixels within the image, either horizontal or vertical. If the image is moving, there can be redundancy between succeeding images. If there are straight lines, this could create another redundancy. There are a number of different techniques for compressing images (Table 3–4).

One of the simplest techniques for image compression is *truncation*. With truncation, data is reduced by throwing away some parts of the bits for each pixel. When you drop digital information, you would expect the image to change, but when you look at the image, you see no apparent loss. What you eliminate is redundancy, or components that are already present in the image. There are usually the least significant bits for every pixel.

Another simple compression scheme is the use of a color lookup table (CLUT). This is usually not a satisfactory approach because photographs

Table 3-4. Types of Image Compression.

Type 30	The type 30 image-compression scheme is a statistical lossless that provided a compression ratio of approximately 3:1. The type 30 is based on adaptive pulse-code modulation (ADPCM). The scheme is attractive because of the low cost software-only implementation. The type 30 runs on the host system in approximately 15 seconds per image. The scheme also is well suited for applications that require exact reproduction of the original image. The compression/decompression process does not result in any loss of image data.
Type 50	The type 50 image-compression scheme, which is also based on adaptive pulse-code modulation, provides approximately 5:1 compression. This scheme, unlike the type 30, is not a lossless compression. In order to obtain the higher compression ratio, some amount of image data is lost in the compression/decompression process. The process does not result in any observable image degradation, and the scheme is ideal for viewing applications. Like the type 30, the type 50 is a software-only scheme.
Type 80	The type 80, which typically provides a compression ratio of 8:1, is based on a fast 2D Hadamard transform. This software provides a user-selectable compression ratio and runs on the host system in 40 seconds. In addition, the scheme is optimized for graphics signal processors (GSP) such as the TMS 34010, on which it will run in 10 seconds.
Type 120	The type 120 (12:1) compression is based on a 2D fast discrete cosine transform (FDCT). This is the highest performance technology and also the most computation intensive. For practical operation, a digital signal processor (DSP) with 5 MIPS integer arithmetic such as the TMS 32020 is required.

usually require a color lookup table of 30,000 or more colors. The CLUT approach works at no more than 8 bits/pixel and has a color lookup table of 256 colors or less.

The third simple method is run-length coding (RL) in which the same pixel is repeated, such as a solid color, and a single value is substituted along with a count of how many times to repeat the value. Again, this is possible only when simple colors exist.

Interpolation compression is another means of reducing the number of pixels in an image. It can be done easily with the chroma portion of a signal; the luminance portion is not interpolated. This is called *color subsampling.* To achieve high-quality color, 8 or 12 bits of colors information is used for each color. If we can reduce this color depth and maintain the color quality, we can substantially compress the image.

With predictive compression, we actually use the previous frame to predict what is different in the next frame. This method is one of the techniques used in colorizing existing black-and-white motion-picture films.

Differential PCM (DPCM) is used commonly for audio compression. With DPCM, adjacent pixels are compared and only the differences transmitted. Because the information is slow to develop, for example a full white, the difference does not really show the changed signal. This causes smearing of high-contrast edges of the images or else an ultimate lack of sharpness.

One means of overcoming this problem is by going to adaptive DCPM (ADCPM). In this case, the step size is changed so that if a sharp change from black to white occurs, such as an edge change, the step size is increased. The problem is that more overhead data and extra processing is required to meet the needs of the adaption.

Transform coding is a process in which data is systematically changed. The most effective transforms used are discrete cosine transforms (DCT) and Fourier transforms. Although these take a great deal of calculating power, with currently available coprocessors and floating-point calculators, these approaches are practical today and very efficient. Statistical coding techniques are either contained within the compression algorithm itself or can be applied separately from a table called a *code book*. The table tells how to decode the bitstream back to the original values.

Storing electronic photographs presents a challenge if photorealistic quality is to be achieved. A minimum of 6 bits per color is required. Then the image can be anywhere from a 1000 × 1000 to 8000 × 8000, depending on the resolution of the equipment and the quality of the image desired. The higher the resolution, the greater the sharpness and the more photorealistic the image.

An example of the need for data compression is the Targa board. Although a full-screen image from an AT&T Targa 16 board uses 410 Kb with overscan for picture borders, the file size goes up to 500 Kb. A 4000 × 4000 pixel image 12-bits/color deep is in the 60 MB range. Image storage and transmission becomes a serious problem.

The option is to compress the image by shrinking the storage requirements without affecting excessively the picture quality. One option is the total software solution, in which all of the compression and decompression is done with software. This would be slow and probably not acceptable for most applications. The alternative is the use of a hardware/software solution, of which several are now or will be available shortly.

Dave Ahlgren heads Telephoto Communications, Inc. a well-known developer of Alice image-compression hardware and software. Here are some of Ahlgren's views regarding image compression.

"Image compression today is important due to the growing popularity of electronic photography and especially the use of electronic photography in computer systems. As soon as you begin to bring TV quality images to computer systems, you are immediately faced with the problem of handling the large amount of data that is required to represent a single picture. One picture is equal to about a minimum of 100,000 typewritten characters.

"Today, there is actually a very large effort in standardization. Image compression research really began approximately 20-25 years ago and found its way into some very high end TV transmission and motion teleconferencing systems, typically $100,000 to $1 million image compressors. Based on this work an international committee, the ISO committee and CCIT committees formed a joint project, Joint Photographic Experts Group (JPEG), to develop a standard for image compression. It is the intent of this standard to produce compatibility between equipment similar to that found between facsimile machines today.

"There is some draft proposal work ongoing now, and an initial decision has been made to use a particular type of compression named Discrete Cosine Transform (DCT). There are a few technical issues yet to be resolved. It is the intent of the committee to attempt to resolve these issues in early 1989 and distribute a formal specification for review. The scheduled release date for a final specification is now June, 1990.

"Standards are a double edged sword for us. Once there are standards, then you are going to have high volume, low cost products. Small players are prohibited from playing in that type of market. One example of that might be a picture phone that you could use to call another business or family member to have face-to-face still frame pictures for communications. Standards will allow a small company to develop specialized products such as an integrated video capture and display devices that include image compression, and allow those specialized devices to communicate in a standard way.

"In the long term, you will have some compression device associated with every image display device, from the electronic still photo cameras to almost everyone's computer screen as well as for security and identification control. The image compressions market will be at least the size of the telephone market, plus the personal computer market."

Alice, a Telephoto Communications product, is a commonly used software/hardware solution for image compression. FOCUSVision and PicturePower are two such imaging database-management systems that use the power of Alice for image compression. With the Alice Type 120 hardware/software package, compression ratios of better than 15:1 are possible on even the most complex images. The Alice Type 80 is designed to run on a Graphic Signal Processor (GSP) such as the TI TMS-34010 and provides approximately 8:1 compression. Alice Type 50 is a software-only image-compression product designed to run directly on a host system and provides a compression ratio of approximately 5:1.

The CVP-2000 color-video-processor family from Discrete Time Systems, Inc., uses images from a standard video camera or alternate video source and then compresses them at ratios as high as 30:1. The design of these boards is based on compression technology that produces quality images that require less data to describe them. The CVP-2800 uses the TI TMS-320C25 digital-signal processor (DSP) at a compression ratio of 15:1. Image compression takes approximately one second. The expansion rate is 5 frames/sec.

Digital Video Interface (DVI) technology was originally developed in the Sarnoff Laboratories. Although DVI technology is software based, special boards and chip sets have been developed to achieve realtime image playback. Intel plans to produce and market these boards.

There are two basic forms of DVI proprietary algorithms. The lossless still-compression algorithm could have a compression of, for example, 11:1 while a scene that has a profusion of similar colors might have only a 2:1 compression ratio. The lossless algorithm, however, results in an output that looks exactly like the input. With a lousy compression, good images are delivered, but they approach a level that might not be as sharp and well defined as the original. Reports indicate that DVI images have been compressed to a level of 100:1.

Manufacturers of workstations, particularly those designed for publication applications, also are exploring compression systems. National Digital Corporation's software allows images to be captured at full resolution (2000 × 3000 pixels × 24 bits of color) and compressed for storage to 1.2 to 1.5 bits of color, yielding a compression ratio of up to 20:1. The results, some say, are identical images with no distinguishable difference between them.

What is still missing is a standard for image compression, but ANSI has set up a subcommittee to develop a standard for some communications transmission systems. Standardization should be a boon to the market of image compression with its savings of both transmission and storage capacity.

The best may be yet to come, however. Another technology has been proposed for image compression—fractal image compression. Using fractal mathematics to compress images, Iterated Systems, Inc., the owners of the process, already have demonstrated 45 seconds of video compressed to a 1.2-Mb floppy disk.

At the same time, Inmos has built a CMOS chip to implement the discrete cosine transform (DCT) for image-compression purposes. At 20 MHz, the chip can perform 320 million operations or instructions/second.

Whether through established DCT compression or new fractal methods, compression systems will be a boon to electronic photo-image storage and processing.

IMAGE TRANSMISSION

Computers have been talking to each other through modems for a number of years. Earlier image-transmission systems such as newspaper wire systems were analog systems that transmitted a simple amplitude-modulated signal. Any noise or other artifacts introduced during the transmission resulted in deteriorated or useless images.

Digital signals, however, have error checking built-in, and this assures that the quality of the delivered signal is a complete reproduction of the original and at higher speeds. The digital transmission of data, be it information from stores, corporations, medical facilities, or even home computers, and the vast network provided by private service, has shown logarithmic growth. Initial modems were slow, with ranges of 10 to 40 bytes/sec. Today, through the use of special fiberoptic lines and equipment, it is actually possible to send 19.2 kbits/sec of information.

For data, this speed might be acceptable; for images, the cost of telephone time combined with the actual wait for images is, for the most part, unacceptable.

To overcome this, special transmitters have been designed by a number of companies for both transmission of still video electronic photographs and conventional film images in electronic form. Generally these images can be received as digital images suitable for digital processing or direct separation in systems such as Scitex systems, an output medium used by many newspaper and magazines.

Sony, in its original announcements of the Mavica, proposed the direct transmission of images. It wasn't until 1988 that their initial still frame communication unit, the SFU-1000, was made available. With Sony's own digital-compression technology along with error correction, high-resolution color and black-and-white still images were sent easily over phone lines.

The SFU-1000 provided a very smart system of monitoring the transmission line and automatically adjusted the transmission rate between three levels of 9600, 7200, and 4800 bits/sec in order to ensure the best quality possible. In addition, a character generator and caption-transmission capability was provided so that a maximum of 40 characters × 22 lines could be superimposed over the video image to provide the recipient with information about the picture content.

The Sony DIH-2000 Digital Image Handler can send color video pictures, audio, and data from point to point in as little as ten seconds, depending on the compression ratio and image density. The unit compresses images in two international formats: ADCT (adaptive discrete cosine transform), a standard recognized by CCITT and ISO that permits a progressive display of the transmitted color images, and ABTC (adaptive block truncation coding), which is the most efficient for text and detailed black-and-white drawings.

The DIH-2000 transmits a 24-bit color image at a viewable resolution of 500 TV lines horizontal resolution over digital leased lines or through an Integrated System Data Network (ISDN) in approximately ten seconds, including image-compression time, depending upon compression ratio and image density. A similar transmission over standard analog telephone lines requires about 1 to 1 1/2 minutes. The unit also has audio capabilities to allow audio information to be added to each image. It also accepts a wide range of signals from other video sources, including composite, analog RGB, and Y/R–Y/B–Y component video.

Highly portable, the Canon RT-611 is a compact battery-powered still video transmitter (Fig. 3–10). It is available with either line connector or with the Canon AC-RT acoustic coupler for connection directly to the

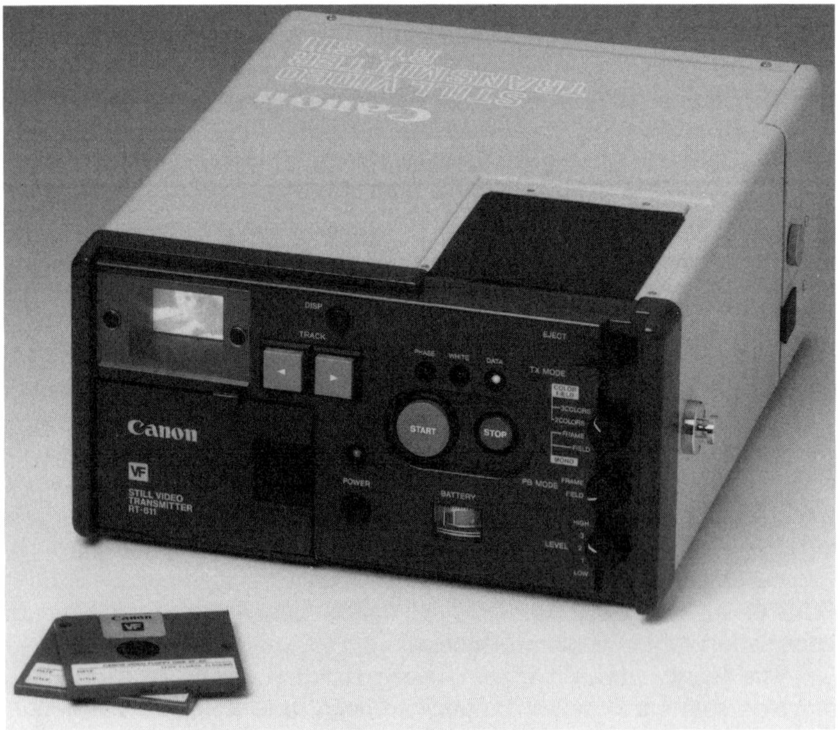

Fig. 3-10. The Canon Still Video Transmitter RT-611.

telephone mouthpiece. Pictures can be sent in field and frame mode, with field mode taking 3 1/2 minutes. A color photo takes 3 1/2 minutes to send, and a monochrome image takes 90 seconds. In frame mode, only monochrome images can be sent, with a transmission time of 3 minutes. Images are viewed on a built-in 1.5-inch monochrome CRT.

The Canon RT-971 still video transceiver is designed for an office or permanent location (Fig. 3–11). With the RT-971, virtually any image can be converted into a video signal and sent over ordinary phone lines to another RT-971 anywhere in the world. In addition, the RT-971 also records still images on a 2-inch video floppy disk that can be viewed on a monitor.

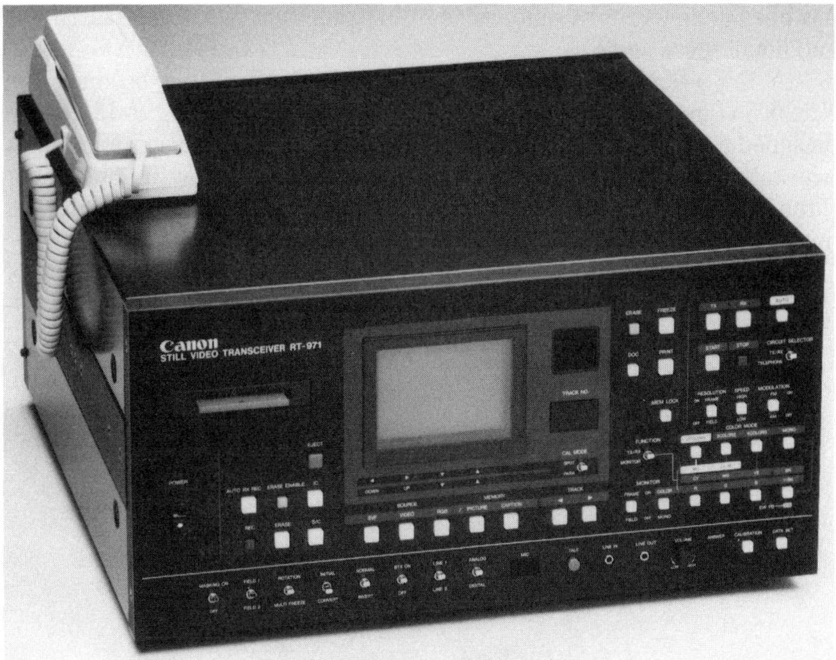

Fig. 3-11. The Canon Still Video Transceiver RT-971.

Compatibility with both analog (AM, FM) and digital (external modem necessary) transmission modes allows you to select the one best suited to an individual telephone system for lowest noise transmission. Color images can be sent anywhere in the world in three minutes (RT-971 to RT-971 in field mode), while monochrome images can be sent in 1 1/2 minutes in black-and-white mode. There are also three- and four-color modes with masking and UCR coefficient setting. With a floppy disk, transmissions are recorded as they are received, with 50 images received consecutively in field mode.

The Kodak SV9600 Still Video Transceiver is a stand-alone tabletop unit designed for transmission and reception of images over standard telephone lines. It interfaces with any standard NTSC or RGB device, including Targas and TrueVistas. Compression ratios range from 8:1 to 20:1, depending on image complexity. Within five seconds of transmission to another SV9600, a recognizable image appears in approximately ten seconds. Final full-color quality appears in less than one minute. There is a function switch for the unit's RS-232C port and also a connector for a remote on/off control.

Another approach to electronic photograph transmission is a combination of the capabilities of scanners with digital-transmission systems. This has been done with several devices from firms such as Nikon, Hasselblad, and major press services.

A few years ago, Nikon unveiled its first electronic product, the NT-2000A film color scanner/direct telephoto transmitter (Fig. 3–12). It was designed to send images from either color negative or transparency films over telephone lines. Full four-color (cyan, magenta, yellow, and black) or three-color (C, M, and Y) separations were sent, as well as monochrome images from either color or black-and-white film.

Optical and electronic zooming (0.7× to 2.8×) permitted cropping of the transmitted image, and the built-in 6-inch monitor displays the transmit-

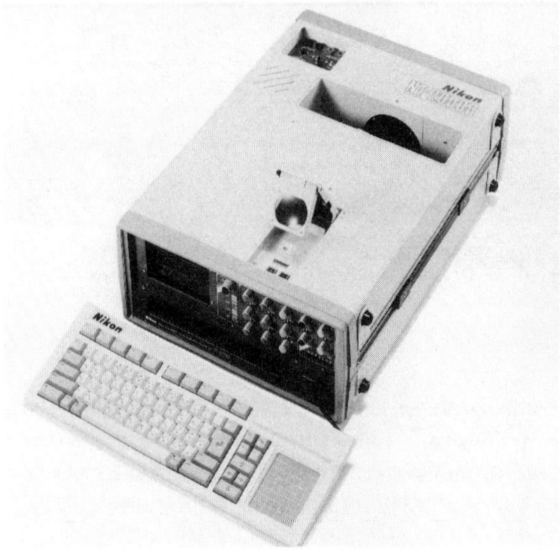

Fig. 3-12. The Nikon 35mm Film Direct Color Telephoto Transmitter.

ted image (negatives are transmitted positive), indicating the gray scale, C, M, Y densities, and progress of transmission. Color compensation was also available, and the results were viewed on the monitor before transmission. Typed or handwritten captions also could be included.

The unit performed automatic compensation for color temperature, color balance, gamma curve, and four-step edge enhancement, along with a masking function for printing. These enhancements minimized post-transmission processing and production time. At the receiving unit, a digital output connected to the NW-100 thermal printer. This provided four (or three) separation prints or a single black-and-white print (Fig. 3–13).

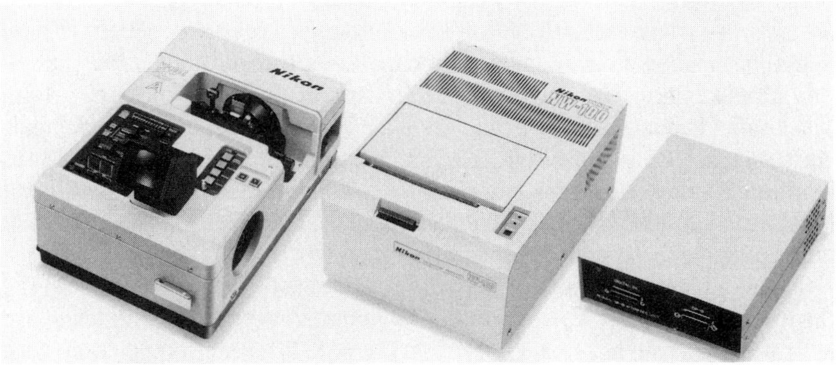

Fig. 3-13. The Nikon NT-1000A System: Transmitter, Monitor Printer, GB-1B Interface Unit.

A further development of this unit was the new LS-3500 Film Scanner and the CP-2 color printer. The Film Scanner was not designed as a portable unit. It is capable of scanning at 4096 × 6144 pixels and representing 16.7 million colors. It provided a 70-Mbyte/image-scanned input for PC–AT computers with TARGA boards.

By using the portable, battery-operated Nikon QV-1010T still video transmitter, a photographer could review images stored on a still video disk with a built-in 4-inch black-and-white monitor. Any selected image could then be transmitted over telephone lines through either a modular connector or an audio output (connected to an acoustic coupler). Information identifying the transmitter, transmission date and other data was sent outside of the image frame. The transmitted information interfaced with existing wire service receiving network equipment.

The most recent Nikon NT-1000A 35-mm film direct transmitter reads 35 mm negatives and positives directly and transmits the images over ordinary telephone lines without sacrificing any of the original sharpness. When compared to the original Nikon 35-mm direct color-telephoto transmitter shown two years before, it was clear that keyboards had been eliminated, the unit had been simplified, and more features had been added to allow more flexibility in handling the image. The original work was not lost, but the improvements were impressive.

The various wire services also provided a form of transmission with AP using the Leafax scanner enclosed in a Haliburton luggage case. Designed for the transmission of 35-mm black-and-white or color negatives, transmission of color separations with captions included was easily done. The AP Leafax 35 transmits analog signals to any photoreceiver from the photo assignment site. The received prints, black-and-white, or color separations are scanned conventionally into the newspaper's prepress system. Using digital transmission, the Leafax 35 is capable of transmitting at high speed (less than a minute) to a newspaper site with an electronic picture system. The Leafax is based on the TransFax—a 35-mm film negative or transparency digitizer and editor that fits into a briefcase. Using an Intel 82716 graphics display controller and a 4.5-inch, 600-line display, the unit has a resolution of 3000 × 2000 pixels with 12 bits/color. Captions of 672 characters can be transmitted with pictures.

New devices for transmitting and receiving still video images and for the transmission of conventional film negatives or transparencies are improving at a rate not seen in the past. The real difference could come with the advent of true digital cameras that will again shorten the process. When combined with good image compression, the result could be a more efficient and more readily used picture-transmission source over available transmission lines.

THE FUTURE OF ISDN

The magic letters ISDN (Integrated Services Digital Network) have been a mystery to some and a source of excitement to other people (Fig. 3–14). Some have said that this very promising approach to communications was something that would happen after the year 2000, much like what has been said about electronic photography, while others feel it is just around the corner. The key advantage of ISDN is that it can use part of the present network for transmission. The problem with the present analog system is the limited bandwidth for analog signals. With digital signals, there is a full error-checking process that assures high-quality transmissions at the 64-Kb rate of transmission. Whereas the normal analog system is noisy, the digital signal is always the same as the original.

In 1984, the International Telephone and Telegraph Consultive Committee (CCITT) defined the initial series of standards for ISDN, the I.400

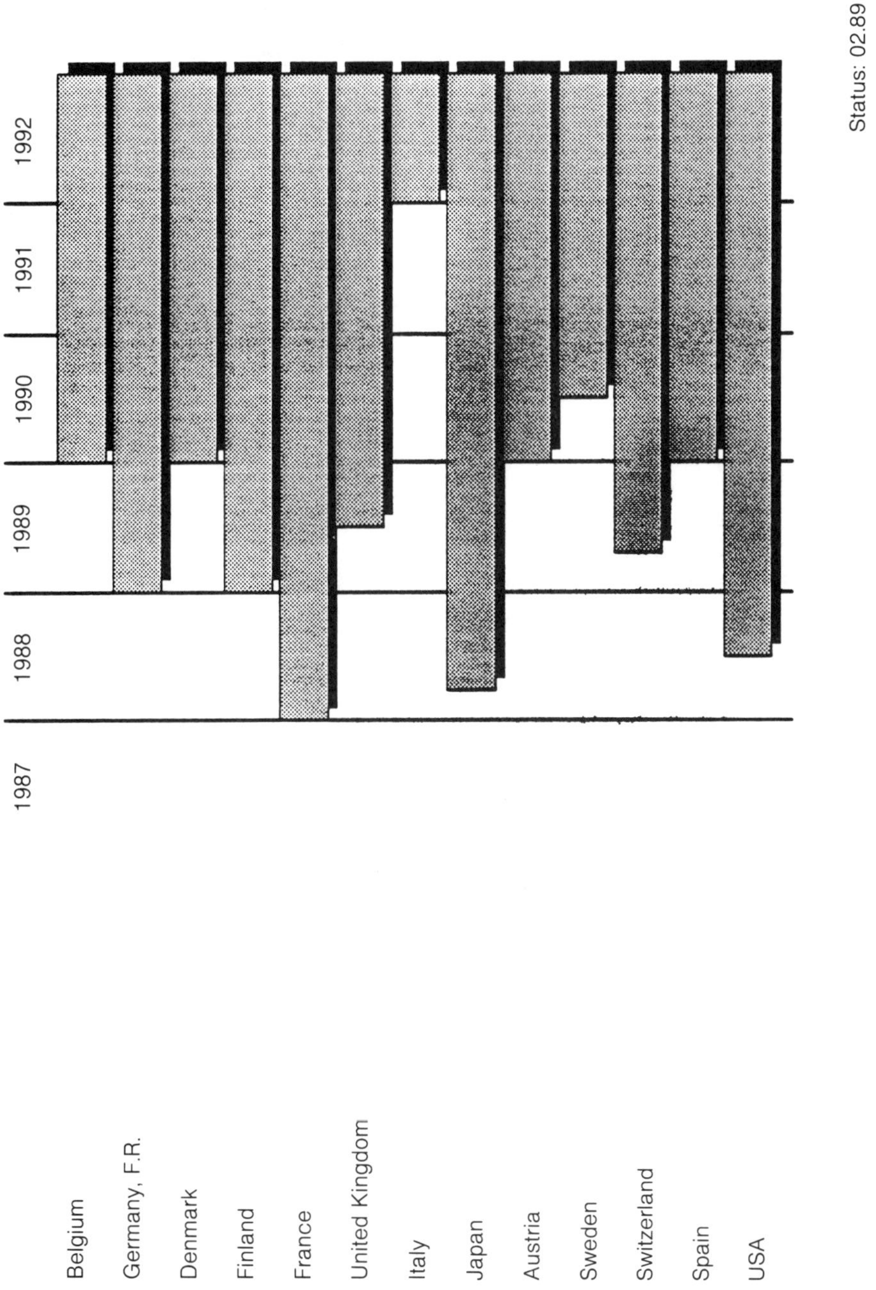

Fig. 3-14. Introduction of ISDN in various countries. SOURCE: SIEMENS

series. The general ISDN concept was "a network evolved from the telephone network that provides end-to-end digital connectivity to support a wide variety of services, including voice and nonvoice services, to which users have access by a limited set of standard, multipurpose customer interfaces."

Already we are beginning to see some of the semiconductor manufacturers—Advanced Micro Devices, Siemens, and Intel—beginning to take the risk to build the necessary chips based on the standards that are just now coming into place. The standards establish tight requirements with unique combinations of analog and digital circuitry on chips, along with filter structures that will meet the needs of this state-of-the-art communication circuit.

One report from The Information Network, "ISDN IC's—Products, Applications and Markets," forecast that the number of installed ISDN access lines in the U.S., Japan, U.K., France, Germany, and Italy will increase from 13,200 in 1988 to 5.4 million in 1992. The growth of IC shipments for use in ISDN terminals, PBXs, and central office switches was expected to be $758 million in 1992, compared with only $4.4 million in 1988.

The growth of ISDN means that finally it will be possible in the 1990's to have true digital-transmission lines at far higher speeds than the analog telephone lines that are available today.

APPLICATION STORIES

Managing Environmental Resources with Electronic Photography

The Bureau of Land Management (BLM) in Portland, Oregon, captures resource information directly from aerial photographs using a video-capture system. The process begins with aerial photographs that are captured and processed using Imaging Technology's PCVISIONplus video digitizer board. From these, line drawings are made on frosted mylar sheets. The images are in a DXF format vector file that is ported to AutoCAD, in which theme-text coordinate labels and other attributes are added to the vector data. Finally, these are taken to the Map Overlay and Statistical Systems family of software and added to the geographic information system database. This direct process allows greater accuracy, increases the speed of data capture, and saves 43,800 manhours a year at the BLM.

Architectural Design with Electronic Photography

Traditional line drawings and watercolor sketches could be a thing of the past through the use of electronic still photography. Initially, an electronic photograph of a proposed building site or a building interior could be digitized using a desktop computer. Options of adding landscaping, a new building, or making changes with the client could be done easily. An imaging board such as the Targa or Vista from TrueVision can provide a basic digitizing capability and present images of the electronic photographs on screen at video- or high-resolution format. Land Development, Inc. (LDL), uses this approach to provide videotape simulation services for land planners and developers.

The images produced have a realistic quality that can include furniture, landscaping, and other finishing touches as they will appear in final form. There are a number of software packages that can be used for this purpose, both for the IBM PC-compatible and Macintosh II computers.

Helix Design Group uses Sony ProMavica products as design and presentation tools on many projects, including a master plan for a St. Louis Historic District and in-store displays for a major retail chain.

The strength of ProMavica, according to Steve Levin, partner, is the ability to capture images from diverse sources, integrate them onto a single medium (the ProMavica diskette), then transfer the files to a computer system for editing on a video monitor. Using ProMavica products in this way helped Helix win an assignment to design display cases for The Limited, the national clothing retailer.

"We created concepts using a variety of media—CAD, drawings, and photos. By capturing all three with ProMavica, we integrated them into a single format, the ProMavica diskette," says Levin. He and his partner, Gina Hilberry, transferred the images to Lumena, a graphics-software paint program running on a Targa-equipped PC. Images were displayed on a monitor, edited, enhanced, and organized into a winning presentation.

Helix also uses ProMavica products in an architectural application: the preparation of a master plan for the Central West End of the city of St. Louis. "Using the ProMavica camera, we can capture and edit real images. For example, we could change the proportions of a street lamp, add flowers to a barren planter, or erase overhead power lines," Levin says. "Clients respond positively to this technique because they can't visualize the consequences of such decisions from drawings nearly as well as they can from an actual video image."

Electronic Photography in Beijing

While I was writing this chapter, the political situation in China grew more and more serious and culminated with students protesting in Beijing. The Army fought with the students, and the government was torn apart on how to handle the situation. It became the main news story in every newspaper, radio, and television broadcast. Last week, ABC, CBS, NBC, and CNN were broadcasting live video from Beijing over the satellite. Then when the trouble started, China cut off all satellite transmissions, and the networks lost their live coverage. At this point, some very creative thinking took place and Sony (in particular, Still Image Systems) had an answer to the networks' dilemma, i.e., transmit images (Mavica stills) back to the states using telephone lines and Still Image Systems cameras, printers, decks, and transmission equipment.

A year ago, this concept was presented to the networks and the perception was "When would you ever lose an up-link?" When the situation unfolded in China, Eric Brobeck of Audio Video of Washington, D.C., along with Cliff Reeves and Tim Justice of Sony, presented the concept to NBC. One day passed from when the concept was presented to its implementation in China. Next, Cliff Reeves went to CNN, and the equipment was on its way to China that day. Tim Justice then talked to ABC and at 5:00 PM on Friday, June 2, ABC gave me a call and stated they wanted the equipment that night to send to China. At this point, Eileen Petrovic, Laura Carlsen, equipment up at the Carson warehouse on Friday and took it straight to the airport for shipment to China. Mr. Tomita and Mr. Tashiro provided some very strong technical support and even arranged for a contact in Beijing. Bob Combs and Paul Berger of Sony Broadcast provided additional sales help.

All in all, through some very creative thinking, a lot of hard work, and excellent cooperation among all parties involved, Sony was able to solve a customer problem with a unique and reasonable solution. When you consider that in less than one week's time, the situation occurred, the equipment was procured, shipped, installed, and images then broadcast back to the networks, it was quite a remarkable achievement.

4

Storage of Images

There are three major types of storage for electronic photographs: magnetic, optical, and RAM. The still video system, with its floppy disk, is an analog recording system, not a digital system. As we reach for digital recording of electronic photographs, we face the challenge of storing large amounts of data. For example, a simple NTSC video image probably will require 500 Kb/image, and this figure can increase to over 150 Mb for very high-resolution images with increased pixel depth for each color.

When you look at the combination of file size along with the need to move these larger and larger amounts of data, it becomes clear that new solutions are required (Table 4–1).

MAGNETIC-DISK MEMORY

Magnetic-disk memories have certain common characteristics. Whether it is an analog-stored still video image or digital data, the information is stored on one circular platter in the case of a floppy disk and several circular disks in the case of a Winchester drive. These disks spin continuously. The information is recorded on the surface of the rotating disk by magnetic heads mounted on arms with the information recorded in bands.

In the case of the still video floppy disk, the disk is a small magnetic disk approximately 5 cm in diameter that uses metal powder as the magnetic recording material. The magnetic disk is contained in a plastic jacket, and the shape is very similar to a conventional 3.5-inch floppy disk. More recently it was announced that 2-inch floppy disks with a different shell and characteristics were to be used commonly in laptop computers. In this form, they would be totally digital with a storage capacity of 1 Mb.

Table 4-1. Digital-Storage Systems Capacity.

	NTSC		HDTV*	
	(000,000)			
	Std.	Comp.	Std.	Comp.
Pixels/Frame	0.26	0.26	1.05	1.05
Bits	4.19	0.65	16.80	1.60
Number of frames per unit media				
Still video floppy (standard)	1.50	9.80	—	4.00
Still video floppy (high density, dbl sided)	6.10	39.40	1.50	16.00
3 1/2 inch disk (vertical recording)	229.00	1476.00	57.10	600.00

*Typical discrete cosine transform

The 2-inch floppy disk drive was developed by Sony Corp. The PDD110 is thinner and lighter than Sony's PDD100, which it will replace. Average access time is 79 milliseconds (4 milliseconds/track), a speed increase of four times. The dimensions of the drive, which provides the still video format standard, are 62.5 × 88.5 × 20 mm. Memory capacity of the 2-inch floppy disk is 819 kbytes. Although designed for still video, the unit is being used by Sony and Sharp for external data storage in portable word processors (Fig. 4–1).

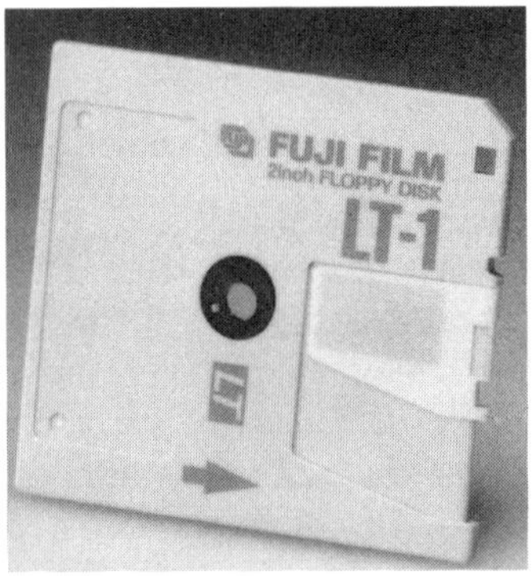

Fig. 4-1. The Fuji 2-inch floppy disk designed for laptop personal computers has a 1-megabyte storage capacity.

For still video recording, the jacket measures 54 × 60 mm and is 3.6 mm deep. It is almost one-third the size of a 3.5-inch floppy. This makes handling, maintenance, and storage of the floppy disk very simple and efficient.

The track pattern for the still video floppy disk consists of 50 main tracks and 1 cue track. The head traces linearly in the radius direction against the rotating floppy. In recording and playback, when a desired track is selected, the head moves and stops at the indicated point. For this reason, precise and stable head-transfer and stop mechanisms are important elements in satisfying the specifications of the still floppy system. The hub, the center of the magnetic disk, plays an important role in mechanical and electrical functions of the unit and disk.

When you insert the floppy disk into the drive, it is important that you center it precisely for stable positioning of the track in the head. The hub specifications and the unit's spindle dimensions require great precision. A spring is incorporated that maintains contact between the surfaces of the hub's center hole and the rotating spindle.

The combination of a pin-yoke (PG yoke) incorporated in the hub and the PG coil of the unit detects the position of the determined starting point at which the recording and playback always begins. The unit's rotating spindle and magnetic sheet rotate as one piece to prevent slipping. The drive spindle and the supported hub surface are maintained in positive contact in order to keep the head-to-disk contact stable. For this purpose, a magnet in the rotating spindle and a magnetic plate in the hub are incorporated to obtain stable head-to-disk contact without any slippage.

If anything happens to the magnetic surface, such as if it is damaged or becomes dusty, the recording and playback requirements will not be met. A flaw in the recording surface can result in the loss of several scan lines or even a complete image. A metal shutter protects the delicate head-to-disk contact portion. The shutter is designed to open and close automatically when the floppy disk is loaded and unloaded into the drive. The shutter will not open accidentally.

The 50 main tracks could be used for video recording. Half of the video scanning lines (for NTSC, 525 lines, for PAL, 625 lines) will be recorded on one track in one interval (one field). To record all of the scanning lines in a frame of video, adjacent tracks are combined (for example, tracks 1 and 2). To record and play back video images, either one track or two tracks can be selected. The recorded image on one track is called a *field picture.* A floppy disk can store 50 field pictures. Recording and playback of two tracks is called a *frame picture.* Twenty-five frame pictures can be stored with a quality higher than that of field pictures. Both field and frame pictures can be recorded on one floppy disk.

In order to play back or record two tracks at once, the head must have two gaps in coils that are only 0.1 mm apart. Special thin-film double-gap heads were developed and were part of the first ProMavica MVR5500.

The quality contained within a video floppy disk is exemplified by a review of one manufacturer's product. The Maxell video floppy disk has a magnetic material with a coercive force of 1400 oersteds with a particle size measuring 0.2 microns. A new binder is used to obtain a high uniformity. The result of these efforts is a higher output and lower noise operation in a wider frequency band. The rf output is 1 db, and the output noise ratio is 1 db, resulting in reproduction that meets the Hi-band specifications for the higher-frequency signals (Table 4–2).

Table 4-2. Maxell Video Floppy Disk Specifications.

	Specification
Basic Specifications	
Magnetic particles	Ultrafine metallic magnetic particles
Coercivity	1400 Oe
Coating thickness	3.5 μm
Thickenss of base film	35 μm
Sides used	single sided
Number of images recorded (still video + use)	50 field recording 25 (frame recording)
Storage capacity (for data)	1 Mb (when unformatted) 819 Kb (when formatted)
Number of tracks	50
Track pitch	100 μm
Track density	254 tpi
Video Characteristics	
RF playback output (7 MHz)I	−20 dB or above**
RF playback output (1.25 MHz)	−20 dB or above**
C/N (7 MHz/6 MHz)	−20 dB or above**
Data Characteristics	
Maximum recording density	64 Kbpi (51.4 Kfci)
Data transfer speed	14.3 Mbps
Record length	4096 bytes/sector
Number of sectors	4 sectors/track
Recording format	8/10 switchable
Disk speed of rotation	3600 rpm
Size	
Disk external diameter	47 mm
Cartridge dimensions	54 × 60 × 3.6 mm (W × L × H)
Weight	8.5 g
Environmental Requirements	
For use	−5 to 53 × C., 8 to 80% relative humidity
For storage	−5 to 53 × C., 8 to 90% relative humidity
For transport	−40 to 60 × C., 8 to 90% relative humidity

*Specifications are subject to change without notice.

**Meets uniform standards for still video floppy format VF.

The surface of the particles is treated with a corrosive-resistant ceramic layer of a very minute thickness that maintains the image quality even after long-term storage of the image.

The special coating used is important because of the extreme proximity of the magnetic head and the very small contact area. The disk operates at 33,600 rpm, more than ten times faster than a floppy disk. Special binders and lubricants have been developed for the floppy disk that assure stable operation in a wide temperature range with more than 500 hours of continuous operation achieved.

The video floppy, particularly the Hi-band, has a high-frequency recording signal so that even a slight variance in head contact decreases output and image quality suffers. The spacing between the head and the disk is maintained at about 1/500th the thickness of a hair.

As mentioned earlier, the hub is important to enhance centering and reduce hub abrasion. The design technology for cartridges and hubs was developed with the earlier experience gained with molding techniques for 3 1/2-inch floppy disks.

For digital storage of electronic photographs, such as those that might be generated by scanners or other video capture systems, magnetic storage on new high capacity floppy disks as well as high capacity Winchester drives offers a practical storage approach. The 5 1/4-inch floppy disks are available in up to 20 Mb configurations while the latest of 3 1/2-inch floppy disk drives pack 16 Mb on a metal disk. These 3 1/2-inch systems use special heads along with metal disk media to achieve the high recording capabilities.

Winchester drives also have increased in capacity, with common sizes of 300 Mb and more in 5 1/4-inch size (Fig. 4–2). At the same time, for

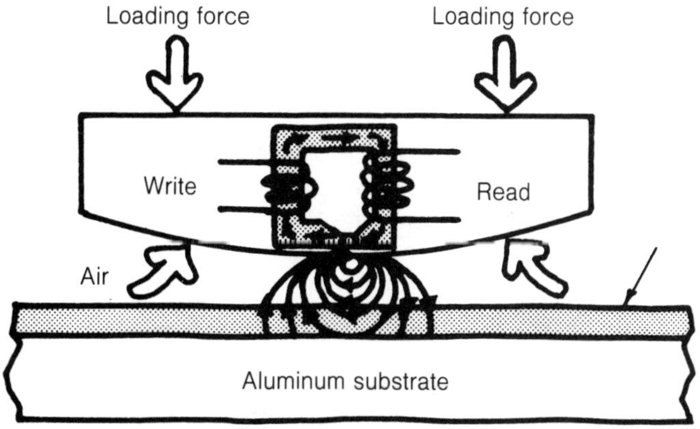

Fig. 4-2. A typical flying head being used in disk memory and showing the right head located above the magnetic surface separated by a thin air cushion.

recording large amounts of data, techniques developed for handling supercomputer data have a potential application to the recording of RGB picture information as well. Parallel writing allows several surfaces of a Winchester drive to be written at the same time so that multiple streams of data can be moved, increasing the writing speed by as many heads as are being used simultaneously. The key problem is synchronization to assure all the information is being written with precisely the same timing so that the information will be readable and will remain in proper sync.

One of the limitations of disk drives is the interface with the computer. The data that can be fed is limited, and one solution is to use a different interface. The Small Computer System Interface (SCSI), sometimes pronounced "scuzzy", allows a faster data transmission with speeds up to 2 Mb/sec as opposed to 1/2 Mb/sec on most systems. Particularly with electronic photographs, this four-fold increase in speed can be a very valuable change. With newly planned buses and existing buses such as the MCA from IBM, faster movement of data is possible as the need for more picture interfaces becomes apparent.

Then there is the new magnetic media recording base. Utilizing BPDA-type polymide film under the brand name Upilex, Ube Industries Ltd. (Tokyo), has developed a new base for magnetic tape and floppy disks. Thin metallic films, which are expected to be used extensively in new media because of the higher-density recording they offer, can be deposited on this new material. It is being offered in two versions: Upilex SX for magnetic tape and Upilex S for floppy disks.

OPTICAL MEMORY

Optical storage media have been in use for more than ten years, primarily in write once-read many times (WORM) disks and in prerecorded laser video disks, which offered a higher-quality image and sound than was available previously on regular VHS tapes for consumers.

The optical disk continues to be a good storage medium for archiving. A rugged, removable medium with a reasonable, projected storage life, it offers low cost per bit storage. Combining these characteristics with nonerasability in a compact format, it offers an attractive medium that has found a place today primarily in document management and storage.

The WORM disk also is becoming an important factor in the storage of photographic images. It offers large capacity and the protected archivability of the images stored.

For the consumer, the main product up to now has been the videodisk. The videodisk contains material on which high-quality image and audio signals can be recorded. A special player, either of the LaserVision disk

(LVD) type, which uses a laser beam, or the Video High-Density System (VHD) type, which uses a stylus, is used for playback.

The optical disk can be prerecorded with the CD audio, for example, in which prerecorded music is available, or with the CD-V, which offers a combination of 20 minutes of digital sound plus 5 minutes of digital sound and moving images.

The CD-ROM is beginning to appear primarily with computer and graphic information. Entire encyclopedias have been committed to CD-ROM forms that can be replayed like any prerecorded material (Fig. 4-3).

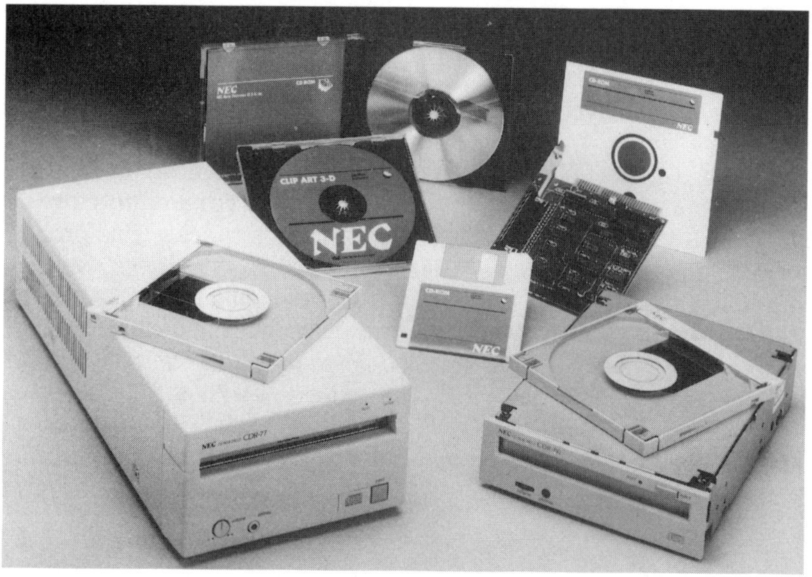

Fig. 4-3. CD ROMs from NEC Home Electronics include two CD ROM readers (one external and one internal), along with two software products and four interface kits.

The WORM disks, or as they are sometimes called, DRAW (direct read after write) disks, allow the user to write once on a disk. WORM and DRAW disks have appeared in sizes from 3 1/2 to 14 inches with the available memory extending all the way to 6.6 gigabytes on the 14-inch materials.

Finally, there are the erasable materials. Erasable direct read after draw (E-DRAW) is one name used for the new family of erasable media.

The erasable materials are not without their problems, however. The access times for retrieving data from optical disks generally has been one-fifth that of magnetic materials. For image transfers of large amounts of data, this is not the most desirable format. The cost of the drives is high, but new products are usually more expensive until volume production brings them down. Most important is the lack of standards. Already an industry group has been formed through ANSI trying to prevent the variations that initially occurred with 5 1/4-inch erasable optical drives when several different standards appeared at the same time. This group is working on a standard for 3 1/2-inch media. There have been three proposals so far. One uses a head with a continuous servo, another uses a sample-type servo, and the third uses a combination of the first two.

Optical media possess several desirable features. Optical-media systems use semiconductor lasers or focusing lenses that are located some hundredths of an inch from the surface of the disk. In addition, the disks generally are coated so that the direct recording material is not on the surface. With magnetic material, heads are located a few microinches above the disk, and the magnetic drive materials generally suffer in a crash as a result.

Although earlier optical WORM disks were 8 and 12 inches in size, these suffered from speed problems because of the time required to move the optical head from the innermost to the outermost tracks. This problem generated a greater interest in 5 1/4-inch optical WORM drives with their removable media (Fig. 4–4). Write-once material, which has been around for more than a dozen years, lacks precise aging data, but testing by several different firms indicate a life of anywhere from 30 to 100 years depending on the accelerated tests that have been run on the material.

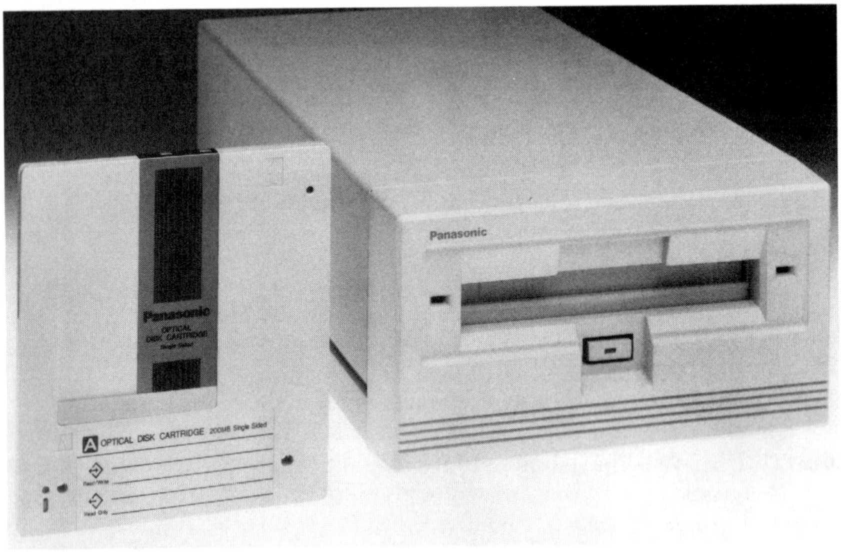

Fig. 4-4. The Panasonic 5 1/4-inch WORM optical disk drive and media.

One example of a WORM optical disk and how it works is the Sony Writable Optical Disk. The aim of Sony is to achieve a 100-year or longer disk life. To achieve this, an SB2S3-BI2TE3 multiple layer structure is used for the recording film. As a substrate material, polycarbonate of special formulation prevents chemical reactions from developing. An additional surface coating was invented by Sony to protect the recording layer from external environmental factors. This is possible with Sony's disk although it might be impractical for other WORM disks that use hole forming or bubble forming because these disks need an air gap to allow the metallic recording material to expand when it melts.

The four-layer film is deposited on a substrate and covered by a protective surface. An adhesive seals the layers together, which are comprised of an adhesive layer, a protective layer, a reflective layer, and recording layers with an antimony-selenide (Sb_2Se_3) bismuth-tellurium (Bi_2Te_3) multiple-layer structure.

The reason for the multiple layers is to extend the usable lifetime to a century or even longer. The reflectance of this series of layers, which includes the reflective layer, a layer of Sb_2Se_3, Bi_2Te_3, and Sb_2Se_3, is as low as 10% to 15% because of multiple interference effects.

To write to the Sony disk, the laser beam switches on and off during the recording process based on the input signal. When a strong laser beam strikes the recording film, the beam is absorbed in the center Bi_2Te_3 portion and converted to heat. This heat causes the diffusion of the atoms in all three layers, resulting in a new formation of a four-element alloy layer that becomes the recorded area. To read the recorded signal, a weak laser beam of fixed strength scans the recorded layer. The beam is reflected back to a photodetector, which converts light-intensity variations into binary data. The recorded alloy area exhibits a reflectance of 30% to 40%, or two to three times higher than that of the unrecorded area.

There are competing materials that can affect the archiving or WORM applications of optical media. Because of their capacity, 8-mm helical scan systems have become a storage medium of choice along with the new 4-mm digital audio tape (DAT). Although these materials are "streamers," or materials that are not available for random access like the optical disk, for most archiving purposes they provide an inexpensive and durable form of storage with a life expectancy similar to that of optical media.

Taiyo Yuden Co., Ltd., of Japan introduced the first recordable compact disk, the CD-R. The new gold-surfaced CD-R is an optical WORM that is fully compatible with existing compact 3.5- and 5-inch disk systems.

Applications are envisioned in both the computer and digital recording industries. The CD-R will be marketed under the brand name That's CD-R, offers 540 Mbytes of WORM and instant record retrieval—attractive features in the fields of archival, medical, and other data storage. For professional audio, the CD-R equals or surpasses International CD Standards Red Book criteria in all categories. Radio station NHK in Japan already has been using music-recorded CD-R to produce some classical FM programs. For stations using a digital music format, commercials, public-service announcements, and full programs can be recorded digitally.

Addressing the press, Taiyo Yuden's president, Mr. Mitsugu Kawanda, said, "First of all, we would like to say that we have been aware of the copyright issue and will continue to be aware of it during the market development for That's CD-R. This means that we are only entering fields that are either free from copyright or where it is strictly protected. For example, we will release That's CD-R for editing and manufacturing CD-ROM and CD-I, and for professional use in broadcasting stations, but do not want to release blank disks in consumer fields until the copyright issue is resolved."

Taiyo Yuden, represented in the U.S. by That's America, spent three years developing the CD-R. As a manufacturer of capacitors, hybrid ICs, ferrite products, solar batteries, and audiotape, the company does not intend to develop hardware for recording (although it does have an experimental system being used to prove the performance of the disks).

Dr. Takashi Ishiguro, product manager, explained how the recording works. The CD-R has pregrooves in a polycarbonate substrate at the standard CD spacing. This is covered by an organic-dye-recording layer, which in turn is covered by a reflection layer and a protective layer. When heated by a laser beam at 780 nanometers (infrared), the dye in the pregrooves diffuses into the polycarbonate material, causing the substrate layer to bulge into these grooves. This results in reflection differences that are read as digital information.

For regular CDs, the laser-produced master disk is a glass-backed platter featuring discrete pits on its surface, representing the 1's and 0's of the digital information. This master then is used to produce a complementary stamping disk, which produces a replica of the original in a special low-defect polycarbonate elastic resin. Once the disk is stamped, a thin layer of aluminum is vacuum-coated on its surface so that low-power lasers can read the pit positions.

From a manufacturing viewpoint, the CD-R process is similar to that used for producing regular CDs, except for the additional dye-layer spin-coating step and the use of gold in place of aluminum. Once full manufacturing begins later this year, the CD-R disks should be available for about $9.00 per disk.

The recent 5 1/4-inch erasable optical drives, such as those from Alphatronix, Hitachi, Maxtor, and Sony, conform to the ANSI/ISO standards. The Canon 5 1/4-inch drive and the Verbatim 3 1/2-inch drive do not conform to the initially established standards. The other concern with the new erasable drives is the seek time. Most of the new drives have a seek time of 70 to 80 msec. or more. Only the Maxtor has an average seek time of 35 msec. This compares to Winchester drives with seek times as short as 12 to 14 msec. The Sony 5 1/4-inch rewritable drive has an average seek time of 95 msec, but the unit offers high reliability.

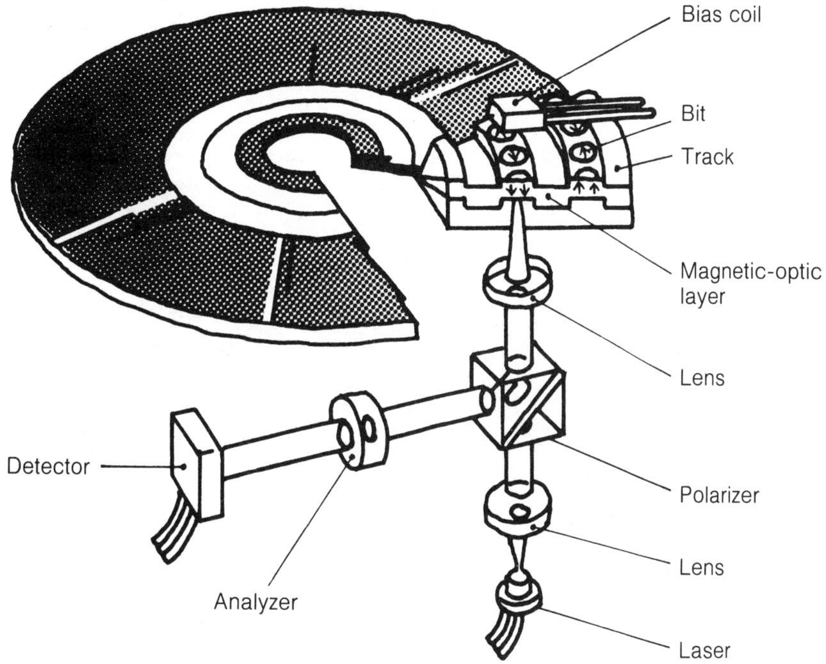

Fig. 4-5. Components of a typical magneto-optical system showing the laser at the bottom, detector on the right for reading, and the optical surface and bias coil for recording and erasing.

The basic principle behind the erasable optical disk is a magneto-optical principle (Fig. 4–5). In normal magnetic recording, such as on hard disks, floppy disks and tapes, particles are reoriented with a magnetic charge. *Coercivity* describes the ease or energy required to reorient the magnetic particles. Low-coercivity materials are easily influenced, whereas high-coercivity materials require greater energy. If a magnetic material of high-coercivity material is heated, then the particles can be reoriented by an extremely weak magnetic field.

To record on a magneto-optical disk, a weak biasing magnetic field is applied to the disk, which has been premagnetized in one direction on the perpendicular axis (Fig. 4–6). A laser rapidly heats a spot 1 micron in width to the Curie point (approximately 572°F). When the temperature of the magneto-optical layer reaches its Curie point, it changes magnetic orientation as determined by the biasing magnetic field. After the laser beam is removed, the exposed disk region cools instantly, and the data, because of its high coercivity, is highly resistive of all but the very strongest of magnetic

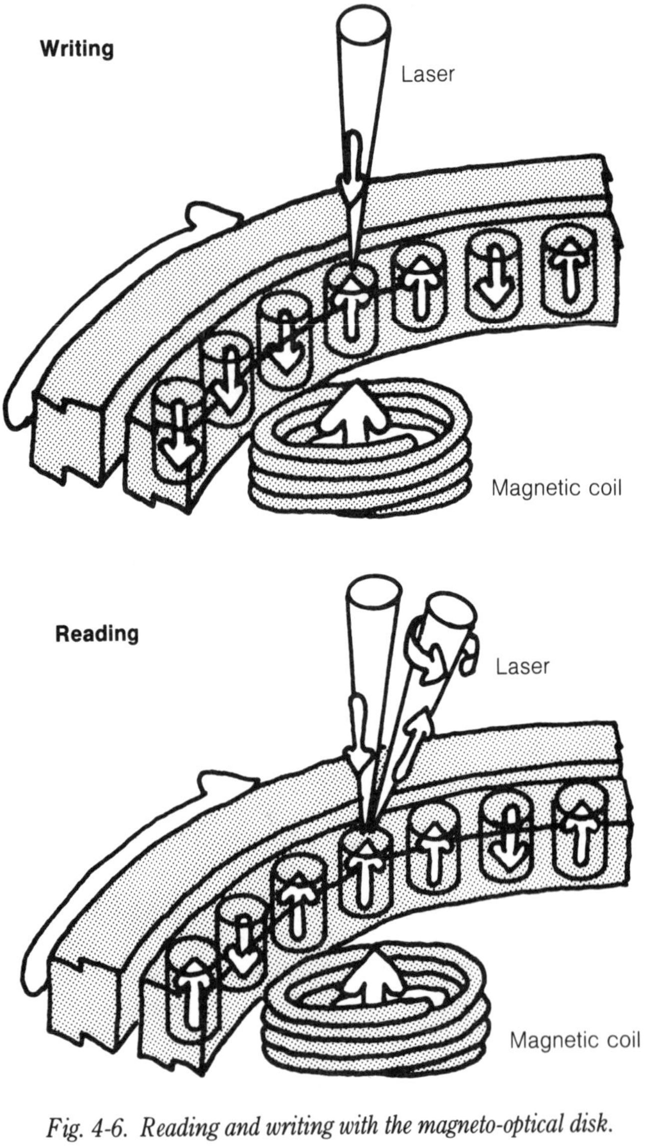

Fig. 4-6. Reading and writing with the magneto-optical disk.

fields. An electromagnet against the surface would affect the recorded material. Because of the small spot size, the data density is extremely high, with up to 512 Mb per 5 1/4-inch side.

In conventional recorded material, the particles are generally flat. The particles in magnetic optical disks are oriented vertically. On a blank disk, all the particles point up and are zeros. Particles reoriented down create a binary 1. A protective covering on the surface shields the particles and eliminates the danger of head crashes or other physical problems.

To read the magneto-optical disk, a weak, linearly polarized laser beam is focused on the recording layer. The plane of polarized reflected light rotates clockwise or counterclockwise according to the magnetization of the recording layer. After passing through a polarizing filter, the light strikes a photodetector that changes intensity or interprets as binary data.

To erase a disk, it is heated with an unmodulated laser-beam spot and exposed to a magnetic field with the opposite orientation to the recording. This returns the medium back to its original state. Current estimates are that the disks can be rewritten ten million times with a data integrity of up to 20 years. The Sony erasable disk uses an ytterbium/iron/cobalt medium.

The Canon 5 1/4-inch erasable drive uses a unique medium that has two magneto-optic layers instead of the single layer specified for the ANSI/ISO standard. The first layer is a low-temperature, high coercivity layer for fast erasing and writing. Reperformance is poor. The other layer is a high-temperature, low-coercivity layer that provides superior reading. The drive writes to the first layer and reads from the second layer, which is magnetized by an exchange-coupling from the first layer. The seek time of the Canon unit is 80 msec.

The one factor that will help the electronic photo-image is the transfer rate of many of these new erasable disks. Whereas the transfer rate of the Winchester drive is 10 Mbits/sec., the transfer rate of the new drives range from 1.2 Mb/sec for the Sony drive to 4 Mb/sec for the Maxtor drive.

Another approach to the erasable field is that of Optical Data, Inc. Using a dye-polymer structure, the structures of the reflectance characteristics are changed physically as a reaction to specific, differing wavelengths of laser light. By varying the infrared-diode laser's wavelength and power, the same device is used to write, read, and erase the optical medium.

The data is written by using a single-frequency infrared-diode laser beam at a higher level. Then at a lower power, the data can be read many times. Erasure is accomplished by using a shorter wavelength of laser light. Apparently there is no limit to the number of erasures with the dye-polymer material.

The Tandy Corporation has licensed the ODI material and added its own proprietary material. A special over-coat allows the platter to be played back on a standard CD audio and CD-ROM drive.

MASS STORAGE WITH WORM DISKS

A number of systems have been produced for mass storage of computer information with WORM optical disks. Called jukeboxes because of the resemblance to the original audio jukeboxes and players, they offer large storage capacities with systems of 50 optical disks not unusual. With systems such as the Kodak 14-inch Optical Disk Jukebox, it is possible to store over 300 gigabytes of information and have any piece of information available in a few seconds. More commonly available, the Sony writable disk automatic changer is currently used in more than 60 installations across the United States. Using a 12-inch WORM optical disk, the information on any disk in the changer is available in ten seconds or less.

A new series of storage units is appearing using the 5 1/4-inch WORM drives with storage capacities of up to 90 gigabytes, such as the 5 1/4-inch jukeboxes from Panasonic, Mitsubishi, and others. These units, with storage capacities up to 90 erasable 5 1/4-inch cartridges, provide media exchange times from 8 to 13 seconds and data exchange rates of 1.5 Mb/sec. The greatest advantage of the 5 1/4-inch units is the *footprint*, or floor space required, which is only 15 × 27 inches and can be placed easily in areas such as a closet.

High-definition optical-disk systems have been shown by firms such as Fuji, Sanyo, and Sony. The high-definition images are the 1125 MUSE standard, which permit the storage of 27,000 still frame images on a single 12-inch disk similar to the standard NTSC optical video disk.

Image database packages are available that provide for the retrieval and archiving of images. PC Album works with a Targa 16 and allows users to merge images, text, and numbers into complete records for easy retrieval. A videodisk unit is integrated into the system with a capacity of 22,000 images in up to 500 different categories (Fig. 4–7). Other database systems allow for the control of jukebox storage to assure complete storage integrity and management of image data files in optical disks.

Because of the large space occupied by electronic photographic images, particularly in their high-resolution form, the application potential of Virtual Disk File Manager (VDFM) systems offer a great deal of attraction. VDFM systems move inactive files to optical disks so that magnetic Winchester drive space is maintained and never fills. The magnetic disk acts as a cache for the most active files in the storage system and retains all optical files on-line by keeping file directory information in place on the magnetic disk. VDFM also uses several tunable parameters to manage which files are moved from the Winchester to the optical disk.

A disk-full fault signal tells the system that a Winchester drive is full and needs to be emptied to a preset level. This preset level eliminates the need for urgent transfers to the optical disk. This system approach will be particularly valuable with the availability of erasable optical disks.

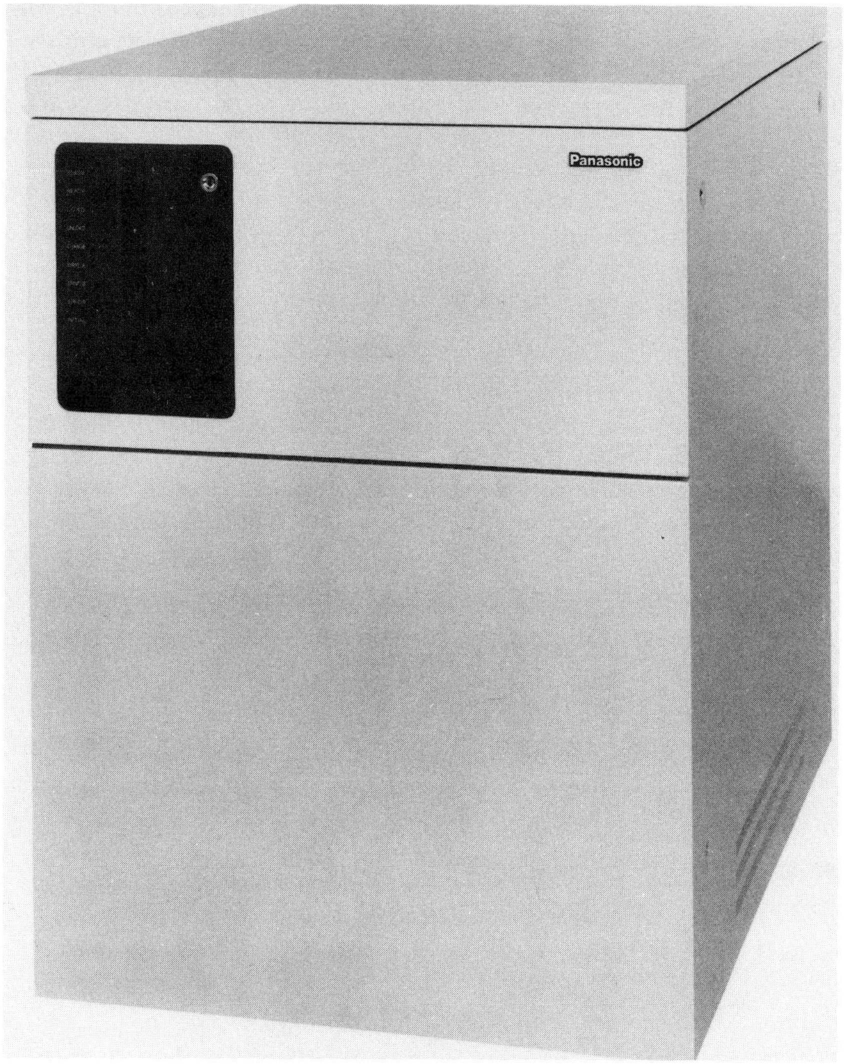

Fig. 4-7. A controller for an optical disk jukebox system from Panasonic.

SOLID-STATE MEMORY

Mechanical devices such as tapes and disks have had a basic role in the development of computers and computer imaging. There have been a few attempts at solid memory such as bubble memory, which involved no moving parts and stored information in magnetic bubbles. This technology was costly, bulky, and never met with favor in the general marketplace.

Today, some of the semiconductor makers' dreams are coming true with the replacement of disk drives by memory chips. The memory chips are costly and require power to maintain them. New developments from Toshiba, such as those predicted for the digital electronic photography cameras, look like a promising answer to this element of memory and storage. The chip designs Toshiba has developed require less than two-thirds the number of transistors and only one-fifth the space needed by today's nonvolatile chips. The new electrically erasable/programmable read-only memory (EPROM) chips could hold 64 Mb on a credit-card-sized chip. More importantly, the data would be available 1000 times faster than the current Winchester drives.

Another approach for semiconductor memory is the use of a series of dynamic random-access memory (DRAM) chips. Fujitsu Ltd., instead of cutting a 6-inch-diameter silicon wafer into several hundred separate DRAMs, simply mounts the whole wafer on a control board. Using a technique for separating the good DRAMs from defective DRAMs developed by Anamartic, Inc., all of the DRAMs on a single king-size chip are available for use. This allows almost 20 Mb/single chip to be available for memory. Although not as effective for permanent storage like the EEPROM, this holds the promise of lower cost memory and greater capacity.

Dataram Corporation produces a solid-state memory device called the Wide Word 2000 Memory System. Using 1 Mb RAM technology, Wide Word array cards can be combined in rack-mountable units to a capacity to 80 Gb. A single Wide-Word System provides a memory transfer rate of 200 Mb/sec and can be interfaced to a wide range of computers, including IBM PC/AT, VME, Q-bus, and Unibus. For example, a 640-Mb very high resolution electronic photograph could be transferred in 3.2 seconds using a single Wide Word 2000 Memory System.

CARD MEMORIES

A variety of memory cards have been produced, ranging from laser-writable cards, smart cards, as well as a variety of other RAM cards.

The Drexon laser memory card from Drexler Technology Corp. is an optical-based storage medium using light sources such as tiny diode lasers to store data and photodetectors to retrieve the information stored on the card's recording surface. Data is recorded using diode lasers or during card production by photolithographic techniques. Optical data recording involves the creation of extremely small holes or patterns representing the digital information. Although optical disk technology is usually 1 micron in diameter, the Laser Card uses a 5- to 10-micron-diameter hole. The card storage capacity can range from 5 million bits to 16 million bits (2 Mb) with ultimately a 10 Mb/side capacity in the future. The material on which the information is recorded is a proprietary Drexler material.

A variety of smart cards have been made available in forms ranging from the original Honeywell Bowl smart card, with a readable and rewritable memory, to a whole host of other cards—cards with simple preprogrammed chips for games and other functions—to battery-backed-up SRAM cards such as those used in the Fujix Digital Still Video Camera System. Available cards today range upwards in size from 2 Mb, and larger cards are expected as the new technologies in memory begin to reach the market. If you think you have heard of everything in the smart-card field, how about the 2- × -4-inch card from Intel, which contains an 88 CPU and all the logic of an IBM PC/XT motherboard. The board even has a socket that can hold an 8087 numeric coprocessor. All of this comes on a board with a 68-pin miniature connector. The possibilities for miniaturization are almost unbelievable.

Smart cards once were considered to be applicable primarily to credit-card usage, such as debit cards. Already we have seen the demonstration of the Fujix and Toshiba digital cameras, which use a different approach to smart cards, but both lean toward the day that a compact card will provide us with our images.

Electronic photography might not displace conventional film, but film might have to share shelf space in dealers' shops with storage cards that will allow images to be made electronically for many applications.

APPLICATION STORY

Storing Art Slides

Louise Bloomberg, curator of slides and prints at the Dorothy Perkins Slide Library (University of Massachusetts at Amherst) hopes that in four to five years viewing great works of art on slides or plates will be a thing of the past. In 1988, Bloomberg began a program that eventually will transfer the library's 25,000 color slides and 10,000 prints to still video floppy disks. The one-ounce disk can replace 50 plates weighing 15 pounds. One goal is to make customized disks that students can use to study for specific exams.

"ProMavica's marvelous flexibility of operation and ease of use allow me to make as many different disks as I need and change them as often as I want," says Bloomberg. The small size and light weight of the Mavipak diskette is a big advantage, she notes, as is the low cost of duplication—approximately $10 per 50 images.

To transfer a 35-mm color slide, Bloomberg inserts a transparency into a Tamron Fotovix and corrects for brightness and color balance. The adjusted image then is blown up on a Sony monitor, where final color corrections are made. "I can enhance the color of a poor slide, crop an image, or zoom-in for an extreme close-up to highlight an artist's brush strokes with exquisite clarity," she says. Once she is satisfied with the video image, it is stored on a diskette in a ProMavica MVR-5500 player/recorder.

In the near future, Bloomberg hopes to equip study carrels in the library with ProMavica player/recorders and Sony monitors for viewing art on diskettes. Even more ambitious is her long-term plan for a system to enable students to retrieve ProMavica images on PCs and view them from their rooms or any location on campus.

5

Display and Output of Images

A key question in electronic photography is "How do you see the image?" With still video images, the standard NTSC television screen provides a commonly available image-viewing source. Even with standard viewing screens, there is a difference in the resolution capability of the individual monitor being used for display.

Equally or more important is the ability to create a hardcopy of the photograph in a photorealistic form. Color printers are not new, but the most recent series of dye-transfer printers have begun to approach the level of photorealism expected of silver-halide prints.

Viewing electronic still photographic images on a screen is referred to as *soft viewing*. This is because no permanent copy is made of the screen image unless a film image or film-capture device is used. The term *hard copy* comes from the copy machines and the various aspects of creating a rigid or permanent copy of an image.

DISPLAY MONITORS

The most common display monitor, whether it is contained in a home television set or a dedicated color display-monitoring device for a video system or computer, is a cathode-ray tube (CRT). The CRT uses a viewing screen that is coated, in the case of a color tube, with either bands of phosphors that produce red, green, and blue or individual dots of phosphor. Electrons are emitted from a cathode in the narrow end of the tube, and these are focused either magnetically or electrostatically into a small spot on the screen and positioned by either magnetic or electrostatic deflection. The cathode and electronic focusing lenses are part of the tube called the gun with the beam being accelerated towards the phosphor by high voltage at an anode (Fig. 5–1). The first CRTs appeared just before the turn of the century and remain today as a major display medium for both video and computer imaging. The CRT is an inexpensive device with many desirable features, including the ability to produce tubes of 35 and even 45-inch diagonal proportions.

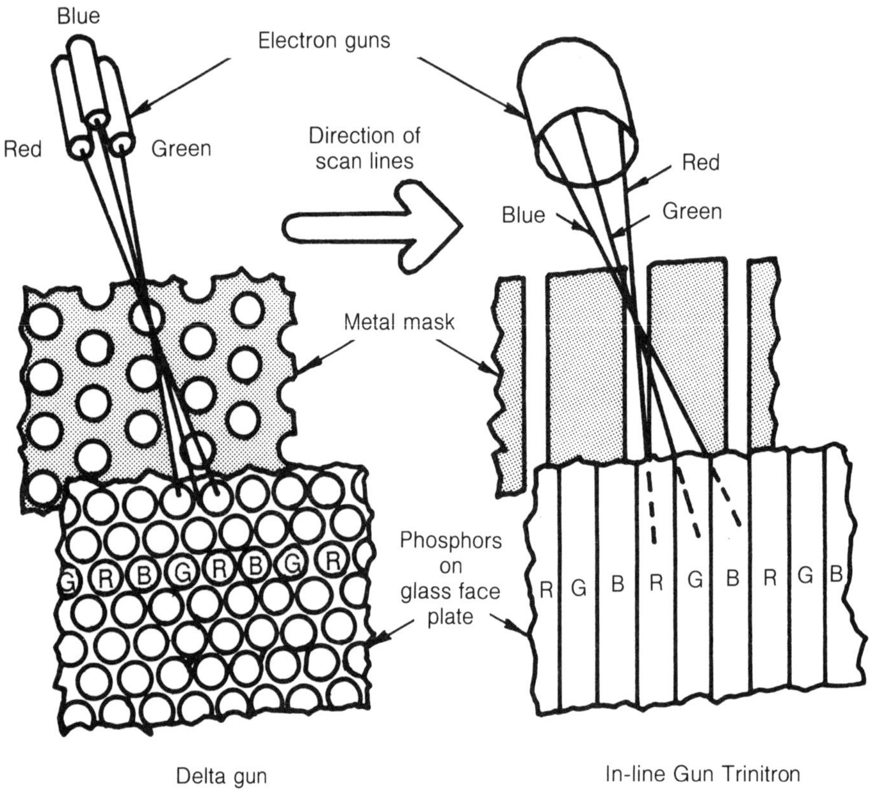

Fig. 5-1. The aperture mask of a color CRT.

The one problem of CRTs is the bulk that they represent. Even some of the newer, much shorter tubes still make it difficult to create wall displays or briefcase-size devices. The CRT needs a considerable distance from the gun to the screen to focus and scan the image.

Because of some of the shortcomings of the CRT, much effort has been expended to find a form of flat display device (Table 5–1). Work on flat-panel displays has been going on for some 20 years, and today the best results have been shown by liquid-crystal displays (LCDs) (Fig. 5–2).

Table 5-1. Flat-Panel Technologies.

TYPE	HOW IT WORKS
Emissive	
Plasma display	AC capacitance-coupled gas discharge
Light-emitting diode (LED)	A display that used diodes that emit light when current is applied. These are now available in all colors and are sometimes used in large displays in open areas.
Vacuum fluorescence	Electrons strike the surface of a phosphor in a hard vacuum but are controlled by a grid.
Electroluminescence	Electron conduction in special crystals due to a high electric field.
Cathode-ray tube (CRT)	Electrons strike a phosphor in a hard vacuum under the control of either a grid or a cathode.
Non-emissive Displays *(Non-emissives requires reflected or transmitted light).*	
Liquid-crystal display (LCD)	Electrostatic rotation of organic compounds that show liquid crystal effects.
Electrochromism	A color change exhibited when charging or discharging a chemical system such as a battery.
Colloidal suspensions	Electrostatic movement or rotation of light-absorbing particles in a colloidal suspension.
Electroactive solids	Certain ferroelectric or magnetic materials which show an electrooptic effect.
Electromechanical	Mechanical motion of elements, creating a contrast change.

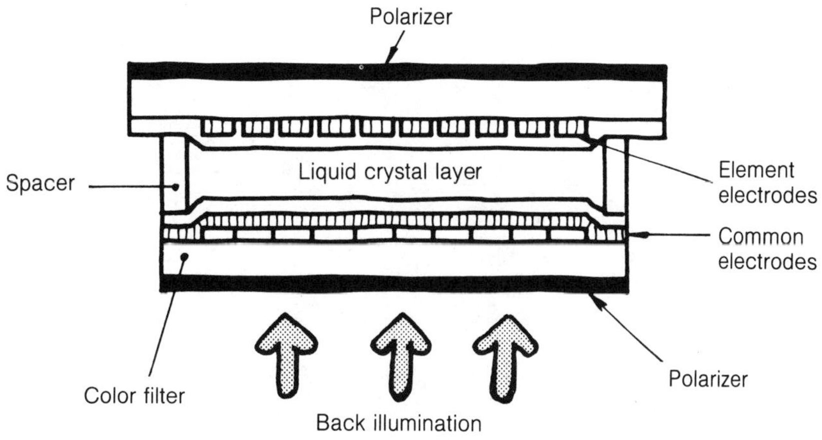

Fig. 5-2. The structure of a liquid-crystal color display.

Liquid-crystal compounds are assembled in a thin film (approximately 0.5 mil in thickness) between parallel transparent conductors. When the electronic field is applied, it creates a scattering effect that allows light to reflect or pass through the conductors. The most recent development of the active screen places a transistor at each pixel location to produce extremely high-resolution results.

Liquid crystals range from unique 2000-×-2000-line liquid crystals produced by Hitachi and written with a laser to control a tungsten light source to color 14-inch LCD screens already suitable for computer graphic display. Color is obtained by using a dichroic dye in the crystal color materials that the light passes through.

LCDs are generally inexpensive, consume little power, and are thin, durable, and lightweight. However, they lack contrast, and it is hard to create large sizes of liquid crystals. Today it is common to backlight LCDs in many applications in which ambient light levels might be low.

In addition, liquid crystals now are beginning to appear in 3-×-3-inch sizes as color projection sources. A new Sharp single-lens projector employs three 3-inch square liquid crystals, each with a resolution of 89,505 pixels (Fig. 5–3). When combined, this projects 268,515 pixels on the screen and no visible lines in the picture area. By using a single lens and mirrors to capture the image from the liquid crystals, it is possible to use such things as anamorphic lenses for the projection of films originally photographed in compressed form and showing these in their original wide-screen appearance.

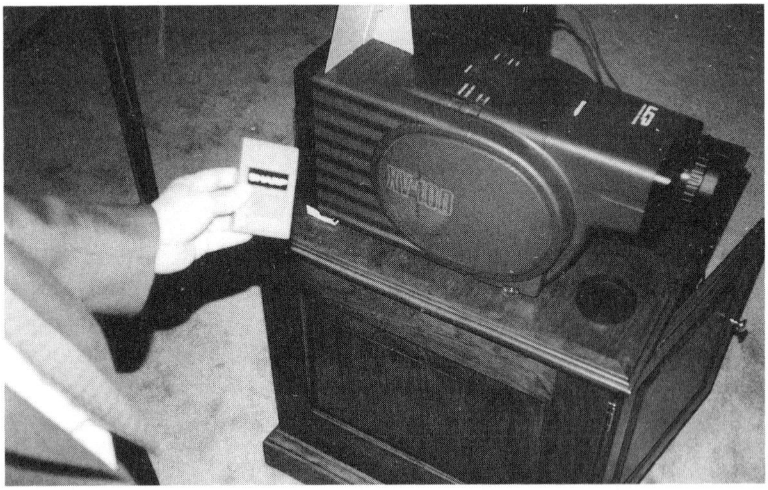

Fig. 5-3. A Sharp single lens liquid-crystal projector uses three square, liquid crystals.

The Omika Works of Hitachi, Ltd. has developed a new way of projecting high-resolution images with 4 million pixels using three liquid-crystal light valves. Images are written to three liquid-crystal light valves (LCLV—approximately 50 × 50 mm) by laser diodes. These images then are collected and use a xenon lamp reflected from the front surface of the LCLV with the image projected to a 2-×-2-meter rear-screen with a 1000 lumens brightness.

The projected image is sharp and contains a seven-color vector image. The seven colors result from the use of each LCLV for a primary color.

The initial application of the display is for industrial or CAD/CAM applications. The currently available system includes both a floppy and hard disk, and it comes with an RS-232C and IBM bisynch communication interface. With further development, both color depth and resolution could offer promise for many other applications such as imaging cameras and other output devices.

A second contender is the electroluminescent display (ELD). ELDs are a direct result of a concept that was envisioned several years ago in which walls would be painted with a compound which, when electricity was applied, would luminesce. ELDs have been used in computer displays with their familiar yellow images on a black background. There are two basic types of ELDs, a thin-film and a thick-film version, with each producing the same amount of light intensity, contrast, and resolution, but being produced by different manufacturers.

Plasma display panels (PDP) contain a gas that glows when subjected to a high voltage (Fig. 5–4). Two sets of electrodes are used, one placed in

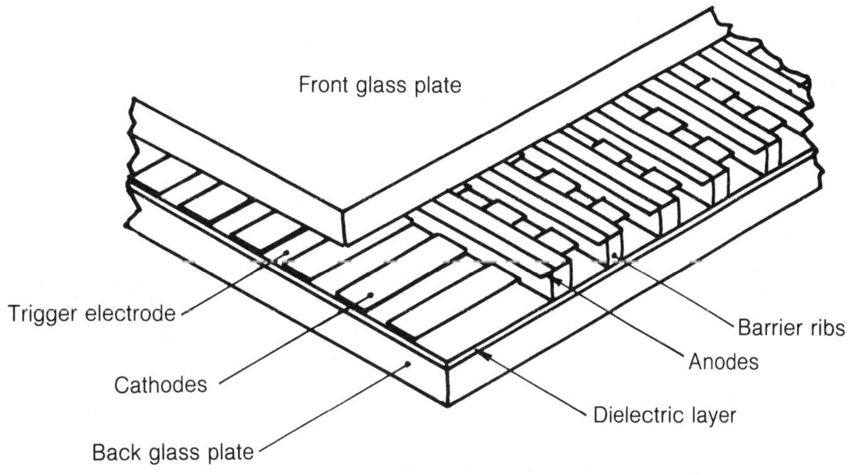

Fig. 5-4. Cross section of a plasma display.

the x axis and one in the y axis, with the gas between the two electrodes. When voltage is applied to the two sets of electrodes, the plasma display exhibits its characteristic orange or red-orange color. Some work has been done to create color plasma displays.

It is expected that much more will be seen of the flat panel devices, particularly the LCDs, because of their size and the potential for projection devices with high resolution (Table 5–2).

Table 5-2. A Comparison of Flat-Panel Displays.

	Electro-Luminescent	Gas Plasma	Vacuum Fluorescent Twist LCD	Double Super-LCD	TFT Color
Viewing angle	±70	±70	±70	±45	± 45
Contrast ratio	40:1	10:1	30:1	17:1	40:1
Response time	10–20 us	10–20 us	10–20 us	300 ms	40 ms
Power consumed with backlight	15 W	30 W	20 W	6 W	5 W
Resolution	Up to 640 × 400	Up to 640 × 480	Up to 640 × 400	Up to 640 × 480	Up to 640 × 200
Color option	No	No	No	Proposed	Yes

Source: Hitachi

Monitors have unique properties that have to be considered as part of the specifications for purchase. First, the resolution of the monitor should correlate to the source that will be providing the information. The ability to handle automatically a variety of outputs is a distinct advantage, and this is available in monitors referred to as *autoscan monitors*. There are models that can be adjusted manually, but the autoscan takes into account any unit that is plugged in. The concern here is the horizontal scanning frequency, which today can reach well above 100 KHz with high-resolution imaging systems. As the resolution of the monitor goes up, so will the requirements for scanning frequency.

Another important consideration is the size of the dot pitch available. Simple monitors for basic home computers might have a dot pitch of .40 mm or larger. The higher-resolution monitors today have a dot pitch of .31 mm or better. This results in a finer trace with the ability to produce more information in the final result.

Francois Gossieaux, Product Manager, Barco Industries, Inc., makes some important points regarding monitors. "The only way you can efficiently use monitors in imaging applications such as photographic imaging or electronic photography or other graphic arts applications is if you can save money in the production process by eliminating some hardcopy output in the process. The only way you can do that is really by relying on the display and that requires that you fulfill a number of requisites. First, there is the need for consistency over time—if you have your display set up in a certain way, you can interpret the image on the display as a representation of whatever the output is going to be and how you want it to stay from day to day.

"The second requisite that is necessary for efficiently using displays in electronic imaging is to have consistency of space, which is [different] from shop to shop. Once you have developed an image on a display at one location and you send it to another location by whatever means, by magnetic tape or direct communication, you want the image at the other end to look exactly the same as the one that you originally looked at. In order to efficiently use displays in electronic imaging, you must fulfill these two criteria.

"One is that it should be stable over time. Traditional displays will not be stable primarily because of aging of the phosphors. Also, there is a very high instability of the dark areas of the display which are dependent on ambient conditions such as humidity, temperature, and pressure. You need to have a display that will keep the color balance in your dark area as well as the color balance of your high brightness area very stable. The second thing that you need in electronic photography images, which is as important in other graphic arts applications, is the high contrast ratio, which is the difference between the high luminance of the white point and the black point. You need a pretty wide gamut there, and also you need a very wide color gamut since dyes have a wider color gamut than inks usually.

"Those are what I would call conventional parameters and they are important in any application. However, in photographic applications where you want to have a true representation of whatever the hard-copy output will be, the color parameters, which so far in the industry have not been specified, are more important.

"A limited number of manufacturers are designing special displays, including special circuitry, to ensure that the colormetric specifications can be set and can be held within certain narrow tolerances. One of the things you see emerging, and I think we've seen that in the broadcast area earlier than in the graphics area, are (sic) intelligent monitors. Intelligent monitors will allow you to automatically recalibrate a display to compensate for the aging of the display phosphors. They also include some automatic circuitry to ensure that the black level stability is maintained. This will vary depending on the ambient conditions.

"Another thing is that intelligent monitors will allow you to get access to the full transfer characteristic of the display—such parameters as gamma and measured chromaticity of phosphors. This is extremely important if you want to compensate in your look-up table in the system side of electronic photography to compensate for the nonlinearity of the display. So you are provided, for example, with parameters such as gamma for red, green and blue separately (these are not the same) for the chromaticity of the phosphors and for just about any other parameter that you can set in the display as far as geometry and linearity are concerned.

"Intelligent monitors will allow you to get access to the many parameters which are usually set differently from one display to another, such as size, timing, picture and brightness. We should use the word picture rather than contrast because picture is really the luminance level of your picture, while contrast will be dependent on your ambient light as well. Once you have control over those parameters you can also retrieve them, [then] send the parameters in a file along with your image file to whatever monitor on which you will view the image. The setting file will set the remote monitor so that it will be at exactly the same settings as the monitor you originally viewed.

"First of all, it is important to understand that the intelligence is not just a 'thing' you have to look for. What is important is how that intelligence is used. If the intelligence is only used to set up some geometrical specifications of the display, then it won't help you to fulfill your colormetric requirements. Intelligence is one thing, but it is more important how you use it.

"In the future you will have a display that is stable over time and stable over space, from one system to another. People will spend increasingly more time in developing spatial color correction as well as compensating for the psychophysical factors, such as ambient light. This is going to affect the way you are going to view the image—surround lighting and observer variability will be more closely checked. People will spend more time on spatial color correction from one part of the image versus (sic) the other.

"Increasingly, you hear about flat panel CRT displays. The advantage of those displays is that they have a much higher light output so that you can fulfill the requirement needed in the photographic market for a greater contrast ratio.

"As far as the liquid crystal display (LCD) is concerned, one of the advantages of LCD displays is that you can have a wider color gamut because you can use more than three primary colors to recreate your image. However, it is strange to see, right now, that people are using color CRTs to simulate the behavior of LCD displays.

"History is a good teacher. In the past, people have said that CRTs were going to be disappearing in the future, but CRTs have caught up every time. I wouldn't be surprised to see CRTs catching up and continue being the most used viewing device for the foreseeable future."

People using monitors are becoming aware of the need for quality control. At least one manufacturer, Barco, has produced a microprocessor-based color imaging display with a backup memory and RS232 capability. The Calibrator imaging display provides an optional resolution of 1280 × 1024 pixels (Fig. 5–5). In addition to the standard 64-KHz Calibrator imaging display, a 32-KHz model also has been developed. Calibration of the monitor is done automatically in about two minutes. An optical sensor, available as an option, measures color and gray-scale values from the display screen and provides direct feedback to the Calibrator circuitry to generate corrections.

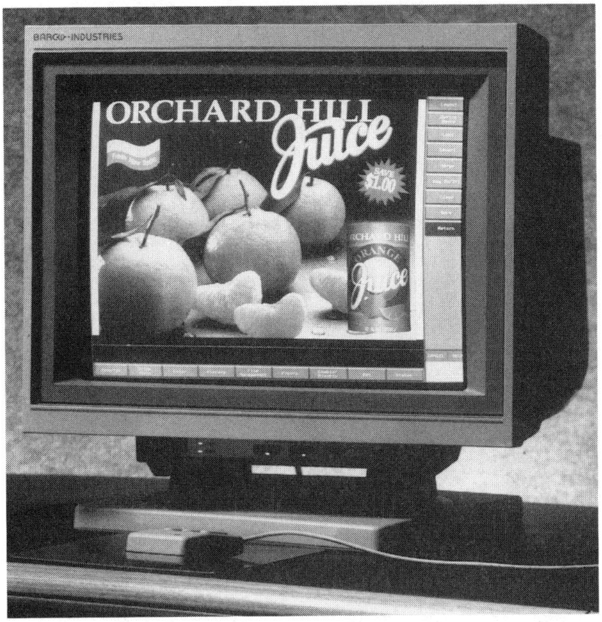

Fig. 5-5. The calibrator display is a microprocessor-based color imaging display from Barco. Here it is used in a Contex design workstation by XYVision Design.

In addition to the calibration devices, new circuits incorporating more stable components are also part of the Calibrator. An ambient-light-controller module with two photocells is placed in opposite corners of the display. This corrects for any changes in room illumination that can affect the user's color perception.

Work continues on other approaches to soft displaying. Matsushita has shown their Beam Matrix flat color display. In the Beam Matrix system, which is unique to Matsushita, 28 linear electrodes about 4.8 inches in length are used instead of the conventional CRT electron gun. These electrodes emit 3200 electron beams, creating a small rectangular "unit screen" (Fig. 5–6). Digital control and drive circuits project the TV image onto these 3200 unit screens. The thickness of the display is 2.6 inches in the 6-inch model and 4 inches in the 16-inch model. Power consumption is almost equivalent to the conventional CRT color TV.

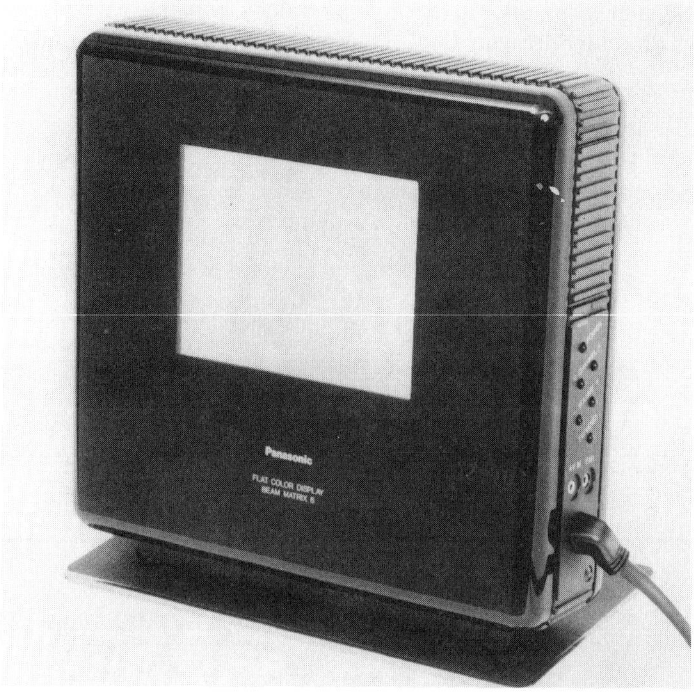

Fig. 5-6. A 6-inch Beam Matrix Color Flat Panel Display from Matsushita.

At the same time, the 40-inch liquid-crystal rear-projection television that they demonstrated used 312,000-pixel LCD panels. This 100-pound projection system was compact and had a depth of only 16 inches, thanks to wide field angle, mirror projection, lenses and a three-lens system (Fig. 5–7).

HARD-COPY PRINTS

There has been talk for many years of the paperless office, and certainly the home-entertainment center is a soft-viewing area for watching home entertainment video programs and events. For both the professional and general user, hard-copy prints are still a significant need.

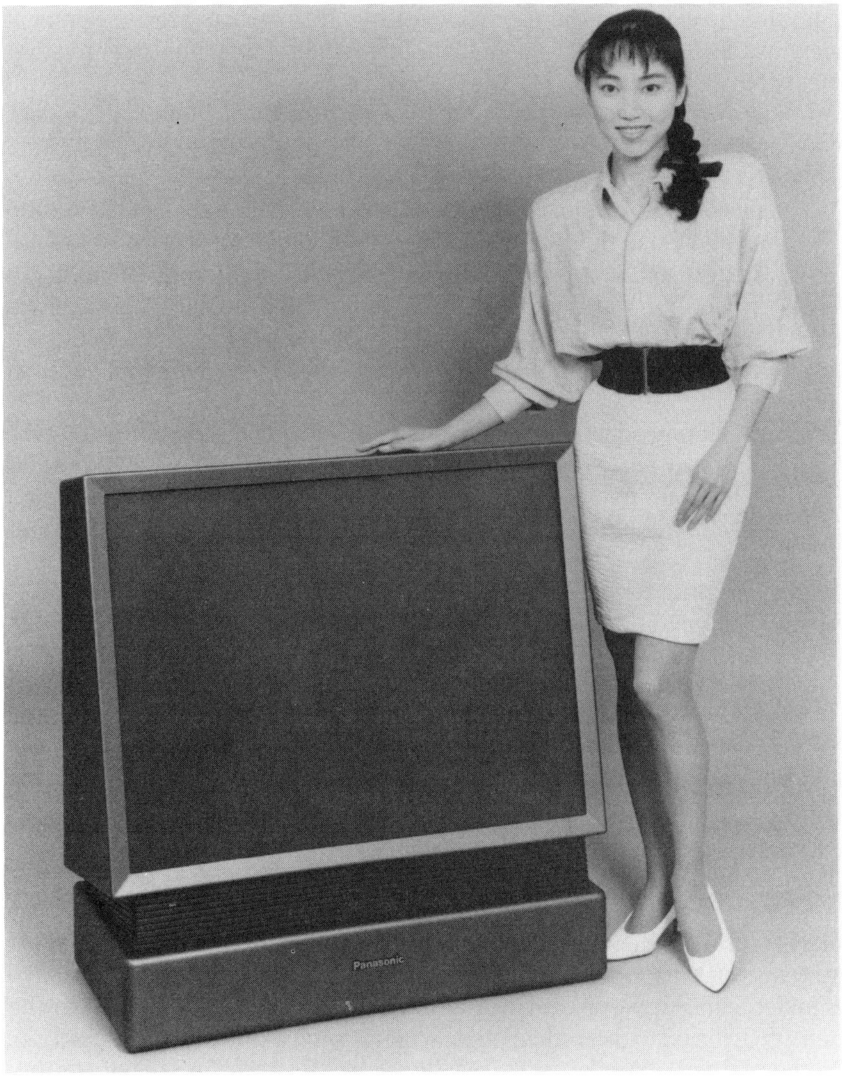

Fig. 5-7. Matsushita's 40-inch Liquid Crystal Rear Projection TV.

There are many approaches to creating prints from electronic images. Some work very well, some are merely adequate, and some leave much to be desired. Much depends on what the application for the prints will be. If prints are for publication, the resolution must match the resolution of silver-halide prints. Otherwise moiré patterns develop because of the inconsistencies between the graphic-arts screening process and the pattern that already exists on the electronic prints. If the prints are for personal viewing, the tolerance for quality can be broader, but some basic requirements must be met.

Some of the basic requirements to meet the needs of good-quality hard copy are:

1. The resolution must be high enough to reproduce all the information contained in the electronic version of the picture. The resolution of images will increase, as we saw with the addition of Hi-band still video. We will continue to see improved systems. This places a major obstacle to some of the available systems. The minimum resolution acceptable to the eye must be at least 200 dots per inch (dpi).
2. Color reproduction must be accurate with good separation of tones.
3. The gray scale reproduction for each color must be a minimum of 6-bits per color with a scale approaching that of conventional silver-halide photography. This could require 12 bits or more per color.
4. The print time must be 1 to 2 minutes for a completed print.
5. The system must be coupled easily to existing computer or video systems.
6. The finished print must give the appearance of a conventional silver-halide color photograph.

When you look at these criteria, there are some judgmental factors that will be based on individual preferences. Other conditions could be added such as storage life, unexposed storage life, as well as environmental impact of the print material and related supplies.

In discussing the various approaches to hard copies, two distinct forms of control over the scale of the images produced become apparent. In systems such as conventional silver-halide photography or thermal-dye transfer, either light or heat will create a proportional value equal to the density of the pixel desired. In other systems such as ink-jet, ion deposition, or thermal wax transfer, this variation is created by the size of the ink deposited or by breaking the single pixel down to micropixels and increasing or decreasing their size. This variation of the two basic systems is one of the reasons why thermal-dye transfer has won popular support today.

ELECTROSTATIC TONER PRINTERS

A number of different approaches are available for color printing. These include lasers, light-emitting diodes (LEDs), liquid-crystal shutter printers using fluorescent or halogen lamps, and ion deposition to create images on the paper using belts or other electrostatic transfer devices.

Although a resolution of 240 dpi does not qualify ion deposition as a prime candidate for image hard-copy output, it is a technology that should not be overlooked. At this resolution, the Delphax S-9000 series duplex printer is capable of outputting 180 pages per minute. Further developments by Delphax (co-owned by Dennison Manufacturing Co. and Xerox Corp.) are aimed at generating graphics at 180 impressions/minute with a resolution of 300 DPI.

Edward R. Pollard, Vice President of Ion Components Division of Delphax Systems described ion deposition this way, "Most people are fairly familiar with the spinning disks, rotating mirrors, dancing laser beams, and belts of laser printers," he said. "In contrast, the ion deposition process/system is quite straightforward; all parts are stationary, except the rotating drum."

Charges are created within the solid-state print cartridge, which houses a pair of electrodes separated by a dielectric. One electrode is exposed to the air by thousands of tiny, precisely pierced holes. The other is not and receives an rf signal that creates a high electric field (between the electrodes). The field breaks down the air molecules, creating a glow discharge at all the electrode intersections (in the dark, these glow points appear as blue specks).

Through a control system, charges are extracted selectively from this "dancing fire" (glow discharge), and deposited on a dielectric surface. Thus, the printing cycle starts with charges being pulled from a stationary solid-state cartridge and deposited directly onto the highly durable dielectric surface covering a rotating drum. This latent electrostatic-charge image is carried past a toning station, in which the charges attract a black toner particle that is a monocomponent magnetic element.

These toner particles, now adhering to the rotating dielectric drum, are carried to a location at which two process steps—transfer and fixation—occur simultaneously. This two-in-one transfixing step is unique to the ion-deposition process. It allows for the rapid and efficient transfer of the toner particles to a blank sheet of paper and the concurrent fixing of these particles to the sheet, creating the print.

The drum is a thick, hard, anodized, large-grain aluminum oxide (which, with certain additives, is commonly called *sapphire*). The surface of this drum can last for well over a million pages, as it is impervious to fingerprints, handling, and so on.

With completion of the fixation step, the faint toner residue on the drum is scraped from the dielectric surface by means of a simple steel blade that is applied against the aluminum oxide. The residual charge pattern, still in evidence, is then removed by bathing the rotating drum in the corona discharge of a special erase rod. This rod is a glass-coated dielectric wire surrounded by tungsten as a ground plane. A glow corona line along the entire length of the rod neutralizes the charge on the drum, in preparation for the next charge pattern/print cycle.

Everything on the periphery of the drum—erase, toner, etc.—stands still. The only moving part is the sturdy, central dielectric cylinder. Therefore, the paper path can be straight and short.

What lies ahead for this technology? Pollard says that the ion charges can be deposited on glass plates, mylar films, leather, and other materials. His company is working on a 480-dpi unit with toner and a 600-dpi unit using a liquid toner. As more research is done with liquid toners, he feels that resolutions of 1000 dpi and higher could be achieved. He also feels that color printing will be possible. Imagine your high-resolution color images being created at 180 pages per minute (3 per second)!

With the introduction of the Canon Color Laser Copier 500 and its intelligent processing unit (IPU), it is now possible to produce full-color copies from video equipment or computers (Fig. 5–8). Images are reproduced in full color with 256 gradations. The 400-DPI color copier produces results that look almost photographic from a variety of images, including still video cameras, computers, and scanned 35-mm slides. Smaller particle toners have been developed that produce even better image quality with higher resolution.

The Colorocs four-color electronic printer utilizes a patented single-pass-to-paper technology that produces color originals in full color or any single color, including true black (Fig. 5–9).

The Kodak Coloredge printer has been demonstrated only in a 1-bit/color depth, which limits the number of colors. The unit does produce 23 copies per minute, but is aimed primarily at graphic reproduction.

The ColorEdge plain paper copier-duplicator uses cyan, magenta, yellow, and black toners to create four-color copies of colored originals. The basic machine is equipped with a top-mounted platen cover and top-exit hopper. Combining superior quality, excellent image quality and 23-pages/minute output speed, the machine is expected to be embraced by quick printers, in-plant printers and in-house reproduction departments. Originals up to 11 × 17 inches can be reduced by as much as 64% to fit a standard 8.5-×-11-inch sheet.

In the carousel projector, a 35mm slide adapter will feature automatic slide advance and a choice of 6×, 4× or 2× magnification. At the 2× magnification setting, the slide image is printed in the right or left upper corner of the paper. Copy can be added subsequently to copies made from the slides.

A companion ColorEdge AC (Accent Color) copier-duplicator is de-

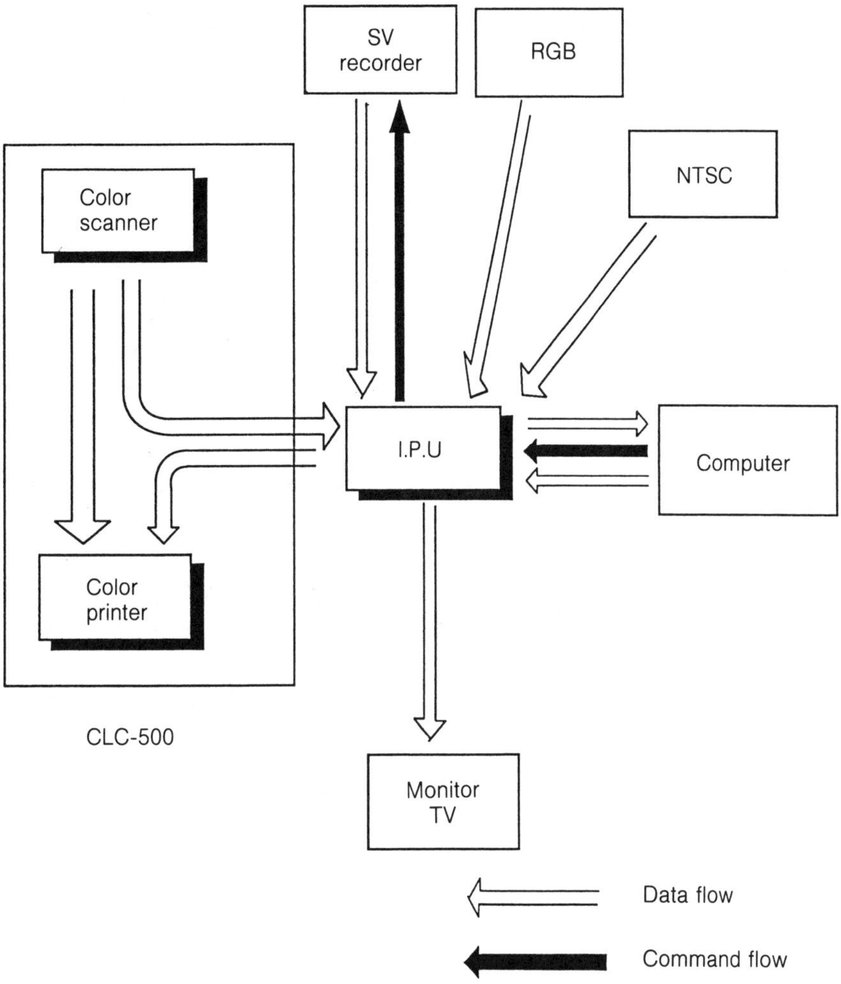

Fig. 5-8. A system configuration for the Canon Intelligent Processing Unit (IPU) showing the flow diagrams from computers, video images, monitor display output, color scanner, and color printer.

signed to add color to copies made from black-and-white originals. Three complete integral toning stations will produce copies in black, plus two colors, or any combination of three colors from a palette of eight (black, brown, green, yellow, cyan, magenta, blue, and red). The operator specifies the areas to be printed in a given color through use of an electronic wand on an editing board mounted on top of the copier. Areas of the original also can be erased selectively or covered up.

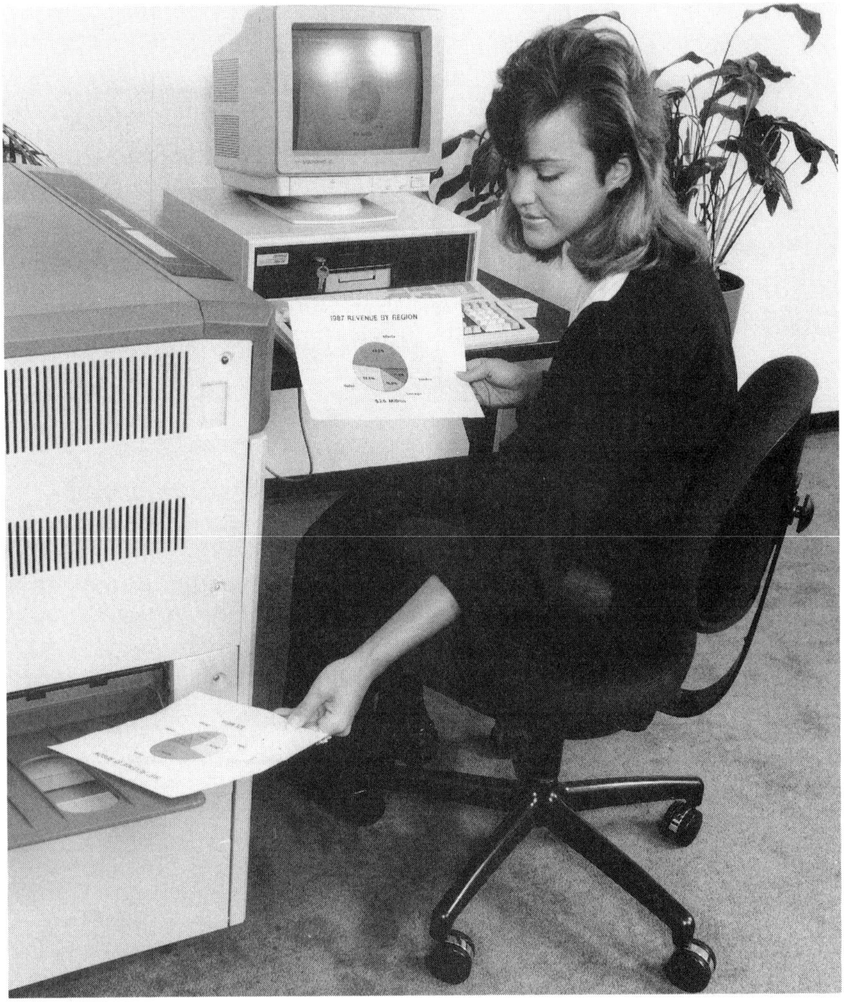

Fig. 5-9. The Colorocs full-color electronic printer operates at a speed of 5.7 pages per minute for 8 1/2-×-11-inch documents in four process colors.

If all three colors are used, the output rate is 23 copies per minute, but this rises to 46 copies per minute for two copies and 70 copies per minute for a single color. The basic machine includes a top-mounted platen, top-exit hopper, and variable zoom reduction from 100% to 64%. A positioner and sorter are offered as options.

New polyester-based small-particle imaging toners are translucent enough to act as filters to produce a rainbow of color combinations. They are designed especially to fuse well with transparency material on Estar base to create high-quality overhead cells.

The ColorEdge ferrite carrier particles that deliver the toner are much smaller than previous Kodak ferrite developers, allowing three color stations to fit in about the same space previously required for a black-and-white toning station alone.

For full-color copies, three exposure flashes are made through red, green, and blue filters to create separations on a moving photoconductive film belt, determining how much of their complementary subtractive color (cyan, magenta, and yellow respectively) is needed in the copy.

The belt moves to a set of three toner stations in which the appropriate toner is conveyed upward to the images on the frames. The belt continues to a transfer roller that conveys the colors consecutively from each frame onto the paper sheet. The paper is held in place on a 3-inch-diameter roller by two rows of vacuum holes that receive the cyan and magenta toners on successive revolutions before being released to receive the yellow toner and continue to the fusing station. There a heated roller fuses the colors to the paper.

The photoconductive belt has a built-in halftone screen on its backsurface so that the screen can be exposed automatically through the belt by an electroluminescent panel. This 133-line screen allows high-quality reproduction of continuous-tone photographs in the "photo" mode.

The electronic wand used with the ColorEdge AC creates a signal from a piezoelectric crystal when it is touched on the original. Two microphones built into the editing board detect the time differences between receipt of the signal, and through triangulation the relative coordinates of the position are automatically calculated.

Edited areas are squares, rectangles, or a combination of the two, and are indicated by touching points on the original to define these shapes. As many as 99 different areas can be indicated on a single original.

Unlike the full-color version, the accent color ColorEdge does not use a filter wheel, because no color information is available on the black-and-white original. The selective editing is actually a selective erase, with the copier deleting all image information except that to be reproduced in a particular color. The image is erased from the photoconductive belt by a light-emitting diode matrix that has 25 LEDs per inch.

The prototype High Speed Electronic Color Printer employs the LED light bar exposing system adapted from the Kodak Ektaprint 1392 printer. This uses a linear array of 3584 separate light-emitting diodes to expose simultaneously the image information over the entire width of the paper. Four exposures are made: black, cyan, magenta, and yellow. Using a negative/positive system, only the pixels representing image information present are exposed onto the photoconductive surface.

For text and graphics, this means that each LED element is on for 0.026 seconds per page, or 7.2 hours per million pages. With a 1000-hour average life for the LED, the array should last for more than 138 million pages. The toning and fusing operation is the same as for the ColorEdge.

Kodak also has demonstrated a feasibility model for an electronic high-speed color printer. The nonimpact 300 dpi LED array printer will output in 3 colors plus black at 17.5 pages per minute in full color, and 70 pages per minute for black and white directly from digital information. It is currently designed to work with input from the Kodak Ektaprint Electronic Publishing System (KEEPS) or to support mainframe color graphics packages for a variety of systems, including IBM and DEC. Potential uses are output of technical documentation and presentation graphics, including transparencies, CAD/CAM, and office publishing.

THERMAL-DYE TRANSFER

The most common and one of the best systems available for photorealistic color imaging is the thermal-dye diffusion process. Also called *dye sublimation* and *dye diffusion*, this process differs from the simple thermal-ribbon printing in a number of ways (Fig. 5–10). First, a color ribbon is used that is the same size as the finished print, with a section of cyan, magenta, and yellow dye each the size of the finished print so that the dyes are applied one at a time.

The receiver papers used are high-gloss finish similar in characteristics to conventional photographic paper. The dyes are partially translucent so that there is very good reflectance of the images through the dyes. Or, if the images are applied to a transparent receiver sheet (in some machines a

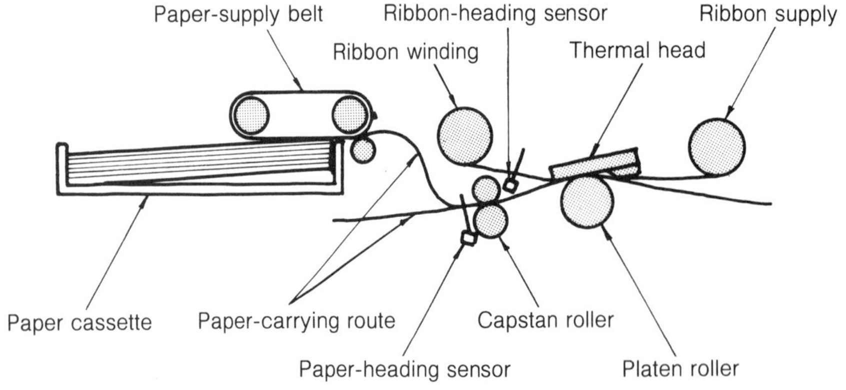

Fig. 5-10. A diagram of a dye transfer color printer.

double pass of color is made to increase the density of dyes), the result is an image that looks much like a conventional color transparency.

The really significant difference in the dye-transfer approach is the ability of the thermal head to heat to different degrees during printing. In this way, the transfer of the appropriate color of the intensity dependent on the number of bits of color called for produces a greater scale than any other electronic color print process except for writing to silver halide color paper or film.

A large variety of dye-transfer printers exist for sizes ranging from snapshots to 11 × 11 inches. The Canon Color Video Printer RP-420 produces 3 15/16-×-3-inch prints on 5 1/2-×-3 15/16-inch paper. In addition to a small print, a two-image print could be produced, with the large print taking 80 seconds and the small print 70 seconds.

The prototype of the Copal Dye-Transfer Printer produces a slightly smaller print than the Canon, with 256 gray scales/color in three minutes. The Fujix VP-6000 Video-Graphic Printer produces a 468-×-527-dot image in frame input mode with a print taking 90 seconds to complete. The Hitachi VY-50A printer produces a standard 100-×-128-mm print in 80 seconds. The VY-5000 printer from Hitachi produces an A4 image of 210 × 297 mm in 3 minutes with a maximum resolution of 1088 × 1728 or 150 dots/inch. The Hitachi VY-55A Color Video Printer prints a 3.9-×-5-inch picture with 260,000 colors and a resolution of 456 × 527 pixels (Fig. 5–11).

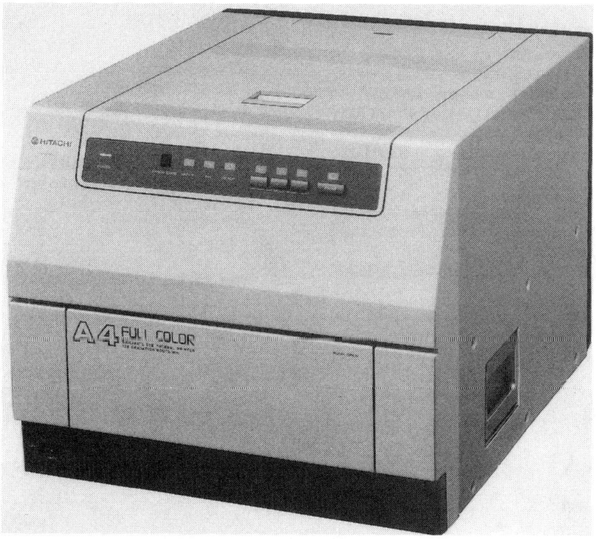

Fig. 5-11. The Hitachi A4 Color Printer produces full-page-size dye-transfer color prints.

Kodak has one of the more popular dye-sublimation printers. The original SV6500 has been upgraded to the SV-6510 color video printer (Fig. 5–12). The 6500 series printers produce 4-×-5.2-inch prints with 1/4-inch borders. A set of 512 individually heated points generates the pulses of energy that are transferred from the donor web to the receiver sheet of plastic coated paper. Up to 256 levels of tone for each primary color can be represented. The Kodak SV6500 series printers will operate not only with the PC, but also will interface with Apple's 32-bit color QuickDraw standard from the Macintosh II computer.

The Kodak XL7700 digital continuous tone printer uses a photographic quality image up to 11 × 11 inches (Fig. 5–13, color section). This printer is produced in a black-and-white and a color model with an actual 10-×-10-inch image area. Using a matrix of 2048 × 2048 pixels, a resolution of 200 dpi is provided.

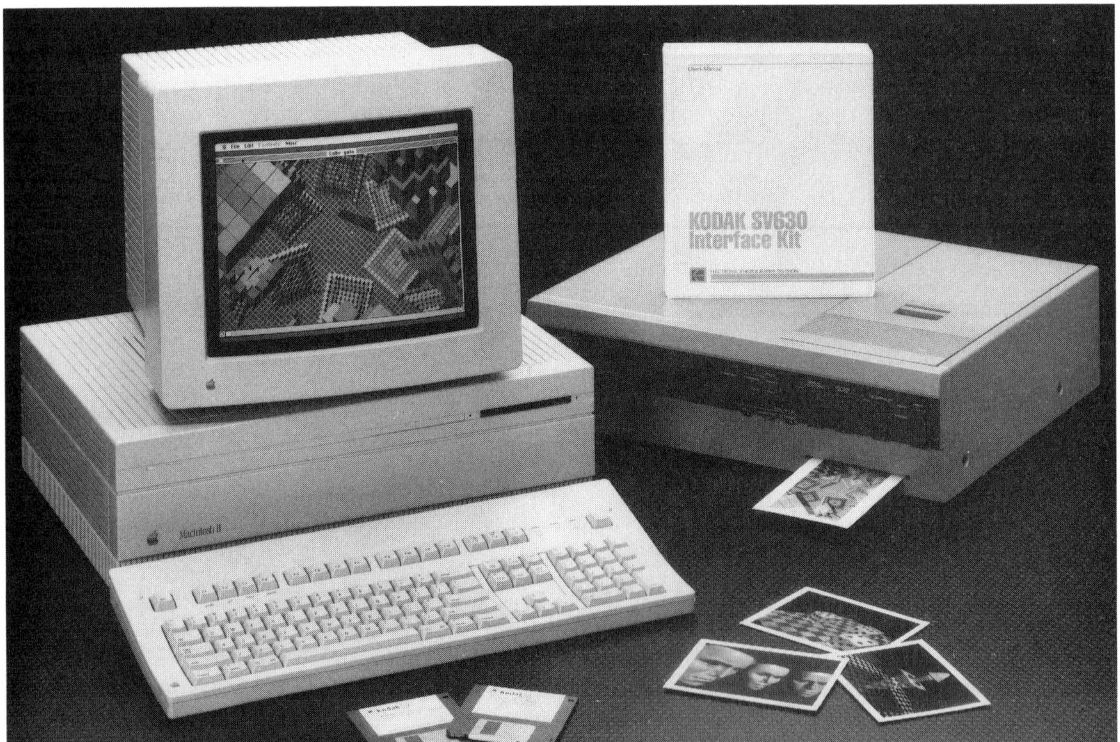

Fig. 5-12. The Kodak SV6500 Series Color Printer now has an interface kit for the Macintosh II, IIx, and IIc computers.

The printer uses Kodak Ektatherm media developed from a library of 15,000 different dyes in Kodak's organic chemical database. Major properties of the dyes are color reproduction, ease of transfer, stability, and solubility. The printing ribbon consists of a six-micron polyester support coated with two layers on each side. A layer on one side faces the print heating elements. The topmost slipping layer provides the lubrication needed to keep the print head from sticking to the ribbon (Fig. 5–14). This layer and the subbing layer underneath also protect the donor web from 300° to 400° Celsius temperatures produced by the print head. The other side of the ribbon comes into contact with the print. The outermost dye/binder

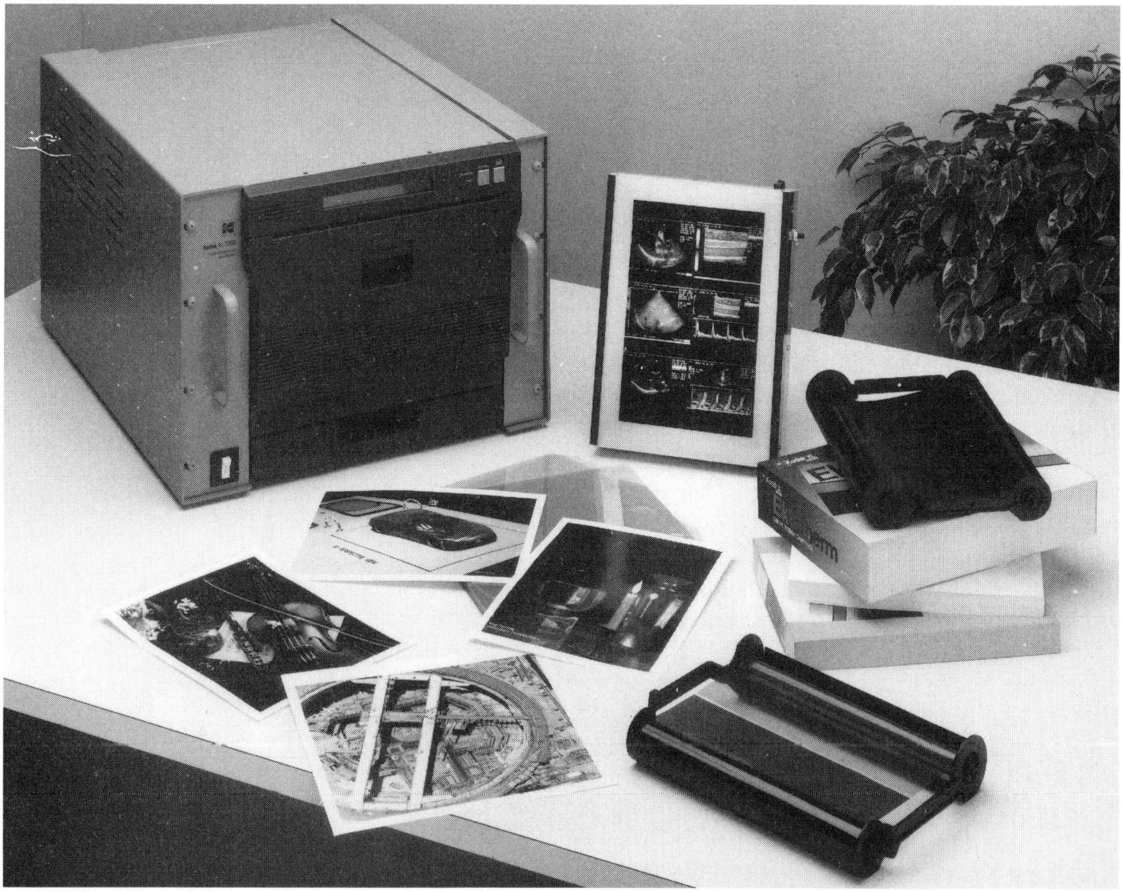

Fig. 5-13. The desktop size Kodak XL7700 Digital Continuous Tone Printer is shown with Kodak Ektatherm media and typical application prints.

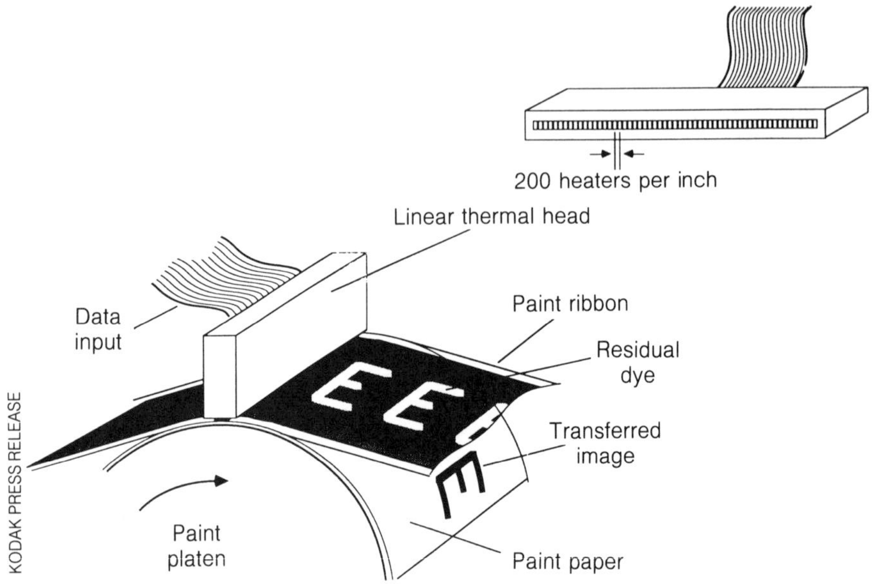

Fig. 5-14. A simplified drawing showing how a thermal image is produced by the Kodak XL7700 Digital Continuous Tone Printer.

layer contains the image-forming dye. Beneath this layer is a barrier subbing layer that provides adhesion to the ribbon and optical dye density in the final print (Fig. 5–15).

The print is made on either a piece of paper or a transparency film that resembles a conventional photographic product. Instead of a photographic emulsion, there is a special dye receiver layer on top followed by a subbing layer and compliant layer. The latter gives under pressure of any dirt sandwiched between the ribbon and paper and helps reduce the effect of any airborne particles on the finished image.

Mitsubishi has created a series of printers that includes the CP-100U for 3-×-4-inch prints that resolve at 640 dots with 64 color gradations. Also, there is a new large-format 6-×-8-inch machine with 162 dots/inch, but at a much lower cost.

The CP2 desktop color printer from Nikon produces a full 8 1/2-×-11-inch copy in 2 minutes, 40 seconds, with 256 steps for each color and a dot density of 8 dots/mm. Up to 10 copies can be printed in sequence. The Nikon full-color printer provides a 128 × 160 mm at 8 dpi on a 5.7-×-7.2-inch print paper (Figs. 5–16; and 5–17, color section).

Panasonic and Sanyo, as part of their introduction of still video

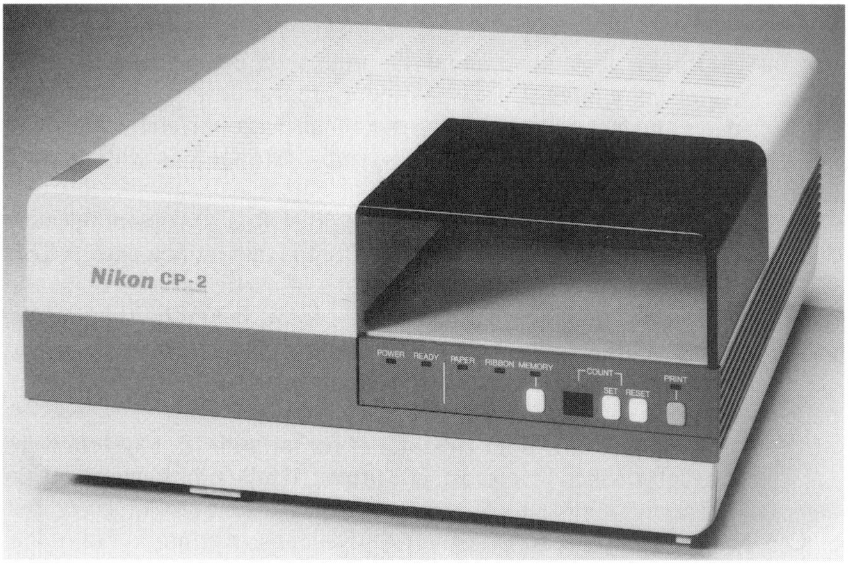

Fig. 5-16. The Nikon CP-2 Thermal Printer.

products, both have created printing units. The Panasonic AGE-EP70 video printer can take a normal print with an image size of 2 15/16 × 3 7/8 and divide that into 4, 9, 16, 25, or 36 squares with a minimum image size of 1/2 × 5/8 inch.

The Sanyo video print system has an image size of 4 3/16 × 3 1/8 inches and can produce multiple pictures of 4, 9, 16, or 25 images on one sheet of paper using an accessory image-processing unit. A 3-×-5-inch floppy disk can be used to store the edited images.

The Sony UP-5000 printer has a thermal head with 512 elements and produces a picture of 6 1/4 × 4 3/4 inches with 256 levels for each color.

Although the quality of the thermal transfer print has constantly improved, the speed of this approach as well as the economics are still shortcomings. In the case of the newer large-format prints, demonstrations generally are made with HDTV images with their 1125-line format or computer-scanned images with resolutions that match the capability of the new large-format printers. Standard still video images or images from conventional NTSC signals are not adequate for large-format printing without some degree of processing such as increasing the resolution through an averaging approach in which additional pixels are created by averaging adjacent pixels.

INK-JET PRINTING

Ink-jet printers have always had the promise of being a cost-effective way of creating color images. Early ink-jet printers suffered from problems of clogged jets and lack of speed. These problems were solved by improved ink jets that self-cleared each time the printing stopped as well as with improved inks.

For photorealistic applications, ink jets presented a problem because in their original form, they create an image that is one bit/color deep. This was improved later by creating different sizes of particles to increase the number of degrees of color shading. Some recent, but rather expensive, ink-jet printers have begun to show photorealistic results through the use of electrically charged particles that can be deposited in a series of micropixel portions to create shadings.

Canon's original color-print capabilities for the still video system were ink jets. The Canon Video Printer RP-601 provided full-color image using an eight-color cartridge system. This provided 64 gradations of color but lacked the saturation of their later thermal-dye-transfer printers (Fig. 5–18). Prints were 3 5/8 × 4 15/16 inches with a total time of 4.5 minutes per print. A Canon laminator was available that provided a protective finish and at the same time brightened the colors of the print.

Canon later introduced the FP510 color printer with the capability of producing 6-×-8-inch prints in approximately 8 minutes, 36 seconds, with 160 dpi. The FP510 printer used a unique diazo electric device to provide an

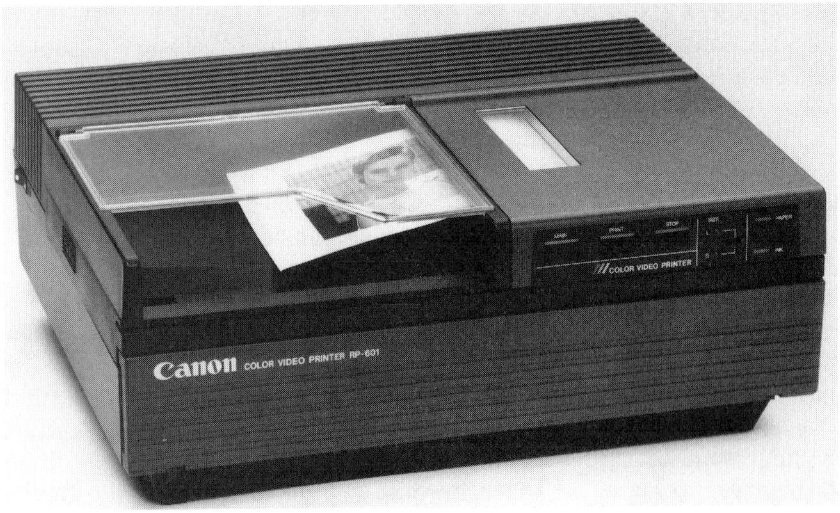

Fig. 5-18. The Canon Color Video Printer RP-601.

analog modulation that allowed microdots to be formed so that the dot diameter was actually changed to provide 64 gradations of color.

Imaging services were developed in the United States using the Fujix Jetgraphy 3000 printer. This printer produced 24-×-30-inch sheets from magnetic tape images. The results were photolike, with 64 gradations/color and a resolution of 2 pixels per mm.

Over the past few years, ink-jet technology has been refined to the point where the Fujix Jetgraphy 3000 printer from Fuji Photo Film, Co. is in regular use for printing large color images. Tone and color reproducibility has been improved by digital techniques to give the 64 gray levels per color necessary to produce a high-quality image. Although the description of the Jetgraphy system is specific to this machine, it will assist you in the understanding of ink-jet printing in general.

The Fujix system uses a Stemme-type drop-on-demand head. The head employs piezoelectric modulation of ink droplets to change the dot size (Fig. 5–19).

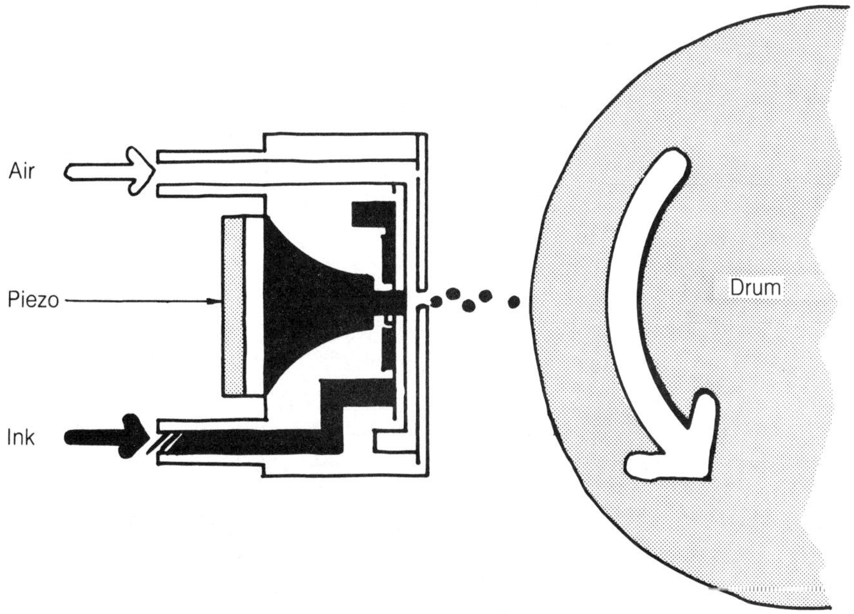

Fig. 5-19. A diagram of a piezoelectric modulated ink-jet printer.

A combination of dot matrixing and dot-size modulation is used to obtain the gray-level range. Each pixel consists of a 2-×-2 or 3-×-3 dot matrix, and the resolution is 6 dots per mm (150 dpi). The density is determined by the structure of the dot matrix, specifically the variation in the number of dots (0 to 4 in a 2-×-2 dot matrix and 0 to 9 in a 3 × 3 dot matrix) and the dot size or density (16 levels). Tone smoothing is provided through software.

As in standard full-color graphic-arts printing, the ink-jet system produces colors by using combinations of cyan, magenta, yellow, and black. For those who understand the conversion from photographic three-color to printing four-color, let's say that a common gray component is removed from the three color inks and replaced by a fourth color—black. This *under-color removal* (UCR) increases the shadow density and minimizes color ink consumption.

The system consists of an image-data-input section (magnetic tape is standard), a system-control section, and the ink-jet printer. It is also possible to read digital images stored on a floppy disk or to scan in and digitize data from colored originals, such as photographs. The processing section executes tone conversion, the UCR/black generation, and color-correction algorithms at high speed. The large drum printer, operating with four ink-jet nozzles, can produce a 728-×-600-mm (28.7 × 23.6 inches) image in 15.5 minutes. Printed images can be up to 2048 × 1800 pixels.

Several solid ink-jet systems were developed in Japan. Designed originally for creating animation cells, a solid wax was melted and projected onto a paper or acetate-base material to form a full-color image. The Howtek Pixelmaster was one such device designed to produce 8-×-10-inch prints in a compact desk-height unit. Based on technology developed by Juki in Japan, the Pixelmaster had a resolution of 240 dpi and could handle paper sizes up to 8 1/2 × 11 inches.

The Iris 3024 Printer is another example of a new, sophisticated level of ink-jet printers (Fig. 5–20, color section). Combining 32 levels of ink density with a 4-×-4 dither pattern, the printer shows 256 shades of gray for each of four colors—cyan, magenta, yellow, and black. The Iris Series 3000 ink-jet technology is an example of how ink jets have evolved in the past few years. The majority of lower cost ink-jet printers use a *drop-on-demand* ink-jet technology. With this technology, the ink is pumped through the ink nozzle only when a mark is to be made on the paper. Continuous ink-jet technology, as utilized in the Iris printer, directs the flow away from the image area when marks are not wanted on the page. The drops are given an electronic charge and the stream is deflected into a gutter.

The Iris 3024 produces photographic quality, continuous-tone prints with the use of variable-dot technology. With this technology, up to 31 different sized dots can be formed and placed on the medium. The printer has resolution options of 200, 240 (Iris standard), or 300 dots/inch. The Iris 3024 printer can handle sheets from 8 1/2 × 11 inches to 24 × 24 inches. The system uses nontoxic water-based dyes, yellow, magenta, cyan, and black.

With four ink cartridges of yellow, cyan, magenta, and black, the Sharp JX-720 printer uses a head-cleaning station that minimizes nozzle clogging problems. A 1024-×-1024-dot color image takes 2.2 minutes.

The Tektronics ColorQuick ink-jet printer is a 216-dpi device designed for use in the Macintosh environment. In addition, the Tektronics has other printers for ink-jet and thermal-wax recording of graphic images.

THERMAL RIBBON PRINTERS

A number of different thermal printers are available that provide a wax medium for creating direct color images at a 300-dpi level (Fig. 5–21, color section). Although these systems appear excellent for photorealistic images, they suffer from a lack of gradation because all of the ink spots are transferred if they are above the melting point. Printers from Bruning, Calcomp, Panasonic, and others are used primarily for graphics applications. Some of their characteristics are small size, quiet, and have the ability to produce full-color pages for graphics presentations. Because of the limited gradation capability, thermal recording printers will probably continue to serve the function of graphics printing in the future.

PHOTOGRAPHIC ELECTRONIC-IMAGING SYSTEMS

Silver-halide color photographic paper and film still provide an excellent medium for the generation of digital imaging using either conventional, nonconventional, or dry processes.

Agfa CRT Scanner Print System

The Agfa CRT Scanner Print System which is a fully electronic image-processing system (Fig. 5–22). Originals are first scanned, converted to digital information, and stored. The stored image can be modified in a variety of ways before it is exposed to conventional color photographic paper in dot form with a CRT. Although the system was designed for printing from slides, it has been used successfully for printing from digitally captured images as well.

Demonstrations of similar products using lasers to print on conventional photographic paper show the promise of reaching levels of 300 to 400 dpi with a quality equal to that of conventional color imaging.

Cycolor

At the end of 1987, Mead Imaging announced a new, full-color reproduction technology called Cycolor, based upon a film coated with light-

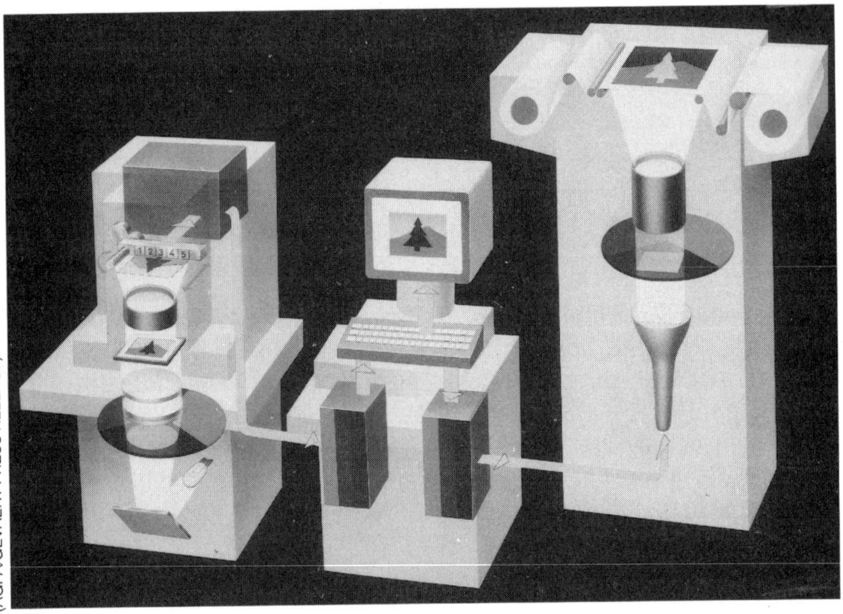

(AGFA/GEVAERT PRESS RELEASE)

Fig. 5-22. A function diagram of the Agfa CRT Scanner Print System with the (left) slide scan unit, digital-image processor, and CRT Printer.

sensitive, image-forming microcapsules that rupture under pressure for transfer to a receiving sheet. This nonsilver color-imaging material is an outgrowth of the technology employed in carbonless paper. Mead Imaging, a division of Mead Corporation, was formed in 1984 to develop and commercialize this new color process. Charles Joiner, Mead Imaging president, stated that the mission of the company is "to bring color to everyday business communications."

The product is expected to find application in markets in which low cost and dry processing are especially attractive. These include office copiers, 35-mm slide printers, color computer printers and color hard-copy devices for electronic cameras. Cycolor should meet the need for low-cost color desktop publishing and a variety of digital-imaging techniques. Mead Imaging plans to continue improving reproduction quality and sensitivity and to manufacture both reflection and transparency materials. The company does not plan to produce any hardware and has forged partnerships with eight companies to produce compatible hardware. These included Noritsu Koki, Dainippon Screen, Greyhawk Systems, Seiko Epson, Seiko Instruments, and Brother Industries as well as two unidentified companies.

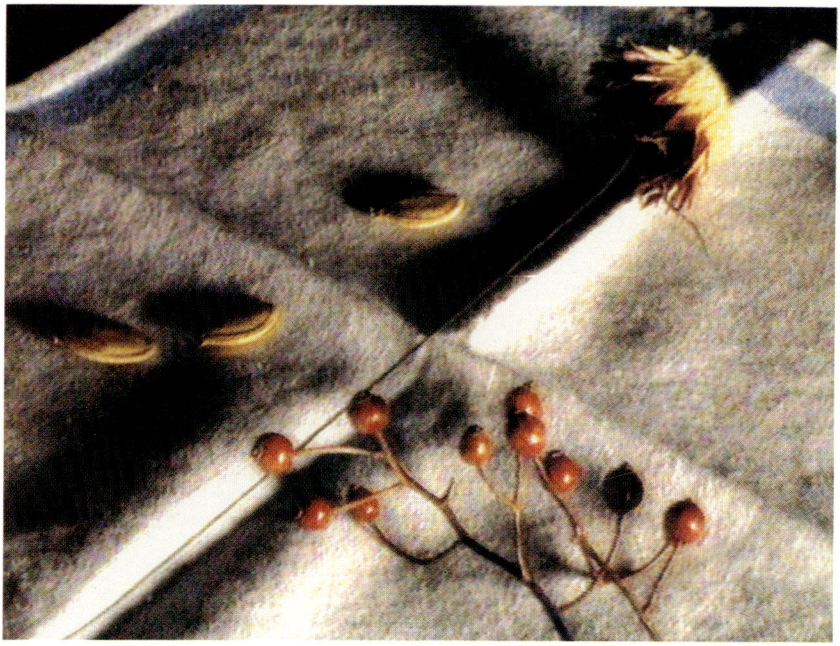

PHOTO BY DOUGLAS FORD REA, 1989

Fig. 1-5. Still life, Canon 701 Still Video Camera and printed on a Kodak 6500 Video Printer.

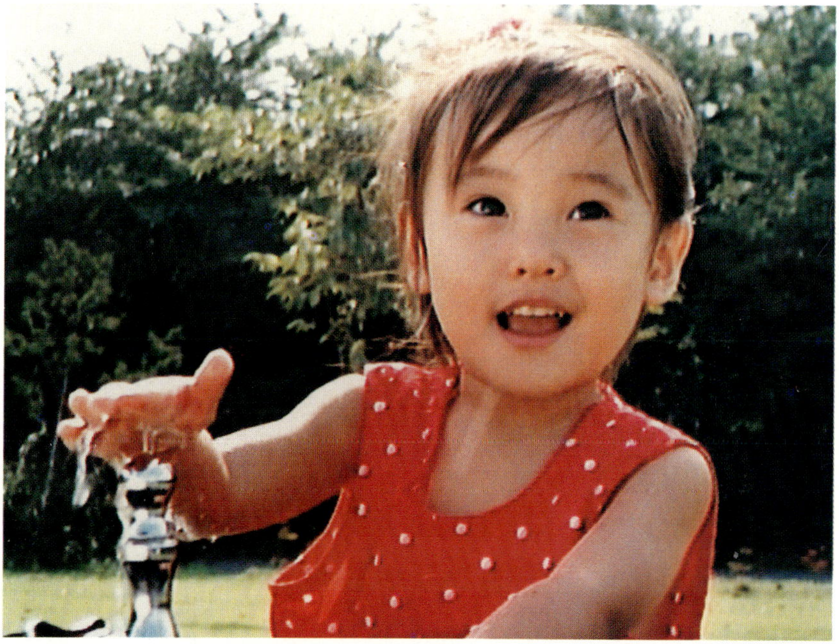

Fig. 1-10. A still video print photographed originally with a Fujix Still Video Camera.

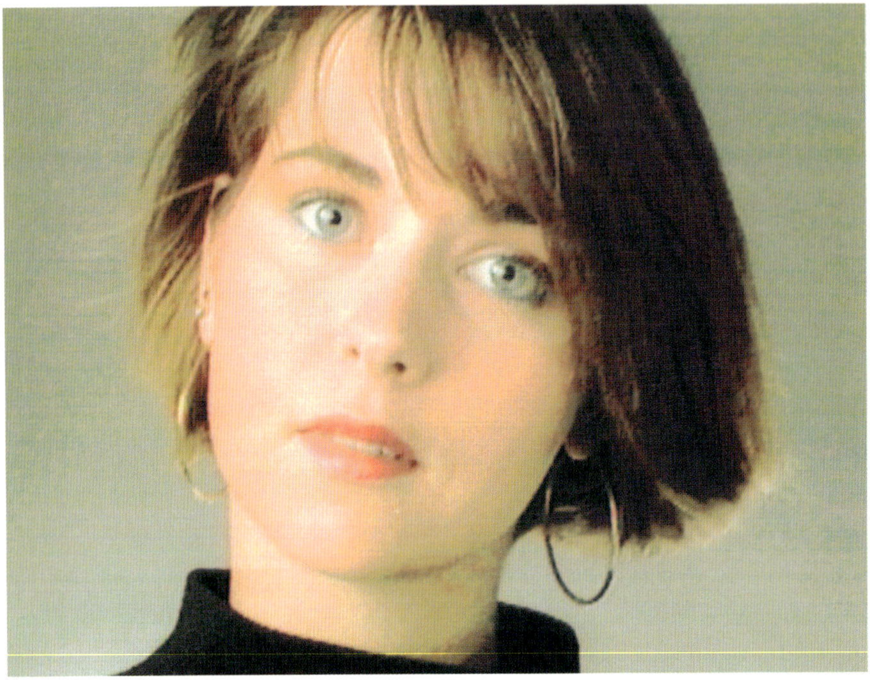

PHOTO BY CHRIS KAHLEY, 1989

Fig. 1-11. (top) Photographed with a Canon Still Video Camera, printed on a Canon ink-jet printer (Courtesy Rochester Institute of Technology).

Fig. 1-12. (right) Photographed with a Canon Still Video Camera, printed on a Canon ink-jet printer (Courtesy Rochester Institute of Technology).

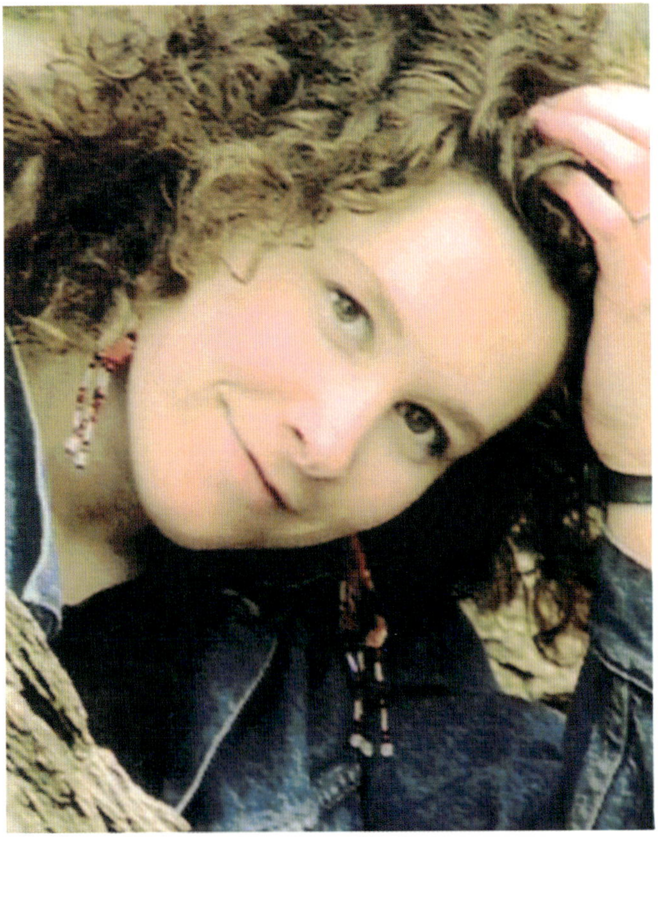

PHOTO BY PAUL MAPLE, 1989

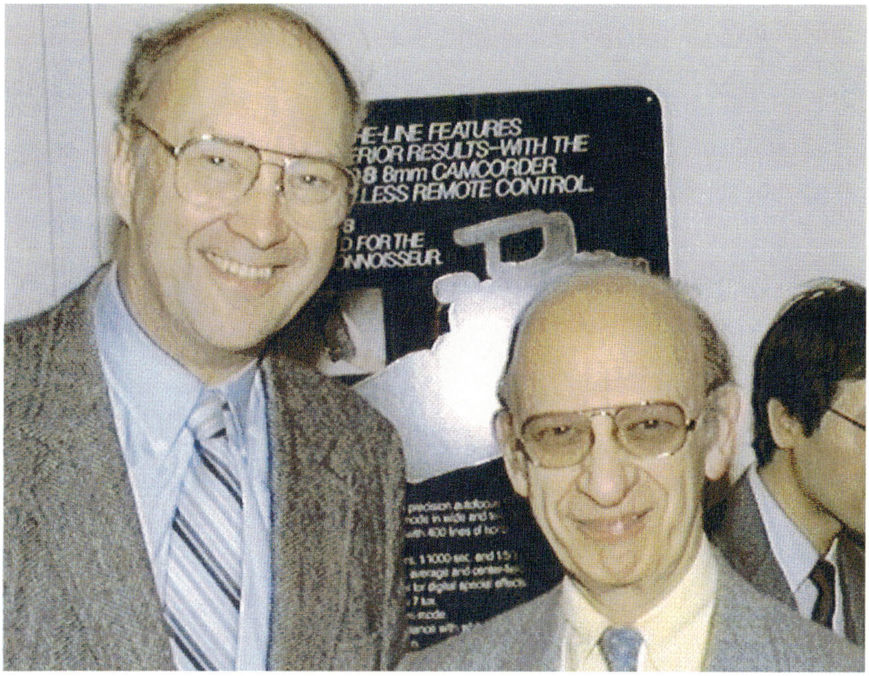

Fig. 1-18. Left, the author; right Herbert Keppler, Publishing Director, Popular Photography. *This is a Canon ink-jet print of an original photograph made with a Canon RC-760 Still Video Camera.*

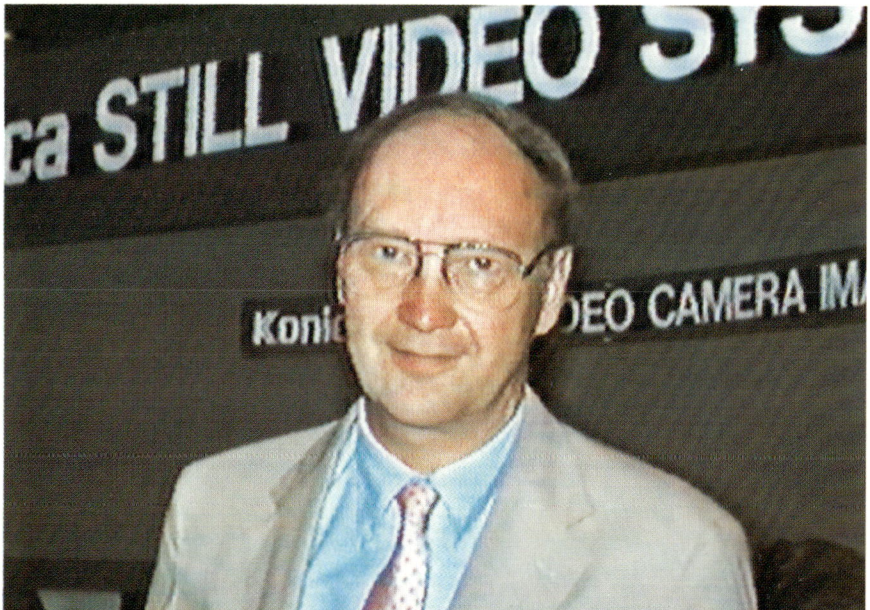

Fig. 1-25. Author photographed with a Konica Still Video Camera and printed on silver halide color paper in the Konica Video printer using smoothing algorithms.

PHOTO BY BRUCE STRONG, 1989

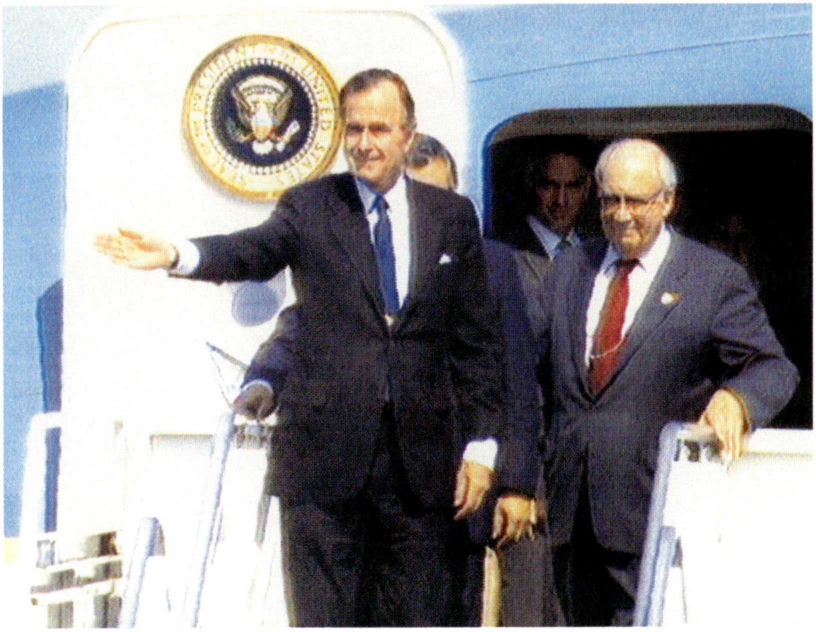

Fig. 1-31. (left) Typical news photograph. Photographed with a Canon 701 Still Video Camera and printed on a Kodak 6500 Video Printer (Courtesy Rochester Institute of Technology).

Fig. 5-17. (bottom) A sample print from the Nikon CP2 Thermal printer (Courtesy Nikon).

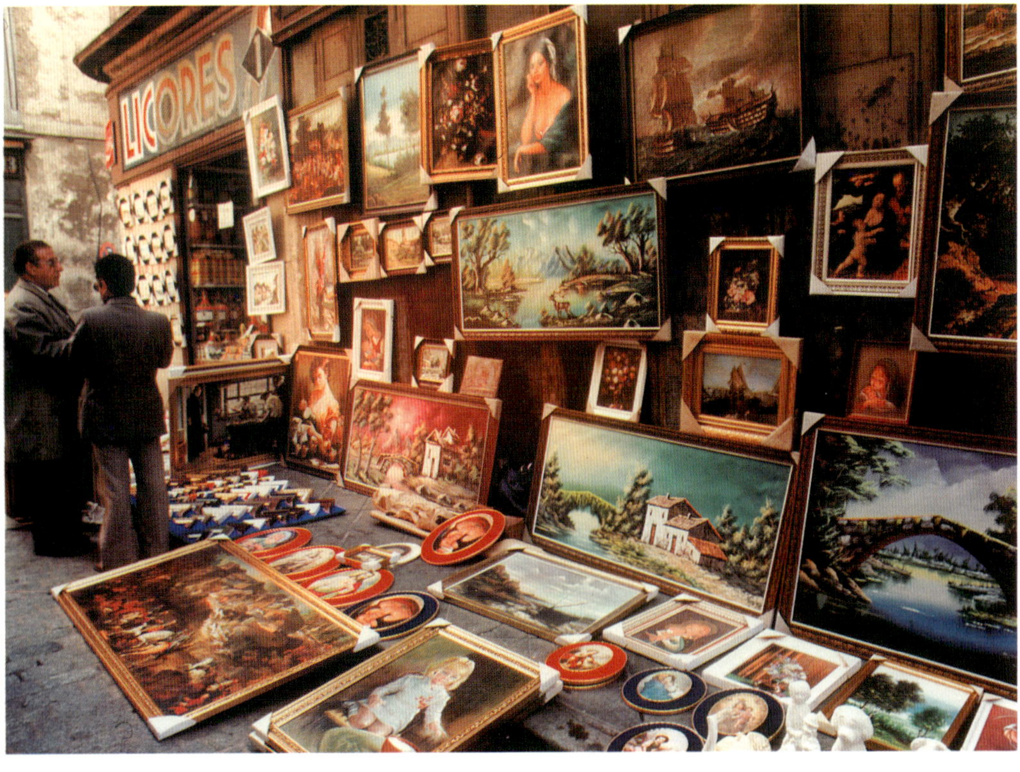

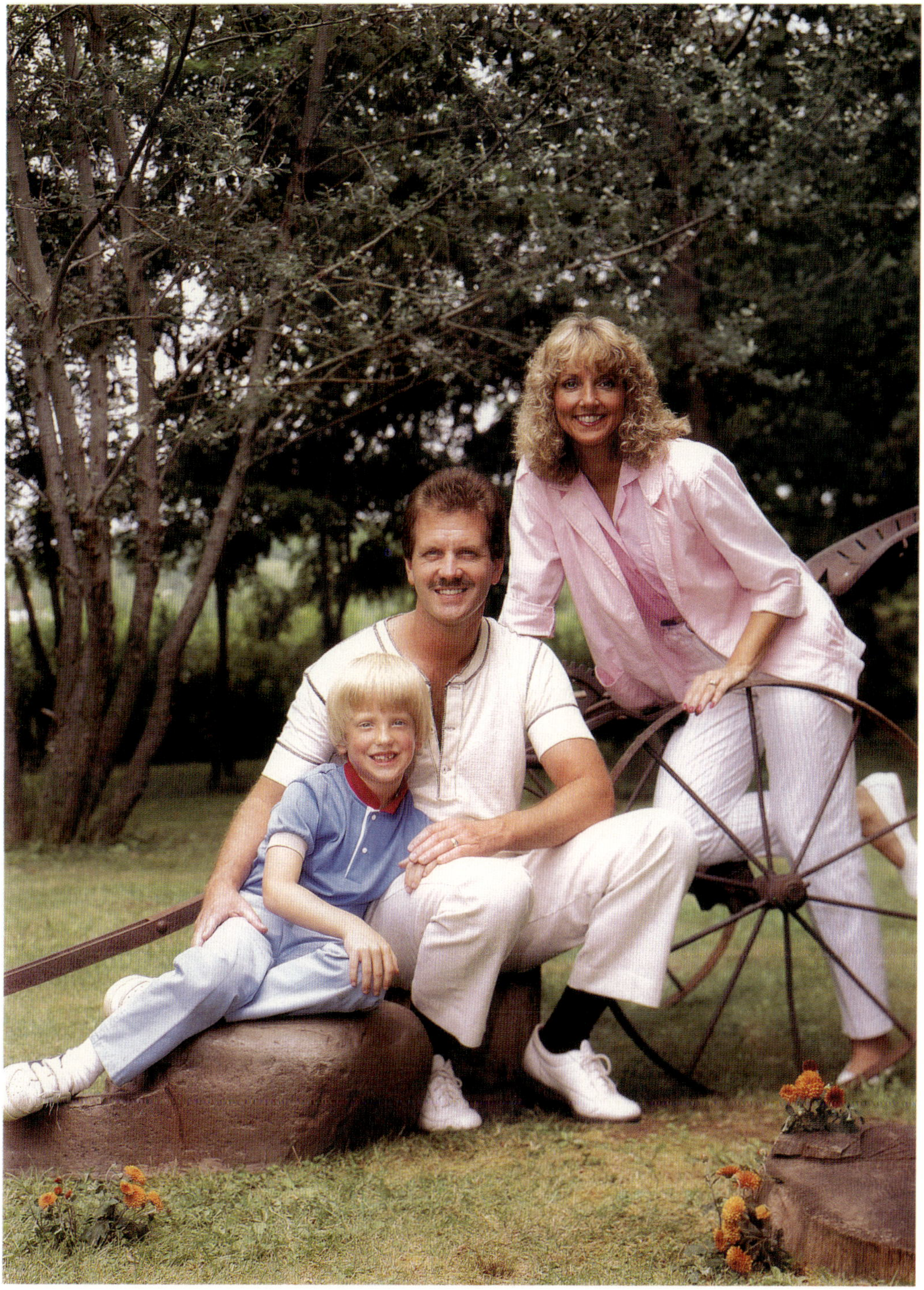

Fig. 5-15. A color print made from a scanned film image and printed on the Kodak XL7700 Digital Continuous Tone Printer (Courtesy Eastman Kodak Co.).

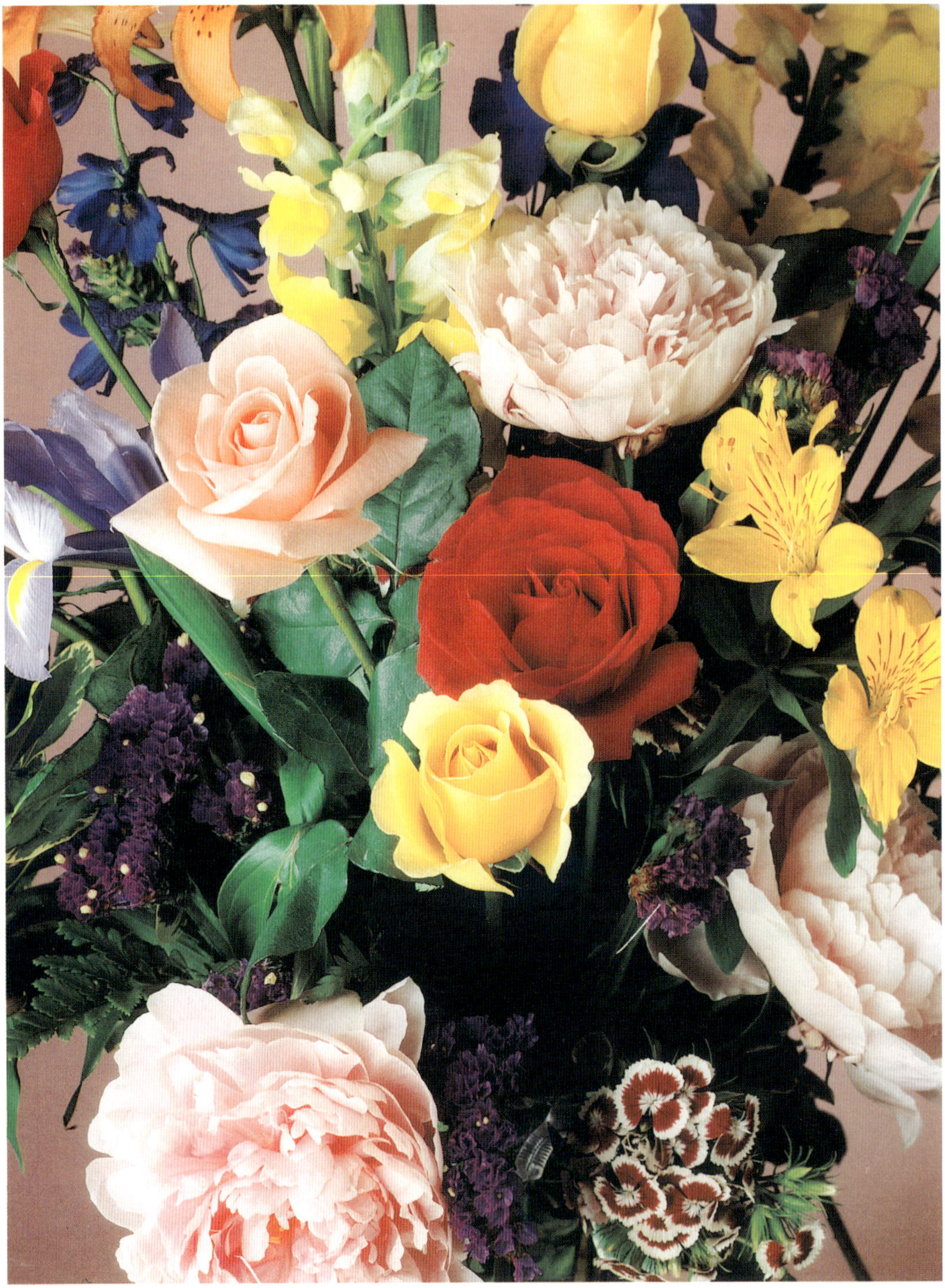

Fig. 5-20. A print from an Iris 3024 Ink-Jet Printer.

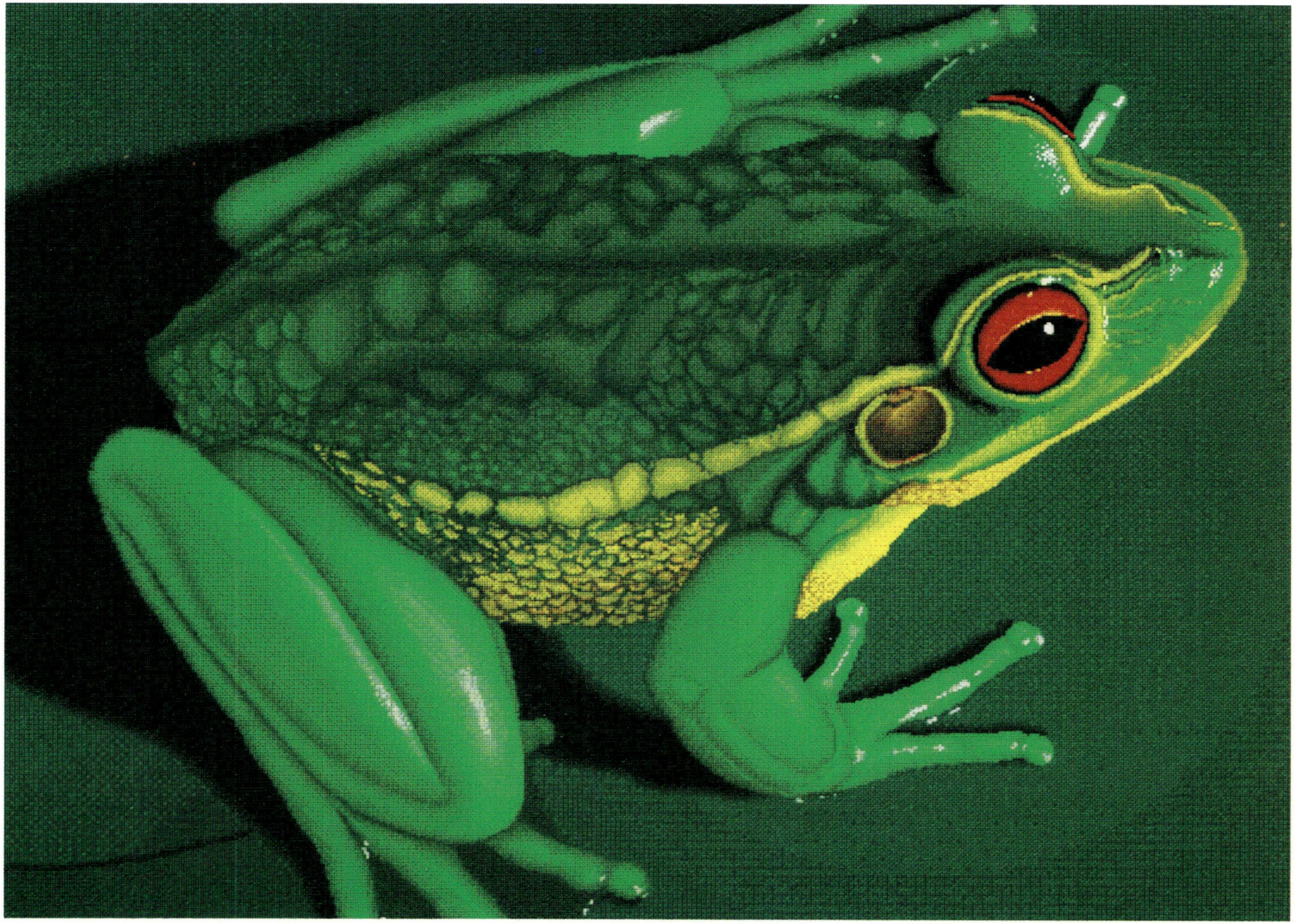

Fig. 5-21. A thermal ribbon print from Seiko Instruments (Courtesy Seiko Instruments USA, Inc.).

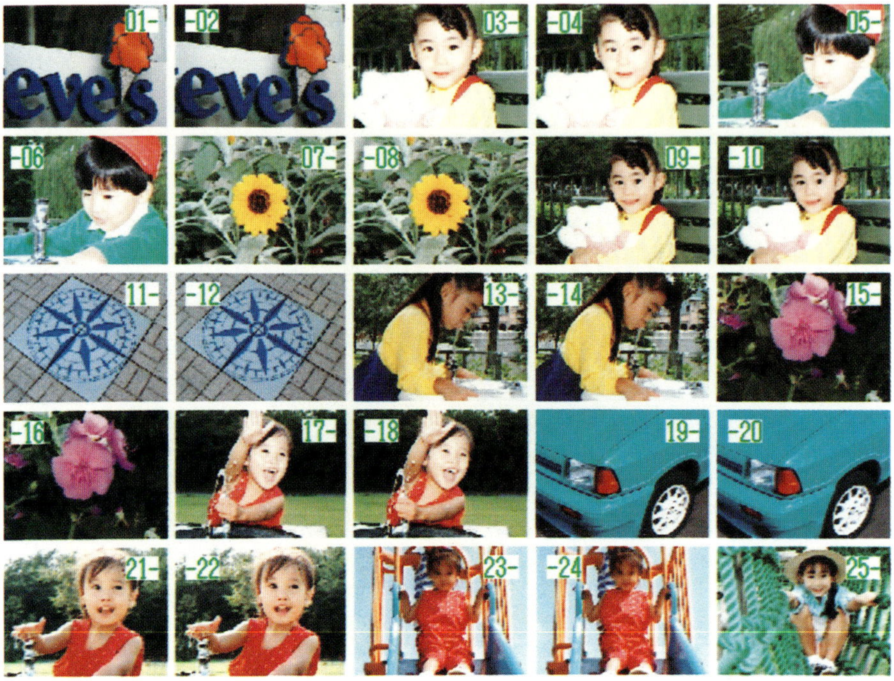

Fig. 7-2. An electronic proof of a still video floppy disk printed by Fuji from a Fujix still video camera (Courtesy Rochester Institute of Technology).

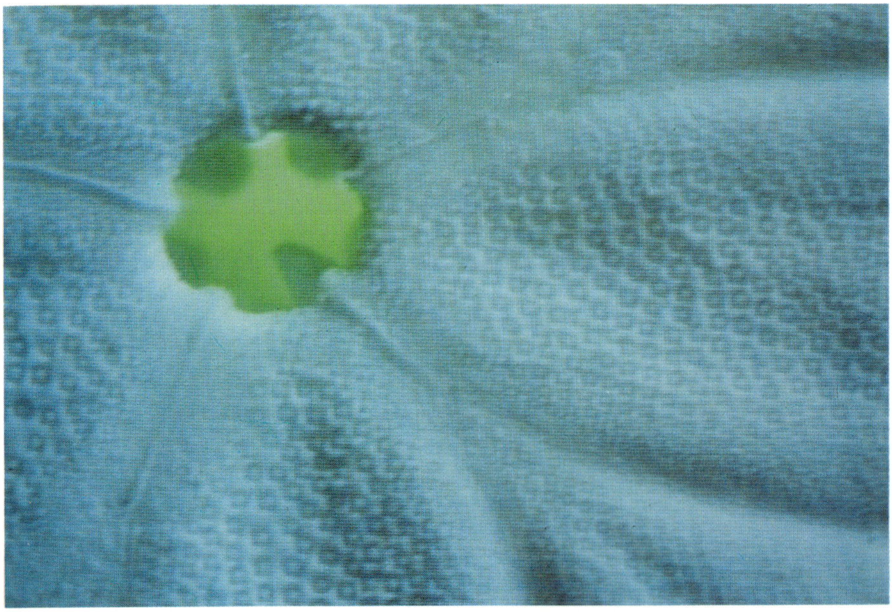

PHOTO BY W.W. DUBOIS

Fig. 7-3. A still video photograph made with a Minolta still video camera back using a Bogen light modulation macro stand (Courtesy Rochester Institute of Technology).

The Cycolor system evolved from work carried out at Mead Corporation over the past several years on the microencapsulation acrylate process. The early Mead color process required UV or blue light to produce images, thus limiting the product to artificial color separation techniques with three narrow exposure bands from 350 to 450 nm (nanometers).

During October 1985, a breakthrough led to the discovery and development of efficient photoinitiators that are sensitive to the visible spectrum, rendering the process panchromatic. The prototype Cycolor product has been optimized for the light emitted by a quartz-halogen lamp. The Cycolor process requires a light-sensitive donor film and a receiving paper or film for the transfer and color-image formation.

The donor film consists of a single coated layer with a mixture of microcapsules that are a few microns in diameter. Each microcapsule contains an acrylate monomer with a photoinitiator sensitive to red, green or blue light, and a color-former (leuco dye) to produce cyan, magenta, or yellow color. These microcapsules are called *cyliths*. Upon exposure to red, green, or blue light, the monomer polymerizes and hardens, making the microcapsule resistant to rupture. Thus, a latent image is formed as an imagewise pattern of hard (exposed) and soft (unexposed) capsules.

The visible image is developed mechanically by compressing the exposed sheet in contact with the receiver sheet (transparency or paper) through a set of rollers. Only the soft (unexposed) capsules rupture and release the leuco dye dissolved in the monomer onto the receiver sheet. The dye former reacts with the coating on the paper or transparency to produce a visible, direct positive of the original image by the subtractive process.

For example, exposure of the film to red light hardens the monomer containing the cyan color-former so that no transfer of cyan occurs. The microcapsules containing the magenta and yellow dye-formers are ruptured under transfer pressure and a red image is formed. In like manner, exposure to green light controls the magenta, and blue light controls the yellow dye transfer. Dyes are formed in the receiving sheet in proportion to the intensity of blue, green, or red light in the original subject. A short heating cycle enhances color saturation.

Although Mead Imaging claims photographic-like color reproduction for the prototype product, the markets selected for the initial applications are more likely to accept the overall quality of Cycolor when coupled with the low-cost and dry-processing features of this color product. Granularity corresponds to a moderate-to-coarse level of graininess in a photographic material. As previously noted, Cycolor can resolve 20 to 30 cycles/mm when optimally exposed through a high-contrast target.

Cycolor compares favorably with thermal transfer and conventional ink-jet printing in overall quality, but recent developments in ink-jet technology applied to color proofing systems has produced enhanced sharpness and tone reproduction characteristics.

Fujix Pictography 1000

Fuji Photo Film Co., Ltd. has created a new color photosensitive material. This material uses silver-halide grains as a sensor to light, and already is producing hard copies in the Fujix Pictography 1000 Series printer.

The process is a heat-development/dye-transfer type, requiring only a small amount of water as the transfer solvent. Because it is free from any specific and coupling process, any diffusible dye can be used.

Separate photosensitive and image-receiving sheets make up the material. For those technical readers, the major components of the image-sensing sheet are photosensitive silver halides, organic silver salts that accelerate development, dye releasing redox (DRR) compounds, and a basic metal compound substantially insoluble in water. The image-receiving sheet consists of a polymeric mordant, a chelating agent that reacts with the basic metal compound and consequently generates a base, and a binder. The two-sheet system provides better preservation of the photosensitive material before processing.

There are four steps in the image-forming process. In a fashion similar to photographic film, step 1 is the exposure of the photosensitive sheet to light forms latent images corresponding to the amount of light reaching the material.

A small amount of water is coated on the photosensitive sheet to assure uniform image transfer (step 2). Ordinary drinking water is suitable for this step. The process requires about 10 grams/sq meter (1 gram/$foot_2$), which corresponds to a water layer thickness of about 10 microns. This is absorbed into the sheet in about one second.

In step 3, the image-receiving sheet is placed on top of the water-absorbed photosensitive sheet. The combination is heated to about 90°C, which stimulates the chemical reactions that develop the dye image in the photosensitive sheet and transfer it to the image-receiving sheet. The time needed for this development/transfer is about 20 seconds.

Finally, in step 4, the image-receiving sheet, now containing the color image, is peeled away. The resulting dye image is quite sharp, providing a resolution of 20 line pairs/mm or better.

The arrangement of the photosensitive layers in the material is similar to that in photographic film. Normally, the layers are sensitive to blue, green, and red light. However, in the Pictography 1000 Series printer, light-emitting diodes are used for exposing the sheet. These are in the yellow, red, and near-infrared regions of the spectrum, and the material has the corresponding spectral sensitivities.

3M Color Dry Silver

Similar to photographic media, 3M Color Dry-Silver media has three distinctive layers: red sensitive, green sensitive, and blue sensitive. When heat is applied after these layers have been exposed to light, they form images of cyan, magenta, and yellow. Processing for 5 to 10 seconds at 270°F (135°C) is required, although temperature variations of up to 5°C can be tolerated without any significant color imbalance or curve shape changes.

Although the dry silver-image-forming mechanism is very different from wet silver halide, the latent image-forming mechanism is analogous. Silver halide is used as the light-capturing compound. The energy required for exposure is less than 50 ergs/cm_2, and no reciprocity law failure has been observed from 240 seconds to less than one millisecond of exposure time. This characteristic makes dry silver a good medium for hard copy from electronic systems. Resolution is in excess of 100 line pairs per mm.

A second-generation dry silver color material (peel-apart) material has already been demonstrated by 3M and is more suited for photographic applications. Applications for color dry silver include industrial design, color flow mapping in medicine, and video printing.

Here is one application for the color dry silver product that was presented by Michael McQuade of 3M Digital Imaging Applications Center. Although specifications for the production version of this laser image remain to be finalized, the prototype provides high-quality continuous-tone color digital hardcopies.

Based on multiple-laser-diode imaging, the printer rapidly outputs photographic-quality images up to 12 × 18 inches on paper that is developed in EP-2 or compatible chemistry in an integral processing system. The proprietary three-color photographic paper and film materials are spectrally sensitive to three infrared wavelengths, producing subtractive color with yellow, magenta, and cyan dyes.

The choice of three infrared-emitting semiconductor laser diodes provides a significant cost savings in comparison to gas lasers in two areas: the inherent cost of the light source itself and the cost of the modulation mechanism (these lasers can be directly modulated). A second advantage is the small size of these lasers, which are little more than the size of a pin head and require only a small optical subsystem. The final advantage is reliability, with an operating lifetime of over 10,000 hours with no warm-up requirements. This means that the lasers are "on" only during actual exposure.

To overcome thermal drifting and a phenomenon known as *mode hopping* (wherein the diode jumps between various internal oscillation modes), a proprietary feedback method monitors and stabilizes the output. The net result is continuous energy control over a dynamic range sufficient to expose conventional photographic materials.

A special photosensitive material has been developed by 3M based upon its color paper technology, which exhibits characteristics typical of conventional photographic color papers. To match the outputs from the laser exposure module, the standard red, green, and blue spectral sensitizing dyes have been replaced by spectral sensitizers peaked in the near-infrared region of the three lasers at 780 nm, 830, nm, and 890 nm. These wavelength separations are substantially narrower than the 150 nm typical of conventional color papers. Consequently, the photographic speed and secondary absorption characteristics of each layer and the relative exposure power of the light sources have been carefully adjusted to provide maximum color separation. Both resin-coated (RC) print and transparent, polyester-based materials have been produced. They give subtractive images based on conventional yellow, magenta, and cyan color-forming dyes. This material can be processed in either washwater or washless (stabilization) EP-2 color chemistry.

The prototype system prints at 300 pixels per inch in both the horizontal and vertical directions. This is sufficient to produce a photographiclike quality when viewed by the unaided eye. Each pixel is imaged as one continuous tone point and is specified by eight bits of red, green, and blue image information. Measurements by 3M indicate that the exposure system/media combination is capable of reproducing greater than 128 unique color levels for each primary color. By using 12-bit output control on each channel, the output has no discernible color quantization.

In contrast to normal photographic exposure systems, which expose one primary at a time and rely on accurate registration, the 3M system exposes all three colors simultaneously. The exposure system, control electronics, and media all are capable of sustaining a continuous exposure speed of 2 inches/second.

The system can expose materials up to 12 inches wide, and the prototype will provide print sizes from 8 × 8 inches up to 12 × 18 inches. Preliminary specifications indicate a production speed of two 8 1/2-×-11-inch prints/minute. From discussions with 3M personnel, the difference between printing speed (2 inches/sec) and production speed is because of constraints in digital-image data processing. If the full printing capabilities of the unit could be utilized, the potential exists for an output of 15 8-×-10-inch prints/minute, or 900 8-×-10-inch prints/hour.

Initial applications of this technology are expected to be in the medical imaging field (3M's monochrome Laser Imager already has become very well accepted in this field); computer design, analysis, and simulation (CDAS); remote sensing; and color electronic prepress systems in graphic arts.

However, the potential for coupling such a printer to an electronic image manipulation system is exciting. Because the system accepts digital signals, it will operate with the data from retouching/manipulating workstations. Initial experimentation in 3M's laboratory shows that the output is capable of being enlarged photographically beyond the maximum 12-inch × 18-inch size, and also is capable of rescanning and retouching using methods appropriate for original art film. This new technology offers great promise in many fields, including electronic photography.

Konica Video Color Printer

Konica developed and demonstrated a Konica color-video printer that produced 111- × 144-mm prints in 7 1/2 minutes with conventional processing. Using a 6-inch fiberoptics tube with a blue, green, and red stripe color filter, the color paper was contact exposed. The density range capability of the prints was 0 to 2.5 reflective density with a gradation of 256 steps.

Light-Valve Technology

Kodak developed new imaging technology in their LVT (Light Valve Technology) Company (Fig. 5–23). As a light-modulation method, PLZT (lead lanthanum zirconate titanate) linear modulators were used. The contrast range of these light modulators is greater than 1500:1, which is more than adequate for good shadow detail on conventional photographic films and papers. The Light Valve Technology Model 1620 image recorder can produce images of up to 16 × 20 inches. The recorder uses three light valves to produce a simultaneous three-color spot that is scanned across photosensitive material as it is rotated on a drum. The exposing system consists of three modulators optimized for selected color bands that match the spectral sensitivity of the material being used. Modulation, triggered by voltage variations, controls the intensity of the red, green, and blue light from the three tungsten halogen lamps. Ten-watt tungsten halogen lamps are used, operating at 2900 degrees Kelvin with a lamp life of more than 2000 hours.

FILM RECORDERS

Film recorders have been a convenient way of taking digital information and placing it on conventional film. Using high-resolution monochrome CRTs, individual exposures are made through red, green, and blue filters to

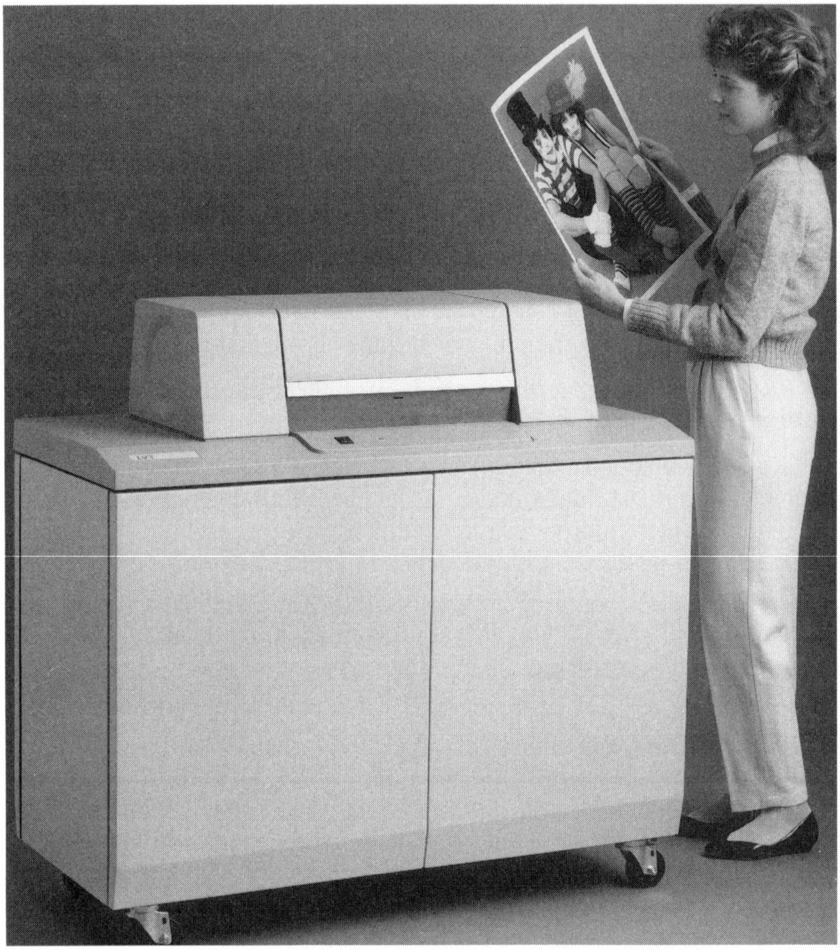

Fig. 5-23. The Light Valve Technology (LVT) Model 1620 Digital Image Recorder produces continuous tone images from digital data on color silver-halide material.

provide the final image. Film recorders are available from 35 mm up to 8 × 10 imaging sizes. Film recorders range in resolution from 1000 × 1000 to 8000 × 8000 pixels. At 2000 × 2000, the pixelation disappears, and it is almost impossible to tell that the image has been generated electronically above that point.

The recording time also is dependent on the quality of the film recorder. A high-resolution 35-mm slide can take up to 20 minutes to record on the smaller, less expensive recorders and can be as short as 15 to 20 seconds on the large, high-priced recorders. Recorders from Pansophic (formerly

Genigraphics), Celco, and Crosfield (formerly called Dicomed) represent a wide range of high-resolution recorders with capabilities of imaging up to 8000 × 8000 pixels (Fig. 5–24). Tabletop or floor-standing recorders from Matrix, Lasergraphics, Mirus, and Polaroid are all examples of recorders that range from 1000 × 1000 to 2000 × 2000. Although perfectly acceptable for many graphics applications, for true photorealistic electronic imaging, pixel patterns will appear in the image and when the image is enlarged, they will appear as artifacts in the image. The image also will suffer from lack of

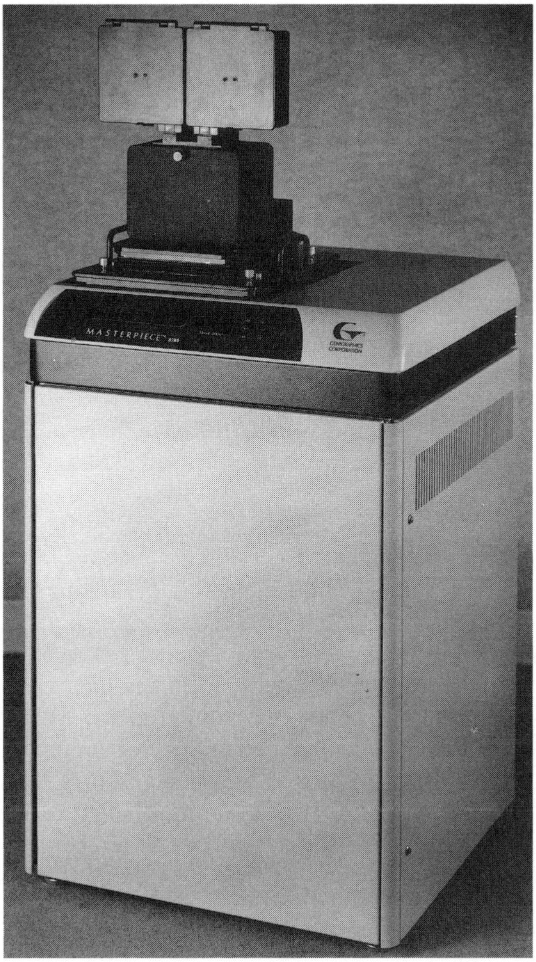

Fig. 5-24. The Pansophic Masterpiece 8780 Imaging System can produce images on 35-mm, sheet, and roll film with up to 65,536 lines of addressability.

sharpness and potentially from lack of sufficient color depth unless it is recorded at 8 or 12 bits/color.

HOW THE EXPERTS SEE COLOR HARDCOPY SYSTEMS

George D. Link
Manager for Business and Product Planning
Advanced Product Concepts
Xerox Corporation:

"There are at least three or four different kinds of media that are going to be available. First, there is electrophotography or xerography. We know, through the work in our own research labs, that very high quality images can be created approaching the very highest quality lithography. With liquid toner development, the particle size of the individual toner is significantly lower. This provides a very great advantage in quality. Our work with DXI (DX imaging) is directly involved in taking that technology, implementing it into products and then taking it and expanding it into the future. Liquid toner technology will have excellent potential in the future.

"Cycolor, from Mead Imaging, is another new technology. I believe that at the present time, it is a rather immature technology which Mead feels has great potential. I have seen some very good examples of that technology and the advantage it has over some other technologies is its simplicity. Essentially the technology is in the media itself.

"Then there is diffusion and sublimation dye thermal transfer that can give significantly higher levels of gray and provide excellent continuous tone output.

"Iris Graphics from Massachusetts, with their ink-jet printer, has certainly demonstrated the ability to combine relatively modest resolution with high levels of gray and provide excellent continuous tone throughput, and if not total proof printing, then certainly near proof printing quality.

"The throughput capability of the liquid toner certainly can be up in the hundreds of A-4 type copies per minute. Like anything else, it is going to relate to development time, costs, operational costs. We are starting out today at relatively low throughput capability in proofing. The ability to digitize images and handle the bitstream is going to be a limiting factor, so there will probably have to be some sort of intermediate utilized to make a proofing master and then to run from that like an offset press.

"Let me break that into a couple of different kinds of applications. First of all, if it's photographic, pictorial, probably your dye transfer technologies are going to be very good for very low throughput capabilities. Certainly ink-jets will be used. However, the ink-jets, for the quality required, are fairly expensive from a marketing standpoint.

"As you move into the xerographic area, probably the productivity and economics don't cross until you're at five, ten, fifteen full color copies per minute.

"When you get into business graphics, it is a different question because the quality output is slightly different. There is the question about tonal rendition and are we spending enough time on tone? In the business graphic you really don't need to be highly concerned about that. What you are looking for is color differentiation. In that case, for your low volume work, I think various types of ink-jets, be they liquid or the solid ink-jet, is (sic) an excellent technology if and when they are able to print on plain bond type paper.

"Thermal transfer is an excellent medium for low volume, especially where you are making an overhead transparency, the chroma of the color coming through is probably the best in the industry of any technology. Those are the technologies I would look at, for instance, for work station type of computer output.

"Cycolor is an example of a new technology. The solid ink-jet, as practiced by Howtek, Data Products and Spectra, is a very innovative technology and has a lot of potential. There are probably some bugs that need to be worked out since it's a rather new technology, but it holds a lot of promise.

"I see phenomenal growth. From a business graphics standpoint, the whole ability to take information and put it in graphical form is just beginning. The next logical step is to transfer the monochrome graphics into color graphics where the communication of information is much more efficient. There is a tremendous amount of growth potential in computer graphics.

"The use of photographs and pictures combined with text and other areas for identification is an excellent application for pictorial input into business type documents. Another example of a color hard copy output is the medical record with a picture of the patient. This could become a standard, and if you make that a standard in all hospitals in the nation, the throughput capability is unfathomable to me at the present time. There are many other applications of that nature possible with color hard copies."

Carl Machover
President
Machover Associates Corporation:

"I think some exciting things are happening: the sublimation techniques for thermal dye transfer are becoming more mature. In the past, the only mechanism that we had to achieve photographic or photo realism in color hard copy was that of silver halide film. Thermal dye transfers, ink jets, etc., were essentially binary devices and therefore to get color, one had to impact the resolution of the image. With the use of dye sublimation techniques as represented by products that are being shown by Kodak and several others, one can get what is essentially photographic quality as an output from the computer at speeds that are highly competitive. In addition to that, the introduction of commercially viable color copying devices offers real promise. Here at the show, for example, the Coloroc unit, which is essentially a color laser engine, is quite analogous to the Canon black and white engine. It represents a commercial step that could make the color copier a dominant technology in the office over the next five years.

"We have for years talked about the electronic office—the paperless office—the paperless engineering office—and today what that really means is that data is stored in electronic form, but still is very often distributed in paper form. We still see growth of paper at 15% a year.

"Finally we are beginning to see some viable electronic techniques for the distribution of information. One example is the digital video interactive technology developed by the Sarnoff Laboratories. This system uses the CD-ROM as a delivery mechanism. The problem with the CD-ROM in the past is that the amount of data that could be delivered is relatively limited. For example, if I put live video on a CD-ROM, I have only about four minutes of data availability. The group at Intel has developed a special set of audio and video compression and expansion chips that reduce band width in real time and expand band width so that we can increase the amount of live video on these systems from four minutes to one hour. Couple that with computer generated imagery and we suddenly have a highly interactive method of delivering information. One has to believe it will have an impact on paper delivery.

"The term that has been broadly used to describe that interactivity is *hypermedia*. For ten years hypermedia was the purvey of people like Ted Nelson and the Media Labs at MIT, but it looks like we are finally getting some practical technology that certainly within the next few years will represent a viable alternate delivery method for data that has historically been delivered on paper.

"One thing that is happening on film recorders is that it is possible today to buy very high quality image film recorders quite economically. I can today buy a film recorder which can be addressed with 4000 lines and can be resolved [with] 2000 lines, and that is comparable to the sort of technology that we expected from Celco, Genigraphics and Dicomed in the $50,000 range. Today these new recorders are under $10,000; that's the good news. The bad new, like in all things, [is] there's a trade-off. The difference is the time it takes to make a slide. I can get that level of resolution on the low cost recorders, but I have to be prepared to spend a half-hour before the slide is produced. This has nothing to do with the computation time, only the recording time. The high production film recorders of the type that I mentioned can produce those slides ten to fifteen times faster. So what it has done is to create an alternate choice. It certainly doesn't replace the production film recorder, but allows someone who doesn't have a production requirement to gain access to high quality imagery at a much more competitive price.

"The term that we have picked up is *photorealism* and increasingly part of the graphics environment includes scanners that allow us to take existing images, put them into our systems and manipulate them—TV generated images or pictures that come from live data and if one looks for a new term besides photorealism, it's the issue of integration. The old separation between vector generated images, image processing and all the artificial barriers are actually being broken down. Today's new systems are integrated."

Peter Testan
Vice President
CAP International
Color Hard Copy (CHC) Market Requirement Service:

"The products that have the capability right now for future survival would be a dye transfer type technology that we are seeing now in video picture type products, and also coming are some A-4 type products. Many companies are looking at this as the type of product that would replace some of the photographic images that we are currently seeing today.

"New products are certainly offering capabilities as far as continuous time type images [go], and costs that are lower than photography at this particular time. [They're] also lower than dye transfer, but perhaps not the same level of print quality as is offered by dye transfer.

"Resolution becomes more of a problem with color because of the memory that is required for the storage of the color, also the processing power that is required for it. For the time being, I think 300 will probably be where we level off. We are starting to see a trend now in the laser printer market toward 600. Color will probably come to that level in the future, but it will be a while before we get there.

"Mainly a lower cost memory at this point would be a major factor for reaching higher resolution levels in printers.

"[But] not until the price of a video printer can get down to the consumer price level, which might be around $500 or lower. At that point then it looks like a viable option for the end user, the consumer, but up to that point it would be difficult to see a large market for it. Dye transfer seems to be the stronger player from an overall imaging point of view and the cost of imaging at this point.

"It will be the early 1990s before we will see significant new printing devices in the market."

APPLICATION STORIES

Video Walls

Complete walls of video screens have become a popular way of highlighting new products and attracting audience attention. Imtech International, the largest producer of video walls, offers Sony ProMavica products to customers as an easy, low-cost way of preparing video wall presentations. Imtech International, the nation's largest producer of video walls, offers Sony's ProMavica products to customers as an easy, low-cost method of preparing video wall presentations. Imtech sells and rents video walls to corporations (for lobby display and trade show uses), clubs, visitor centers, museums, retailers, and others.

"Unless you have high production value, which usually means a high budget, live action video can look cheap," says Imtech president Paul Noble. "Video demands extensive post-production and editing. Sony ProMavica is a less demanding form of production. You can take 25 or 50 still images, arrange them in sequence, and generate an effective presentation of continuous still images easier, quicker, and less expensively than you can produce a moving video."

"Playing ProMavica through the video wall increases the level of animation," notes Noble. "For instance, you can program the wall to gyrate between large and small images, so the visual production is greatly enhanced." At their own trade show booth, Imtech uses ProMavica to take candid shots of clients and potential clients, then immediately displays their images on a video wall.

A big advantage of ProMavica is its ability to provide direct RGB input for the video wall—result—better picture quality for Imtech's customers. Noble also praised the ProMavica camera for its close-up capabilities, which he finds useful for shooting product stills.

Another positive factor is ease of use. Says Noble: "With a good eye and a little experimentation, a nonskilled person using a ProMavica can, in minutes, create and display a video wall presentation that looks far more professional than if they (sic) try it with live-action video."

The ProMavica is a less demanding form of production. With 25 to 50 still images, arranged in sequence, you have an effective fast-moving and inexpensive presentation.

The electronic still video images provide better picture quality and allow the customer to use a camera similar to the 35-mm cameras they are familiar with.

Fuji Photofilm Company has used video walls with images from their Fujix still video players.

Selecting Hair Colors with Electronic Photography

In the past, the only way a woman could really tell how she would look with a different hair color was to actually color her hair, a step many were afraid to take.

So several years ago, Clairol, a leading manufacturer of quality hair color and hair-care products, began looking for ways to make the hair-coloring decision an easier one. The result is Clairol Color Visions, a computerized hair-color makeover system that shows women how they would look in hair-color shades from black to the palest blond.

"We knew from the start we wanted people to walk away with before-and-after images of their hair-color selections," says Lisa Carvalho, manager of Consumer Education Services at Clairol. "We knew, too, that we had to be able to produce high-quality prints on the spot that would show all the subtleties of hair color."

Designed for use in malls and on the hair-color aisles of drug stores, Clairol Color Visions marries real-time video with computer graphics. It's an electronic system that enables people to visualize what they could not otherwise see. Today the Kodak SV6500 Color Video Printer is an important member of this system.

With Color Visions, a video camera and framestore device capture and digitize a customer's image. With the image displayed on a computer monitor, a Clairol haircolor consultant changes the haircolor on the display. Because of the system's split-screen capability, the customer can see before-and-after images comparing her natural color with her new look.

At the end of the session, the consultant activates the Kodak SV6500 Color Video Printer to produce a high-quality color print of the before-and-after images on the screen.

"The print is a key part of the Color Visions process," says Carvalho. "The customer goes home with more than just a memory. Because she can show it to others, the print reinforces the hair-color decision and encourages follow-through."

Carvalho also stresses the importance of giving customers high-quality prints. "We selected the Kodak printer for its ability to accurately reproduce the nuances of hair color. Hair colors can have up to 11,000 shades. With Kodak still video prints, we can reproduce even the most subtle hair-color changes," she says.

Cataloging Images with Electronic Photography

Three years ago, the Image Center at Eastman Kodak, Rochester, New York, embarked upon an ambitious project: the development of an electronic cataloging system to provide fast access to the growing collection of images produced within the company.

"Today our computerized system provides a description and full-color video display of more than 25,000 photographic images," says David Fox, Image Center supervisor. "Users can select images for viewing based on up to 20 criteria such as subject, film type, image size, photographer, location, special effects, and company product."

At the heart of the cataloging system is a laser video-disc system. Twelve-inch video discs store up to 54,000 still images. A video-disc player, controlled by an IBM personal computer and software developed by Kodak, offers random access to any image within seconds. The computer also maintains the database of image information and the location of each image on the laser disc.

"When a user selects an image for reproduction, the original photographic slide or negative is retrieved from the archive vault and reproduced using traditional photographic techniques," Fox says.

With the cataloging function in place, Image Center staff turned their attention to two other problems: 1) providing users with reference copies of the displayed images, and 2) cataloging new images in a timely, cost-effective fashion.

"People often need hard copies of images before selecting any for reproduction," says Bob Parrett, senior engineer and imaging systems specialist. "In the past, we maintained five reference slides for each photograph in the system. That meant keeping an inventory of more than 100,000 slides. Also reviewing the slide required a light table, projector or some other viewing device. We wanted a better method."

The Center also needed a way to keep the system up to date. As Parrett explains, "We're adding 2-3,000 images to the system each year. While video discs store a tremendous number of images, adding new ones requires 'remastering' of the laser discs. This is an expensive process, so we don't want to do it until we have enough images for a new disc."

The Image Center solved both problems with two Kodak still video products: the Kodak SV6500 Color Video Printer and the SV750 Still Video Multidisk Recorder.

"By connecting the SV6500 printer to our video disc player, we've eliminated the reference slides," Fox says. "Now our users can capture and print any image they see on the monitor. Within 90 seconds they have a 4-×-5-inch continuous-tone color print to use as a reference. The response has been very enthusiastic."

Integrating the printer with the video disc system was easy, Fox says. "Since the SV6500 accepts NTSC video input and the player output a standard NTSC video signal, we were able to make a direct connection," he explains.

To handle new images coming into the Center, Parrett added the Kodak SV7500 Still Video Multidisk Recorder to the existing computer system.

"We use in-house video production equipment and the multidisk recorder to transfer new images to the still video floppy disks used by the recorder," he says. "When the recorder is connected to the computer, the users sort through the images on the floppies just as they would using the laser disc system and are unaware of where the image resides."

Each still video floppy holds up to 50 images, and the recorder's removable disk tray holds up to 30 disks. Parrett says the Center has about 800 images stored on still video floppies.

Electronic Photography in Sports Medicine

Centinela Hospital Medical Center in Inglewood, California is a 403-bed, nonprofit acute care facility and leader in the field of sports medicine. It was an official hospital for the 1984 Summer Olympic Games and currently serves most professional sports teams in the Los Angeles area.

An anxious athlete wonders if or when he'll play again after undergoing surgery for a career-threatening injury. The surgeon must give his worried patient more than a yes or no answer. One common practice is to review with the patient a video tape of the surgical procedure. However, that requires playing an entire 20-minute-plus cassette.

At Centinela Hospital Medical Center, sports-medicine specialists whose surgical procedures involved the use of video asked for a practical way to make hardcopy color prints from video sources.

Centinela's director of medical photography, Alan Goldstein, responded to the physicians' need by purchasing a Kodak SV6500 Color Video Printer. "We put a Kodak color video printer along with a VCR and television monitor in one of the surgeon's lounges," Goldstein says. "Physicians can view tapes documenting procedures at their leisure. When they see an image they want, they just push a button. In 90 seconds or less they have a color print." Many orthopedic surgeons at Centinela are enthusiastic about this new capability.

Biomedical Electronic Photography

Biomedical Media at The Ohio State University's College of Veterinary Medicine, is the world's largest veterinary school. It includes photographers, videographers, medical illustrators, computer artists, and production technicians who provide audiovisual services to more than 150 faculty as well as to veterinarians and outside veterinary organizations.

"Medicine—human and veterinary—is taught with images," says C. Allen Shaffer, assistant director for Biomedical Media. "In fact, for the past

18 years our group has been producing 8000 to 10,000 images per month for the faculty here." Slides have many uses at the school. Instructors routinely use them in the classroom and for conferences and seminars. It's not unusual, Shaffer says, to see a faculty member carrying 15 to 18 slide trays to a conference or 3 to 4 trays to a class.

Slides also are used in the school's media lab, in which students can study slide programs to supplement their classroom experience.

Many images are produced during the treatment of animals. "Through our small and large animal clinics, we do everything that is done in a human hospital and generate many of the same images," Shaffer says. "We then use these images for diagnosis, documentation and instruction." Not surprisingly, Biomedical Media has accumulated "an enormous pile of media."

"To provide the media services our faculty need, we must find better ways to organize, store and retrieve the images we collect," Shaffer says. "In addition, we want to provide these people with tools they can use to create their own presentations and teaching aids."

Michael Q. Bailey, DVM, a veterinary radiologist, teacher, and practitioner at Ohio State, is especially enthusiastic about still video. He regularly performs ultrasound examinations in the field. In the past, he used a thermal-paper recorder connected to the ultrasound machine to capture and print still ultrasound images. However, these prints lacked the range of tones needed for diagnosis and comparison.

"I could have taken the format camera from the lab into the field, but it's expensive equipment and moving it from site to site is risky," Bailey explains. "Instead I take the SV7400 still video recorder, connect it to the ultrasound machine and quickly record the images I want on still video floppies. Once captured, these images can be transferred in the lab to the format camera, which yields much higher quality images than the paper prints."

Bailey uses the still video recorder in the classroom, too. "I can project images from the still video floppies directly without going through another transfer process, he says. "This has two advantages. First, it saves time. Second, and more importantly, we don't have to worry about image quality.

"It's important to have the highest quality image possible for diagnosis, but transferring always causes some loss of detail. With the Kodak recorder, I can say to students, 'This is what you'll see on your ultrasound or CAT scan machine.' "

Computer Graphics at Telesis Productions, Inc.

Telesis Productions, Inc., located in Rochester, New York, is a full-service video-production company. With its state-of-the-art facilities and experienced staff of producers, writers, directors, and graphic arts specialists, Telesis creates video programs for corporate presentations, sales meetings, new product instructions, commercials, and training. Computer graphs have become an important part of video productions today. Images and text generated on the computer introduce programs, bridge video sequences, explain difficult concepts, and reinforce information presented.

Throughout the design process clients need to see and approve the artist's work. However, reproducing a computer monitor's display in hardcopy form has not been easy for video producers.

"In the past, we used a black-and-white thermal printer or a 35-mm camera to produce hardcopy of the graphics we created," says Telesis president David Rose. "We then gave these prints to clients for their review and approval."

However, although the thermal printer produced prints quickly, Rose says, they were black and white; clients had to imagine the color, look at color sketches along with the prints, or come to Telesis.

Telesis recently purchased a Kodak SV6500 Color Video Printer, a tabletop unit that uses a thermal-dye sublimation transfer process to produce a full-color 4-×-5-inch print in about 90 seconds.

"Now, by connecting the SV6500 to the computer graphics system, we can produce a continuous-tone color print of any image displayed on the screen simply by pressing a button," Rose says. "Our clients don't have to imagine how the graphics will look. They see the design and color together and can make changes or give approvals based on a complete picture."

Telesis has also found other uses for the SV6500: in storyboarding, image management, and marketing. A *storyboard* serves as a road map for a video production and is an important Part of a video project.

"The conventional method for producing storyboards—sketching graphics and scenes from video sequences with colored markers—is a very time-consuming task," Rose explains. "Now that we have the Kodak printer, we create the images for our storyboards on the computer-graphics system. We can also capture and print scenes from video sequences. These still video storyboards give the client a much better idea of what is going on. It is also much faster than the traditional storyboard technique."

In the area of image storage the SV6500 helps Telesis with image management. Each graphic Telesis creates is stored digitally on streamer tape. According to Rose, literally thousands of images—about 50 per tape—have been archived. Tape contents are noted on a paper filed with each tape.

For marketing once a video program is completed, Telesis captures a scene/image from the program and makes a still video print. The print is framed and sent to the client as a thank you and a reminder of the work Telesis did.

Video People Postcards

An automated postcard vending system designed for sale to theme parks and other tourist locations uses a Kodak SV 6500 color video printer to make full-color 4-×-5.2-inch postcards.

After inserting money, customers press a button to select tone of four different postcard backgrounds. The choice of custom-created backgrounds is almost unlimited and can incorporate city skylines, landscapes, historical landmarks, and theme and amusement-park characters or mascots. Because backgrounds are maintained electronically, they can be changed easily for holidays, special events, etc.

Customers see their picture on a monitor, composed with the background. After a few seconds lapse, which allows the customer time to position the live portrait image, the composite image is frozen. The system then resets itself to begin generating another postcard, and 90 seconds later the system provides a unique postcard ready to mail. A ledge in the booth allows customers to address the postcard, and a stamp dispenser provides postage. The booth occupies 18 square feet, about the same size as traditional self-serve photo booths, according to Pamela Barber, president of Practically Perfect Productions, Inc.

Dry Color Silver at Work

3M's Dry Silver Color technology will be combined with Honeywell's manufacturing of color hardcopy recorders for the computer-aided design, manufacturing, and engineering (CAD/CAM/CAE) market and medical and nondestructive testing markets. Honeywell has developed two new hardcopy recorders using fiberoptic cathode-ray-tube (FO-CRT) technology.

David W. Powell, vice president of 3M Photo Color Systems Division, and Dr. Ira Langenthal, vice president/general manager of Honeywell's Test Instruments Division, recently held a video-telecast news conference. Powell identified five major fields in which the use of color hardcopy is expanding rapidly: business graphics, engineering, scientific/medical, printing/publishing, and home use. He quoted Datek research that indicates a 34% compound annual growth in color hardcopy products from 450,000 units in 1985 to 2 million in 1990. Hardware revenue in 1990 should reach $5.5 billion, with the supplies adding another $20 billion.

For the medical ultrasound market, the recorder will print full, continuous-strip records as well as page prints on black-and-white or color paper. The CAD/CAM/CAE unit will be a page copier. Exposure is *one-pass*, meaning that all three colors are exposed during the same pass. It will take about 11 seconds to print an 8 1/2-×-11-inch page. Developing is achieved through heating to 275° F for 5 to 10 seconds.

Resolution is in excess of 100 line pairs/mm, and the cost per 8 1/2-×-11-inch sheet should be in the 90¢ to $1.00 range (compared to 30¢ to 40¢ for black and white dry silver). The Dry Silver Color material is still first generation and probably not suited for photographic applications, although the second generation Dry Silver Color (peel-apart) material already has been demonstrated by 3M—and is more suited for photographic applications.

Honeywell's Test Instruments Division has been making video graphic recorders for many years and has sold more than 10,000 units of all types for the medical market. The new recorders are expected to sell at around $10,000 in a basic configuration, with a cost/print (8 1/2 × 11 inches) of approximately 90¢ to $1.00. The comparable black-and-white dry silver cost would be 30¢ to 40¢. After three years of selling the new units, Honeywell expects to have placed 5000 recorders worldwide, the majority into the medical market.

This version of the Dry Silver Color product is designed for industrial applications, and no photographic applications are envisioned presently. However, using the "writing engine" of this versatile recorder, planned video interfaces could expand applications into satellite imaging, reconnaissance, and other markets. With a grain size smaller than "wet" silver halide, resolution can be quite acceptable. However, because it uses a thermal development process, the material is temperature-sensitive, and degradation of images begins above 140°F. Ultraviolet radiation also affects the images (as it does in regular silver halide images). However, the material can be used for overhead transparencies without any problems.

Ink Jets and Billboards

Ink-jet printers have been used to make even larger images. Nate Accardo, president of Custom Color Corp. in Kansas City, MO spoke on "The Next Decade—A Professional Color Lab's Viewpoint" at the recent SPSE Symposium on Business Issues in Photographic and Electronic Imaging. He cited an example of hybrid imaging with an ink-jet output. The Patrick Media Group in New York received a visit from a touring delegation from the Peoples Republic of China in regard to a possible contract to modernize outdoor advertising in China.

The company took a transparency of all the delegates and sent it overnight to Los Angeles where Computer Images of Los Angeles scanned the image and used an ink-jet system in San Francisco to create a 14-×-48 foot billboard. This was erected where the delegation could see it when they arrived the following day—an example of modern outdoor advertising. In this context, the application of ink-jet technology offers many new opportunities for marketing.

6

The Electronic Darkroom

The photographic darkroom has been a way of life for practitioners of photography since before the turn of the century. Photographic darkroom operations have been a combination of chemistry, manipulation, and the artistry of the retoucher.

Electronic retouching has been in existence for two decades using equipment available to printers for page composition, scanning, and output. It was not unusual to see a single location spending several million dollars for a digital-retouching area.

Sony showed a prototype retouching system for electronic still video photography in 1982, one year after its original introduction of the Mavica. In a small console unit of less than one yard square, Sony was able to take a still video image and do all of the necessary retouching that had been done previously in studio darkrooms. This included air brushing, spotting, retouching, or even combining other backgrounds. Sony never marketed this product.

Canon also has shown retouching systems with the ability to make caricatures from standard electronic still video photographs and other novelty effects, but Canon has not created a true electronic retouching station.

In his classic article, "Towards the Electronic Studio," L. Mills Davis in 1986 pointed the way to the new technologies that are transforming the traditional studio into an electronic studio. Today, we have seen what Davis and others foresaw. We now have a variety of digital software and hardware for retouching at a variety of prices.

A California company has put together a system that allows anyone to copy black-and-white photos, retouch them, and create a new negative for conventional silver-halide printing. Photocraft in San Diego, California uses an Apple Mac II with 8 megabytes of RAM and a Big Picture IQ monitor that produces 256 shades of gray at 1024 × 808 resolution. For scanning original photographs, the Microtek 300G scanner is used for image input. It has a resolution of 300 DPI. For film output, a Matrix Slidewriter is operated at a 4000 × 4000 resolution. Kodak TMAX 400 film is underdeveloped one stop. In addition, there is a Kurta 12-inch × 12-inch digitizing tablet and Digital Darkroom software from Silicon Beach Software.

The software is slightly modified for Photocraft. The station is able to track the time on each job and print an invoice. Digital Darkroom software has the ability to stretch, distort, rotate, resize, and contain the same retouching tools that most programs have. The software has a menu for various "plug in filters". In the future, Photo Craft will be adding other menu items, including sharpening, despeckle, dot-screen elimination, noise reduction, and other filter algorithms. These will speed the process of restorations without having to rely totally on labor-intensive hand painting of global defects in an image (Fig. 6–1). An example would be the smoothing of skin surfaces using the despeckle filter function.

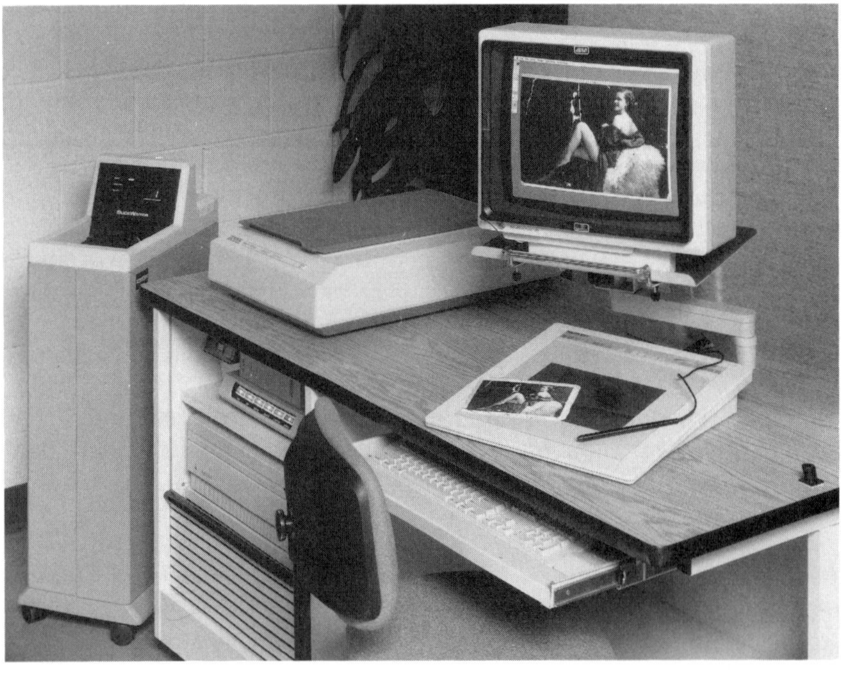

Fig. 6-1. The digital darkroom for retouching black-and-white photographs.

The average current time for Photocraft artists to retouch a typical old photograph is 1.5 hours. With experience the time will be reduced to under an hour.

Tom Reid of Photocraft makes several important points. They use technology that is available now. Even resolution—which many people consider a limitation of electronic-imaging systems—is better than the results from a conventional photographic copy camera. Most important, the system is practical, profitable, and low in cost compared with giant color systems requiring a considerably higher investment.

ELECTRONIC DARKROOMS AND PUBLISHERS

The third largest cost for U.S. companies is publishing. Publishing in all forms averages 4% to 8% of gross annual revenues. This is especially true for information companies. A $100 million company could easily spend $4 million to $8 million per year on publishing materials, both internally and for distribution to the public. At the moment, a small percentage of printing is in color. Because of color electronic publishing, this share is expected to grow tremendously.

Tasks you couldn't afford to do electronically are becoming affordable because of computers like the Macintosh II, and software like PhotoMac (Fig. 6–2). In early 1989, the Avalon Development Group started shipping PhotoMac, the first full-fledged photodesign software for the Macintosh II. Targeted for graphic design and corporate electronic-publishing professionals, PhotoMac is the first software that manipulates color photographs on the Macintosh II platform (Fig. 6–3). With the introduction of desktop scanners, low-cost film recorders, and faster imagesetters, the lower cost of electronic publishing is driving down the cost of prepress technology. Corporate publishers can afford to do more color printing—and color sells.

According to Clay Gordon of InterConsult (Cambridge, Mass.), "Until now, many kinds of color printing were too expensive to produce electronically. And the costs associated with traditional color prepress (separations and stripping) limited its use in areas like catalog production." Gordon predicts that the innovators in color electronic publishing will be companies who already purchase large-volume color printing.

Although the prospect for color electronic publishing is bright, consumers are confused. There are many options for input and output devices to work with their color workstations. Let's take a look at some of these devices. To get photographs into the Macintosh II, there are two choices: video or scanners.

A number of desktop scanners that convert color photos to digital format have appeared recently on the market. Many provide software

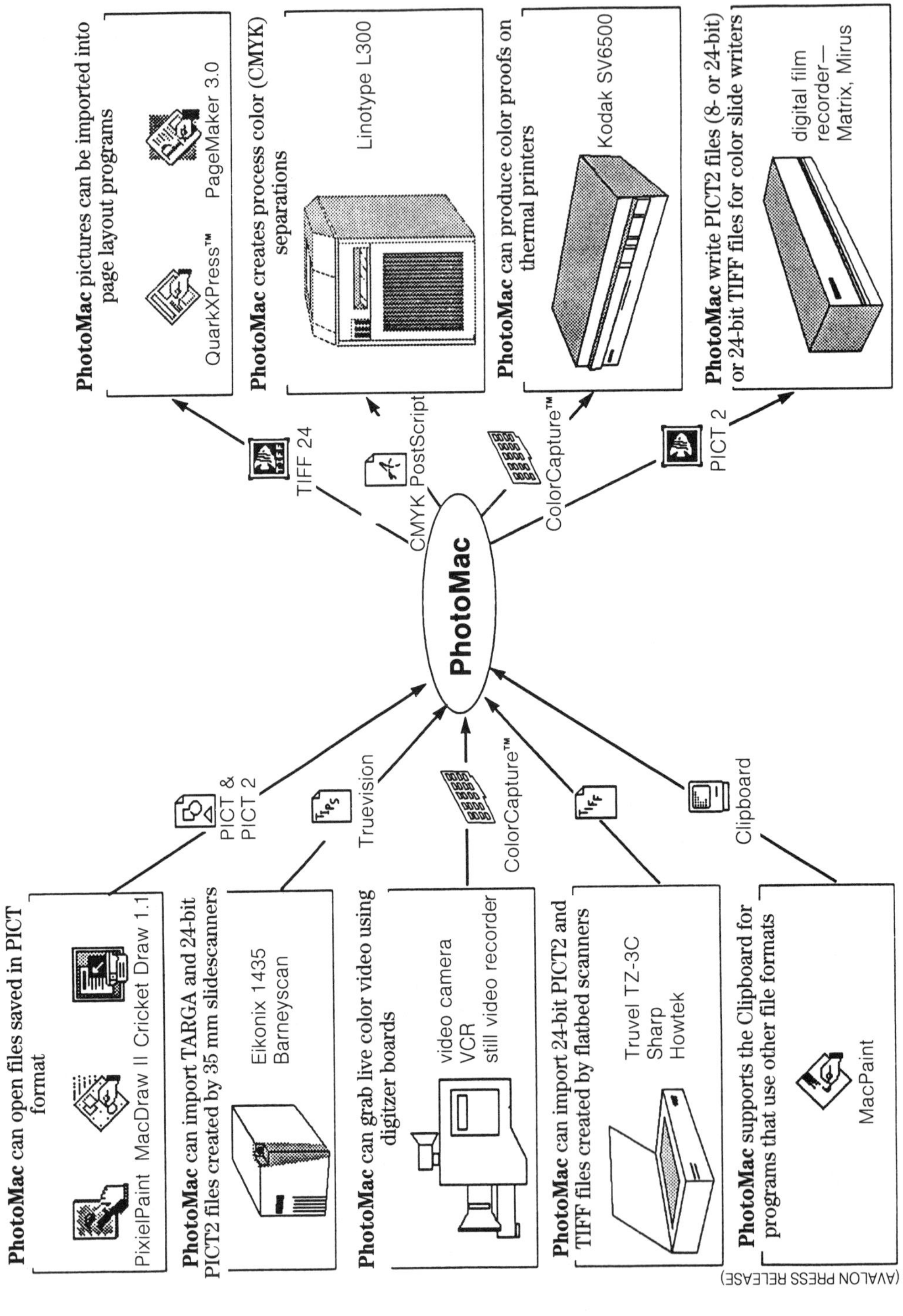

Fig. 6-2. Input and output options for PhotoMac software.

(AVALON PRESS RELEASE)

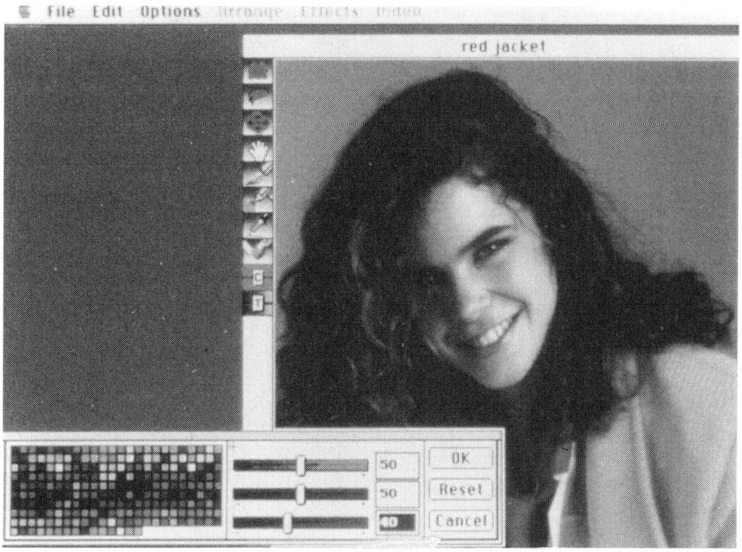

Fig. 6-3. A sample screen from PhotoMac.

interfaces to a range of computers, including the IBM PC and compatibles, Macintosh, and Sun Microsystems.

Although there are three types of scanners—flatbed, camera and drum—only the first two are desktop units. The flatbed scanner looks like a small copier. You lay a piece of artwork or photograph on a glass plate, put a cover over it, and the scanner digitizes the image. A specialized version of the flatbed scanner is the slide scanner, which digitizes 35-mm slides. The camera scanner uses a video camera to read the image and can digitize slides, photographs, artwork, and even three-dimensional objects.

Many corporate publishers will scan flat art or slides. However, for some, video is a viable solution for capturing images. The PhotoMac software works directly with the ColorCapture frame grabber from Data Translations. ColorCapture grabs video images at 480-×-640-pixel resolution. With video menus, images generally can be captured from, and outputted to, video cameras, still video cameras, and VCRs.

Virtual memory or *addressable main memory* is a term that will crop up more and more in color software and hardware for one simple reason: high-resolution scanned images. In fact, images in general are space/memory intensive. Suppose you make a 300 DPI scan of a 4-×-6-inch image, producing an 8.64-Mb file. Even if the Macintosh II has the maximum installed working memory of 8 Mb (an expensive option), this is still insufficient to handle an image file this large.

Most color paint packages now available limit the user to working with images that fit into RAM. Some color scanners also have memory-based systems that limit the size of images. PhotoMac has a virtual-memory architecture that lets users work with very large images. The size of the image is limited by available hard disk space, not by available RAM. This is absolutely crucial in a design or production setting. To compete in this area, future products that handle scanned images will, of necessity, have virtual memory systems.

PhotoMac is the first color-photo-manipulation software for the Macintosh II. What image manipulation is offered? The graphic arts features allow the user to:

- Cut out unwanted pieces of the image
- Copy or clone portions of the image to create duplicate items, mirror images, or water reflection effects
- Combine images into a montage, or create a collage of images on a white or tinted "canvas"
- Use a paintbrush or airbrush to pull back part of a picture in order to highlight another area

The photographic operations include the ability to:

- Retouch the image by adjusting color, brightness, or contrast
- Change the colors of an image or part of an image down to the pixel level
- Invert colors to dramatically transform an image
- Invert negatives to positives
- Produce images up to 256 levels of gray
- Rotate the image or portions of the image through any angle (*free rotation*)
- Resize the image or portions of the image proportionally, or create special effects through distortion

With PhotoMac Version 1.1, electronic stripping has been added. The program features separation controls with which the user can set screen rulings, screen angles, and separation dimensions. This allows the automation of the electronic prepress system by generating four PostScript files that contain the separations for all the photographs in position on a page. With QuarkX Press and PhotoMac, four negatives are produced that include text and separations of the images. With PageMaker and Ready,Set,Go, five negatives are produced: four for the separations in position, and one for the text and line art.

On a technical level, PhotoMac handles 24-bit per pixel images scanned at resolutions of up to 32,000 × 32,000 pixels. The virtual memory lets you open large images of 10 Mbyes or more if your hard disk can handle it. The software is designed to run on the Macintosh II with only 2 Mb of RAM, although additional RAM memory will provide faster performance. Also, although the program manipulates 24-bit images, it runs on the standard 8-bit monitor using an adaptive display that chooses the best colors for the image, minimizing color banding.

Several other software packages are available for color-image processing on the IBM PC. Media Cybernetics has its Image-Pro Color that uses the TrueVision Vista board. The Picsus package, called The Darkroom, includes a Pixie video board and software and provides 256 levels of gray and tools for image manipulation.

Beyond the simple capture of images, there is the opportunity, with the digitized image, for creating entire new expressions of images. ImagePaint allows a user to take a digitized image and make it look hand-drawn in any number of classical drawing and painting styles—from watercolor, oil, charcoal, pencil or crayon, pastels, ink, or lithography to more exotic special effects such as reflective chrome and refractive glass.

There are several ways of outputting information. Desktop publishing has moved from the black-and-white era to full photographic color. Part of that picture is color separations, which can be generated by several software packages now available. Some do process color, others do spot color. What's the difference between them?

Spot color is a solid area of a single-colored ink. *Process color* is an area that has been overprinted by the four process ink colors: cyan, magenta, yellow, and black (CMYK). Spot color typically is used to print a few solid colors (a bar or a line, for instance) on a page with black type. If you magnified spot color, you would see solid ink, no dots.

Some Macintosh software now includes Pantone colors for designating spot colors. The Pantone Matching System (PMS) is used widely among graphic artists. Essentially, it is a standardized system of printing inks. You can use a swatch book called a Pantone Color Specifier to choose from over 1000 color ink samples on coated or uncoated stock. When you choose a PMS color and tell your printer the corresponding number, the printer can reproduce the color precisely using the ink formula supplied by Pantone, Inc.

Adobe Illustrator is one software package that includes Pantone color. You can select an object on the screen and fill it with a Pantone color. When the software creates separations, each Pantone color is run out on a separate negative. This is a great way to get reliable spot color very simply. However, if you specified five Pantone colors and created separations, you would need five negatives—negatives that must be stripped accurately together to make the plates.

In this case, it might be wiser to consider switching to process color, which uses the four basic colors to create all others and requires only four negatives. In process color, if you look at the printed image through a magnifying glass (or loupe), you would see that it is actually made up of clusters of tiny, overlapping dots. Each cluster is a rosette pattern of four dots, each a different process color ink. The pattern, density, and colors of the dots create the illusion of color shadings.

To understand color separations, you need to understand some basic concepts of color printing. Process color printing uses three transparent inks: cyan, magenta, yellow (C, M, Y), and black (K). A screen is used to break the image into tiny dots of each color. During printing, the dots are overlaid in a rosette pattern, with each color offset at a different screen angle. Software packages like Avalon's PhotoMac and LaserWare's Laserpaint Color II convert the image you see on the screen into CMYK separations that can be printed on a PostScript printer. A 1-Mb image takes about 3 minutes to separate with PhotoMac; a 6-Mb file about 8 minutes, and a 13-Mb file can take 15 minutes.

The time needed to run off a separation depends upon the size and line screen of the separation. Maximum size is 7½ × 10 inches; films from the Linotronic are typically 8½ × 11 inches, and the header information (registration and crop marks and color bar) takes up about half an inch on each side of the image. If the printer has a raster image processor (RIP), which acts as an accelerator, the output time can be cut in half or less.

These packages specify line screen rulings (dots/inch) and screen angles, as well as adjust for ink and press conditions. This information also can be combined with page layout software to create full pagination. In addition to outputs for printing, the PhotoMac outputs to any 8-bit color device and even to film recorders.

"In developing PhotoMac, it became clear to us that the Macintosh world does not need another 8-bit color paint package," said Rudy Burger, Avalon's president. "The software is easy to use, handles 24-bit photographic pictures, and provides real cost and time savings in design and production environments."

New photo image software has been released by Letraset in the form of Color Studio and Adobe with their Photo Shop. Both packages have photo retouching and paint capabilities and can produce color separations for printing.

PROFESSIONAL ELECTRONIC DARKROOMS

At the end of 1987, there were only three full-color electronic prepress systems (CEPS) operating in professional labs in the United States. By the beginning of 1989, that number had grown to 11. Several labs have been

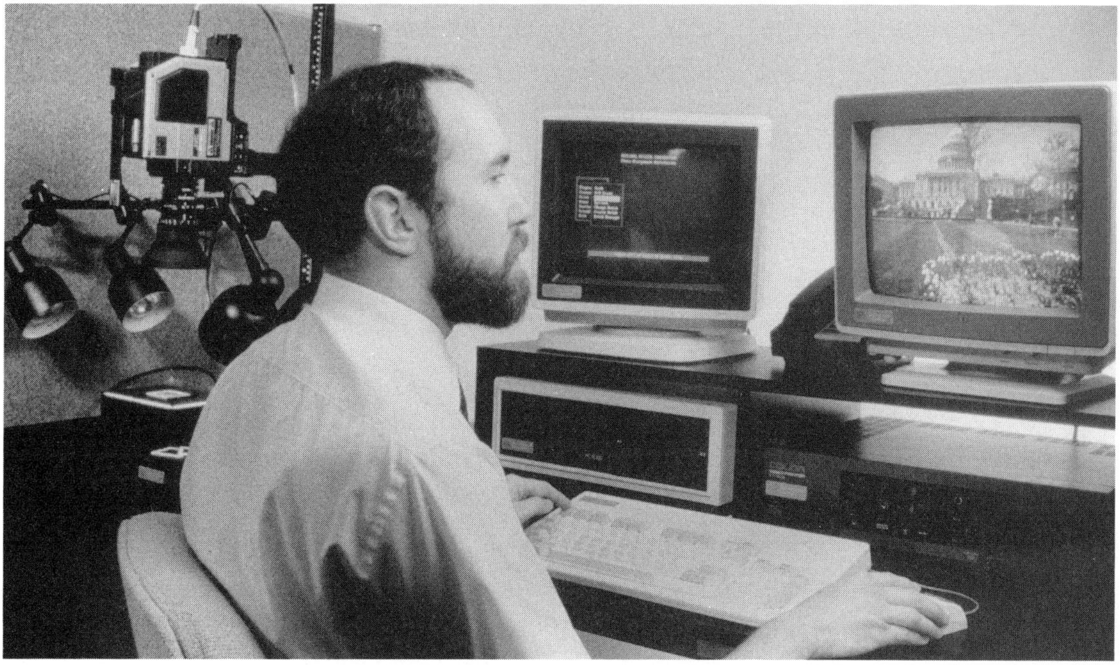

(PRESS KIT PHOTO)

Fig. 6-4. A typical digital darkroom.

investigating alternatives and probably will purchase one of these sophisticated digital-image manipulation systems. Many others possess equipment suitable for the production of high-quality computer-generated presentation and image slides. Figure 6–4 shows a typical digital darkroom.

Driven by the fear of losing customers to prepress companies, which only need to add a high-quality film recorder to provide similar capabilities, labs are rushing out to entertain overtures from digital darkroom suppliers. Another concern is the mistakenly perceived demise of silver halide in favor of electronic image capture.

Don Hutcheson, National Photo Sales Manager at Crosfield Color Graphic Systems, says that in the hands of an experienced artist, the digital darkroom can achieve some awesome effects that would be more expensive or even impossible to achieve by any other means. The main concern of labs must be to obtain the necessary digital darkroom to produce saleable work.

The four basic components in a digital darkroom are:

- The Input Scanner, which is used for digitizing the image information from an original negative, photograph or transparency

- The mass storage system required to store the large amount of digital data generated by the input scanner
- A workstation, which allows the artist to electronically manipulate the image, incorporating such functions as eliminate, clone, retouch, resize, local and global color change, contrast change, edge enhancement, pagination and even merging text and images, according to Vern Meier of 3M
- And the output film recorder for converting the digital data into a photographic image.

The hard-copy output from such a system is often called a *second generation original*, and it can be on transparency or color negative film or even direct onto color print material. This second-generation original can be used for making murals, display transparencies, or even color separations for dye transfer. However, it usually serves as a new original that will be scanned again to produce color separations for use in four-color lithography. The way in which the electronically generated image ultimately will be used determines how it should be produced.

In photographic images, resolution is measured in lines/inch. In electronic images, the number of pixels (picture-elements) is used. Without delving into what is acceptable or unacceptable, a simple rule-of-thumb can be used: "If you can see the individual pixels, you don't have enough resolution." Because the amount of resolution in a digital darkroom is a primary criterion, let's look at it in detail.

To digitize an original photograph without losing any of its sharpness, an image-processing system is required with a resolution that is equal to or greater than the maximum resolution of the color film. The published resolving power of a transparency film is typically 40 line pairs per mm. Each line pair consists of two lines: one white and one black. So this resolution is 80 individual lines per mm, which equates to about 2000 lines per inch (25 mm per inch).

Unfortunately, there seems to be a general misconception about what scanning resolution is really needed to produce an image equivalent to the theoretical resolving power of color film. Electronic information theory tells us that to record accurately the analog information (location and magnitude) of an image, it must be scanned at three times the highest resolution. Thus, we must scan a film image with a scanner having a resolution of about 240 lines per mm, or 6000 lines per inch to insure photographic like quality.

The total number of pixels that must be recorded is calculated by multiplying the resolution by the image area. For example, the image area of a 35-mm negative frame is 24 × 36 mm, or about 1 × 1.5 inches. Therefore, the number of pixels that would need to be recorded is (6000 × 1) × (6000 × 1.5) = 54,000,000 pixels.

Larger originals with more image area require an even greater number of pixels. However, from a practical viewpoint, the lenses used by view cameras to create 4″ × 5″ and larger sheet negatives/transparencies are not as sharp as those made for small format cameras. In practice, you can record extremely sharp images on 8″ × 10″ film with only 1000 to 1200 scan lines per inch; so the number of pixels needed to digitize an 8-×-10-inch image would be about 125,000,000.

Remember that in digitizing we must consider not only the number of pixels, but also the three component colors: cyan, magenta, and yellow. Because one byte of data is generated for each pixel and for each color, the digital memory required to store the image information from a 35-mm image is 3 × 54 million, or 162 megabytes. Similarly, an 8″ × 10″ image would require 375 megabytes of memory. However, these systems store an extra byte to permit transparency effects to be added to the image, so that the actual file sizes might typically be over 200 Mb for a 35-mm image and 500 Mbyte for an 8-×-10-inch image. This is more than ten miles the file size required for graphic-arts image manipulation.

For high-quality photographic work, the drum scanner is unrivaled. It is more expensive than either a video camera or flatbed/CCD scanner, but the photomultiplier tubes used for detecting the image data have an inherently higher sensitivity. The design of the drum scanner utilizes a narrow beam to illuminate only a small portion of the image at any time, eliminating any degradation due to lens flare.

Our first judgment of any image, even before we look at the sharpness, is based on color. Regardless of what scanning method is used, the raw data, if sent directly to the output recorder, does not match the colors of the original. This is because of problems with the color filters in both the input scanner and the output recorder, as well as limitations in the sensitivity of the color film itself. Fortunately, the color computer that is an integral part of high-end drum scanners not only compensates for the color-filter errors but also permits the contrast changes that normally occur in duping film-to-film to be overcome. Although conventional duping film will reproduce the tones of the original in a nonlinear way, which results in loss of highlight detail and an increase in overall contrast, the scanner's computer automatically compensates for these film characteristics, producing a straight-line reproduction. This ability of the color computer to provide not only overall corrections but also very localized corrections enables a digital darkroom to be used for such application as:

- Perfect copies/chromes from original reflection art/chromes
- Restoring poor originals

- Repairing damaged originals
- Digital retouching
- Photo composites

The type of corrections that can be applied directly from the scanner's computer, without the need for a retouching workstation, are:

- Lightening middle tone details without lightening highlights
- Extracting details from the shadow tones while leaving highlights untouched
- Correcting color casts, such as the tungsten cast on daylight film

However, the retouching workstation provides the added abilities to clone or duplicate a particular area of the image and repeat it elsewhere, paint over an unwanted part of the image with adjacent image information, or alter the local color of a specific region of the image (a single pixel can be changed, if desired). Usually, such retouching functions can be performed faster, easier, cleaner, and more realistically digitally, with no trace of change, than can be done optically.

NEWSPAPER ELECTRONIC DARKROOMS

Several dedicated systems have been developed for retouching. The digital darkroom uses a 80386-base computer with a digital copy camera and a film recorder with capability up to 8 × 10. The digital darkroom not only allows retouching, but also page composition by integrating a variety of images.

The Photographics 3000 from Imapro brings together a flatbed scanner, 35-mm film scanner, special software, and the ability to capture images, retouch them, lay out pages, and finally produce copy for either scanned or camera output.

National Digital Corporation provides a Photo Management Workstation for capturing, compressing, storing, and transmitting batches of color photographic images. Many modifications can be made to the stored image. Communications are in digital form and can be made directly to prepress equipment.

Sun workstations are beginning to offer a range of products that compete actively with PC products but with much more powerful image-processing capability (Table 6.1). These systems, with their Scalable Processor ARChitecture (SPARC), offer a uniqueness that is being adopted by many other companies as a standard way of processing images.

The 4cast Digital Color Imager from Dupont provides an interface computer, a thermal-dye-transfer printer and all the necessary software

Table 6-1. Sun Workstation Comparison.

SPARCstation 1 vs. Personal Computers (16" color, 8-MB hard disk, floppy)	SPARC station 1 208 MB	Mac IIx* 160 MB	IBM PS/2 Model 70* 120 MB
MIPS	12.5	2.2	5
Accelerated graphics	Yes	No	No
Standard Ethernet	Yes	No	No
Standard UNIX	Yes	No	No

*Mac II and PS/2 features based on published data as of April 12, 1989.
Source: Sun Microsystems

housed in a single cabinet. The thermal printer achieves 256 levels of gray for each color at each pixel location and can address 16.7 million colors. Printing with cyan, magenta, yellow, and black, the imager provides photorealistic images as well as output for checking page designs in graphics applications. Dupont also has RISC computers for high performance on networks (Fig. 6–5).

The electronic darkroom (ED), also called the *picture desk*, is becoming important to newspapers. In their daily use, they are important where time is at a premium because of the ever-present deadlines for the various daily editions. In view of the size and quality requirements involved, the EDs are costly systems. More recently, low cost EDs have been shown based on the Apple MacIntosh II computer with its excellent graphics capabilities. Such devices are much too slow for all but the smallest news publications. For that reason, the EDs discussed are only the larger systems designed for daily newspaper usage and are typically tied in with an elaborate electronic color pagination setup of Scitex, Crosfield, and Hell.

The term *electronic darkroom* is a misnomer because the ED is actually an elaborate computer system with input and output ports, digital enhancement capability and, most important, extensive electronic memory storage, typically a large hard disk, to store the memory-hungry digital images. No chemistry is involved, and the viewing of the photographic images is done by the use of a soft display such as a CRT monitor. Any desired print or hardcopy is either produced on-site using peripheral electronic printing equipment or by remote transmission, with the print being made on a unit such as the AP dry-silver wire-photo printer.

There are only four companies producing large electronic darkrooms. Three of the four are major wire services. Associated Press (AP) is

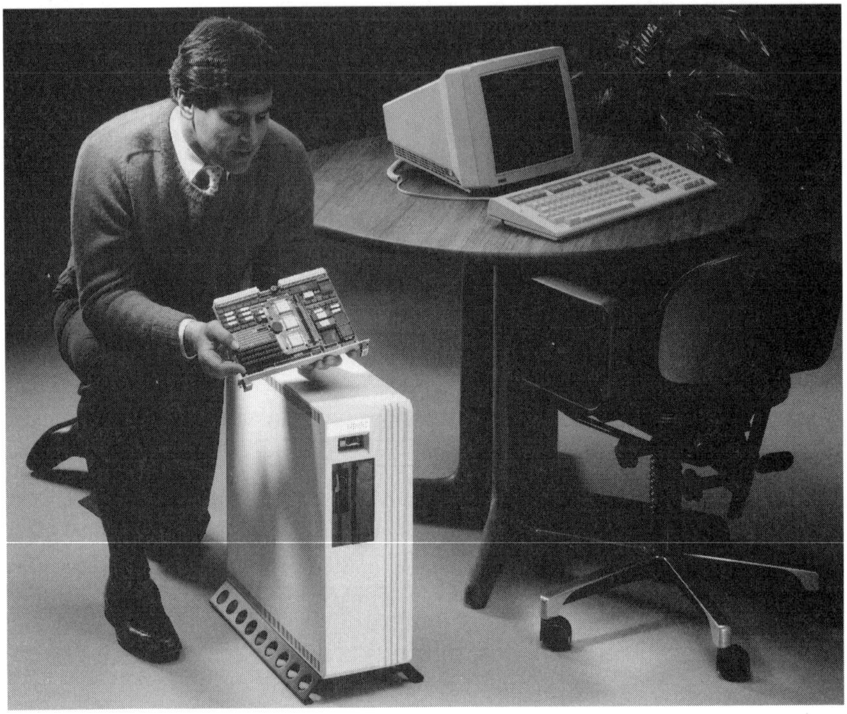

Fig. 6-5. bRISC from Dupont Pixels Systems is a new VME-based single-board UNIX computer that uses reduced-instruction-set computing (RISC) technology to provide over 13 MIPs of sustained performance. It provides parallel processing with separate on-board processors for applications and for I/O handling and is ideal for intensive multi-user networking environments.

discussed first because the AP has used EDs internally for over ten years and has the greatest influence, especially in the U.S.

The AP offers two different sizes of EDs. The larger ED is based on DEC minicomputers, has more input/output ports, greater speed, and greater storage capability. The new, smaller ED is PC based and uses the Intel 80386 microprocessor. The AP has used the DEC PDP-11/70 and 11/84 internally but is in the process of changing to the DEC MicroVax line of minicomputers. This is being done because DEC's main effort is now on the MicroVax line of minicomputers. The current configuration being marketed to member newspapers is ten ports and as many as six display terminals. The system can store 400 photos with an increase to 800 possible (at additional cost).

At present, the large ED has been installed in the *St. Petersburg Times* (FL), the *Minneapolis Star Tribune*, the *Chicago Tribune*, and *USA TODAY*. The display monitors can show 16 photos on the screen or *ups* at a time, in either black and white or color. The ED can also provide a video as well as digital output.

The four large AP EDs are essentially the same system that the AP has in its bureaus outside of its New York City headquarters. As of this time, the large EDs are considered commercial. The four units out in the field are 10-port models. When the typical analog image is transmitted to the large ED, it is captured and digitized. At the time the image is captured, two images are created. One is the TV image seen on the screen, and the other is the digital image (requiring over 3 Mb of storage) that contains all of the information. Manipulation and/or enhancement actually is done on the TV image on the monitor in a WYSIWYG (what you see is what you get) fashion. The coding for any changes is kept for the stored digital image. When the work is completed, the information on the changes is transferred to the digital image just prior to its conversion to analog and subsequent transmission over the AP wire-photo network.

The AP's well-established LaserPhoto I and II wire-photo networks use both input and output ports configured as part of the big 60-port ED in AP's New York City headquarters. Every port in the ED is duplexed and thus can be used for either input or output. In addition, a given photo can be queued and sent out through a single port if time is not a factor or distributed through multiple ports if the timing is critical. The AP has found that this kind of flexibility is essential in meeting the requirements of its member news publications.

AP calls their smaller unit a PC Electronic Darkroom. Several other companies also use the 80386 as the basis for their PC-based EDs, and I will discuss these subsequently. It has enough memory to store 360 black-and-white images, and the standard I/O port configuration is three input and one output ports. An interface to the Scitex pagination unit is available and also a digital interface for the Leafax 35 scanner.

In contrast to the large ED (which the AP calls its mainframe ED), only two or three test sites are planned for the PC version. Of these two or three sites, one is at the Chicago Tribune and at least one other will be in Europe. The smaller, 386-based ED receives the same analog signal, converts it to digital, and compresses the image 4 to 1 to save disk storage space.

One of the major driving forces behind the current newspaper industry interest in EDs is the AP PhotoStream satellite photo-transmission system. With PhotoStream and an ED, it is possible to transmit a color project—three filtered, black-and-white images that produce a color photo—in two minutes and 40 seconds, instead of the 30 minutes presently required. In addition, the transmission will be all-digital, thus eliminating any image degradation such as that produced by the present analog-transmission systems.

Although the AP's new PhotoStream system includes a transmission component with both ground and satellite links, the ED is a key element in the total PhotoStream system. PhotoStream is currently in operation internally by the AP, which is testing it daily.

With its PC-based ED called Image Terminal, Agence France Presse or the AFP has the lowest priced unit on the market. The device has three ports, compared to the AP's four-port ED and has only a black-and-white monitor. Picture storage is 100 to 120 depending on the wire service system. There are two input ports and one output port.

Impact Systems is the AFP's large ED. Impact Systems consists of a sizable bank of computers and memory storage: a large, high-resolution black-and-white monitor, a smaller color monitor, a keyboard, and a mouse. At the upper end, the system can have 24 input and/or output ports with 450 picture storage. This storage capability will be increased shortly to 600 pictures.

The AFP appears to be ahead of the AP in overseas commercialization, but the wire service has chosen to push its low-end unit first rather than the large unit, which is approximately equivalent to the large AP ED. AFP is second only to the AP in its phototransmission efforts.

Crosfield offers four models of its ED for newspapers that are sold under the name of Newsline. Crosfield is the largest electronic pagination firm supplying EDs. With the acquisition of Muirhead and its Picture Desk in June 1987, Crosfield has become an aggressive factor in the ED or picture-desk field. Unlike its wire service competitors, Crosfield is in the equipment business and offers a full line of color pagination equipment as well as the EDs.

Crosfield has four ED versions. The Model 2610, which is black-and-white only, is based on a 80386 CPU. It has one workstation, two terminals, three I/O ports, and can store up to 126 photos. The 2610 is black and white only while the Model 2615 is a color ED.

The Models 2620 and 2630 are based on the PDP-11/73 minicomputers and thus are larger and more costly EDs. In terms of number of I/O ports and photo storage, the 2620 and 2630 are the same. The 2630 has more terminals, can do more manipulations including making color separations, and has other additional features. The larger, multiuser 2630 has four workstations with a DEC minicomputer file server. The 2630 fills a gap in terms of I/O ports and other capabilities between the large AP ED and the PC-based EDs.

Crosfield has been working extensively with the *Los Angeles Times*. All of Crosfield's North American manufacturing facilities are at the old

Hastech plant in Manchester, NH, a location that should provide a good, low-cost situation.

Interfacing with the Autokons has been a problem because the individual Autokon units vary. Crosfield has stated that the firm has worked on this problem longer than anyone else and even they cannot guarantee full compatibility. Because Crosfield is a competitor to Scitex in color pagination, no Scitex interface was mentioned. Others, such as AP, have indicated that an interface to the Scitex pagination unit also was being developed.

Crosfield has stated that the Chicago Tribune is testing a Crosfield Newsline system in addition to the AP ED already in place. The *L.A. Times*'s Crosfield 2630 has 10 I/O ports, seven input and three output. The times also has a Crosfield Studio System color pagination installation.

Reuters has had a low-key presence with its News Picture Terminal. Reuters News Pictures Terminal (or RNPT) is based on the Intel 80286, not the 80386 as is the AP's and Crosfield's. The RNPT can only handle black and white. In addition, Reuters leases rather than sells their ED to customers of the Reuters news service.

There are two models, with the smaller one capable of storing 120 black-and-white photos (in the lower-resolution CCITT format) while the larger ED can handle 220 images. The Picture Desk is based on a NCR PC and has only one output and three input ports. Reuters transmits only black-and-white images at present. In terms of the wire-services ED, Reuters ranks a distant third behind the AP and AFP in the newsphoto area.

Reuters has indicated that there are 50 News Picture Terminal placements worldwide, with the majority being outside of the U.S. Reuters has said that U.S. requirements are the highest in the world, with most Reuters' subscribers being small to medium newspapers.

Reuters is a relative newcomer in wire-photo transmission as the UK based organization entered this field when the international operation of UPI was acquired several years ago. The key component of Reuters ED is the Reuters News Picture Terminal, which is already in the marketplace in Western Europe. Because the lease prices appear high, they might well decline once both AFP and AP achieve full commercial availability.

An example of the electronic darkroom is the publication produced through the efforts of Professors Eiler and Carr and their associates. It was distributed as The VisCom Tribune by Ohio University, Athens, Ohio. This issue consisted of a duplex, double broadsheet paper printed on conventional newsprint.

A color photo of acceptable resolution was printed in the same four-page issue. Although the original intent was to develop a system that a university could afford for teaching students about electronic prepress pagination (including both black and white and color photos), Carr saw a definite potential for its usage by small newspapers to run color photos. At present, only the largest newspapers can consider purchasing the multimillion-dollar color-pagination systems of Scitex, Crosfield, Hell, and other suppliers in order to run color photos.

According to Professor Carr, a number of steps were required to create the printed newspaper with the black-and-white photo. These were:

1. The image of a girl was originally recorded in an analog form with a Canon RC-701 Still Video Camera onto the standard 2-inch still video floppy disk.
2. The 2-inch floppy was placed in a Canon RR-551 Recorder/Player. The analog image was transferred into a two-megabyte Macintosh Plus computer equipped with a Magic Video Digitizer. LaserMagic software was used to control the digitizer.
3. The image was saved in 8-bit (256 gray levels) gray-scale TIFF format and imported into Letraset's Image Studio software. Several enhancements were made using Image Studio. These included sharpening the image's density curve. Contrast and brightness were set to produce a proper halftone for offset reproduction on newsprint. A sharpening filter was applied to small areas of the picture that included metallic or other strong highlights.
4. Graphics were prepared using MacDraw and Cricket Draw software. The stories were written with Microsoft Word. The pictures, text, and graphics then were combined into a broadsheet page layout using Aldus's PageMaker software.
5. The final page was printed on a Linotronic 300 Postscript typesetter. The three 11-×-17-inch files from the Linotronic were pieced together to make the camera-ready mechanical. The final page was offset printed.

A key element was that at no time in this process was a hard copy of the photo made: the entire production was done electronically until the final steps of making the mechanical and the actual printing.

NEW WAYS

In addition, existing and potential product advancements would have dramatically reduced the steps involved and considerably improved the output. There are a number of improvements that are already available, such as the new Macintosh II, with its higher speed, greater memory, and color graphics boards capable of displaying some 16 million colors or shades of gray.

In early 1989, National Digital Corporation introduced the last piece of their Photo Management Workstation—the piece that turns a preview system into a true production tool for publishers.

Imagine receiving developed film of European or Middle Eastern events from a press photographer outside of Paris, France and digitizing the images through a high-resolution scanner into a portable, PC-compatible computer-based Photo Management Workstation at a location outside of Paris, France. Once the information has been entered into the system, the local office places a telephone call to the picture editor of a prominent magazine in Washington, D.C.

The picture editor, seeking late-breaking news for a tight deadline weekly uses a regular Photo Management Workstation to call up the different images in a preview mode. Several are selected and individually cropped, enlarged, and manipulated to fit the magazine's format. When the final manipulated images are chosen, the editor orders reproduction-quality images that are sent digitally in a form compatible with the prepress electronic pagination system being used. Photos of news breaking at the magazine's deadline have been integrated into the story (Fig. 6–6).

This very scenario has been successfully demonstrated over ordinary telephone lines by National Digital Corp. for a prominent newsweekly that has already been using the preview capability of the system in regular production decisions, and then having the final photographic images—made to the specifications determined by the picture editor—flown to the printer. Now, when there is insufficient time to wait for the photographic pictures to arrive, the digitized images can be used.

Software is the key to the success of the Workstation. National Digital has developed software for compressing the digitized information along with error detecting and correcting software that allows the images to be transmitted without loss of information due to the drop-outs, spurious noise, etc., that accompany telephone line transmissions.

The core product of the image management system is the workstation. This consists of a PC-compatible computer (Compaq 286 or 386), two monitors, and a mouse. Usually, this workstation operates in conjunction with a preview scanner, a removable hard disk for extra storage and a 3-×-4-inch or 8-×-10-inch color video thermal printer.

Let's review the functions of this workstation. They include:

- Capturing (i.e., digitizing) images in color or black and white
- Compressing images so that many can be stored on a small disk and transmission time is reduced
- Storing and retrieving pictures electronically in just seconds.
- Transmitting digitized pictures at high speed over normal telephone lines

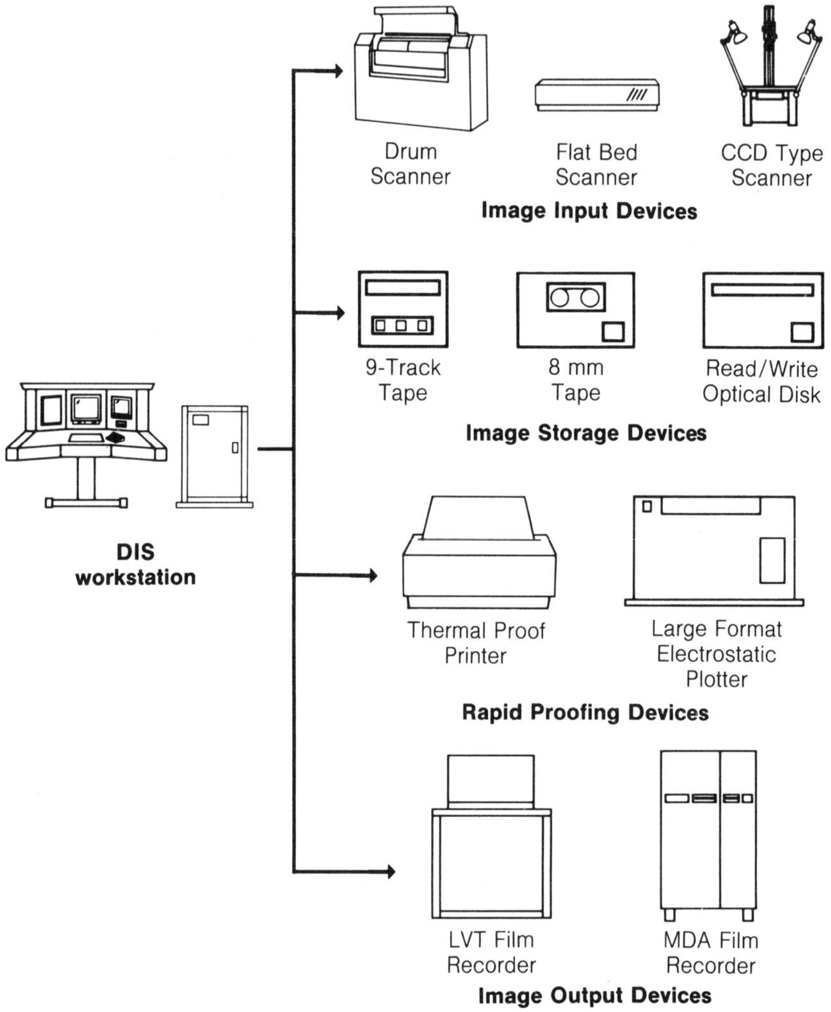

COURTESY DIS

Fig. 6-6. The DIS Workstation shows typical input and output capabilities for newspaper or magazine-publishing systems.

- Displaying and previewing the images
- Modifying and editing pictures, including the ability to flop, crop, tint, etc., and to convert the pictures to black and white.
- Printing the images in various formats and sizes for layouts or as reference copies

- Transferring the images to prepress systems such as Scitex, Crosfield, Hell, or DDES
- Maintaining statistical and other management data

Looking at each step in more detail, there are two scanners available. The medium-resolution preview scanner will convert a 2″ × 2″ (35 mm) color negative or slide into an 8-bit (256 gray levels) 512-×-341 pixel digital image in about 1 minute. The Production Resolution Scanner, just introduced, converts the same image into an 8-bit (256 gray levels) 3072-×-2048 pixel digital image.

However, because 36 times the information is being stored from the same original picture, the scanning time is also extended to about 15 minutes. (The analog-to-digital converters provide 12 bits of input per pixel, although the stored information is saved at only 8 bits.)

Besides photographic or other copy inputting from the two scanners, the system also can receive video input in NTSC format. This opens up the possibility of getting information from broadcast TVs, videocassette recorders, video disks, video cameras, or even electronic still cameras recording on the 2-inch diskette. A VCR can be used to grab incoming images, with later frame-by-frame compression into computer memory.

To reduce the memory required to store these images, they are compressed. Typically, the preview resolution image receives a 5:1 compression, while the production resolution images undergo a compression of 15:1 or more. A typical system is able to store 500 preview images. The removable hard disk drive, available for the full workstation, is provided with software, interface, and two 15 Mbyte cartridges (4 × 4 × 0.5 inches). These greatly extend the storage capacity, and additional disks can be filled as required.

Image storage ranges from 3000 to 50,000 bytes per preview image, depending upon the user-selected image size. Typically, 20 to 320 images are stored per Mbyte of memory. Along with the digitized image information, there is a caption box for up to 245 characters for each image. For preview resolution images, the Compaq 286 computer is used, while high-resolution images require the Compaq 386. In addition to the workstation version already discussed, a portable version and a desktop version are also available.

The portable version consists of a computer with mouse and keyboard and a single ruggedized monitor. It is capable of working with either the preview or production scanner for entering images into the system, and can receive and display pictures transmitted from other locations. One of the video printers also can be hooked up to the portable unit to provide a hard-copy output of the images.

For the desktop version, two color monitors and a copystand with video camera for inputting preview images are provided. High-speed modems along with error detecting and correcting software permit the digitized information to be sent at a 9600 baud rate over any POTS (plain ordinary telephone system), according to NDC vice president of Engineering Raoul Drapeau. Transmitted images are stored automatically at the receiving site, without the need for any operator to be present. The system also can be set to transmit at a predetermined time to take advantage of lower telephone rates, line availability, etc. In addition to the 245-character caption box with each image, unlimited messages also can be sent with each batch of photos.

Transmission time varies with the image size. For a preview image, it would typically be from 15 to 90 seconds. However, it takes 22 minutes to transmit a production resolution, full-color image. Because ordinary voice-grade telephone lines are used, the cost is at the minimum rate.

In addition to error detection and correction, the Photo Management Workstation software will also sense noisy lines and temporarily slow transmission to ensure that all the information is received. In the event of a broken transmission, the system redials and continues without the need to start from the beginning and resend previously transmitted data. These features also permit the system to be used over almost any telephone system in countries throughout the world.

Any workstation can display 1, 4, 9, or 16 images for previewing. The displayed images also carry an adjacent identifying number.

The easy-to-use menu-driven software offers a variety of operational functions: camera, display, communicate, print, alter, statistics, transfer, and exit. Under the camera mode, the user can select grab, H/V format, or adjust, and options, change, create, or batch. Under the options are frame, caption, default, video, grab, and compose.

Any individual image can be selected for manipulation. Although the system will not provide electronic retouching capability, it does offer the ability to flop up/down, flop right/left, reverse (negative), provide black and white, crop, or rotate. In addition the magnification can be changed, the brightness adjusted, tints changed (red, green, blue, or all) and the color balance altered. For publication purposes, it is possible to create the final high-resolution image on the screen and put the information into prepress pagination format for use without further manipulation other than placement.

The 3-×-4-inch video printer generally is used for outputting preview images, although a single image up to the full size can be printed. For larger images, the 8-×-10-inch video printer is used.

Color output can be obtained either as RGB (red, green, blue) or CMY (cyan, magenta, yellow). For printing, the black information is interpolated.

IMAGE INTEGRITY

With the advent of highly sophisticated electronic darkroom capabilities comes great concern over the integrity of photographic images. Once it was thought that photographs could be admissible in court, that they were difficult to alter without experts being able to recognize the alterations.

With the electronic darkroom, undetectable alterations to original photographs are possible. Ethics is a new issue raised by electronic photography. Here is the way that Hal Buell, Assistant General Manager for News Photo, Associated Press, New York sees the problem.

"The ethics problem with electronic digital photography is that it is easier to manipulate pictures. In fact, the changed picture cannot be shown as having been manipulated. For example, historically, as far back as Lincoln's time, pictures were altered, but when they were changed, an expert could tell they were modified. If they were altered with such skill that an expert could not tell that there was a modification, you could always ask for the original photographer's negative. The negative was very difficult to alter, if not impossible.

"With digital manipulation, you literally create a new picture that cannot be proved or disproved as being authentic. Today, there is the widespread availability of these manipulative skills. Someone operating a computer with keys needs no artistic talent to make the actual alteration. In the old days you had to be skillful with a knife, airbrush and all the other paste-up equipment needed to change the picture. The ease of manipulation makes the digital problem more complicated.

"Electronic photography and digital manipulation have not settled into the area of journalism yet. It is still a new capability and it is not widespread in the editorial and journalistic community. Advertisers for years have used manipulation of one kind or another to improve, change, or create the kind of picture that they wanted to use in an ad, but that facility is only now entering into the journalistic scene with the placement of sophisticated production prepress systems available today. It's really too early to comment on anything that has happened, but there have been some recent examples of pictures that were altered. The famous one was the cover of the book "A Day in the Life of America" where the cowboy was moved around on the hill and a moon was added.

"There is also the *National Geographic* photo in which the pyramids were moved to make a more pleasant and better composed picture. But those are unusual cases and there's really not enough experience yet.

"A couple of years ago when we began to realize that electronic photography was going to be part of the still picture scene, the first sensitivity that photographers expressed was the fear that editors were going to be looking over their shoulders on remote consoles if they moved to the right or left. They thought they might become like TV cameramen covering a football game and getting all their instructions from a director. That issue has not materialized, maybe it died because of its own silliness. That type of control is not going to happen. Photographers are still going to make pictures the way they have always made them.

"The second sensitivity relates to a kind of psychological romance between the photographer and the print. The making of a print is an artistic step, it's a pleasurable step in photography for most people, particularly when the photographer is dealing with his or her own negative. Even in the art world, prints made by the photographer who made the original negative go for higher rates at auctions than prints made by [someone] other than the photographer. There is a love affair between the photographer and the making of the print. I think it's a psychological problem that we could deal with. Given those two aspects, overall, photographers are excited about electronic photography. As a group, photographers are technically minded and see it as a way to get better pictures faster into the papers.

"Editors are only now beginning to be sensitized to the problems that electronic photography and digital processing are going to pose and there hasn't been a lot of discussion about it. In the next year or two it's going to be a buzzword and a hot item at journalistic seminars for editors. It's really too soon to give you any kind of definitive answer. Those editors who are into electronic photography and are aware of the problem are concerned about it. There has always been the ability to manipulate words to make them say what the writer or editor wants them to say, but historically, that has not been available to photography. Editors are very careful about the way they handle words. The same philosophy, attitudes, discipline and training that goes on in newspapers to develop words properly will apply to pictures also.

"Editors and publishers are becoming sensitive to electronic photography. There is going to be a period of some acceleration and then there will be a leveling off. Then there will be the longer pull as the system spreads more completely throughout the industry. In the newspaper industry there is that group that is very technically advanced and adapts quickly to new technology. They will be the people active towards the end of next year and into 1989. As those systems are developed, corrected and proved, more newspapers will gradually come in and probably over a period of five to seven years, we will see widespread use of digital handling within the newspaper and the transmission of pictures. I just can't predict when we will make pictures digitally for publication. It's a complicated engineering problem which people are working on, but today the solution is unclear."

THE FUTURE OF THE ELECTRONIC DARKROOM

Welcome to the hybrid world of digitized color imaging, where electronics and silver halide-based technologies are converging to define new frontiers of visual creativity! A number of professional labs have invested over a million dollars each in preparation for the future by offering hybrid electronic lab services.

"Digital image processing adds a new dimension to photography," said Bill Lamberg, Spectrum Photo Services president. "Digital color imaging systems are the way of the future," Lamberg continued, "because they expand our creative options while allowing us to meet critical deadlines and quality standards."

According to Los Angeles-based GP Color vice-president John Portaro, digital color-imaging systems offer tremendous capacity for experimentation. GP Color uses a Crosfield electronics PhotoTouch II system and serves clients ranging from movie studios to ad agencies.

"We can look at something on the workstation screen and if we don't like what we see, we can try something else. All we've lost is a few minutes.

"There's also more synergy between the lab and designer," Portaro added. "In a way, we're co-designers. Art directors or designers can present us with a concept and ask us to experiment. They can look over the system operator's shoulder and help discover the desired look."

Raymond H. DeMoulin, Kodak vice president and general manager, Professional Photography Division, said that new paths being blazed by the union of silver halide and digital imaging technologies are provocative.

"Digital color imaging is a hybrid which erases conventional imaging boundaries and provides an opportunity for us to create a new kind of aesthetic artform," he said.

The decision to implement hybrid imaging technology is not a casual one. Digital color imaging systems require substantial capital investment.

"It's easy to spend a million dollars entering this marketplace," said Portaro. "That's beyond the reach of most custom photo labs."

For Spectrum Photo's Lamberg, the high cost of installing of digital imaging system is offset by the capabilities it affords, which are far beyond what can be achieved manually. For example, every transparency generated through a digital imaging system is a first-generation original.

"Because the system stores information in computer memory, you can make numerous first-generation originals of any single image," he said. "And when you compare an electronically-generated transparency to an image that's been manually retouched, airbrushed or composited, many times you'll see a quality difference. Because of production limitations, the manually manipulated image may be four or five generations away from the original."

"In addition, once an image is digitized the original can be put away for safekeeping," said Lamberg. "All work is done electronically. The original piece of film or artwork may never have to be handled again."

"Digital imaging is tremendously efficient," noted Lamberg. "For instance, with the system we've altered a photograph of a European-version car so it appears as the American version. A photographer who shot a truck on location, and then discovered it was lacking part of its grille, had us clone in the missing portion.

"We've even created photographs of product prototypes before the prototypes have been built. We've done this by photographing the prototype parts separately and then digitally assembling these photographs into one final image."

Lamberg predicts the cost of digital-imaging technology will drop as 'downsized' systems are introduced. "A downsized system may not offer a full range of capabilities," he said. "Perhaps it might only be a retouching system. However, such a system will bring digital imaging technology within reach of more photo labs."

GP Color's Portaro envisions the use of an electronic paintbox to create digital proofs that will be communicated to an art director via modem. "By following a menu, the art director can alter or correct the image. Then the electronic image will be sent back to the lab, where a high-resolution image on film will be generated."

However, Portaro emphasized the electronic lab won't provide the solution for every problem. "GP Color has three skilled photo retouchers on staff," Portaro said. "I tell them not to plan on retiring anytime soon."

APPLICATION STORY

Electronic Photography in the Portrait Studio

Portrait photographers can choose several new systems using electronic photographs to show customers instead of traditional paper proofs. Customers find the video selection process easy, with final pictures delivered on conventional color photographic paper.

An electronic-image-previewing system for portrait photography that has been undergoing extensive field-testing was unveiled during the Professional Photographers of America convention held in Orlando, FL in 1988. A model of "The Studio of Tomorrow" was set up at Kodak's booth, with John and Trish Perrin from Portland, OR demonstrating how the equipment has helped them sell a wall portrait with almost every sitting, averaging $500 in sales per sitting, with 5 sittings/day, 5 days/week.

The Kodak Prism system uses a still video disk to capture the images of a portrait sitting. These can be shown later on a color monitor so that the customer can select the photograph for finishing. The overall system consists of a studio station and a sales station. The studio station features a beamsplitter that directs identical images into both a conventional camera and an electronic CCD color camera. The system design has a rigid rail for mounting a variety of film cameras, allowing the photographer to use his/her standard camera. Demonstration equipment was set up to accommodate a 6-×-4.5-mm format camera (Mamiya RZ67), but the system is designed to accommodate all medium-format cameras (6 × 6 mm and 6 × 7 mm), 35 mm, 4 × 5 view cameras, and even long-roll cameras for 46-mm and 70-mm formats, equipped with normal or longer focal-length lenses.

At the studio station, the photographer can view the subject either through the camera lens or on the video monitor (a 13-inch unit, the SV1300 is supplied as part of the system), but the demonstration system also featured a larger 19-inch monitor for the subject to see. The electronic system operates in a live mode until the image is snapped, when it stores (and displays) the captured image for a time that is controllable from 3 to 99 seconds. This gives the photographer a chance to review the recorded film and electronic image for closed eyes, awkward subject positioning, and other flaws. The subject also can see the captured image if the photographer provides a convenient monitor.

With the beamsplitter, about 1.5 stops of light are lost, according to Paul Ness of Kodak's Professional Photography Division. The normal light level of the modeling lights produce a relatively dark video image in the live mode, but John and Trish Perrin did not appear to have any difficulty working with it. Modeling light levels could be increased and a faster film would overcome any problems that might arise.

The electronic images are recorded on a 2-inch video floppy disk, using full frame storage (25 images per disk) for higher resolution. Although the preproduction models display the tracks/frames as 1:2, 3:4, etc., production models will show 1,2, etc. The mask color surrounding the electronic image also can be changed. In addition to black, choices include light and dark selections of gray, blue, and brown. User-friendly software allows the different masks, image display time, format (and vertical/horizontal orientation), etc., to be selected easily. The video floppy also can store such pertinent data as customer, roll number, and photographer number.

At the sales station, a customer-supplied 19-inch monitor is connected to a still video recorder. John and Trish Perrin provided soft music as the customer is shown the images for 1 to 8 seconds. These are treated like transparency-proofs, although a hard-copy output is not necessary. An optional color video printer can provide hard-copy prints if desired. Customers select the poses they want enlarged "at the time of the sitting", eliminating the need to return to review paper or transparency proofs.

What benefits will this new system (and the similar AutoStudio being sold by Noritsu) offer? "Having portraits taken can become fun," says Paul Ness. "Making your customer King or Queen for a day enhances the portrait experience." Seeing instant results should help to fine-tune lighting, sharpen technical skills, permit creative techniques to be developed and evaluated, and provide just what the customer wants. It can be used as a training tool for conveying principles easily to students. In a program to photographers at the convention, he concluded, "I predict that newer technology will be as significant a part of your business in the future as the telephone is today."

Another system is available in the form of the AutoStudio, shown first in early 1988 by Noritsu America Corporation in a preproduction form.

The patented AutoStudio uses a professional long-roll camera combined with a video pickup; the studio photographer can see the camera image in a handviewer. Camera height, lens zoom, and exposure can be done, using controls on the hand-viewer, from almost any location in the studio.

The same images captured on film are held in a unique electronic storage device that allows the customer to see all six proofs or any two proofs or one proof instantly at the touch of a button on a television monitor. Customer reactions to the system, with its projected backgrounds, has been good.

7

Tomorrow's Electronic Image

Electronic still photography is no longer a theory or a prophecy. Yesterday's promise has become today's reality. The only things yet to be defined are the various roles electronic photography will play in our everyday lives.

Today there are analog still video and digital still cameras. We are moving to higher-resolution systems both in the picture-taking side as well as the processing and output side. With the beginning of HDTV, we will be moving to new levels of electronic image quality, but it doesn't stop there.

There are new three-dimensional systems that allow you to turn your head and use your hands as part of a computer image. There are the miniature monitors that clip onto your eyeglasses and produce a full monitor image at that distance.

How about the new picture telephones that give you color and slow-motion video? Everywhere you look you see electronic images.

Much of the future depends on a combination of technological advancements and consumer acceptance. Judging by the trends in camcorders and the other new electronic products, the consumer likes the electronic image, and technology is moving at a pace beyond most of our abilities to cope with the changes.

OPTICAL COMPUTERS

One of the products that could affect electronic photography is the potential development of optical computers. Although IBM appears negative, AT&T has supported research on this product for several years and has already shown a working model. Individual devices already have been created for memory and switching, and the potentials of superconductors have been reviewed for possible application to optical switching devices.

The value of optical computers for electronic photography is the ability to switch rapidly large amount of data. There is even the potential of moving from an image to the processing and back again to a new form of image either in hardcopy, silver halide, or some other new material, using fiberoptics technology.

Optical computing is not immediately foreseeable, but it could be part of the beginning of the 21st century.

THE SILVER HALIDE/ELECTRONIC MARRIAGE

K. Bradley Paxton, Kodak vice-president and general manager, Electronic Photography Division, believes electronic photography will have its biggest impact as a tool for more effective communications in professional areas, including business, education, medicine, science, and government.

"We are a visually literate society," he said. "We use images to communicate information, concepts and emotions. I look for a happy marriage between traditional silver halide imaging and electronic photography. People will use silver halide technology to record high-resolution color images on film. They will use electronic imaging technology to store, transmit and display representations of these images in soft viewing and hard-copy formats."

Looking to the mid-1990s and beyond, Paxton said, "In the office, expect to see more color images output via electronic photography—and transmitted across the country or around the world in minutes. Electronic still imaging also should find wide acceptance in industry, schools and government, and at events such as athletic competitions," said Paxton.

As corporations, event promoters and the air-travel industry look for ways to beef up security, photo-identification card systems are becoming more in demand. With those systems employing electronic still image technology (for example, the Kodak Video ID card system), high quality, tamper-resistant cards can be produced quickly. During the 1988 Olympic winter and summer games, the Kodak Video ID system was used to produce thousands of photo ID cards.

Continuing, Paxton said, "In fields ranging from architecture and advertising to medicine, photorealistic imaging should take off. And the military is exploring still video for reconnaissance, since electronic images can be transmitted with high security to a command post for evaluation minutes after being taken."

Kodak introduced a broad line of electronic still image products in mid-1987. Those first products included two still image recorder/player models, a color electronic printer utilizing state-of-the-art thermal-dye-transfer technology, an electronic still-image transceiver, and an RGB monitor.

More recently, the company introduced the Kodak SV5035 slide/video transfer unit, and for government agencies requiring secure communications, a transceiver compatible with a STU-III telephone encryption scrambling device. Kodak also is manufacturing thermal-imaging media for a consumer color video printer being developed by Hitachi, Ltd.

However, Paxton predicted that despite the rapid advancement and acceptance of electronic photography, silver-halide imaging is still in the forefront as the high-tech photo capture and display technology. According to Paxton, the growth in popularity of hybrid imaging systems during the 1990s will be nothing short of explosive. In addition, computer technology will play a key role in the equation as image databases are compiled and managed.

Photorealistic imaging should become firmly established during the 1990s, said Paxton. The technology will cut across a broad range of professions. For example, industrial designers will utilize the technology for solid modeling applications. In advertising, storyboards will be configured by imaging workstations. Photorealistic imaging also will find a place in medicine.

Plastic surgeons, for instance, will manipulate images on-screen to show to a patient—prior to reconstructive surgery—the expected results of that surgery. Other physicians will use imaging workstations for diagnostic purposes, such as the evaluation of CAT scans.

"The imaging workstation will revolutionize the management of photographic images," noted Paxton, "much as computers have revolutionized information management. And as the photorealistic imaging market develops, the cost of workstations will drop."

When it comes to the future of electronic image capture technology, Paxton said Kodak is "leapfrogging" still video floppy (SVF) technology, and looking far down the pike toward digital still electronic cameras.

There are clear-cut advantages to utilizing digital technology over SVF technology, said Paxton. The image quality achievable through digital technology is much higher than what's possible with the analog still video floppy, noted Paxton, and a digital electronic still camera can be rugged and compact. There's also one drawback, however, at least for now. The problem lies in price.

Currently, technology for capturing, digitizing, and storing high-resolution images with anything close to film-like quality is very expensive, beyond the reach of most potential users. For that reason, until demand for the new cameras calls for high-volume manufacturing and a resulting price break, something that will take several years, high-resolution digital cameras are likely to be used for specialized government, industrial, and scientific applications.

In the meantime, Paxton predicts research and development efforts in electronic image capture will focus on two points: utilizing digital technologies, such as optical disk and rotary digital audio tape (R-DAT), to store image data, and developing higher-grade imaging sensors to complement digital-storage capabilities.

"A still video floppy holds 50 fields of analog video data," explained Paxton. "In order to hold the digital equivalent for 50 high-resolution images requires media with tremendous storage capacities. That's where optical disk and R-DAT come in. The still video floppy just doesn't have the capacity."

In terms of advancements in image sensors, and corresponding rises in image resolution, Paxton said recent improvements have seen sensors in consumer still video cameras go from 0.25 megapixel (250,000 pixels per image) to 0.4 megapixel (400,000 pixels per image). For commercial and industrial applications, a 1.4-megapixel sensor from Kodak recently became available, and the company now has a 4-megapixel sensor.

Despite these advances in sensors and the other progress electronic photography will make over the next few years, Paxton said the technology is still far from realizing its full potential. "There's no question that as time goes on, more applications will be discovered, and newer and better electronic photography tools will be developed. And as that happens, you'll find Kodak in the forefront," he promised.

PREDICTIONS

Here are some predictions from experts in the photographic field.

Benedict J. Fernandez
Chairman of the Department of Photography
Parsons School of Design/New School for Social Research
New York, New York

"Educators are in a panic not to be left off of the electronic bandwagon. They think video imaging is in and silver halide is out. But there really isn't any need to panic. At Parsons and the New School we are taking the position that electronic technology isn't going to replace silver halide processes; it is simply going to augment the silver image because people will have more choices. And more choices are good.

"Electronics definitely will have a big impact in amateur photography. By the early 21st century, the majority of people will be using still video cameras. They want its rapid capability and they love to project pictures on their home televisions. Eventually everyone will have the technology to product hard copies from their still video cameras.

"Electronics will change the face of professional photography as well, but it won't replace traditional photographic methods. It will, however, separate commercial photography from fine art photography. As electronics takes over the commercial business, it will move silver halide photography into the art world where it has always wanted to be. The silver halide photographers of the future are going to be the artists and photography will finally achieve stature as an art form.

"We are seeing an increase in enrollment in traditional—even non-silver—processes. We keep getting students for a class in dye-transfer printing. We sell basic photography classes to 800 students a semester. And on demand, we are introducing a four-day workshop on non-silver processes.

"Both electronic systems and silver halide systems will become tools for the creative process. Hybrid systems will emerge. The video image will support the silver halide image. A person will be a fine artist and make silver halide prints, but show work as an electronic portfolio, and carry an electronic portfolio.

"Ultimately the electronic image will help support the fine art of the silver halide image. And that is how we will be approaching it here.

Ron Scott
Advertising and Commercial Photographer
Houston, Texas:

"I am excited about the potential for computer manipulation. In silver halide processes, a photographer manipulates the tool—the camera—not the medium. He operates the equipment; he doesn't actually move the dots around, like a painter moves paint around on a canvas. Sometimes I've wanted to be able to go in there and move those silver halide crystals around. I'd like to move or remove elements. Purity is great, but in the real life we've got problems to solve and jobs to do. The computer will enable me to manipulate the image like a painter manipulates a canvas. I will be able to see and move those dots around. I think this will only enhance creativity, not threaten it.'

Eli Reed
Photojournalist, Magnum Photo Agency
New York, New York:

"I think that electronic imaging is still too far away to worry about, particularly with the advances in film stocks, both color—Kodachrome 200 professional film and Kodak Ektachrome 100 Plus professional film—and black and white—T-Max P3200 professional film.

"It will be a long time before pixels will rival film as a cost-effective high-quality medium on which to produce and store images.

"That aside, the notion of the electronic still camera is intriguing, more for color, though, than black-and-white. The problem with shooting color is that you begin to think about exposure and color temperature which distracts you from the image itself. On my wish list is a camera that would automatically compute color temperature and provide the proper exposure and filtration, like a video camera does, so I shoot in available light and concentrate on the image.

"I wonder though, if it will be possible to make the video images work in a form as successful as a traditional still photograph. I think people will always want the printed image. For example, everyone remembers that Pulitzer Prize-winning photograph that Eddie Adams took of the Vietnamese officer shooting the prisoner in the head. Most people don't realize that they also saw that same image on television. We simply don't remember it.

"Electronic images are somehow fleeting. It's as if we are programmed to think of them as transitory, while photographs that we can hold and carry around stick with us. This may be because visual communication in this form spans all cultural, language and literacy barriers."

Bill Pierce
Contract Photographers, *U.S. News & World Report*
New York, New York:

"Film and electronics will coexist because they each offer advantages. Electronics offers speed. Film is portable and cheap and provides an incredible 'pixel' count. The only drawback is that I have to get it back to a darkroom.

"Right now the factors determining the viability of electronic still cameras are the size of the equipment and the storage medium.

"When you think electronic you think journalism, particularly fast-breaking news. Transmitting is the key. You may be able to record a super high-fidelity image, but right now it takes too long to transmit it. I'm told that Bell Labs is devoting some effort towards programs that will allow us to store and transmit more efficiently. That will make a difference.

"I see a place for super high-quality electronic photography, even in its current bulky size, for fixed position work like presidential conventions or inaugurations. The lens itself could be small, and the camera would be mobile, with a remote control. The bulky equipment would be stored in a van somewhere. Just as ENG (electronic news gathering) cameras got more compact and handheld, we'll see that happen with electronic still video.

"Photographers will choose a faster transmission rate for editing purposes, and a slower, more high-quality rate for the final selects.

"There will be very good film photography and very good electronic photography. The question will be when do I use what. If I want an inexpensive high-quality system, I will use film. Even a dye transfer print from Kodachrome film is still more economical than something output from a fancy CEPS (color electronic prepress system).

"The question of manipulating photographs doesn't worry me. We have always been able to manipulate the image. I am worried about the seduction of electronic manipulation, even for hard nosed editors who insist that they wouldn't alter news images until they see just how easy it is to change that color a bit. Electronic manipulation is simply more seductive than darkroom manipulation because it provides immediate feedback.

"Manipulation raises its head as an issue of ethics in journalism. The question of ethics is far more serious than that of manipulation. The dwindling marketplace for serious news stories worries me more than using an electronic system to turn the sky blue.

"The problem of ethics does not lie with the equipment, it lies with the photographer. The reason we have problems of ethics is not because we can manipulate images electronically, but because we are at a time where the photojournalism publications are having an identification struggle. Instead of grappling with that, we are worried about whether we are taking the telephone poles out electronically.

"One real problem with manipulated images will be that of ownership. If copyright is a Gordian knot now, it is going to become a treble Gordian knot.

"I look forward to electronic photography because of the things it will allow us to do. I won't get out of my darkroom, though, let that be clearly understood.

"Photographers are terrified of electronics, but then they were terrified when they were handed autofocus cameras. The electronic camera itself is the easiest thing to adjust to. Photographers shouldn't be afriad. If they can get through autofocus, they can get used to a camera with a wire coming out the back.

"The real threat from electronic still equipment will be the wires. The true Gordian Knot will be whether someone can fight his way through all the power cords. If a photographer were using several bodies with flash units, well, he or she could literally strangle on the cords. And what will happen if it rains? We could all be electrocuted.

Carl Machover
Machover Associates
White Plains, New York:

"Electronic photography, it seems to me, gives us some new arrows in our quiver, so to speak. It gives us an opportunity to move further along in this concept of a paperless society, although the presence of electronic photography will probably give rise to even more paper. One of the things that it is leading to (which becomes part of other trends) is the ability to store images which historically had been stored on paper and distributed as prints. Now we can store them in electronic files as optical memories and distribute them as raster images. A significant amount of work is going [on] in that area and many of us believe that, in the not to distant future, most large volume image distribution will be done by these electronic images.

"Today, resolution is the problem. My understanding is that the current range of commercial product has resolutions which are a quarter that of 35-mm film, which means that for high quality images, it is just not adequate. The second issue is that right now, the costs are very high. The electronic cameras are in the order of several magnitudes more expensive than conventional cameras, and unless that price comes down, the market for them will be narrowly limited. I think also we need to see further improvements in relatively low-cost hard copy devices. It seems to be a conflict, but we do need to have the portability of carrying images and that image typically will now be taken from a video environment which comes from electronic photography. I have always been struck by the difference in value that an industrial user places on this environment compared to a consumer.

"A few years ago when Sony first introduced the Mavica System and they talked about the hard-copy unit associated with it, the editor of the consumer magazine in photography was just livid because it was projected, in the future, to cost almost $1000. For us in an industrial environment, the ability to get fast, hard copy in color for as little as $1000 is always remarkable. A consumer market is a much broader one, but today's price factors are simply too high. The last issue which is just beginning to be resolved is a way of recovering the data. We really aren't sure how to recover graphic images. Most of the time in the past we have recovered in a numeric scheme of one kind or another, and in fact there are products today like Pictureware, a company in Philadelphia, which has a database system which includes visual images, but the information is recovered on a word-type basis. Somewhere along the line it would be great if we could recover images by visual features rather than alphanumeric features.

"Electronic photography is the AT&T Targa boards as well as the many plug-in cards that come from a variety of other sources, the digital paint systems like Imapro, and I think these are very significant because they offer essentially electronic retouching, whether that's to retouch consumer photographs to make them look better or to retouch page images or advertisements, or what have you, I think this is a vast field that just has started and I see some major growth areas occurring.

"If we look at electronic imaging as a market and don't look at the electronic photography, the consensus is that in '86 the electronic imaging market was somewhere in the $4 billion range. It probably had a growth of about 30 percent. The digital paint and animation portion of that market was about $200 million in '86 and is probably growing at the 30 to 35 percent range. Right now the scanning part of that market [is] 10 percent or under and electronic photography is part of that area. We are starting from a fairly small base, but I think the growth opportunities are enormous."

Richard D. Schwarz
Shearson Lehman Hutton, Inc.
New York, New York:

"Electronic imaging, at a macro level, is a wide variety of markets that are now being served by systems that employ digital imaging processing technology. Within each of those markets—there are over 20 of them—there are application clusters that a particular image-based processing system will address.

"There are some very big markets. Graphic arts is a market that is going digital. Will it go entirely digital? Of course not, but it is going digital and it's huge—a hundred billion dollars plus. For defense systems, weapons guidance and that area, this technology is increasingly important. It's important to realize that digital image processing is going into so many markets, a number of which are absolutely huge (Fig. 7–1).

"As a product system that captures the imagination and pocketbooks of the mass market, I don't think electronic photography is going to happen in

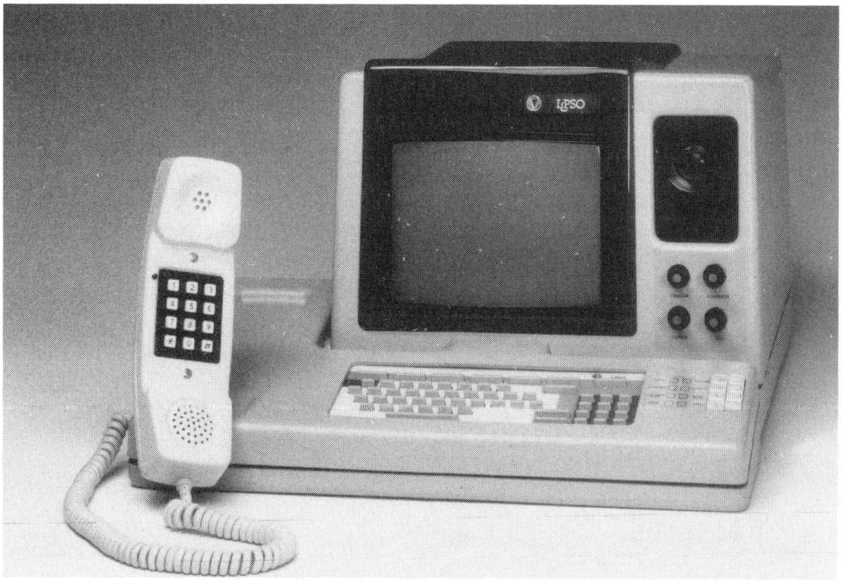

Fig. 7-1. The Vuphone allows users to carry on a telephone conversation with eye contact, as well as other video tasks such as holding a remote conference or remote teaching and fault finding.

the next couple of years. What's happening with image processing is not that dissimilar to what happened to computer technology. It was manifest initially in very large, centralized, costly systems. As the computer got smaller, cheaper, faster and easier-to-use, it diffused through the economy till it ultimately met the parameters of the consumer market. But long before we had the personal computer or the home computer, it was used in much more sophisticated applications. In a sense, the home computer is the analog of electronic still photography. That will be the last market tackled.

"As to how long it will take, first of all, digital imaging technology is not a new technology, it's been around for a couple of decades. It has burst on the commercial scene in the last four or five years because some of the components have became a lot cheaper in a very short period of time. It's not a new technology in that sense. Secondly, all of these technology cycles are accelerating. If it took 25 years at some past time frame, the new technology is not going to take that long now. It's a long way of saying that we will have in five to seven years electronic still photography that is going to be a significant factor with the consumer. Will it dominate film? I doubt it. One thing about the film based systems—they're getting better all the time. You've got a hundred dollar 35-mm format auto-everything camera out there now [so] that even I can't botch up the picture. And the new films like Kodak's Gold are superb. That's not an easy target.

"Medical research and diagnostics is clearly going with digital imaging. The technology is embedded in CAT scan units, nuclear magnetic resonance units and other systems. Graphic arts, military, law enforcement for fingerprint identification—these markets are clearly drifting toward digital.

"Small companies are in the market by the hundreds. All the big companies that are in the peripheral [area] are going into electronic imaging. In most cases, it's a small part of their total business. If you look at companies like the De La Rue Company, a British based company, they're going into the field. 3M has [made] a number of forays into electronic imaging and I certainly don't view the company as a play on electronic imaging. Kodak is going into it—it is a ubiquitous area—it is going everywhere. But the pure plays are with the smaller higher risk companies."

COMPARING ELECTRONICS AND SILVER-HALIDE PHOTOGRAPHY

For too long people have been drawing eye-for-an-eye comparisons of electronic still photography with silver-halide imaging. These are the same folks who think that apples are oranges.

They haven't given the soft (video screen) image a chance. Maybe the owners of 160 million television sets in the United States are all wrong. Maybe the massive use of video tapes for entertainment, communication, and education is just a passing fancy. Maybe the extensive use of color computers (some say almost entirely color by 1990) is just a fluke.

Electronic photography is a medium of its own, with unique characteristics that can entertain, inform, educate, and contribute much to science, medicine, and business. However, it's a new medium and that's the way we should be looking at it. It shouldn't be limited to just a hard-copy approach as some have thought.

Why can't video tape do the same job as the new generation of electronic still video cameras? First, try to find an exact frame in a video tape. Then there is the problem of the videographer. Few people know how to make a good video tape. Most people play slide-trombone with the zoom—panning on everything to the point of video sickness (directly related to car and motion sickness)—and don't know when to take their fingers off the take button.

Still, electronic photography today can be the medium you use in your living room. You will be a lot less bored looking at 25 or 50 still images, being able to oh-and-ah over the baby, vacation scenes, or family events rather than at a boring, two-hour show (Fig. 7–2, color section; courtesy Fuji Photo).

How about the businessman who can now make a dramatic desktop presentation or show a story board through selected video images. Then there is the scientific worker who can use the computer with a number of available analog-to-digital converters to make the images into measurable, variable images that can be processed at the touch of a computer key.

Don't forget the artist. For two decades, the artist has used video as a medium. Now with electronic still video, he or she has a new, exciting medium for the capture of entirely new images in whatever dimension or time space he desires.

Yes, it's apples and oranges. Electronic still photography is a new tool that should be appreciated in its own right. It can create true, instant images that are processable and viewable in a variety of available video equipment, and editable, printable, and even projectable with the excellent video projectors available today. Electronic still video is different, but viva la difference (Fig. 7–3, color section)!

THE FUTURE IMPACT OF HDTV

In Europe, the Eureka research group demonstrated all the elements of a full chain of compatible HDTVs at the International Broadcasting Convention in Brighton, England, at the end of 1988. It covered studio facilities, satellite and terrestrial transmission, home-video recorders, laser-disc players, and TV receivers. Led by N.V. Philips of the Netherlands, Thomson S.A. of France, and Robert Bosch GmbH of West Germany, the Eureka group includes 26 other European manufacturers, broadcasters, and research laboratories. The HDTV effort, started in 1986, uses 1250 lines and 50 Hz to meet European requirements, and provides a 16:9 aspect ratio on the screen display. It is compatible with standard Phase-Alternation Line (PAL) and Secam systems as well as Multiple Analog Component (MAC), the European direct broadcasting by satellite standard.

Following the FCC decision in September 1989 that any HDTV standard adopted in the U.S. be compatible with existing systems, Philips started promoting its High Definition System for North America (HDS-NA), which is NTSC compatible. P.W. Boegels, a Philips executive who is president of the Eureka HDTV group, stated that Philips believes its system has a chance of being adopted in the U.S., although "other systems, which are also compatible, are being developed. "We need to get together in the United States, review all the systems being proposed, and agree on which is the best."

A meeting of the European Community-Japan HDTV Working Group in London was followed by a communique that said it recognized the importance of unified world-production standards, but recognized that this goal will be difficult to achieve.

The Japanese Hi-Vision HDTV system, based on 1125 lines and 60 Hz, was demonstrated publicly during the Seoul Olympic Games. However, it is incompatible with existing studio equipment and domestic receivers (Japan uses the NTSC standard). As a result, the Japanese appear isolated from the U.S. and European efforts.

THINGS THAT WILL AFFECT THE FUTURE

Digital images are the future of electronic imaging. Storage and transmission of digital images are a real challenge because of the size of the storage space required. Iterated Systems, Inc. of Atlanta, GA has come up some unique approaches to the analysis, compression, storage, transmission, and synthesis of images.

For example, a 1024-×-1024-bit per pixel image can be transmitted over a 2400-baud modem in just under three hours. However, Iterated Systems produces a similar image in less than 10 seconds using the same 2400 baud modem.

Using a variety of mathematical functions, including fractals obtained from an iterated function system (IFS) and several other mathematical tools, it is possible to compress an image up to 10,000:1 and reconstruct the image in a highly creditable form.

The work being done by Iterated Systems can be described as one of the first practical applications of the Chaos Theory being expounded in scientific circles today. Plans are under way for a demonstration of the feasibility of real time-video compression using these new techniques.

The work being done by Iterated Systems is designed for large computer systems, but it does offer the hope of new ways of compressing images and increasing the use and capability of electronic-imaging systems.

HOW DIGITAL IMAGING WILL AFFECT US

Imagine the future of the moving image. Imagine pictures and sound beamed down from satellites or transmitted over fiberoptics, providing greatly enhanced television reception. Imagine high-definition TV displayed on flat, wall-size screens.

Imagine movie theaters with bigger, wider, and brighter screens. And how about colors so deeply saturated that viewing them is a tactile experience—images so crisp and sharp that every seat is the best one in the house—even in the front row.

The question isn't if. The question is when? Inventors and dreamers have always shared a quest for learning how to write with light. It's natural; in a sense, man's mind is a camera. But the images it records are imperfect and fleeting. There are no words, drawings, or paintings that accurately describe the images you can capture on film.

"There is good technology today for transferring images recorded on video tape to film," said Joerg Agin, Kodak vice-president and general manager, Motion Picture Division. He went on to add that there was no practical way to go in the other direction.

Digital postproduction will change that equation. Agin noted that the technology needed to develop film to digital interface tools already exists, and the challenge now is to effectively integrate the parts. Much behind-the-scenes progress has been made already.

"We need to develop a 'filmreader' which will economically scan and convert all of the subtle imagery recorded on the emulsion into digital output," Agin said. "Then, we can use sophisticated digital imaging workstations for editing, visual effects, titling and everything else that you would ever want to do during electronic postproduction."

Agin noted that at this stage it would also be easy to alter such imaging characteristics as grain, sharpness, contrast, and color by applying digital technology. This could be done without altering the artistic content of the original negative.

The next step would be to translate the digital imagery into release format. If that format is television, digital transfers could be made directly onto video tape or laser disk. Tapes could be customized for different television systems used in various countries. The 35-mm film used for origination will be compatible with all of the proposed high-definition TV systems under consideration around the world.

A 'filmwriter' will be used to convert digital image information to an analog printer. Agin said this probably will be some sort of a laser device that writes with bursts of intense light onto either high-resolution film intermediates or print film.

"Both approaches have some merit," Agin noted. "If you go directly from digital output to prints, you are saving the time and costs associated with making a film intermediate. You also are making first-generation quality-release prints. However, you are using the filmwriter to make thousands of prints. If you make a film intermediate, you still get excellent image quality, and you can make your prints with existing high-speed equipment in laboratories."

What else can we anticipate for the 1990s and beyond? "Digital optical sound should definitely be in theaters by the early 1990s," Agin went on. "That will add a new dimension to the movie-going experience. We also look for a resurgence of big screen and special-venue presentations."

As for HDTV, he said, "I expect that it will have the same impact on film production as home video. It will give people more and better viewing options, and it will make film look better on television than it ever has before. That is likely to boost film production. The 1990s could be a new golden age for filmmakers."

Another Kodak view of the future comes from Kodak VP Larry Matteson. He explained how vendors such as Kodak were researching future new avenues of technology. He said "Future growth of print media will be fueled by customer expectations for color in all their documents." He also said, "The major impact of electronics will not come from initial image capture, but from the dramatic improvement in imaging work stations."

"Electronics and silver halide are not locked in a technology struggle," said Raymond H. DeMoulin, Kodak vice-president and general Manager, Professional Photography Division. "We believe the relationship between traditional and electronic technologies is synergistic."

That synergy envelops all aspects of the professional photography industry worldwide. Whatever the eventual marriage between film and electronics, film will continue to be the yardstick for measuring image quality, DeMoulin predicted.

Industry analysts forecast that for most market segments—photojournalism being the potential exception—film will remain the most cost-effective medium for some time. The reasons are clear: a single 35-mm color negative frame contains some 15 million pixels. A transparency on Kodachrome 64 professional film, 120 format, contains some 60 million pixels. In contrast, today's highest resolution electronic sensor can provide 16 million pixels of image information, but at a very high cost.

Electronics will have the biggest impact on professional photography in the image-enhancement stage. This mirrors today's marriage between motion-picture film and electronics: film is preferred by most for origination while electronic manipulation is firmly established for postproduction.

The photojournalist of the 21st century will use different tools than his 20th century counterpart. Films with speeds in the ISO 3200 range, for both black and white and color, will be commonplace and combined with the quality found today in films of lower speed. Electronic still cameras will make their debut for fast-breaking news stories in situations where time is more critical than quality. Electronic systems will continue to be used to transmit and store images originated on film. This type of hybrid film-electronic system will become standard in news situations.

"Photojournalism is the first market for electronic still cameras," said DeMoulin. "We will see the current type of still video camera used in situations where time, not quality, is paramount. Wire services will use them first."

The barriers to acceptable still electronic systems are speed, image quality, and size. Currently storage presents another obstacle for still video. Digital still video cameras use a 2-megabyte SRAM (static random-access memory) card for storage. Although DRAM (dynamic random-access memory) technology is moving towards 4- and 16-megabit capacity at low prices, SRAM is at least two generations behind.

DRAM requires too much power to refresh the fading memory; SRAM circuitry corrects that problem but at significant cost. A 2-megabyte SRAM card (containing 16 one-megabit chips) today is estimated to cost between $3000 and $5000.

This price range is expected to drop significantly to the $100 range by the late 90s. With data compression, this card could store over 50 low-resolution images.

In the immediate future, color will be the driving force in newspapers. Currently, 1400 of the 1600 Sunday newspaper inserts in the U.S. and Canada have some color. In Europe, newspapers are just moving into color.

On another front, the portrait studio of the 21st century will be an interactive playground with the subject-customer playing a key role. The new Kodak Prism electronic previewing system will help portrait photographers increase their business because it will bring the buying process closer to the creative process.

Based on patented Kodak technology, the Kodak Prism system simultaneously captures on still video floppy disk an image identical to that captured on film. With this hybrid system, the photographer and portrait customer can view the electronic preview image both during and after a sitting.

"In the future, it (Prism) will aid commercial photographers as well.

With improved color on the monitor, a commercial photographer could use the Prism system in lieu of instant photographs and transmit images to a similar system on the art-director's desk," DeMoulin said.

Commercial photographers will have an array of products to choose from: color films that are even more consistent, color films to satisfy our color palette, and wonderful electronic tools for image enhancement and manipulation.

Professionals have indicated that electronic image-enhancement systems could be crucial to the professional photography industry. They want a system that can accept a variety of input materials, including transparencies and negatives.

The system should be able to merge, crop, rotate, and clone images as well as write to color negative and transparency films. It should also be able to change color balance, saturation, and contrast and do it all with terminology that is common to the commercial lab industry. These labs will offer a complete selection of electronic processing services. Photographers who choose not to own electronic systems will be able to affiliate with a color lab that does.

"Kodak is committed to applying its technology expertise to enable commercial labs to move into electronic image enhancement," said DeMoulin. "Film will continue to be the preferred input because it's of the highest quality. It will be digitized and manipulated electronically and output digitally onto either negative or positive film."

In early 1990, Kodak announced and demonstrated the Kodak Premier Image Enhancement System for commercial photo labs.

To crystallize a perspective on the future of imaging and photography, just look at how far we've come. Sensitized metal plates that could record an image in only 30 minutes under full sunlight were considered a breakthrough 150 years ago. Today you can purchase black-and-white and color negative films that are up to 16 million times more sensitive.

The first human photographic subjects had to remain motionless for long periods. Today, modern cinematography can capture high-speed action sequences with tack-sharp detail under the most demanding lighting conditions.

Frenchman Louis Daguerre's plates measured 6 1/2 × 8 1/2 inches. Today, full-color images that can be enlarged easily to 20 × 24 inches with virtually no grain come from a negative no larger than one inch by an inch and a half. The technology that photohistorian Beaumont Newhall called "The Mirror With a Memory" had indeed come a long way.

Will electronics overtake conventional silver-halide films despite a 150-year head start?

The answers to this question can be found at Kodak Research Labs. The company's scientists have been pioneers not only in exploring conventional photographic technology, but in electronics. What do these experts have to say about the film/electronics horse race?

"If you consider all the factors, including image quality and economy, electronic systems won't catch up to silver halide photography for a dozen years or more. Even so, electronics offers some potent advantages," said Dr. Rajinder P. Khosla, director of the Microelectronics Technology Division at Kodak Research Laboratories. "Electronics and film breakthroughs can be combined to build products that could not be achieved with one technology alone."

"When you look at a print made from Ektar 25 film, it's difficult to imagine how anything could look better. Yet, there is a considerable margin for improvement in silver halide films. In fact, electronics are helping us make film work even better," noted Dr. Gerhard Popp. Popp is director of the Color Negative Technology Division at Kodak's Research Laboratories.

These two men lead teams of scientists who have developed the world's most advanced imaging systems in their respective technologies. Khosla's crew, for example, recently unveiled a solid-state sensor with a resolution of 2048 $\times$ 2048 picture elements, or pixels. That's more than four million pixels. To put that in perspective, consider the sensors in a video camcorder that can capture only about 250,000 individual pixels.

However, a four-megapixel sensor is far from the ultimate. Kodak already has brought to market a product that can capture at least twice that much information: Kodak Ektar 25 film. The world's best "sensor" is, in fact, a film that has set new standards for image quality.

Both Dr. Popp and Dr. Khosla feel that electronics and conventional film technology will complement each other into the 21st century. "There are some applications where electronic imaging systems are ideal," Khosla said. "Tiny sensors can be built into internal probes to provide physicians with close-up, real-time views inside a patient's body. Astronomers can use mosaics built of many sensors to photograph the skies over long periods of time."

For the time being, the cost of electronic still imaging will limit applications in the consumer area, he noted. However, there is growing use of the technology in commercial, scientific and government applications. Electronic still systems are used by real-estate professionals, security experts, astronomers, manufacturing engineers, and others who can justify a trade-off in picture resolution and higher expense for the flexibility of electronic storage and display.

"In the future, electronic still photography will coexist with traditional photography to add value to a wide range of imaging applications," said Khosla. "There will continue to be growth in traditional photography, as the cost-performance of film systems will remain highly attractive to picture-takers. In addition, the film-electronics interface will provide users with a high degree of flexibility and capability."

Designers and fabricators of very high-resolution sensors face stiff technological challenges because requirements for defect-free devices are more demanding than for computer memory chips, according to Khosla. This makes the production of high-resolution sensors the most complex and costly of all integrated-circuit-manufacturing processes.

Costs will drop and image quality will improve, Khosla promised. "It's almost impossible to tell the difference between a 3R print made from a film negative from one made with the best experimental electronic systems," Khosla said. "For many applications, this is good enough. After all, people watch television for hours a day and don't complain about the image quality."

Electronic still systems will have to drop to the $500 price point to see widespread acceptance, he added. Khosla doesn't expect to see that happen soon. Meanwhile, we will see more hybrid systems, imaging systems that combine the strengths of electronics and silver halide technologies.

The Kodak Prism electronic-previewing system is a prime example, he noted. The product allows capturing an image identical to that captured on film on a still video floppy disk.

The film image can be processed and used to produce high-quality prints, yet the photographer and portrait customer can view electronic images during and after a sitting. They can select poses for printing immediately, without waiting for the film to be processed. The consumer gains instant gratification. At the same time, the photographer gains the opportunity to sell prints when the customer's enthusiasm is highest.

Another example of a hybrid system is the Kodak Create-a-Print 35-mm enlargement center. This product allows consumers to blow up, crop, and print their own enlargements easily and quickly. Customers insert their processed color negatives into the Create-a-Print unit (Fig. 7–4).

A video monitor displays an image of the snapshot as it will appear in the enlargement. Once the picture is composed to the customer's liking, a press of a button starts the printing process. A few minutes later a finished print emerges.

Other hybrid systems abound. Motion-picture companies are producing television programming and theatrical features on film to obtain the best available image quality. However, where time is a factor, they find that transferring to videotape for editing offers additional speed and flexibility.

Digital imaging and electrophotographic techniques are used in some of the most advanced copiers today. Businesses have found that microfilm has unmatched archival permanence and economy. However, microfilm databases also can be digitized for transmission over computer networks.

These are only a few of the hybrid systems in use today. In the future,

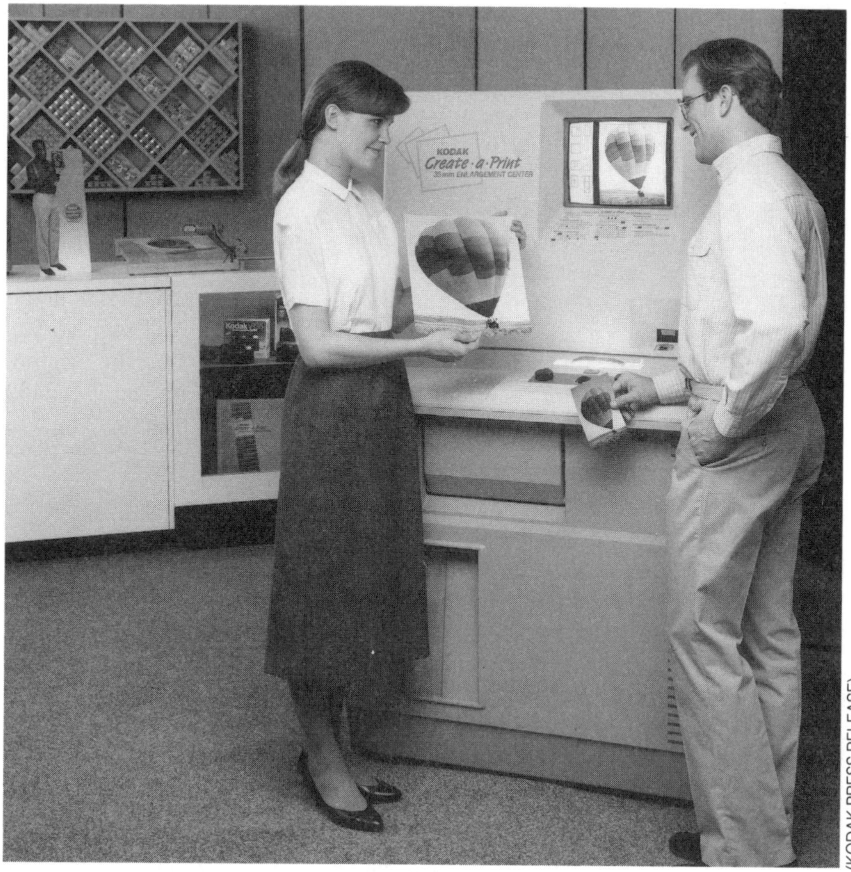

(KODAK PRESS RELEASE)

Fig. 7-4. An example of hybrid technology in the Kodak Create-a-Print Station, which allows customers to take their color negatives and make their own enlargements using the television screen for composing their photograph.

we will see even more extensive combinations of film and electronics technologies, the two scientists predict.

For example, electronic systems are helping Kodak produce better films, reported Popp. "We make extensive use of computer modeling to predict how a new film will behave," Popp explained. "The computer can calculate the grain, color, sharpness, contrast, and other characteristics of a film when we supply information about the emulsion. That lets us play 'what-if' games. For example, what would happen if we changed the order of the film layers, or added this new color coupler?"

The computer simulation is no rough 'guesstimate,' either, he emphasized. Laser printers can be used to produce sample prints that look exactly like those that would be produced by the new film. "Now, when our researchers begin work on a new film program, they have target prints available telling them what that film should look like," Popp said.

How much room for improvement is there in film technology? Former director of Kodak Research Laboratories, Dr. Jack Thomas, used to say that a one-stop gain in imaging efficiency came every seven years. That is, a new film with an ISO rating of 200 could have the same image characteristics as one at ISO 100 seven years earlier.

This pace has accelerated considerably in recent years, with that same one-stop gain coming in about three to four years, according to Popp. Today, films like Ektapress Gold 1600 provide image quality as good as the original Kodacolor 400 of 1977. Popp said he could visualize some day an ISO 6400 film with the image quality of today's Kodacolor Gold 400 film.

In that case how will these gains in imaging efficiency be applied? How sharp or how fast does a film need to be?

"Improvements in film provide a great deal of flexibility in terms of picture-taking and camera design," Popp explained. "We might find that totally available-light photography is practical. Or we might use those gains to reduce the size of the negative, making smaller cameras possible."

Camera manufacturers, in particular, are quick to exploit the features of new films. Leica and other manufacturers already have announced that they will redesign some of their lenses to take advantage of the sharpness of Ektar 25 film. For the first time in many years, they said, the film is not the limiting factor in image quality.

Breakthroughs in photographic technology could provide benefits the average consumer might not even think of. Films with less silver and smaller film sizes use less processing solution. That would be good news for the photofinisher because both costs and effluents would be reduced.

It's inappropriate to think of the growth of film and electronics technology as a horse race. Silver-halide systems, after all, have had a significant head start and are still moving ahead at top speed. Instead, electronics and film might best be considered as a team hitched to the same wagon. Working together, they can provide the consumer with capabilities neither could provide alone.

HDTV AND A DIGITAL TOMORROW

Probably the two most meaningful developments that will affect electronic photography are HDTV and the continued progress in digital technology. HDTV is predicted to be available in the mid-1990s. Along with it will come new cameras, new chips to meet the needs of these higher-resolution cameras, and new TV sets and output devices to match. Industry predictions are that 25% of homes will have HDTV sets by the end of the 1990s. Although no match to the 160 million homes with NTSC sets now, that still is a tremendous growth in a product that will afford greater quality and a totally different format for viewing. With its 9:16 ratio, HDTV promises to present a much more interesting image to the eye.

Already new cameras from NEC Corporation have been demonstrated, using 2-million pixel CCDs. These CCDs reach that magic level of 1 megapixel in image information that has been one of the horizons needed for electronic still photography. The cost of these CCDs will be high initially, but as volume gains and new technologies CCDs appear, it might even be possible to reach well beyond the level of these new CCDs.

Memory chips also are rapidly increasing in capability. Although we have 1-megabit DRAMs today, 4-megabit DRAMs are reaching the market, and promises of 16-megabit DRAMs or higher are expected in a short time. As these larger memory chips become available, it becomes easier to build the necessary memory to handle higher-resolution images. Actually, the change in the capabilities of chips, integrated circuits, and CCDs has been logarithmic, and it is not expected to slow with the advent of the greatly increased worldwide competition for both research, development, and manufacturing (Fig. 7–5). What all this means is that the tools necessary for electronic photography will be lower in cost and higher in quality in the reasonably near future (Table 7–1).

It might be good for each of us to follow the admonition of George Bernard Shaw, "You see things and ask why; I see things and ask why not." The real message is why not electronic photography? The tools are available today to begin to learn and the future promise is outstanding.

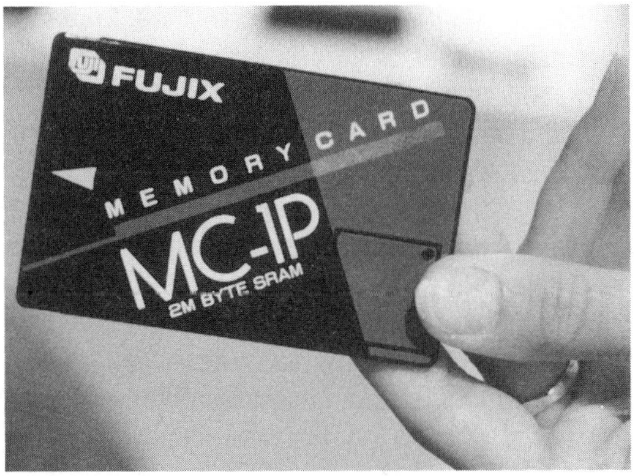

Fig. 7-5. The Fujix Memory Card is a promising development on the road to digital still photography in the future.

Table 7-1. Still Video Market Forecast.

	1987	1988	1989	1990	1991	1992
Still Video Cameras*						
(000 Units)	0.18	1.85	3.3	10.0	20	32
($MM)	0.70	3.60	6.3	15	25	35
Still Video Printers						
(00 Units)	5.0	7	10	15	22	40
($MM)	16.4	20	25	35	55	95

*Includes commercial and general market still video cameras
Source: Concord Associates, Inc.

APPLICATION STORIES

Using Still Video in Japan

At a recent still video seminar for salespeople, Fusanosuke Togashi, general manager of Fuji's Electronic Imaging Division, spoke about the immediate future of the technology and its possible impact on the photographic market. This was reported in JPEA Photo Electro News.

"In comparison with a video movie, still video images are produced easier, quicker, and at far lower costs," he said. The video floppy disks used in still video cameras sell for only 920 yen each, and one can erase the recorded images anytime he likes. Once stored, still video images can be played back at the desired speed and sequence repeatedly."

Emphasizing the relative convenience and benefits of using still video rather than moving video for presentations, he said, "Since the still image on display remains unchanged, one can look at the image, think about it, and then go back and look at it again. It helps a great deal when one wants to study an image. That is the reason that still video has begun displacing video movies in the field of presentations."

Mr. Togashi stated that the quality of present video images is too poor to qualify as serious photography, so applications are confined to low-resolution reproduction. However, he has a very optimistic outlook for the market acceptance of amateur still video systems, encouraged by the phenomenal popularity of the video movie in recent years.

"Already as many as 1.4 million camcorders have been sold nationwide, capturing 10 percent of all Japanese households," he said. "My impression is that when it comes to picture quality, consumers tend to be far more forgiving of images produced on CRT displays than those printed out on photographic paper. They seem satisfied with moving images with sound, regardless of quality. Therefore, we can familiarize them with Still Video through our promotional efforts with video movies."

He stressed that Fuji's new DS-1P digital card camera prototype represents the ultimate development in still video. "Images recorded on digital memory cards can be reproduced on a player as stable, smearless and distortion-free video pictures," he commented. "Other benefits include simple image processing, quick transfer speed, and no image distortion during duplication. We are expecting to commercialize this camera within three years. We anticipate that other makers will follow suit sooner or later."

Here are some uses found for still video systems in Japan.

- Department stores—as an information tool for introducing events, attractions, new products, special sales, seasonal gifts and many other items. In an automatic mode, the TV display will change regularly.
- Flower shops—various seasonal flower arrangements are stored on a floppy disk "catalog." Customers can review these on the TV monitor to assist in making their selection, or it can be used as a sales aid.
- Beauty salons—before and after styles can be recorded for customers. Also, a record of the different hairstyles for customers can be maintained on their individual floppy disk. A still promotion for cosmetic sales can be shown to customers.
- Used car dealers—particularly those with more than a single outlet, can exchange information on their various cars, and use the TV display to aid in selling cars not on their own lot.
- Real estate offices—realtors can record both the exterior and interior views of houses. This permits customers to review many houses in a short while to select those that they wish to visit.
- Design houses—presentations can be assembled quickly without the need for a darkroom. Existing images can be duplicated quickly.
- Educational facilities—using full color capability, chemical procedures can be demonstrated easily, showing color changes, phase changes such as precipitations, types of apparatus, etc. Images of distant places can be shown large enough for classes to view easily. Some teachers using the system state that a major benefit is their ability to control/change the demonstration sequence based upon the response of students, and that they can modify or create the program themselves.
- Public locations—the system provides effective visual guidance by combing actual pictures, graphics, and text in museums, libraries, cultural centers, hospitals, banks, etc.
- Exhibitions—the 16 TV Monitor/Player Multivision system permits one big picture or numerous small ones to be created.

- Sports clubs—with its ability to record 15 shots/second, the Fujix still video camera can be useful in analyzing an athlete's movements and in improving skills.
- Traffic control—by recording traffic flow in 1 to 10 second intervals, patterns can be determined for review and analysis.

Electronic Photography in Broadcasting

WCIU, an independent broadcaster serving Greater Chicago, Milwaukee, and South Bend had to fit a much needed film chain into a tiny, over-crowded master control room. In Rehoboth, MA, station WNAC, a UHF station reaching approximately 2.5 million households, sought a low-cost alternative to a large still store system for on-air graphics.

These are common problems, with a common solution. Both stations went with Sony MVR-5500 ProMavica player/recorders.

"ProMavica allows smaller stations to have the same on-air look as the big stations, without spending all the money," says Dick Castanie, a consultant to WNAC. He adds, "What initially drew me to ProMavica was one-inch quality video at a price affordable for smaller stations."

"We use ProMavica in place of a film chain," says WCIU chief engineer Bernie Hoelting. "Upstairs, in production, we have a system that takes up 25 square feet of floor space. Downstairs, in master control, the ProMavica requires only a few inches of rack space."

WNAC's Castanie notes that the station might acquire a second ProMavica MVR-5500 deck for use as a production system. Aside from the low cost, one advantage of ProMavica over larger systems is automatic shut-off, preventing graphics from being left on the air accidentally.

California Heads for Tomorrow

A recent California State Request for Proposal concerned setting up an electronic-driver's-license program for the state, a first in the nation.

Although proposals are still in the submission stage, every indication is that Californians will be getting an electronic photo license and signature along with a stored electronic thumbprint. The world of electronic photography is truly catching on and expanding.

Glossary

access time In mass-storage devices, the time from issuance of a command to read or write a specific location until reading or writing actually begins at that location.

ACTV Abbreviation for Advanced Compatible Television, techniques for advanced television transmission. ACTV 1 is a channel-compatible, receiver-compatible system utilizing many different techniques to add widescreen panels and increase horizontal and vertical resolution. ACTV II is ACTV 1 with improved resolution and sound.

A/D *See* analog-to-digital conversion.

additive color system A color reproduction system in which an image is reproduced by mixing appropriate amounts of red, green, and blue lights.

algorithm A group of processing steps that perform a particular operation, such as drawing a line, or compressing a digital image.

aliasing Also called *stairstepping* or *jaggies*. In sampling, the flaw is produced when the input signal contains frequency components higher than half of the sampling rate. Typically produces jagged steps on diagonal edges. *see* anti-aliasing.

AM Abbreviation for amplitude modulation, a form of modulation in which the level of the baseband information affects the level of the carrier. The carrier frequency remains unaltered by the process.

analog Of or referring to a signal that is a likeness of a physical process and is continuously variable, rather than different.

analog-to-digital conversion (A/D) The process of converting an analog signal into a digital bit stream. Includes the steps of sampling and quantizing.

analog video Video in which all the information representing images is in a continuous-scale electrical signal for both amplitude and time.

ANSI Abbreviation for American National Standards Institute, the United States organization responsible for American standards.

anti-aliasing The process of reducing the visibility of aliasing by using gray-scale pixel values to smooth the appearance of jagged edges.

aperture As applied to television, the specific size and shape of the point of the electronic beam in a camera or picture tube. When the beam does not come to a unique point, it affects the area around it by reducing resolution.

artifact In video systems, something unnatural or unintended observed in the reproduction of an image by the system.

aspect ratio The ratio of the width of an image to its height, sometimes expressed as two numbers separated by a colon (e.g., 4:3). For broadcast television, the standard aspect ratio is 4:3.

bandwidth Of or referring to the frequency range transmitted by an analog system. In video systems, specifying the highest frequency value is sufficient, because all video systems must transmit frequencies down to 30 Hz or lower. The greater the bandwidth, the more information is carried. In television, bandwidth is usually expressed in MHz.

base bandwidth The amount of bandwidth required by an unmodulated signal, such as video or audio. In general, the higher the quality of the signal, the greater the base bandwidth required.

binary Of or referring to a digital signal having two levels, usually referred to as 0 and 1.

B-ISDN Abbreviation for broadband integrated digital network, a mechanism by means of which telephone companies will be able to carry television signals digitally, probably through optical fibers. ISDN systems are considered broadband if they carry at least 45 Mbps, the DS3 rate, currently used for delivery of broadcast television signals. If and when B-ISDN reaches homes it will be a powerful competitor to other delivery mechanisms, potentially able to perform a computer-television function.

BitBlt Abbreviation for bit boundary block transfer, a data transfer function that moves a rectangular region of pixels within or between bitmaps. This function often is used for displaying pop-up windows, cursors, and small symbols such as text. BitBlt traditionally is capable of performing a Boolean (e.g., XOR) operation between the source and destination during the transfer.

bitmap A region of memory or storage that contains the pixels representing an image arranged in the sequence in which they are normally scanned to display the image. If a bitmap can be directly displayed on the screen, it is referred to as a *frame buffer* or *display memory*. If the bitmap cannot be viewed directly, then its data must be moved to display memory to be viewed. For example, a text font can be stored in an off-screen bitmap, and each character is moved to the proper place on the screen (using BitBlt) as it is needed.

bit plane In digital video display, hardware that has more than one video memory array contributing to the displayed image in real time. Each memory array is called an *image plane*; however, if the arrays have only one bit per pixel, they can be called *bit planes*.

bits per pixel The number of bits used to represent the color value of each pixel in a digitized image.

bit stream A serial sequence of bits.

bit rate The digital equivalent of bandwidth.

blanking The process, and period of time when it takes place, when the beam from the electron gun in a television is turned off. Blanking is used to prevent the beam from being visible on the screen when it resets from right to left or bottom to top of the screen; also that portion of the time that a video signal is transmitted when it is at or below blanking. These time portions can be divided into a horizontal blanking interval (HBI) and a vertical blanking interval (VBI).

The blanking intervals are used for descrambling codes, text transmission, time code, and test and reference signals.

blanking level In a video signal, the signal level during the horizontal and vertical blanking intervals, typically representing zero output.

blur A state of reduced resolution. Blur can be a picture defect, as when a photograph is indistinct because it was shot out-of-focus or the camera was moved during exposure. Blur also can be a picture improvement, as when an unnaturally jagged-edged diagonal line or jerky motion is blurred to smoothness. *See* aliasing.

broadcast television Conventional, common, television broadcasting.

bubble memory A computer memory technology that makes use of magnetic bubbles generated from a single-crystal sheet. In addition to being nonvolatile, bubble memory requires small amounts of power.

burn An image or pattern appearing so regularly on the screen of a picture tube that it ages the phosphors and remains as a ghost image even when other images are supposed to be shown. On computer terminals, the areas occupied by characters are frequently burned, particularly in the upper left corner. In television transmission centers, color bars are sometimes burned onto monitors. In production, burn refers to long-term or permanent image retention of camera pickup tubes when subjected to excessive highlights.

C Abbreviation for chrominance; also compatible.

CCD Abbreviation for charge-coupled device, a semiconductor device that can produce an electrical output analogous to the amount of light striking each of its elements.

CD Abbreviation for compact disc.

CD-I Abbreviation for Compact Disc-Interactive.

CD-ROM *See* compact disc-read-only memory.

CD-V Abbreviation for compact disc-video.

CGI Abbreviation for Computer Graphics Interface, an ANSI/ISO graphics standard currently being developed to specify how to interface directly to graphic devices. The proposed standard describes commands for such things as drawing lines, curves, text, and performing BitBlt. Originally called the Virtual Device Interface (VDI).

CGM Abbreviation for Computer Graphics Metafile. An American and international standard that specifies the format for storing a picture (e.g., on magnetic tape). Originally called the Virtual Device Metafile (VDM).

chroma See chrominance.

chroma crawl An NTSC artifact also sometimes referred to as moving dots, a crawling of the edges of saturated colors in an NTSC picture. Chroma crawl is a form of cross-luminance, a result of a television set decoding color information as high-detail luminance information (dots).

chroma resolution The amount of color detail available in a television system, separate from any brightness detail. In almost all television schemes, chroma resolution is lower than luminance resolution, matching visual acuity. Horizontal chrome resolution is only about 12 percent of luminance resolution in NTSC. *See also* resolution.

chrominance In an image-reproduction system, the signals that represent the color components of the image, such as hue and saturation. A black-and-white image will have chrominance values of zero. In the NTSC television system, the I and Q signals carry the chrominance information (sometimes abbreviated as chrome).

chrominance signal The part of the video signal that contains the color information. Also called the chroma signal or color signal.

codec Abbreviation for coder/decoder.

color balance In a color video system, the process of matching the amplitudes of the red, green, and blue signals so that the mixture of all three makes an accurate white color.

color bars A test pattern composed of eight rectangles of different colors: white, yellow, cyan, green, magenta, red, blue, and black.

color corrector An equipment for adjusting the color values of a color video signal. Color correction usually is required for proper reproduction of images from motion picture film.

color depth The number of bits per pixel. One bit per pixel allows two colors (often black and white) to be displayed, two bits per pixel allow four colors, three bits allow eight colors, and in general, n bits allow 2^n colors.

colorimetry The characteristics of color reproduction, including the range of colors that a system can produce.

color noise Random interference in the color portion of a composite video system. Because of reduced color bandwidth or color subsampling, color noise appears as relatively long streaks of incorrect color in the image.

color subcarrier A subchannel created by the second NTSC to carry color information within the original NTSC's black-and-white signal with minimal interference to black-and-white sets. The color subcarrier, an interlaced carrier at 3.579545 MHz, is quadrature modulated with a wideband (I) and a narrowband (Q) signal.

color table A table of color values that are displayed in an indexed color system.

color value The three numbers that specify a color. *See* also pixel value.

comb filter A filter designed to deal with periodic signals (i.e., signals that are repetitive), such as scanning lines or frames. Comb filters are so named because a chart of their effect on a signal appears similar to the teeth of a comb. They are used most often to separate luminance and chrominance signals in NTSC.

Compact Disc-Interactive (CD-I, also referred to as CD-IV Compact Disc-Interactive Video) A format that would include either many of the capabilities of reflective optical videodiscs in the 4.75-inch compact-disc medium, or would include features of the compact disc-interactive format, plus full-screen, full-motion video.

compact disc-read-only memory (CD-ROM) An adaptation of the compact disc for use with general digital data.

compact disc-write once (CD-WO) A variant on CD-ROM that can be written to once but read many times. Also known as CD-write once/read many (CD-WORM) and compact disc-programmable read-only memory (CD-PROM).

component video The three color video signals that describe a color image. The typical component systems are R,G,B; Y,I,Q; or Y,U,V.

composite video signal The complete color television-picture signal, including all blanking and sync signals. Typical composite television standard signals are NTSC, PAL, and SECAM.

compression A digital process that allows data to be stored or transmitted using less than the normal number of bits. Video compression refers to techniques that reduce the number of bits required to store or transmit images.

constant luminance principle A rule of composite color television that any change in color not accompanied by a change in brightness should not have any effect on the brightness of the image displayed on a picture tube. The constant luminance principle is generally violated by existing NTSC encoders and decoders. *See* also gamma.

contouring In a digital system, the appearance of patterns in a digitized image because the quantization did not have enough levels.

CRT Abbreviation for cathode-ray tube, a phosphorus-coated tube used for direct viewing of television or digital images.

cyan The color obtained by mixing equal intensities of green and blue light. It is also the correct name for the subtractive primary color sometimes called blue.

D/A Abbreviation for digital-to-analog converter.

data rate The speed of a data-transfer process, normally expressed in bits per second or bytes per second. For example, the data rate of CD-ROM is 150,000 bytes per second.

DBS Abbreviation for direct broadcast satellite, a distribution scheme involving transmission of signals directly from satellites to homes. It does not carry common broadcasting's restricted bandwidth and regulations. DBS is the most effective delivery mechanism for reaching most rural areas, but it is relatively poor in urban areas and in mountainous terrain, particularly in the north. Depending on frequency band used, it can be affected by factors such as rain.

definition Synonymous with resolution or quality.

detail Resolution; finer detail means higher resolution.

differential PCM (DPCM) Abbreviation for a digital system in which the data transmitted or stored represents the difference between data elements (for images it is pixels), rather than the data elements themselves.

digital Of or referring to a quantity that is expressible numerically. *See* also digitization.

digital audiotape (DAT) An audiotape designed for use in systems that employ digital, rather than analog, recording technology. DAT cassettes are more compact than conventional audio cassettes and are used now for data and image storage as well as audio.

digital video Video in which all the information representing images is in some kind of computer data form that can be manipulated and displayed by a computer.

Digital Video Interactive (DVI) A technology that allows real-time compression and decompression of graphics and full-motion video for recording on CD-ROM, videodiscs, magnetic disks, or other digital storage media.

digitization The process of changing an electronic analog signal such as a television signal into a discrete numerical form. Digitization is subdivided into the processes of sampling the analog signal at a moment in time, quantizing the sample (assigning it a numerical level), and coding the number in binary form. The advantages of digitization include improved transmission and repeatable quality; the disadvantages include the need for more storage space than the analog signal. Data compression works to reduce that disadvantage.

digitizing The process of converting an analog signal into a digital signal. With images, it refers to the processes of scanning and analog-to-digital conversion.

direct-view A CRT or Projected image that is watched directly, as opposed to a hard-copy print.

display The cathode-ray tube used to display

the ultimate image to a viewer; the process of presenting that image.

dithering A method for making digitized images appear smoother using alternating colors in a pattern to produce a new, perceived color. For example, displaying an alternating pattern of black-and-white pixels produces gray. Also, a technique of adding random noise to pixel values before quantization.

dot pitch The distance between phosphor dots in a tri-color, direct-view CRT. It can be the ultimate determinant of resolution.

DRAM Abbreviation for dynamic random-access memory. This is the standard type of RAM used in personal computer main memory. Dynamic RAM requires a periodic refresh operation in order to retain its data.

driver A software entity that provides a software interface to a specific piece of hardware. For example, the DVI video drive provides software access to the video-board hardware.

dub A copy of a video or audio tape recording made by replaying the original tape and simultaneously recording the signal onto a new tape, which becomes the dub. Also used as a verb meaning to copy a tape.

dye sublimation A method of hard-copy output using a thermal head and a controlled spreading of the dye image to achieve a smoother, finished blend of dyes.

ED-Beta Extended definition Betamax. A consumer/professional videocassette format developed by Sony offering 500-line horizontal resolution and Y/C connections.

edge A boundary in an image. The apparent sharpness of edges can be increased without increasing resolution. *See* also sharpness.

EEPROM Abbreviation for electrically erasable programmable read-only memory.

EGA Abbreviation for enhanced-graphics adapter, a standard that specifies 640 × 350 pixels with 16 color capability from a palette of 64 colors.

EIA standards Standards set by the Electronics Industries Association (U.S.), including television-broadcast standards.

Electronic Still Camera Standardization Committee (ESCSC) A committee of over 40 corporations established in the late 1970s to create standards for the new still video format.

encoders Devices that change component signals to composite signals; sometimes devices that change analog signals to digital (*see* A/D). All NTSC cameras include an encoder. Because many of these cameras are inexpensive, their encoders omit many of the advanced techniques that can improve NTSC. Component analog video facilities can use a single, advanced encoder prior to creating a final NTSC signal.

engine A computer-processing platform such as a PC or Macintosh computer.

field In an interlaced scanning system, all of the odd-numbered or all of the even-numbered scanning lines comprise a field, and two sequential fields comprise a frame. For NTSC video, one complete vertical scan of 262.5 horizontal lines is one-half of a complete picture "frame," which contains 525 lines. The second field provides the other 262.5 horizontal lines between the first 262.5. This is called *interlaced scanning.* Sixty fields or thirty frames are scanned each second.

field rate The number of fields per second.

filtering Calculating a single pixel value from multiple samples taken in the neighborhood of a pixel.

flat-panel display An electronic display with a package thickness that is a fraction of the display's height or length.

flicker A visible fluctuation in the brightness of an image, often a problem in CRT displays if the vertical scan rate is lower than about 50 Hz.

fm Abbreviation for frequency modulation, a method of modulation in which the frequency of the carrier voltage is varied with the frequency of the modulating voltage.

frame The result of a complete scanning of one image. In motion video, the image is scanned repeatedly, making a series of frames.

frame buffer Memory that can be viewed directly on the display surface. Also called display memory.

frame grabber Hardware that takes the analog signal from a TV and digitizes the image into RAM. A single video field or frame can be captured by a frame grabber.

fringing In a color display, the effect caused by incorrect superimposition of the red, green, and blue images. Incorrect colors appear at the edges of objects in the image. Also called color fringing.

gamma In video systems, gamma refers to the gray-scale reproduction or amplitude characteristic of the system, a measure of how much a graph of display brightness versus scene brightness varies from a straight line. Picture tubes have gammas of more than one; cameras, therefore, use gammas of less than one, so the overall brightness-in/brightness-out characteristic will be linear (a straight line). Current CRT gammas do not match those in the NTSC standard, creating nonlinear gamma. Because camera gamma is introduced prior to encoding (which lowers chroma resolution), the constant-luminance principle is violated.

gamma correction The process of correcting the amplitude transfer characteristics of a video system so that equal steps of brightness or intensity at the input are reproduced with equal steps of intensity at the display.

genlocking The process of synchronization to another video signal. It is required in computer capture of video to synchronize the digitizing process with the scanning parameters of the video signal.

granularity The density with which a viewing surface is divided into physical sensors such as pixels in an image or grains of emulsion in film.

hard copy Output onto permanent media such as paper or film as opposed to a CRT screen.

Hi-band A new standard recording format for still video that will allow resolutions of up to 500 horizontal TV lines from the original format of 360 lines. New recording heads and processing circuits are used to improve the luminance frequency response.

high-definition television (HDTV) High-resolution, wide-screen television broadcasting with digital sound. Until an international standard is decided for HDTV, improvements in the quality of equipment used to receive standard broadcasts are being made, and these are referred to as improved-definition television (IDTV) or extended-definition television (EDTV).

horizontal blanking interval The period of time when a scanning process is moving from the end of one horizontal line to the start of the next line.

horizontal resolution The specification of resolution in the horizontal direction, meaning the ability of the system to reproduce closely spaced vertical lines, or detail across the screen, usually specified as the maximum number of alternating white and black vertical lines (lines of resolution) that can be individually perceived across the width of a picture, divided by the aspect ratio. This number usually is expressed as TV lines per picture height. The reason to divide by the aspect ratio and express the result per picture height is to be able to compare easily horizontal and vertical resolution. Horizontal chroma resolution is measured between complementary colors (rather than black and white) but can vary in some systems (such as NTSC), depending on the colors chosen. Horizontal resolution in luminance and/or chrominance can vary in some systems between a stationary (static resolution) and moving (dynamic resolution) picture. It is usually directly related to bandwidth.

hue The color of a colored point, such as red, green, yellow, or violet.

IDTV Abbreviation for improved-definition television, a term widely accepted to mean improvements restricted to television sets.

IEEE Abbreviation for the Institute of Electrical and Electronics Engineers.

image enhancement Techniques for increasing apparent sharpness without increasing actual resolution. This usually takes the form of increasing the brightness change at edges.

image A still picture, or one frame of a motion sequence.

image file A file of data that represents an image.

image plane In a digital video display, hardware that has more than one video memory array contributing to the displayed image in real time. Each memory array is called an image plane. *See* also bit plane.

image processing Techniques that manipulate the pixel values of an image for some particular purpose. Examples are brightness or contrast correction, color correction, changing size (scaling), or changing the shape of the image (warping).

ink jet A method of creating a hard copy using jet(s) of black and/or cyan, magenta, and yellow solid or liquid inks to create hard copies from digital images.

interlaced A system in which the electron beam makes two complete passes on the screen to display the image. In television, a 2:1 interlace is used. On the first pass, the odd lines (1,3,5,...) are displayed. On the second pass, the even lines (2,4,6,...) are displayed. This means it takes twice as long to display the entire image, which often results in flicker in a computer graphics system. Home TVs are interlaced displays.

interlaced scanning Television scanning employing interlace.

interpolation Calculating values or locations of intermediate points as a smoothly varying function between end points.

ISDN Abbreviation for Integrated Services Digital Network. A telecommunications concept and series of standards whereby one universal, digital-transmission network can carry computer data, voice, still and moving pictures (at any quality level), and high-fidelity sound. ISDN is in the process of being implemented slowly by telephone companies worldwide.

ISO Abbreviation for the International Standards Organization, the international organization responsible for international standards. The United States is a member.

jitter A rapid, small shift in image position.

jittering A technique for reducing the effects of aliasing by randomly displacing samples from a uniform distribution.

JPEG Abbreviation for Joint Photo Experts Group, an image-compression standards committee.

keying In a video system, the process of inserting one picture into another picture under spatial control of another signal called the keying signal.

LCD Abbreviation for Liquid-crystal display.

LED Abbreviation for light-emitting diode, a display that uses diodes made of gallium arsenide, gallium arsenide phosphide, or SiC to emit light when current is applied.

line In scanning, a single pass of the sensor from left to right across the image.

linearity In television, usually refers to the geometric accuracy of scanning. However, linearity is also used sometimes to refer to the accuracy of gray-scale reproduction (linearity of the amplitude-transfer characteristic), but it is less confusing to use the word gamma for the gray-scale characteristic.

linear matrix transformation The process of transforming a group of n signals by combining the signals through addition or subtraction. It is used, for example, to convert RGB into YIQ.

line pairs A measure of resolution often used in film and print media. In television, lines are used instead, creating confusion when comparing film and video.

lines Scanning lines or lines of resolution. The later are hypothetical lines alternating between white and black (or, in the case of chroma resolution, between complementary colors). The combined maximum number of black-and-white lines that might be perceived in a particular direction is the number of lines of resolution. Vertical resolution is measured with horizontal lines; horizontal resolution is measured with vertical lines. Diagonal resolution is measured with diagonal lines (no current television system or proposal favors one diagonal direction over the other, so the direction of the diagonal lines does not really matter).

look-up table (LUT) Same as color table.

luminance In an image, refers to the brightness values of all the points in the image. A luminance-only reproduction is a black-and-white representation of the image. The human visual system is more sensitive to luminance detail than to chrominance detail.

luminance signal The portion of the video signal that controls the luminance of the picture. Also known as the "Y" signal.

magenta The color obtained by mixing equal intensities of red and blue light. It is also the correct name for the subtractive primary color sometimes called red.

Mavica Magnetic video camera.

MBps Abbreviation for megabyte per second, a data transmission rate in millions of bytes per second.

Mbps Abbreviation for megabits per second, a data transmission rate in millions of binary digits per second.

MHz Abbreviation for megahertz, or millions of cycles per second. A normal U.S. television transmission channel is 6 MHz. The base bandwidth of the video signal in that channel is 4.2 MHz.

MIPS Abbreviation for million instructions per second.

modulation The process (or result) of changing information (audio, video, data, etc.) into information-carrying signals suitable for transmission and/or recording. In NTSC-M television transmission, video is modulated onto a picture carrier using AM-VSB, and audio is modulated onto a sound carrier using FM.

moiré A wavy pattern, usually caused by interference. When the interference is cross-color, the pattern is colored, even if the picture is not.

monochrome Literally, of or pertaining to a single color, usually used to indicate black and white. There have been monochrome high-line-rate cameras and displays for many years. The EIA has standardized rates of up to 1225 scanning lines per frame. NHK developed a monochrome HDTV system with 2125 scanning lines per frame. Even higher numbers of scanning lines are used in conjunction with lower frame rates in cathode-ray-tube scanners used in printing and in film. These extremely high rates are possible because monochrome picture tubes have a single phosphor instead of three phosphors.

nonimpact printer Printers that form images on paper or film without stamping or inking through a ribbon. Examples include laser, thermal, and ink-jet printers.

NTSC Abbreviation for National Television Standards Committee, an advisory group established in the USA in the 1940s. In 1953, it was responsible for establishing the present color standards used in TV in the USA, Japan, etc. The abbreviation NTSC is used to designate signals that conform to these standards. Basically, the NTSC standard is a 525-line, 60 field/30 frame per second format.

NTSC standard The documentation on the characteristics of NTSC. NTSC is defined primarily in the FCC Part 73 technical specifications. Many of its characteristics are defined in EIA-170A.

overscanning Displaying less than the complete area of an image to a viewer (i.e., scanning beyond the visible area). All TV sets are overscanned at least slightly, so that viewers do not see blanking (the size of which can vary). The restricted areas of the SMPTE Safe Action Area and the SMPTE Safe Title Area take this overscanning into account. Newer TV sets have less overscanning then their predecessors.

PAL Abbreviation for phase alteration line, the color-television broadcast standard used in a number of European countries, including Germany and the United Kingdom. A common composite color transmission system (like NTSC) in which there are 625 scanning lines per frame and 25 frames per second. Brazil is the only country in the world transmitting PAL on a 525/30 system.

PC Abbreviation for personal computer, a software-controlled system containing general-purpose computer functions and intended for use by one user.

PCM *See* pulse-code modulation.

pels Picture elements, the smallest dots that can be transmitted for any given bandwidth and scanning system. *See* pixel.

PHIGS Programmer's Hierarchical Interface to Graphics, a graphics standard currently being developed by ANSI/ISO for three-dimensional graphics.

piezo Of or pertaining to a piezoelectric crystal, a crystal that changes its shape when an electrical signal is applied between its faces.

pixel The smallest dot that can be turned individually on and off on a device. Derived from the words "picture element." For flat-panel displays, pixels and dots are interchangeable.

pixel operation The process of modifying a pixel value for some specific purpose.

pixel value A number or series of numbers that represent the color and luminance of a single pixel. *See* also color value.

pixellation In a digital image, a subjective impairment in which the pixels are large enough to become visible individually.

plane Bitmap memory organization that contains a single bit for all of the pixels. Thus, if you have one bit per pixel you have one plane, for two bits per pixel you have two planes, etc. Reading a 16-bit word from a plane will return a single bit for each of 16 pixels. Packed pixel is an alternative way to organize memory.

plasma An ionized gas containing an approximately equal number of positive and negative charges. The gas emits light when subjected to a sufficiently high voltage.

polygon A simple type of primitive surface composed of three or more vertices connected by straight edges.

P–P Abbreviation for peak-to-peak, the total difference between the most positive and most negative peaks of a waveform.

primary color In a tri-stimulus color video system, one of the three colors mixed to produce an image. In additive color systems, the primary colors are red, green, and blue. In subtractive color systems, the primaries are cyan, magenta, and yellow.

pulse-code modulation (PCM) A digitization technique that uses fixed frequency sampling and linear quantization.

Q In NTSC video, Q refers to the quadrature color difference signal. It is 90 degrees out of phase with the color subcarrier.

RAM Abbreviation for random-access memory, a memory providing access time that is independent of address.

random-access In digital memory or mass storage, the ability to access to any point or address without any limitation.

raster The pattern of motion used in scanning, usually left to right, and repeated over the image from top to bottom as a series of horizontal lines. Also the type of image sampling using scanning lines (as in raster scanning) or a rectangular array of dots (pixels).

raster image processing The process in which a printer controller converts text and graphic images from a computer into a grid of dots (raster pattern) that the printer prints onto paper or film.

RasterOp Abbreviation for raster operation, or another term for BitBlt. Unfortunately, the same term also is used to refer to the boolean operation that can be performed as part of the BitBlt.

resolution The perceivable detail, or the ability of an image reproducing system to reproduce fine detail. There are two resolution figures in video: horizontal and vertical. Video resolution is specified in lines per picture height, which is the total count of black and white lines that can be reproduced in a distance equal to the picture height. Video resolution is measured per frame rather than lines per millimeter. There is no direct correlation between resolution measured in pixels (digital environment) and horizontal resolution measured in TV lines. An approximation is 2 pixels = 1 TV lines of resolution. In digital systems, resolution is the number of pixels on a display surface. CRT resolutions are usually given as number of pixels per scan line and the number of scan lines, e.g., 640 × 480. Laser printer/plotter resolutions usually are given in dots per inch, e.g., 300 DPI. *See* also chroma resolution, vertical and horizontal resolution.

RGB Abbreviation for red, green, blue.

RMS Abbreviation for root-mean square.

ROM Abbreviation for read-only memory. A memory unit in which data or instructions are stored permanently. The information is read out nondestructively and no information can be written into this memory.

sample A measurement of a particular property at a specific point in time and/or space.

sampling The process of dealing with something continuous in discrete sections. In the process of digitization, the value of a signal is read at evenly spaced points in time.

sampling rate The clock frequency for sampling, or the number of samples per second.

saturated color A color as far from white,

black, or gray as possible (e.g., vermilion rather than pink).

saturation The depth of color intensity. Zero saturation is white (no color), and maximum saturation is the deepest or most intense color possible.

scaling Changing the size of something.

scan line A complete horizontal row of pixels on the display surface.

scanner A device that performs scanning.

scanning The process of converting an image to an electrical signal by moving a sensing point across the image, usually in a pattern from left to right, and repeated from top to bottom as a series of horizontal lines.

scanning lines Horizontal or near-horizontal lines sampling a television image in the vertical direction. In tube-type cameras and displays equipped with CRTs, the scanning lines are caused by electron-beam traces.

SECAM Abbreviation for Sequential Couleur Avec Memoire, the color-television broadcast system of France, the USSR, and other countries.

sector In a mass-storage device, the smallest physical unit of storage.

seek time In a mass-storage device, the time required to position the read head over the track containing the desired data.

sensitivity The amount of signal a camera can emit from a particular sensor illumination at a particular S/N, sometimes expressed as a certain scene illumination (in lux or footcandles) at an assumed reflectance and signal strength, a particular lens transmission aperture, and a particular S/N. The sensitivity of a camera can be increased by improving its image sensor, increasing its transmission aperture, or slowing its frame rate; it can be increased by allowing the S/N to be reduced.

sharpness Apparent image resolution. High sharpness can be the result of high resolution, or it might be an optical illusion caused by image enhancement or by visible edges in a display, such as the vertical stripes of an aperture grille CRT (e.g., Trinitron). Visible scanning lines actually can increase perceived sharpness.

signal-to-noise ratio (S/N) In analog video systems, the ratio between the peak-to-peak black-to-white signal and the rms value of any superimposed noise. The eye's sensitivity to noise varies with the detail of the noise.

smear An analog artifact in which vertical edges in the display show a spreading to the left or right, typically caused by midfrequency distortions in an analog system.

S/N *See* signal-to-noise ratio.

SMPTE Abbreviation for Society of Motion Picture and Television Engineers.

square pixels Pixels generated in a television system having the same horizontal and vertical resolution. There is some evidence that a large mismatch between horizontal and vertical resolution prevents the higher resolution from being fully perceived by the human visual system. NTSC was created with square pixels with a resolution of approximately 330 by 330 lines.

SRAM Abbreviation for static random-access memory.

standard A set of rules or characteristics defining a particular television system. Some standards (such as those contained in FCC rules and regulations) are mandatory. Most (including those of the EIA, IEEE, and SMPTE) are voluntary. The establishment of a standard often freezes development at a certain level but allows users and manufacturers to deal with a much larger array of products than might be available without a standard.

standards converter A device for converting signals from one standard to another. Converting between different color schemes with the same scanning structure is called *transcoding*. Converting between different scanning structures requires line and field interpolation, which usually introduces artifacts. Conversion is performed regularly between 525 and 625 scanning-line signals.

still-video format An analog video-production system that stores fields or frames of video information on 2-inch floppy disks.

streaking An analog artifact in which bright objects in the picture cause a shifting of level that extends horizontally all the way across the picture. Typically caused by distortions to the frequency components below the horizontal line frequency.

subtractive color system Color reproduction by mixing appropriate amounts of the subtractive primary pigments, cyan, magenta, and yellow.

S-VHS A very high-resolution videotaping mode. S-VHS videotapes, which offer significantly enhanced picture quality, can be viewed only on S-VHS equipment, although S-VHS VCRs are compatible with standard VHS-format tapes. It allows component recording and playback without cross-luminance or cross-color artifacts through a four-pin S-Video connection.

sync information In television, refers to the part of the video signal devoted to making sure that the display scanning will move in synchronism with the camera scanning.

system gamma The overall light-in/light-out characteristic of a television system, from camera through receiver. In an ideal system, the gamma should be one. In practice, it appears to be about 1.4.

thermal printing head A heat-emitting resistor, also known as a *heat pen* or *print head*, designed to form an image or letter on heat-sensitive paper. Thermal heads often are composed of dozens or hundreds of resistor elements and are used widely in office equipment such as facsimile machines and printers.

threshold In a digital circuit, a dividing line between circuit signal levels representing different digital values.

tint *See* hue.

transform In data compression, a process that converts a block of data into some alternate form that is more convenient or efficient for a particular purpose.

transformation The combination of any or all of rotation, scaling, and translation to modify an image.

TTL Abbreviation for through-the-lens; usually refers to viewfinding or focusing in a camera.

U,V The chrominance components of the PAL color-television system.

underscanned Scanning of a display so that the edges of the raster are visible.

VDI Abbreviation for Virtual Device Interface, the original name for the CGI.

VDP *See* video display processor.

vertical resolution The specification of resolution in the vertical direction, meaning the ability to reproduce closely spaced horizontal lines. Also the amount of detail that can be perceived in the vertical direction, or the maximum number of alternating white-and-black horizontal lines that can be counted from the top of the picture to the bottom. It is not the same as the number of scanning lines. It is the number of scanning lines minus the vertical blanking interval times the Kell factor (and, where appropriate, times the interlace coefficient).

VGA Abbreviation for video-graphics array, an electronic-display standard that defines a resolution of 640 × 480 pixels with a 16-color capability and 320-×-200-pixel resolution with a 256-color capability from a palette of 256k colors.

video compression *See* compression.

video coprocessor A separate CPU for video functions, operating in parallel with the main system CPU.

video-display adaptor In the IBM PC and PC AT systems, the plug-in board that provides the video display hardware for the system.

video-display processor (VDP) A custom chip set that provides the video hardware for a digital computer.

video RAM *See* VRAM.

video signal The varying electrical signal coming from a scanning image sensor.

video signal In order for a TV receiver to reproduce the scene captured by the video camera produced at a television station, it must receive a vast amount of information on luminance, color, and color balance. Because sending all this information as separate color signals is not feasible, it is combined into one *composite signal.* The brightness information is contained in the *luminance signal*, sometimes called the *Y* signal, and the other information of what is normally called color is contained in the *chrominance signal*, sometimes shortened to *color signal.* Hue and saturation are both carried by the chrominance signal. These two signals contain all the information necessary for either color or black-and-white reproduction (the luminance signal contains both color and black-and-white information). The video signal occupies about 4 MHz of the total 6-MHz channel with luminance in the lower portion and color riding a 3.58-MHz carrier (called the *chrominance subcarrier*). The subcarrier is phase shift modulated to carry the hue and amplitude modulation for the saturation information. In addition to all the picture-related information a *synchronizing pulse* is added to start the scan at the correct time.

viewing ratio In video displays, the ratio between the viewer's distance from the screen and the height of the display screen.

virtual device A software entity that defines the interface characteristics of a specific physical device, such as a video display.

visual acuity The amount of detail perceptible by the human visual system. It depends on many factors, including brightness, color, orientation, and contrast.

VRAM Abbreviation for video RAM. A variation of DRAM that has two ports: the usual random-access port for access by a CPU, and a separate serial port which can output or input a serial stream of data at high rates independent of the activity on the random-access port. Designed to reduce the conflict between trying to draw into the frame buffer while having to read the frame buffer to display the image on the CRT.

white balance A means of adjusting, either manually or automatically, the color balance of a camera by shooting a white object and adjusting for a white image on the monitor. With a still video camera, white balance is achieved instantly as the subject is photographed.

white noise Electrical noise whose energy content is uniformly distributed over the system bandwidth.

workstation A high-end computer system having many of the characteristics of a personal computer; intended for use by engineers or professionals.

Y In color video, the abbreviation for luminance. The Y signal is the luminance signal, so named because it is the y-axis of the chart of the spectral sensitivity of the human visual system.

yellow The color obtained by mixing equal intensities of green and red light.

YIQ The color component format used by NTSC television. *See* luminance; chrominance.

YUV The components of the PAL system: luminance and chroma.

Index

J

K

L

M

N